THE PORTABLE

Emerson

Selected and arranged
with an Introduction and notes by

MARK VAN DOREN

THE VIKING PRESS

CONTENTS

INTRODUCTION

BY MARK VAN DOREN

THERE is no danger that Emerson will not survive, but opinions differ as to why this is so. The opinions are mainly two: his ideas were good, his writing was good. If the present selection tends to express the second opinion, it does so in full understanding of the fallacy which lurks in so sharp a division between what is said and the way it is said. Things well said—as well said as Emerson could say them—must somehow have deserved the attention thus bestowed upon them by the muses of verse and prose. Nor is it to be ignored that the simplicity with which an author believes what he writes has much to do with the fact that he writes well. The ideas of Emerson cannot be dismissed, for he did not dismiss them. "Virtue is the business of the universe." Emerson meant this with all his heart, as he meant the words which preceded it in his journal: "Literature is an amusement." He wrote in order that he might tell the truth, and the multitude that was affected by him in his time thought he had told the truth. Perhaps he did. His ideas, with certain possible exceptions, are not to be called wrong or bad.

But neither are they to be separated from the circumstance of his having stated them with a peculiar charm. This charm is nothing like the honey which Lucretius said he rubbed on the edges of his cup so that a bitter doctrine might get swallowed. Emerson's

1

doctrine, such as it is, was believed by him who mixed it to be as sweet as any words he could use to convey it; indeed, the idea sweetened the word, the truth trimmed the lamp. Nor is the reverse instance of Rabelais applicable to Emerson's case. The creator of Gargantua promised his reader that the box of mockeries and lascivious jests before him would when opened be found to contain most serious, most precious matter, as the grotesque exterior of Socrates had but concealed the "heavenly drug" of Plato's truth. The instance is not without point, for one of Emerson's charms is wit. But the wit of Emerson, indeed the humor of Emerson, reveals rather than conceals. It is inseparable from what is inside him. It has everything to do with the way he looked upon the world.

Nevertheless, it will be plain to any instructed reader that the following pages were selected to show the writer in Emerson, not the philosopher. The representative Emerson, the influential Emerson, gives way here to the man who at the moment is most readable—at the moment and, one may have the faith, for a long time to come. Some of his best-known works, of course, survive into the classification. But not all of them, as for example the essay on Compensation and many another essay which used to lie in leather on parlor table tops. *English Traits,* which aimed less at eternal truth, seems now, by a familiar paradox of art, to have hit more of it after all. *English Traits* is still a book which historians of Emerson's influence can be doubtful what to do with. But most of it is here, for the simple reason that the book is powerful and delightful, and therefore cannot be overlooked. It is Emerson not at his most sententious but at his best; it is Emerson gazing at a portion of the world and giving, without self-consciousness, his amazed, his amusing, his mature report.

For he was at his best not when he was basic, not when he was trying to understand the man he was, but when he was being that man, when he was applying the ideas which that man had furnished him. He needed matter to illuminate. The light he held in his hand was one he had made as bright and steady as it could be, but his attention henceforth was upon the things, the people, to be scrutinized. These he saw with an astonishing clarity—astonishing, unless we are prepared to grant that saints and angels have good vision. Emerson by all the evidence of his time was something of both. The terms, however, were not always intended seriously. Intended quite seriously, they mean a power to see more reality than most men see. Reality, refined and unrefined. The perfect angel sees either sort without difficulty. Emerson, oddly enough, is imperfect only when he tries to see truth in its disembodied state. Then he vaporizes, tautologizes, and dissolves. He needed body about him—objects and persons. Then he grew busy and became his best.

The man in Emerson who made the fine writer we have before us was completely generous and candid. He was always somehow personal, but his nature was ventilated to the core. His modesty was equal to his pride. He was an aristocrat who thought all could be aristocrats. When he said there were no common people he meant that he was not common and that he had never met a man who was. He asked the most of everybody because he truly believed it could be given. "I am always made uneasy," he once wrote in the solitude of his journal, "when the conversation turns in my presence upon popular ignorance and the duty of adapting our public harangues and writings to the mind of the people. 'Tis all pedantry and ignorance. The people know as much and reason as well as we do. None so quick as they to discern brilliant genius or solid parts. And I observe that all those who use this cant most, are such as do not rise above mediocrity of understanding." This was when he was twenty-five, and perhaps only hopeful. But ten years later he was saying it still better. "Remember that the hunger of people for truth is immense. The reason why they yawn is because you have it not." When, almost twenty years later still, he observed frontier audiences walking out on his lectures because he had not given them jokes, he regretted that he was not master of the hearty laugh. "These are the new conditions to which I must conform. The architect who is asked to build a house to go upon the sea must not build a Parthenon, or a square house, but a ship. And Shakespeare, or Franklin, or Aesop, coming to Illinois, would say, I must give my wisdom a comic form, instead of tragics or elegiacs, and well I know to do it, and he is no master who cannot vary his forms, and carry his own end triumphantly through the most difficult."

Emerson never learned to joke, but from the beginning he studied how to "command the whole scale" of human discourse. "Every one has felt," he said, "how superior in force is the language of the street to that of the academy. . . . The speech of the man in the street is invariably strong, nor can you mend it by making it what you call parliamentary. You say, 'If he could only express himself'; but he does already, better than any one can for him. . . . The power of their speech is, that it is perfectly understood by all. . . . And observe that all poetry is written in the oldest and simplest English words." He admired Plato not least for the language he knew how to put into the mouth of Socrates —a language, by the way, which he did not suppose with Rabelais to be merely a cover for the content

within. The language was the content, or at any rate
the seal of its sincerity, the index to its authority. "From
mares and puppies; from pitchers and soup-ladles;
from cooks and criers; the shops of potters, horse-
doctors, butchers and fishmongers"—thence, said Emerson, came Plato's illustrations, and it was the right place
for them to come from. For the language of the street
"is always strong. What can describe the folly and emp-
tiness of scolding like the word *jawing*? I feel too the
force of the double negative, though clean contrary to
our grammar rules. . . . Cut these words and they
would bleed; they are vascular and alive; they walk and
run. Moreover they who speak them have this elegancy,
that they do not trip in their speech. It is a shower of
bullets, whilst Cambridge men and Yale men correct
themselves and begin again at every half sentence."
Dear Bronson Alcott was indeed his friend, but he shied
from Alcott's solemn suggestion that the things they
said to each other should be set down in "a historical
record." "I say, how joyful rather is some Montaigne's
book which is full of fun, poetry, business, divinity,
philosophy, anecdote, smut, which dealing of bone and
marrow, of cornbarn and flour barrel, of wife, and
friend, and valet, of things nearest and next, never
names names, or gives you the glooms of a recent date
or relation, but hangs there in the heaven of letters, unrelated, untimed, a joy and a sign, an autumnal star."

Emerson never learned to joke, and he disliked
laughter. But the wit of the foregoing is as natural as
the humor behind it—well behind it, as is always the
case with Emerson. The presence of that humor, loving
the fact of life and recommending it, must have been
one of the things Carlyle had in mind when he wrote to
Emerson in 1860: "There is but one completely human
voice to me in the world; and you are it." If Emerson

was ever pleased by a compliment, it must have been by this one. For his chronic fear was lest he sound cold to those who heard or read him. He supposed he had too much in him of New England's "hesitation and reserve." "Now listen to a poor Irishwoman recounting some experience of hers. Her speech flows like a river—so unconsidered, so humorous, so pathetic, such justice done to all the parts! It is a true substantiation—the fact converted into speech, all warm and colored and alive, as it fell out." He envied the Irishwoman, as he envied the talkers of Sicily—"they crow, squeal, hiss, cackle, bark, and scream like mad." And of course Emerson was not like that. But he had his animal spirits, and they are what set a strange, wild current moving even among his most abstruse remarks. The excitement of reading him is the excitement of feeling just this current, this tide of an intense interest in what he sees and would have us see, either with mind or eye.

"We must use the language of fact," he advised himself, "and not be superstitiously abstract." The language of fact for Emerson was the way truth spoke in time. "Fact is better than fiction if only we could get pure fact." Pure fact—it was what he searched for wherever he looked; the hope of finding it sharpened his gaze, and the feeling that it had been found expressed itself in the ecstasy of his style. "I like that poetry which, without aiming to be allegorical, is so. Which, sticking close to its subject, and that perhaps trivial, can yet be applied to the life of man and the government of God and be found to hold." This is an excellent theory of poetry—one more excellent, as it happens, than Emerson was able to state in the formal essay he composed and called *The Poet*. When he puts on robes to discuss poetry he rarefies the subject. The subject is common, not rare, as at his best he knew. It has much to do with what he chose to call fact. Philosophers can debate the question what a fact is, and whether there are any. The poet in Emerson, and indeed the writer generally, recognized them with lightning ease.

The perversity of fact inspires the paradox of his style. "It makes men very bad to talk good." The truth here is an imp of heaven, sitting on his shoulder and beseeching him not to be less tart than truth is, not to be less total in his view. In the journal which he kept through most years of his life he revealed how irresistible to him were the successful sayings of other men. His quotations, both in the journal and in the books of which it was the source, have an all but creative power. They are the diamonds he mixes with his dust—which in turn learns how to be diamonds too. The art of quotation, which for Emerson was scarcely an art since it was native to his daily breath, has seldom been practised with an equal perfection. It is not strange that one of his works should deal with the subject and be called *Quotation and Originality.* "He believed in quotation," says Oliver Wendell Holmes, "and borrowed from everybody and every book. Not in any stealthy or shamefaced way, but proudly, as a king borrows from one of his attendants the coin that bears his own image and superscription." Emerson, in other words, felt himself to be the peer of those he borrowed from. He was their partner in the enterprise of speaking suddenly and well. He liked best the sudden saying, with a hook on it perhaps, a hidden barb. "It makes men very bad to talk good." There is one of his own—one of his many, for he returned as many diamonds as he stole.

He read in his own fashion, for conclusions instead of arguments, for epigrams and graces instead of triumphs in development. His piece on *Memory,* as his journal for 1850 makes clear, owes much of what is in it to the great tenth book of St. Augustine's *Confessions*. "Admirable analysis," remarks Emerson, conscious no doubt that this was understatement, for there is nothing grander than the book he had been reading. But his own attempt to render back what he had read yields a collection of sentences rather than a frame of gigantic discourse. Emerson's unit was still the sentence. The shining sentence, he hoped, but still the sentence.

His journal was what he called it, a "savings bank" of sentences. Into it went daily the irreducible essence of what he thought or read, and out of it came his lectures and his essays. The chapters of *English Traits*, however much they may seem to read right on as if they had been written so, were nevertheless a series of drafts on Emerson's precious bank. They were pieced together from sentences he had written to himself over decades, and latterly from lectures he gave while he was preparing *Representative Men* for the press. The book he was publishing was never the book he was thinking about. The books of Emerson formed slowly, as coal forms, underground.

Emerson himself formed slowly, after gropings and false starts. Born in Boston in 1803 of a line which on his father's side ran back through generations of preachers to the founding of the colony, he was manifestly destined to be a preacher in his turn, and he wasted years in trying to be one. When he knew he could not he was in his thirtieth year. Before this he had been a sober boy in Boston—not nearly so much liked by children, he once remarked, as he grew to be in middle age. Within the circle of his family he might be called frivolous, as sometimes he was, but toward the world he carried his head loftily. His youth came late, like his genius. Perhaps it took time for him to absorb the influence of his remarkable aunt, the picturesque and

formidable Mary Moody Emerson whose visits were so
frequent and whose preoccupation with death could be
so pungently stated. Emerson's portrait of her is one of
his best writings in its important kind. And her contribution to his success is something we cannot doubt. It
could not be felt at once, however, in its right force and
ratio.

At Harvard, where Emerson studied between 1817
and 1821, he commenced keeping his famous journal.
He began there, in other words, the one long book which
we may consider, as he did, his private masterpiece. As
now printed it is thousands of pages long, and stretches
in time over more than five decades. In its early shadows
we may trace his doubts of himself as he sought first to
be a teacher and then a preacher. The bulk of its entries
is speculative. His first marriage, to Ellen Tucker in
1829, is given only a line, as his second marriage, to
Lydia Jackson, was in 1835. His marriages were important to him, but it was not of them that he wrote.
He wrote of Plato and Swedenborg, of morals and the
human myth, of science and the soul. And it might have
been clear to any stranger looking on that the young
man who wrote would never in the end be satisfied with
the ministry. His speculation was unlimited, his language was that of a lay genius, not of a divine.

It was fortunate for Emerson that when he resigned
as pastor from the Second Church of Boston he was able
almost at once to make the first of his three voyages to
Europe. For in Scotland, in the summer of 1833, he met
Thomas Carlyle. He also met Landor, Coleridge, John
Stuart Mill, and Wordsworth before he came home; but
Carlyle was his great discovery, as he was Carlyle's.
The long friendship of these two men is strange, or is
perhaps not strange, in view of the differences between
them. Their correspondence, lasting forty years, is tem-

pestuous on the one side, serene on the other, yet mutually tempered by an affection which based itself upon a sincerity which each found in his opposite. Emerson came home, then, with memories of at least one man he could never have met in America; and with his mind set in the areas where it would continue to operate while it lasted. The native Unitarianism, republicanism, skepticism were henceforth not enough. Emerson "transcended" these in search of the headier, more dangerous realities which he identified with what he called the soul. German philosophy and Oriental scriptures were new fields in which he was to read. He preached a little longer, but it was not very long. He was preparing himself now to be the lecturer and writer whom the world of the nineteenth century knew so well.

It was by lectures that he made his living, and his manner on the platform was much like what it had been in the pulpit—where, as an observer once said, he seemed "the most gracious of mortals. . . . Our choir was a pretty good one, but its best was coarse and discordant after Emerson's voice. I remember of the sermon only that it had an indefinite charm of simplicity and wisdom, with occasional illustrations from nature which were about the most delicate and dainty things I had ever heard." Lowell's account of the lecturer is quite in harmony with this. Emerson seemed cold but was not —if one listened. And people did listen, if only to the voice. "I have heard some great speakers and some accomplished orators, but never any that so moved and persuaded men as he. There is a kind of undertow in that rich baritone of his that sweeps our minds from their deeper waters with a drift we cannot and would not resist. And how artfully (for Emerson is a long-studied artist in these things) does the deliberate utterance, that seems waiting for the fit word, seem to admit us partners in the labor of thought, and make us feel as if the glance of humor were a sudden suggestion, as if the perfect phrase lying written there on the desk were as unexpected to him as to us!"

Emerson lectured everywhere—in Boston, of course, but in every other city too, and in many lesser places farther west. It was a hard life, of which he often complained; for he loved his family and his study in Concord, and the conditions of travel were rugged. He found himself in a burning hotel, on a blazing Great Lakes Steamer; he traveled over ice and snow; he came uncomfortably close to cholera; he missed trains, had his pockets picked, borrowed money, and in general suffered the exhaustions incident to "a puppet show of Eleusinian Mysteries," as he once called his trade. Yet he believed in the trade, and so could find the courage to go on with it. When he returned to Concord he had his family and books again, and he had the friends—Thoreau, Alcott, Hawthorne, Margaret Fuller—with whom it was so rich a pleasure to converse.

He published his first book, *Nature*, in 1836. It was also his most systematic one. Its symmetry he never captured again, though its ideas are distributed through all of his other works—in maturer language, for this manifesto still has something in it of the callow and the incomprehensible. It is Emerson hoping to be a philosopher, which he never was. "Our age is retrospective," he begins. "It builds the sepulchres of the fathers. It writes biographies, histories, and criticism. The foregoing generations beheld God and nature face to face; we, through their eyes. Why should not we also enjoy an original relation to the universe? . . . There are new lands, new men, new thoughts. Let us demand our own works and laws and worship." So far so fine, but in the ensuing chapters Emerson is less successful when he attempts an ordered statement of the functions Nature has in man's life. He was more successful in the series of ringing addresses he delivered during the next half-dozen years: addresses in which he repeated the gist of the foregoing sentences, and applied it where it was needed. *The American Scholar,* his Phi Beta Kappa oration at Harvard in 1837, is still the most famous of these addresses, though a close rival is the one he made next year to the graduating class of the Divinity School at Cambridge. Both were electric in their effect, and together they set a foundation beneath the career Emerson was now about to build.

Between 1840 and 1844 he was occupied with *The Dial,* a Transcendental journal of genuine if now dated distinction, and with the publication of his *Essays* (1841, 1844). The *Essays* are still his best-known writings, though it can be doubted that they are his best. In them he is the writer preaching—with grace and learning, and with an ethical passion which would be proper to any man, yet with a tendency to abandon art for unction, to lose the subject in an attitude that takes the place of principle. Having found a tone, Emerson makes the most of it: too much of it, in fact, as many readers after the passage of a century attest. They speak of a monotony in the inspiration, a too-great rarity in the discourse, and a drift in all the *Essays* toward a single end at which Emerson seems unable to arrive. Detached paragraphs are better than the wholes which are their contexts. The sentences are all. And this is Emerson's genius at work, but under less favorable conditions than his future volumes will provide.

Representative Men (1850), for instance, gains by possessing a theme which can be stated. "The uses of great men"—that is the point to which the chapters on Plato, Swedenborg, Montaigne, Shakespeare, Napoleon, and Goethe are addressed. If the chapter on Montaigne is the best of these, the reason is not that Emerson loved Plato or Shakespeare less. His praise of them, in the *Journals* and elsewhere, is constant. It is rather that in Montaigne he met the talker and the skeptic he himself was on weekdays. This fellow always fascinated him. He was not of the highest repute, and the report he gave of the world was horizontal, not erect. Montaigne, in other words, was not high; and Emerson was high. But he was low also, and loved facts. The admission makes rare reading.

The volume of *Poems* which Emerson published at the end of 1846 (it was dated 1847) was not followed by another such collection until 1867, when *May-Day and Other Pieces* appeared. Emerson as a poet has been variously praised, but no reader of his finest lines has missed in them the strange, rapt music which is easier to hear than to explain. Emerson's theory of poetry was that it comes suddenly or not at all; it too is sentences —golden sentences which arrive as odors do in spring, fitfully, from no named source. He was not interested in the craft of such men as Dryden or Pope, or even in the sustained glories of certain still greater poets whom he admired without reservation. He preferred the wild notes; and caught many of them in his pages. Hardly a poem of his, with the exception of "Brahma," "Days," and "The Rhodora," is even in its excellence. He usually begins better than he finishes—his intelligence, somewhat against his theory, working out what his inspiration has deserted. But at his top he reaches excellence indeed; the best of him belongs with the best American poetry.

He made his second visit to Europe in 1847, seeing Carlyle again and a dozen others who were as eager as he was for the meeting. His *Essays* had made him famous on both sides of the ocean. Matthew Arnold was to venture the opinion at a later date that no prose had been more influential in the nineteenth century than Emerson's had been. Here now was that influential man, and the addresses he gave in London were well attended—by Carlyle among others, who would have sat and listened to few other living persons. While he was in England Emerson added to the stock of impressions and ideas which eventually were to find such brilliant expression in *English Traits* (1856). This book, published after eight years of further thinking and lecturing on the subject, may well prove in time to have been his surest success. He told Margaret Fuller that he admired the English people more than he liked them, and this perhaps is the key to the unique accomplishment of his volume. A certain conflict between the two states of admiration and repulsion may be what gives the work its tension, its effect of a special energy released in full and even comic force. Few books are more intoxicating or infectious. The people he describes —and no people has been better described by a stranger to them—becomes in his hands both heroic and preposterous, both magnificent and odd. Spiritually they are declared to be less than men should be—unideal, indifferent, sluggish, and complacent. Yet even as this is suggested it is also borne in upon the reader that the English, consciously or not, have developed a health of tone, a vigor in virtue, an unparalleled personal strength of every sort, which men everywhere must find glorious. The net finding is such as only the book itself can set forth. In the reading, however, it works its own charm as it goes. It is the wittiest work of America's wittiest writer.

The Conduct of Life (1860) was the outgrowth of perhaps the most popular lectures Emerson ever gave, and Carlyle thought it his best book. It may not be that. but its last chapter, called "Illusions," is a candidate for being its author's most beautiful achievement in prose. *Society and Solitude*, published ten years later, is still noteworthy if only for a sentence of six words, in the essay called "Civilization," which has often been misinterpreted: "Hitch your wagon to a star." Emerson means both more and less than merely this: "Aim high." The context is plain, and should have left nobody in doubt concerning the author's full intention. "Now that is the wisdom of a man, in every instance of his labor, to hitch his wagon to a star, and see his chore done by the gods themselves. That is the way we are strong, by borrowing the might of the elements. The forces of steam, gravity, galvanism, light, magnets, wind, fire, serve us day by day and cost us nothing." It is civilization as all men understand it that he is speaking of— the conspiracy of men to make the most of nature as they build and work. When, two pages on, the sentence appears again in its classic form—"Hitch your wagon to a star"—the reference is broader, to the gods of love and justice, but the meaning has not changed. The title-essay of the volume returns Emerson to one of his favorite themes: the conflicting claims upon us of society and ourselves. He could never make up his mind in this difficult area. He loved both solitude and society; and now he lets it go at that. "If solitude is proud, so is society vulgar." "Solitude is impracticable, and society fatal." He believed as much as his young friend Henry Thoreau did that society defeats the individual, but he could not forget that the world is full of interesting persons. He knew it was, for he had seen them. And they had seen him; the admiration was mutual.

Letters and Social Aims was published while Emerson still lived, in 1876, but his faculties had so far failed

him as to make it necessary for another, James Elliot
Cabot, to sift the manuscript notes and prepare them
for the press. Emerson had begun to lose his memory
and his concentration of mind only a few years after the
close of the Civil War, which itself was a hard period
for him to live through. His interest in it was both intense and bewildered. He had seldom lent his tongue to
public causes, being doubtful of reformers and skeptical
of social programs. The reform he asked for was personal
—each citizen a prince. Yet in 1838 he had written a
letter of protest to President Van Buren against the removal of the Cherokee Indians from Georgia; and in company with other New Englanders he had disapproved
of the annexation of Texas, the Fugitive Slave Law,
the treatment of John Brown, and slavery as an institution. "Sometimes gunpowder smells good," he said when
war broke out; but the progress of hostilities distressed
and depressed him, and in 1866—not necessarily as a result—he wrote the poem "Terminus" in which he confessed that "the god of bounds" had said to him: "No
more!" In 1871 he was taken by friends on an outing to
California. In 1872 his house in Concord burned—a
blow to his strength which a third trip to Europe, when
he saw Carlyle for the last time, but partially repaired.
His death in 1882 left manuscripts still calling for publication. His correspondence with Carlyle came out the
next year. In 1884 appeared *Lectures and Biographical
Sketches,* notable particularly for its pieces on Thoreau,
Mary Moody Emerson, and Carlyle: pieces which revealed to many readers a hitherto unsuspected genius in
portraiture. They are now among his best-known works,
along with *Historic Notes of Life and Letters in New
England,* an exercise in social and intellectual history
such as few men could have carried through so wittily
and triumphantly. There was a volume of *Miscellanies*

in 1884, and in 1893 appeared *Natural History of Intellect and Other Papers,* which now stands as the last volume in his collected works. But the *Journals* were still to come, in ten volumes published between 1909 and 1914. With them the tale was substantially complete.

Emerson wanted no followers. His wish, he said, was to bring men not to him but to themselves. His message to each man was that each man is great and should think for himself. The reason he distrusted communities—as he makes clear in *New England Reformers* and *Historic Notes of Life and Letters in New England*—was that communities made thought common; the members leaned on one another. He liked only the best of everything, in philosophy, in farming, or in dancing, and believed it to be the fruit of individual endeavor. Most individuals were not aware of the greatness within them; to them, then, he addressed his counsel of perfection. If it sometimes seems too bland a counsel, too confident a hymn to certain success, that is Emerson's optimism at work. His optimism could be childish, and at worst it could be dangerous. At its most harmless now it sounds like commercial inspiration. At its most harmful it says things such as this at the end of the essay called *Circles:* "A man never rises so high as when he knows not whither he is going." Cromwell is being quoted, but the sentiment is approved. Emerson trusted the world not to be tragic, as his essay on tragedy reveals. It is an interesting essay because it comes from him, but it suggests how seriously he was limited by having no theory of evil. He counted on things to take care of themselves. He could not be angry, he could not be sad. He could only throw up his incessant fountain of angelic epigrams, of saintly acceptances. In his journal he could reflect that his reputation for good nature was not always deserved. "I too, like puss, have a retractile claw." But he did not show this claw in public. From birth to death he beamed—a long time to be occupied with only half of man's duty. Yet his beaming was in itself beautiful; and it was sweeter for the wit with which the action was performed.

Intellectual isolationism, a vice to which Americans are regularly and fatally drawn, was scarcely Emerson's vice, though *The American Scholar,* which asked its audience to forget Europe, might seem to say so. Emerson, like Whitman who echoed him, meant better things than he said. He meant that Europe should be forgotten only after it had been mastered. His own effort was to master a tradition which embraced not only the Greeks but the Hindus, not only Plato but the *Bhagavad-Gita* (from which he took his poem "Brahma"). Not to speak of Shakespeare and Montaigne, or—nearer home—of Goethe and Carlyle. In his own way Emerson was a scholar, and proud to be one. It was the proud scholar he wanted in America: one who knew all the ways of life, old as well as new, and who then could choose for himself. His complaint of his contemporaries was that they lacked self-reliance and fresh force. When he said of the English that they had "more personal force than any other people," he was thinking of his own people, and criticizing them. It may be only a legend that Americans are not lazy. Emerson found them lazy, and labored to wake them up. But his appeal was not to their ignorance. It was to what they might become if they grew into scholars. As his first book declared, a theory of nature was needed. Too many phenomena were unexplained—"as language, sleep, madness, dreams, beasts, sex." He never produced the theory, but he never gave up trying. He never gave up hoping that Americans were as superior as he suspected they were.

ooo

Programs

EDITOR'S NOTE

BETWEEN the publication of *Nature* in 1836 and the completed publication of the *Essays* in 1844, Emerson delivered a series of addresses which announced him as the prophet of his generation. They were prophetic by intention as well as in tone. Like many another American of his time, Emerson conceived himself in the orator's role. The new republic—for it was still new—needed voices to declare its future greatness and to warn it of the dangers in its way; for prophecy is critical too, and reminds the people of their destiny when they show signs of wandering from it.

The audience Emerson presupposes is the young men of America. To them he addresses his trumpet notes, to them he delivers his analysis of the perils in the path. *The American Scholar* is intended for what his listeners in fact took it to be, a declaration of intellectual independence. The Divinity College address measured the possible future of religion in America, and moved its audience to consider whether the realities of that future had yet been taken into account. *Man the Reformer* and *The Conservative* were political and social in their bearing. They did not depart from the ground on which their predecessors had stood, but they attempted a statement of the secular role which any young man might hope to play in the society to come. They were at once —and this baffled certain listeners—radical and conservative. Emerson expected more changes from the individual than he expected from the crowd; indeed, the crowd would increase its virtue only as its members perfected themselves. Emerson invested no hope in mechanical improvements of man's state. This is why he never could take quite seriously the experimental communities which dotted his America. *New England Reformers,* known now as one of the *Essays,* was originally an address in the manner of its fellows in this section. He is kinder to the zealots than he will be again, yet even now he lets his humor play over their programs. His own programs were in the end one program. "Union must be inward. . . . Union must be ideal in actual individualism."

THE AMERICAN SCHOLAR

*An Oration Delivered before the Phi Beta Kappa Society,
at Cambridge, August 31, 1837.*

MR. PRESIDENT and Gentlemen, I greet you
on the recommencement of our literary year. Our
anniversary is one of hope, and, perhaps, not enough of
labor. We do not meet for games of strength or skill, for
the recitation of histories, tragedies, and odes, like the
ancient Greeks; for parliaments of love and poesy, like
the Troubadours; nor for the advancement of science,
like our contemporaries in the British and European capitals. Thus far, our holiday has been simply a friendly
sign of the survival of the love of letters amongst a
people too busy to give to letters any more. As such it is
precious as the sign of an indestructible instinct. Perhaps
the time is already come when it ought to be, and will be,
something else; when the sluggard intellect of this continent will look from under its iron lids and fill the postponed expectation of the world with something better
than the exertions of mechanical skill. Our day of dependence, our long apprenticeship to the learning of
other lands, draws to a close. The millions that around
us are rushing into life, cannot always be fed on the sere
remains of foreign harvests. Events, actions arise, that
must be sung, that will sing themselves. Who can doubt
that poetry will revive and lead in a new age, as the star
in the constellation Harp, which now flames in our

zenith, astronomers announce, shall one day be the pole-star for a thousand years?

In this hope I accept the topic which not only usage but the nature of our association seem to prescribe to this day—the AMERICAN SCHOLAR. Year by year we come up hither to read one more chapter of his biography. Let us inquire what light new days and events have thrown on his character and his hopes.

It is one of those fables which out of an unknown antiquity convey an unlooked-for wisdom, that the gods, in the beginning, divided Man into men, that he might be more helpful to himself; just as the hand was divided into fingers, the better to answer its end.

The old fable covers a doctrine ever new and sublime; that there is One Man—present to all particular men only partially, or through one faculty; and that you must take the whole society to find the whole man. Man is not a farmer, or a professor, or an engineer, but he is all. Man is priest, and scholar, and statesman, and producer, and soldier. In the *divided* or social state these functions are parcelled out to individuals, each of whom aims to do his stint of the joint work, whilst each other performs his. The fable implies that the individual, to possess himself, must sometimes return from his own labor to embrace all the other laborers. But, unfortunately, this original unit, this fountain of power, has been so distributed to multitudes, has been so minutely subdivided and peddled out, that it is spilled into drops, and cannot be gathered. The state of society is one in which the members have suffered amputation from the trunk, and strut about so many walking monsters—a good finger, a neck, a stomach, an elbow, but never a man.

Man is thus metamorphosed into a thing, into many things. The planter, who is Man sent out into the field to gather food, is seldom cheered by any idea of the true dignity of his ministry. He sees his bushel and his cart, and nothing beyond, and sinks into the farmer, instead of Man on the farm. The tradesman scarcely ever gives an ideal worth to his work, but is ridden by the routine of his craft, and the soul is subject to dollars. The priest becomes a form; the attorney a statute-book; the mechanic a machine; the sailor a rope of the ship.

In this distribution of functions the scholar is the delegated intellect. In the right state he is *Man Thinking*. In the degenerate state, when the victim of society, he tends to become a mere thinker, or still worse, the parrot of other men's thinking.

In this view of him, as Man Thinking, the theory of his office is contained. Him Nature solicits with all her placid, all her monitory pictures; him the past instructs; him the future invites. Is not indeed every man a student, and do not all things exist for the student's behoof? And, finally, is not the true scholar the only true master? But the old oracle said, "All things have two handles: beware of the wrong one." In life, too often, the scholar errs with mankind and forfeits his privilege. Let us see him in his school, and consider him in reference to the main influences he receives.

I

The first in time and the first in importance of the influences upon the mind is that of nature. Every day, the sun; and, after sunset, Night and her stars. Ever the winds blow; ever the grass grows. Every day, men and women, conversing, beholding and beholden. The scholar is he of all men whom this spectacle most engages. He must settle its value in his mind. What is nature to him? There is never a beginning, there is never an end, to the inexplicable continuity of this web of God, but always circular power returning into itself. Therein it resembles his own spirit, whose beginning, whose ending, he never can find—so entire, so boundless. Far too as her splendors shine, system on system shooting like rays, upward, downward, without center, without circumference—in the mass and in the particle, Nature hastens to render account of herself to the mind. Classification begins. To the young mind every thing is individual, stands by itself. By and by, it finds how to join two things and see in them one nature; then three, then three thousand; and so, tyrannized over by its own unifying instinct, it goes on tying things together, diminishing anomalies, discovering roots running under ground whereby contrary and remote things cohere and flower out from one stem. It presently learns that since the dawn of history there has been a constant accumulation and classifying of facts. But what is classification but the perceiving that these objects are not chaotic, and are not foreign, but have a law which is also a law of the human mind? The astronomer discovers that geometry, a pure abstraction of the human mind, is the measure of planetary motion. The chemist finds proportions and intelligible method throughout matter; and science is nothing but the finding of analogy, identity, in the most remote parts. The ambitious soul sits down before each refractory fact; one after another reduces all strange constitutions, all new powers, to their class and their law, and goes on forever to animate the last fibre of organization, the outskirts of nature, by insight.

Thus to him, to this school-boy under the bending dome of day, is suggested that he and it proceed from one root; one is leaf and one is flower; relation, sympathy, stirring in every vein. And what is that root? Is not that the soul of his soul? A thought too bold; a dream too wild. Yet when this spiritual light shall have revealed the law of more earthly natures—when he has learned to worship the soul, and to see that the natural philosophy that now is, is only the first gropings of its gigantic hand, he shall look forward to an ever expanding knowledge as to a becoming creator. He shall see that nature is the opposite of the soul, answering to it part for part. One is seal and one is print. Its beauty is the beauty of his own mind. Its laws are the laws of his own mind. Nature then becomes to him the measure of his attainments. So much of nature as he is ignorant of, so much of his own mind does he not yet possess. And, in fine, the ancient precept, "Know thyself," and the modern precept, "Study nature," become at last one maxim.

II

The next great influence into the spirit of the scholar is the mind of the Past—in whatever form, whether of literature, of art, of institutions, that mind is inscribed. Books are the best type of the influence of the past, and perhaps we shall get at the truth—learn the amount of this influence more conveniently—by considering their value alone.

The theory of books is noble. The scholar of the first age received into him the world around; brooded thereon; gave it the new arrangement of his own mind, and uttered it again. It came into him life; it went out from him truth. It came to him short-lived actions; it went out from him immortal thoughts. It came to him business; it went from him poetry. It was dead fact; now, it is quick thought. It can stand, and it can go. It now endures, it now flies, it now inspires. Precisely in proportion to the depth of mind from which it issued, so high does it soar, so long does it sing.

Or, I might say, it depends on how far the process had gone, of transmuting life into truth. In proportion to the completeness of the distillation, so will the purity and imperishableness of the product be. But none is quite perfect. As no air-pump can by any means make a perfect vacuum, so neither can any artist entirely exclude the conventional, the local, the perishable from his book, or write a book of pure thought, that shall be as efficient, in all respects, to a remote posterity, as to contemporaries, or rather to the second age. Each age, it is found, must write its own books; or rather, each generation for the next succeeding. The books of an older period will not fit this.

Yet hence arises a grave mischief. The sacredness which attaches to the act of creation, the act of thought, is transferred to the record. The poet chanting was felt to be a divine man: henceforth the chant is divine also. The writer was a just and wise spirit: henceforward it is settled the book is perfect; as love of the hero corrupts into worship of his statue. Instantly the book becomes noxious: the guide is a tyrant. The sluggish and perverted mind of the multitude, slow to open to the incursions of Reason, having once so opened, having once received this book, stands upon it, and makes an outcry if it is disparaged. Colleges are built on it. Books are written on it by thinkers, not by Man Thinking; by men of talent, that is, who start wrong, who set out from accepted dogmas, not from their own sight of principles. Meek young men grow up in libraries, believing it their duty to accept the views which Cicero, which Locke, which Bacon, have given; forgetful that Cicero, Locke, and Bacon were only young men in libraries when they wrote these books.

Hence, instead of Man Thinking, we have the book-worm. Hence the book-learned class, who value books, as such; not as related to nature and the human constitution, but as making a sort of Third Estate with the world and the soul. Hence the restorers of readings, the emendators, the bibliomaniacs of all degrees.

Books are the best of things, well used; abused, among the worst. What is the right use? What is the one end which all means go to effect? They are for nothing but to inspire. I had better never see a book than to be warped by its attraction clean out of my own orbit, and made a satellite instead of a system. The one thing in the world, of value, is the active soul. This every man is entitled to; this every man contains within him, although in almost all men obstructed, and as yet unborn. The soul active sees absolute truth and utters truth, or creates. In this action it is genius; not the privilege of here and there a favorite, but the sound estate of every man. In its essence it is progressive. The book, the college, the school of art, the institution of any kind, stop with some past utterance of genius. This is good, say they,—let us hold by this. They pin me down. They look backward and not forward. But genius looks forward: the eyes of man are set in his forehead, not in his hindhead: man hopes: genius creates. Whatever talents may be, if the man create not, the pure efflux of the Deity is not his—cinders and smoke there may be, but not yet flame. There are creative manners, there are creative actions, and creative words; manners, actions, words, that is, indicative of no custom or authority, but springing spontaneous from the mind's own sense of good and fair.

On the other part, instead of being its own seer, let it receive from another mind its truth, though it were in torrents of light, without periods of solitude, inquest, and self-recovery, and a fatal disservice is done. Genius is always sufficiently the enemy of genius by over-influence. The literature of every nation bears me witness. The English dramatic poets have Shakespearized now for two hundred years.

Undoubtedly there is a right way of reading, so it be sternly subordinated. Man Thinking must not be subdued by his instruments. Books are for the scholar's idle times. When he can read God directly, the hour is too precious to be wasted in other men's transcripts of their readings. But when the intervals of darkness come, as come they must—when the sun is hid and the stars withdraw their shining—we repair to the lamps which were kindled by their ray, to guide our steps to the East again, where the dawn is. We hear, that we may speak. The Arabian proverb says, "A fig tree, looking on a fig tree, becometh fruitful."

It is remarkable, the character of the pleasure we derive from the best books. They impress us with the conviction that one nature wrote and the same reads. We read the verses of one of the great English poets, of Chaucer, of Marvell, of Dryden, with the most modern joy—with a pleasure, I mean, which is in great part caused by the abstraction of all *time* from their verses. There is some awe mixed with the joy of our surprise, when this poet, who lived in some past world, two or three hundred years ago, says that which lies close to my own soul, that which I also had well-nigh thought and said. But for the evidence thence afforded to the philosophical doctrine of the identity of all minds, we should suppose some pre-established harmony, some foresight of souls that were to be, and some preparation of stores for their future wants, like the fact observed in insects, who lay up food before death for the young grub they shall never see.

I would not be hurried by any love of system, by any exaggeration of instincts, to underrate the Book. We all know, that as the human body can be nourished on any food, though it were boiled grass and the broth of shoes, so the human mind can be fed by any knowledge. And great and heroic men have existed who had almost no other information than by the printed page. I only would say that it needs a strong head to bear that diet. One must be an inventor to read well. As the proverb says, "He that would bring home the wealth of the Indies, must carry out the wealth of the Indies." There is then creative reading as well as creative writing. When the mind is braced by labor and invention, the page of whatever book we read becomes luminous with manifold allusion. Every sentence is doubly significant, and the sense of our author is as broad as the world. We then see, what is always true, that as the seer's hour of vision is short and rare among heavy days and months, so is its record, perchance, the least part of his volume. The discerning will read, in his Plato or Shakespeare, only that least part—only the authentic utterances of the oracle —all the rest he rejects, were it never so many times Plato's and Shakespeare's.

Of course there is a portion of reading quite indispensable to a wise man. History and exact science he must learn by laborious reading. Colleges, in like manner, have their indispensable office—to teach elements. But they can only highly serve us when they aim not to drill, but to create; when they gather from far every ray of various genius to their hospitable halls, and by the concentrated fires, set the hearts of their youth on flame. Thought and knowledge are natures in which apparatus and pretension avail nothing. Gowns and pecuniary foundations, though of towns of gold, can never countervail the least sentence or syllable of wit. Forget this, and our American colleges will recede in their public importance, whilst they grow richer every year.

III

There goes in the world a notion that the scholar should be a recluse, a valetudinarian—as unfit for any handiwork or public labor as a penknife for an ax. The so-called "practical men" sneer at speculative men, as if, because they speculate or *see*, they could do nothing. I have heard it said that the clergy—who are always, more universally than any other class, the scholars of their day—are addressed as women; that the rough, spontaneous conversation of men they do not hear, but only a mincing and diluted speech. They are often virtually disfranchised; and indeed there are advocates for their celibacy. As far as this is true of the studious classes, it is not just and wise. Action is with the scholar subordinate, but it is essential. Without it he is not yet man. Without it thought can never ripen into truth. Whilst the world hangs before the eye as a cloud of beauty, we cannot even see its beauty. Inaction is cowardice, but there can be no scholar without the heroic mind. The preamble of thought, the transition through which it passes from the unconscious to the conscious, is action. Only so much do I know, as I have lived. Instantly we know whose words are loaded with life, and whose not.

The world—this shadow of the soul, or *other me*, lies wide around. Its attractions are the keys which unlock my thoughts and make me acquainted with myself. I run eagerly into this resounding tumult. I grasp the hands of those next me, and take my place in the ring to suffer and to work, taught by an instinct that so shall the dumb abyss be vocal with speech. I pierce its order; I dissipate its fear; I dispose of it within the circuit of my expanding life. So much only of life as I know by experience, so much of the wilderness have I vanquished and planted, or so far have I extended my being, my dominion. I do not see how any man can afford, for the sake of his nerves and his nap, to spare any action in which he can partake. It is pearls and rubies to his discourse. Drudgery, calamity, exasperation, want, are instructors in eloquence and wisdom. The true scholar grudges every opportunity of action past by, as a loss of power.

It is the raw material out of which the intellect molds her splendid products. A strange process too, this by which experience is converted into thought, as a mulberry leaf is converted into satin. The manufacture goes forward at all hours.

The actions and events of our childhood and youth are now matters of calmest observation. They lie like fair pictures in the air. Not so with our recent actions—with the business which we now have in hand. On this we are quite unable to speculate. Our affections as yet circulate through it. We no more feel or know it than we feel the feet, or the hand, or the brain of our body. The new deed is yet a part of life—remains for a time immersed in our unconscious life. In some contemplative hour it detaches itself from the life like a ripe fruit, to become a thought of the mind. Instantly it is raised, transfigured; the corruptible has put on incorruption. Henceforth it is an object of beauty, however base its origin and neighborhood. Observe too the impossibility of antedating this act. In its grub state, it cannot fly, it cannot shine, it is a dull grub. But suddenly, without observation, the selfsame thing unfurls beautiful wings, and is an angel of wisdom. So is there no fact, no event, in our private history, which shall not, sooner or later, lose its adhesive, inert form, and astonish us by soaring from our body into the empyrean. Cradle and infancy, school and playground, the fear of boys, and dogs, and ferules, the love of little maids and berries, and many another fact that once filled the whole sky, are gone already; friend and relative, profession and party, town and country, nation and world, must also soar and sing.

Of course, he who has put forth his total strength in fit actions has the richest return of wisdom. I will not shut myself out of this globe of action, and transplant an oak into a flower-pot, there to hunger and pine; nor trust the revenue of some single faculty, and exhaust one vein of thought, much like those Savoyards, who, getting their livelihood by carving shepherds, shepherdesses, and smoking Dutchmen, for all Europe, went out one day to the mountain to find stock, and discovered that they had whittled up the last of their pine trees. Authors we have, in numbers, who have written out their vein, and who, moved by a commendable prudence, sail for Greece or Palestine, follow the trapper into the prairie, or ramble round Algiers, to replenish their merchantable stock.

If it were only for a vocabulary, the scholar would be covetous of action. Life is our dictionary. Years are well spent in country labors; in town; in the insight into trades and manufactures; in frank intercourse with many men and women; in science; in art; to the one end of mastering in all their facts a language by which to illustrate and embody our perceptions. I learn immediately from any speaker how much he has already lived, through the poverty or the splendor of his speech. Life lies behind us as the quarry from whence we get tiles and copestones for the masonry of today. This is the way to learn grammar. Colleges and books only copy the language which the field and the work-yard made.

But the final value of action, like that of books, and better than books, is that it is a resource. That great principle of Undulation in nature, that shows itself in the inspiring and expiring of the breath; in desire and satiety; in the ebb and flow of the sea; in day and night; in heat and cold; and, as yet more deeply ingrained in every atom and every fluid, is known to us under the name of Polarity—these "fits of easy transmission and reflection," as Newton called them—are the law of nature because they are the law of spirit.

The mind now thinks, now acts, and each fit reproduces the other. When the artist has exhausted his materials, when the fancy no longer paints, when thoughts are no longer apprehended and books are a weariness—he has always the resource *to live*. Character is higher than intellect. Thinking is the function. Living is the functionary. The stream retreats to its source. A great soul will be strong to live, as well as strong to think. Does he lack organ or medium to impart his truth? He can still fall back on this elemental force of living them. This is a total act. Thinking is a partial act. Let the grandeur of justice shine in his affairs. Let the beauty of affection cheer his lowly roof. Those "far from fame," who dwell and act with him, will feel the force of his constitution in the doings and passages of the day better than it can be measured by any public and designed display. Time shall teach him that the scholar loses no hour which the man lives. Herein he unfolds the sacred germ of his instinct, screened from influence. What is lost in seemliness is gained in strength. Not out of those on whom systems of education have exhausted their cul-

ture, comes the helpful giant to destroy the old or to
build the new, but out of unhandselled savage nature;
out of terrible Druids and Berserkers come at last Alfred
and Shakespeare.

I hear therefore with joy whatever is beginning to be
said of the dignity and necessity of labor to every citizen.
There is virtue yet in the hoe and the spade, for learned
as well as for unlearned hands. And labor is everywhere
welcome; always we are invited to work; only be this
limitation observed, that a man shall not for the sake of
wider activity sacrifice any opinion to the popular judgments and modes of action.

I have now spoken of the education of the scholar by
nature, by books, and by action. It remains to say somewhat of his duties.

They are such as become Man Thinking. They may
all be comprised in self-trust. The office of the scholar
is to cheer, to raise, and to guide men by showing them
facts amidst appearances. He plies the slow, unhonored,
and unpaid task of observation. Flamsteed and Herschel, in their glazed observatories, may catalogue the
stars with the praise of all men, and the results being
splendid and useful, honor is sure. But he, in his private
observatory, cataloguing obscure and nebulous stars of
the human mind, which as yet no man has thought of as
such—watching days and months sometimes for a few
facts; correcting still his old records—must relinquish
display and immediate fame. In the long period of his
preparation he must betray often an ignorance and shift-
lessness in popular arts, incurring the disdain of the able
who shoulder him aside. Long he must stammer in his
speech; often forego the living for the dead. Worse yet,
he must accept—how often! poverty and solitude. For

the ease and pleasure of treading the old road, accepting the fashions, the education, the religion of society, he takes the cross of making his own, and, of course, the self-accusation, the faint heart, the frequent uncertainty and loss of time, which are the nettles and tangling vines in the way of the self-relying and self-directed; and the state of virtual hostility in which he seems to stand to society, and especially to educated society. For all this loss and scorn, what offset? He is to find consolation in exercising the highest functions of human nature. He is one who raises himself from private considerations and breathes and lives on public and illustrious thoughts. He is the world's eye. He is the world's heart. He is to resist the vulgar prosperity that retrogrades ever to barbarism, by preserving and communicating heroic sentiments, noble biographies, melodious verse, and the conclusions of history. Whatsoever oracles the human heart, in all emergencies, in all solemn hours, has uttered as its commentary on the world of actions—these he shall receive and impart. And whatsoever new verdict Reason from her inviolable seat pronounces on the passing men and events of today—this he shall hear and promulgate.

These being his functions, it becomes him to feel all confidence in himself, and to defer never to the popular cry. He and he only knows the world. The world of any moment is the merest appearance. Some great decorum, some fetish of a government, some ephemeral trade, or war, or man, is cried up by half mankind and cried down by the other half, as if all depended on this particular up or down. The odds are that the whole question is not worth the poorest thought which the scholar has lost in listening to the controversy. Let him not quit his belief that a popgun is a popgun, though the ancient and honorable of the earth affirm it to be the crack of doom. In silence, in steadiness, in severe abstraction, let him hold by himself; add observation to observation, patient of neglect, patient of reproach, and bide his own time—happy enough if he can satisfy himself alone that this day he has seen something truly. Success treads on every right step. For the instinct is sure, that prompts him to tell his brother what he thinks. He then learns that in going down into the secrets of his own mind he has descended into the secrets of all minds. He learns that he who has mastered any law in his private thoughts, is master to that extent of all men whose language he speaks, and of all into whose language his own can be translated. The poet, in utter solitude remembering his spontaneous thoughts and recording them, is found to have recorded that which men in crowded cities find true for them also. The orator distrusts at first the fitness of his frank confessions, his want of knowledge of the persons he addresses, until he finds that he is the complement of his hearers—that they drink his words because he fulfils for them their own nature; the deeper he dives into his privatest, secretest presentiment, to his wonder he finds this is the most acceptable, most public, and universally true. The people delight in it; the better part of every man feels, This is my music; this is myself.

In self-trust all the virtues are comprehended. Free should the scholar be—free and brave. Free even to the definition of freedom, "without any hindrance that does not arise out of his own constitution." Brave; for fear is a thing which a scholar by his very function puts behind him. Fear always springs from ignorance. It is a shame to him if his tranquility, amid dangerous times, arise from the presumption that like children and women his is a protected class; or if he seek a temporary peace by the diversion of his thoughts from politics or vexed questions, hiding his head like an ostrich in the flowering bushes, peeping into microscopes, and turning rhymes, as a boy whistles to keep his courage up. So is the danger a danger still; so is the fear worse. Manlike let him turn and face it. Let him look into its eye and search its nature, inspect its origin—see the whelping of this lion—which lies no great way back; he will then find in himself a perfect comprehension of its nature and extent; he will have made his hands meet on the other side, and can henceforth defy it and pass on superior. The world is his who can see through its pretension. What deafness, what stone-blind custom, what overgrown error you behold is there only by sufferance—by your sufferance. See it to be a lie, and you have already dealt it its mortal blow.

Yes, we are the cowed—we the trustless. It is a mischievous notion that we are come late into nature; that the world was finished a long time ago. As the world was plastic and fluid in the hands of God, so it is ever to so much of his attributes as we bring to it. To ignorance and sin, it is flint. They adapt themselves to it as they may; but in proportion as a man has anything in him divine, the firmament flows before him and takes his signet and form. Not he is great who can alter matter, but he who can alter my state of mind. They are the kings of the world who give the color of their present thought to all nature and all art, and persuade men by the cheerful serenity of their carrying the matter, that this thing which they do is the apple which the ages have desired to pluck, now at last ripe, and inviting nations to the harvest. The great man makes the great thing. Wherever Macdonald sits, there is the head of the table. Linnæus makes botany the most alluring of studies, and wins it from the farmer and the herb-woman; Davy, chemistry; and Cuvier, fossils. The day is always his who works in it with serenity and great aims. The unstable estimates of men crowd to him whose mind is filled with a truth, as the heaped waves of the Atlantic follow the moon.

For this self-trust, the reason is deeper than can be fathomed—darker than can be enlightened. I might not carry with me the feeling of my audience in stating my own belief. But I have already shown the ground of my hope, in adverting to the doctrine that man is one. I believe man has been wronged; he has wronged himself. He has almost lost the light that can lead him back to his prerogatives. Men are become of no account. Men in history, men in the world of today, are bugs, are spawn, and are called "the mass" and "the herd." In a century, in a millennium, one or two men; that is to say, one or two approximations to the right state of every man. All the rest behold in the hero or the poet their own green and crude being—ripened; yes, and are content to be less, so *that* may attain to its full stature. What a testimony, full of grandeur, full of pity, is borne to the demands of his own nature, by the poor clansman, the poor partisan, who rejoices in the glory of his chief. The poor and the low find some amends to their immense moral capacity, for their acquiescence in a political and social inferiority. They are content to be brushed like flies from the path of a great person, so that justice shall be done by him to that common nature which it is the dearest desire of all to see enlarged and glorified. They sun themselves in the great man's light, and feel it to be their own element. They cast the dignity of man from their downtrod selves upon the shoulders of a hero, and will perish to add one drop of blood to make that great heart beat, those giant sinews combat and conquer. He lives for us, and we live in him.

Men such as they are, very naturally seek money or power; and power because it is as good as money—the "spoils," so called, "of office." And why not? for they aspire to the highest, and this, in their sleep-walking, they dream is highest. Wake them and they shall quit the false good and leap to the true, and leave governments to clerks and desks. This revolution is to be wrought by the gradual domestication of the idea of Culture. The main enterprise of the world for splendor, for extent, is the upbuilding of a man. Here are the materials strewn along the ground. The private life of one man shall be a more illustrious monarchy, more formidable to its enemy, more sweet and serene in its influence to its friend, than any kingdom in history. For a man, rightly viewed, comprehendeth the particular natures of all men. Each philosopher, each bard, each actor has only done for me, as by a delegate, what one day I can do for myself. The books which once we valued more than the apple of the eye, we have quite exhausted. What is that but saying that we have come up with the point of view which the universal mind took through the eyes of one scribe; we have been that man, and have passed on. First, one, then another, we drain all cisterns, and waxing greater by all these supplies, we crave a better and more abundant food. The man has never lived that can feed us ever. The human mind cannot be enshrined in a person who shall set a barrier on any one side to this unbounded, unboundable empire. It is one central fire, which, flaming now out of the lips of Etna, lightens the capes of Sicily, and now out of the throat of Vesuvius, illuminates the towers and vineyards of Naples. It is one light which beams out of a thousand stars. It is one soul which animates all men.

But I have dwelt perhaps tediously upon this abstraction of the Scholar. I ought not to delay longer to add what I have to say of nearer reference to the time and to this country.

Historically, there is thought to be a difference in the ideas which predominate over successive epochs, and there are data for marking the genius of the Classic, of the Romantic, and now of the Reflective or Philosophical age. With the views I have intimated of the oneness or the identity of the mind through all individuals, I do not much dwell on these differences. In fact, I believe each individual passes through all three. The boy is a Greek; the youth, romantic; the adult, reflective. I deny not however that a revolution in the leading idea may be distinctly enough traced.

Our age is bewailed as the age of Introversion. Must that needs be evil? We, it seems, are critical; we are embarrassed with second thoughts; we cannot enjoy any thing for hankering to know whereof the pleasure consists; we are lined with eyes; we see with our feet; the time is infected with Hamlet's unhappiness—

> Sicklied o'er with the pale cast of thought.

It is so bad then? Sight is the last thing to be pitied. Would we be blind? Do we fear lest we should outsee nature and God, and drink truth dry? I look upon the discontent of the literary class as a mere announcement of the fact that they find themselves not in the state of mind of their fathers, and regret the coming state as untried; as a boy dreads the water before he has learned that he can swim. If there is any period one would desire to be born in, is it not the age of Revolution; when the old and the new stand side by side and admit of being compared; when the energies of all men are searched by fear and by hope; when the historic glories of the old can be compensated by the rich possibilities of the new era? This time, like all times, is a very good one, if we but know what to do with it.

I read with some joy of the auspicious signs of the coming days, as they glimmer already through poetry and art, through philosophy and science, through church and state.

One of these signs is the fact that the same movement which effected the elevation of what was called the lowest class in the state, assumed in literature a very marked and as benign an aspect. Instead of the sublime and beautiful, the near, the low, the common, was explored and poetized. That which had been negligently trodden under foot by those who were harnessing and provisioning themselves for long journeys into far countries, is suddenly found to be richer than all foreign parts. The literature of the poor, the feelings of the child, the philosophy of the street, the meaning of household life, are the topics of the time. It is a great stride. It is a sign—is it not? of new vigor when the extremities are made active, when currents of warm life run into the hands and the feet. I ask not for the great, the remote, the romantic; what is doing in Italy or Arabia; what is Greek art, or Provençal minstrelsy; I embrace the common, I explore and sit at the feet of the familiar, the low. Give me insight into today, and you may have the antique and future worlds. What would we really know the meaning of? The meal in the firkin; the milk in the pan; the ballad in the street; the news of the boat; the glance of the eye; the form and the gait of the body—show me the ultimate reason of these matters; show me the sublime presence of the highest spiritual cause lurking, as always it does lurk, in these suburbs and extremities of nature; let me see every trifle bristling with the polarity that ranges it instantly on an eternal law; and the shop, the plough, and the ledger referred to the like cause by which light undulates and poets sing—and the world lies no longer a dull miscellany and lumber-room, but has form and order; there is no trifle, there is no puzzle, but one design unites and animates the farthest pinnacle and the lowest trench.

This idea has inspired the genius of Goldsmith, Burns, Cowper, and, in a newer time, of Goethe, Wordsworth, and Carlyle. This idea they have differently followed and with various success. In contrast with their writing, the style of Pope, of Johnson, of Gibbon, looks cold and pedantic. This writing is blood-warm. Man is surprised to find that things near are not less beautiful and wondrous than things remote. The near explains the far. The drop is a small ocean. A man is related to all nature. This perception of the worth of the vulgar is fruitful in discoveries. Goethe, in this very thing the most modern of the moderns, has shown us, as none ever did, the genius of the ancients.

There is one man of genius who has done much for this philosophy of life, whose literary value has never yet been rightly estimated—I mean Emanuel Swedenborg. The most imaginative of men, yet writing with the precision of a mathematician, he endeavored to engraft a purely philosophical Ethics on the popular Christianity of his time. Such an attempt of course must have difficulty which no genius could surmount. But he saw and showed the connection between nature and the affections of the soul. He pierced the emblematic or spiritual character of the visible, audible, tangible world. Especially did his shade-loving muse hover over and interpret the lower parts of nature; he showed the mysterious bond that allies moral evil to the foul material forms, and has given in epical parables a theory of insanity, of beasts, of unclean and fearful things.

Another sign of our times, also marked by an analogous political movement, is the new importance given to the single person. Everything that tends to insulate the individual—to surround him with barriers of natural respect, so that each man shall feel the world is his, and man shall treat with man as a sovereign state with a sovereign state—tends to true union as well as greatness. "I learned," said the melancholy Pestalozzi, "that no man in God's wide earth is either willing or able to help any other man." Help must come from the bosom alone. The scholar is that man who must take up into himself all the ability of the time, all the contributions of the past, all the hopes of the future. He must be an university of knowledges. If there be one lesson more than another which should pierce his ear, it is, The world is nothing, the man is all; in yourself is the law of all nature, and you know not yet how a globule of sap ascends; in yourself slumbers the whole of Reason; it is for you to know all; it is for you to dare all. Mr. President and Gentlemen, this confidence in the unsearched might of man belongs, by all motives, by all prophecy, by all preparation, to the American Scholar. We have listened too long to the courtly muses of Europe. The spirit of the American freeman is already suspected to be timid, imitative, tame. Public and private avarice make the air we breathe thick and fat. The scholar is decent, indolent, complaisant. See already the tragic consequence. The mind of this country, taught to aim at low objects, eats upon itself. There is no work for any but the decorous and the complaisant. Young men of the fairest promise, who begin life upon our shores, inflated by the mountain winds, shined upon by all the stars of

God, find the earth below not in unison with these, but are hindered from action by the disgust which the principles on which business is managed inspire, and turn drudges, or die of disgust, some of them suicides. What is the remedy? They did not yet see, and thousands of young men as hopeful now crowding to the barriers for the career do not yet see, that if the single man plant himself indomitably on his instincts, and there abide, the huge world will come round to him. Patience— patience; with the shades of all the good and great for company; and for solace the perspective of your own infinite life; and for work the study and the communication of principles, the making those instincts prevalent, the conversion of the world. Is it not the chief disgrace in the world, not to be an unit—not to be reckoned one character—not to yield that peculiar fruit which each man was created to bear, but to be reckoned in the gross, in the hundred, or the thousand, of the party, the section, to which we belong; and our opinion predicted geographically, as the north, or the south? Not so, brothers and friends—please God, ours shall not be so. We will walk on our own feet; we will work with our own hands; we will speak our own minds. The study of letters shall be no longer a name for pity, for doubt, and for sensual indulgence. The dread of man and the love of man shall be a wall of defence and a wreath of joy around all. A nation of men will for the first time exist, because each believes himself inspired by the Divine Soul which also inspires all men.

AN ADDRESS

*Delivered before the Senior Class in Divinity College,
Cambridge, Sunday Evening, July 15, 1838.*

IN THIS refulgent summer, it has been a luxury to
draw the breath of life. The grass grows, the buds
burst, the meadow is spotted with fire and gold in the
tint of flowers. The air is full of birds, and sweet with
the breath of the pine, the balm-of-Gilead, and the new
hay. Night brings no gloom to the heart with its welcome shade. Through the transparent darkness the stars
pour their almost spiritual rays. Man under them seems
a young child, and his huge globe a toy. The cool night
bathes the world as with a river, and prepares his eyes
again for the crimson dawn. The mystery of nature was
never displayed more happily. The corn and the wine
have been freely dealt to all creatures, and the never-
broken silence with which the old bounty goes forward
has not yielded yet one word of explanation. One is constrained to respect the perfection of this world in which
our senses converse. How wide; how rich; what invitation from every property it gives to every faculty of
man! In its fruitful soils; in its navigable sea; in its mountains of metal and stone; in its forests of all woods; in
its animals; in its chemical ingredients; in the powers
and path of light, heat, attraction and life, it is well
worth the pith and heart of great men to subdue and
enjoy it. The planters, the mechanics, the inventors, the

47

astronomers, the builders of cities, and the captains, history delights to honor.

But when the mind opens and reveals the laws which
traverse the universe and make things what they are,
then shrinks the great world at once into a mere illustration and fable of this mind. What am I? and What is?
asks the human spirit with a curiosity new-kindled, but
never to be quenched. Behold these outrunning laws,
which our imperfect apprehension can see tend this way
and that, but not come full circle. Behold these infinite
relations, so like, so unlike; many, yet one. I would
study, I would know, I would admire forever. These
works of thought have been the entertainments of the
human spirit in all ages.

A more secret, sweet, and overpowering beauty appears to man when his heart and mind open to the
sentiment of virtue. Then he is instructed in what is
above him. He learns that his being is without bound;
that to the good, to the perfect, he is born, low as he
now lies in evil and weakness. That which he venerates
is still his own, though he has not realized it yet. *He
ought.* He knows the sense of that grand word, though
his analysis fails to render account of it. When in in-
nocency or when by intellectual perception he attains
to say—"I love the Right; Truth is beautiful within and
without forevermore. Virtue, I am thine; save me; use
me; thee will I serve, day and night, in great, in small,
that I may be not virtuous, but virtue"—then is the end
of the creation answered, and God is well pleased.

The sentiment of virtue is a reverence and delight in
the presence of certain divine laws. It perceives that
this homely game of life we play, covers, under what
seem foolish details, principles that astonish. The child
amidst his baubles is learning the action of light, motion,
gravity, muscular force; and in the game of human life,

love, fear, justice, appetite, man, and God, interact.
These laws refuse to be adequately stated. They will
not be written out on paper, or spoken by the tongue.
They elude our persevering thought; yet we read them
hourly in each other's faces, in each other's actions, in
our own remorse. The moral traits which are all globed
into every virtuous act and thought—in speech we must
sever, and describe or suggest by painful enumeration of
many particulars. Yet, as this sentiment is the essence of
all religion, let me guide your eye to the precise objects
of the sentiment, by an enumeration of some of those
classes of facts in which this element is conspicuous.

The intuition of the moral sentiment is an insight of
the perfection of the laws of the soul. These laws execute
themselves. They are out of time, out of space, and not
subject to circumstance. Thus in the soul of man there is
a justice whose retributions are instant and entire. He
who does a good deed is instantly ennobled. He who
does a mean deed is by the action itself contracted. He
who puts off impurity, thereby puts on purity. If a man
is at heart just, then in so far is he God; the safety of
God, the immortality of God, the majesty of God do
enter into that man with justice. If a man dissemble,
deceive, he deceives himself, and goes out of acquaintance with his own being. A man in the view of absolute
goodness, adores, with total humility. Every step so
downward, is a step upward. The man who renounces
himself, comes to himself.

See how this rapid intrinsic energy worketh everywhere, righting wrongs, correcting appearances, and
bringing up facts to a harmony with thoughts. Its operation in life, though slow to the senses, is at last as sure
as in the soul. By it a man is made the Providence to
himself, dispensing good to his goodness, and evil to his
sin. Character is always known. Thefts never enrich;

alms never impoverish; murder will speak out of stone walls. The least admixture of a lie—for example, the taint of vanity, any attempt to make a good impression, a favorable appearance—will instantly vitiate the effect. But speak the truth, and all nature and all spirits help you with unexpected furtherance. Speak the truth, and all things alive or brute are vouchers, and the very roots of the grass underground there do seem to stir and move to bear you witness. See again the perfection of the Law as it applies itself to the affections, and becomes the law of society. As we are, so we associate. The good, by affinity, seek the good; the vile, by affinity, the vile. Thus of their own volition, souls proceed into heaven, into hell.

These facts have always suggested to man the sublime creed that the world is not the product of manifold power, but of one will, of one mind; and that one mind is everywhere active, in each ray of the star, in each wavelet of the pool; and whatever opposes that will is everywhere balked and baffled, because things are made so, and not otherwise. Good is positive. Evil is merely privative, not absolute: it is like cold, which is the privation of heat. All evil is so much death or nonentity. Benevolence is absolute and real. So much benevolence as a man hath, so much life hath he. For all things proceed out of this same spirit, which is differently named love, justice, temperance, in its different applications, just as the ocean receives different names on the several shores which it washes. All things proceed out of the same spirit, and all things conspire with it. Whilst a man seeks good ends, he is strong by the whole strength of nature. Insofar as he roves from these ends, he bereaves himself of power, or auxiliaries; his being shrinks out of all remote channels, he becomes less and less, a mote, a point. until absolute badness is absolute death.

The perception of this law of laws awakens in the mind a sentiment which we call the religious sentiment, and which makes our highest happiness. Wonderful is its power to charm and to command. It is a mountain air. It is the embalmer of the world. It is myrrh and storax, and chlorine and rosemary. It makes the sky and the hills sublime, and the silent song of the stars is it. By it is the universe made safe and habitable, not by science or power. Thought may work cold and intransitive in things, and find no end or unity; but the dawn of the sentiment of virtue on the heart, gives and is the assurance that Law is sovereign over all natures; and the worlds, time, space, eternity, do seem to break out into joy.

This sentiment is divine and deifying. It is the beatitude of man. It makes him illimitable. Through it, the soul first knows itself. It corrects the capital mistake of the infant man, who seeks to be great by following the great, and hopes to derive advantages *from another* —by showing the fountain of all good to be in himself, and that he, equally with every man, is an inlet into the deeps of Reason. When he says, "I ought"; when love warms him; when he chooses, warned from on high, the good and great deed; then, deep melodies wander through his soul from Supreme Wisdom. Then he can worship, and be enlarged by his worship; for he can never go behind this sentiment. In the sublimest flights of the soul, rectitude is never surmounted, love is never outgrown.

This sentiment lies at the foundation of society, and successively creates all forms of worship. The principle of veneration never dies out. Man fallen into superstition, into sensuality, is never quite without the visions of the moral sentiment. In like manner, all the expressions of this sentiment are sacred and permanent in proportion to their purity. The expressions of this sentiment affect us more than all other compositions. The sentences of the oldest time, which ejaculate this piety, are still fresh and fragrant. This thought dwelled always deepest in the minds of men in the devout and contemplative East; not alone in Palestine, where it reached its purest expression, but in Egypt, in Persia, in India, in China. Europe has always owed to Oriental genius its divine impulses. What these holy bards said, all sane men found agreeable and true. And the unique impression of Jesus upon mankind, whose name is not so much written as ploughed into the history of this world, is proof of the subtle virtue of this infusion.

Meantime, whilst the doors of the temple stand open, night and day, before every man, and the oracles of this truth cease never, it is guarded by one stern condition; this, namely; it is an intuition. It cannot be received at second hand. Truly speaking, it is not instruction, but provocation, that I can receive from another soul. What he announces, I must find true in me, or reject; and on his word, or as his second, be he who he may, I can accept nothing. On the contrary, the absence of this primary faith is the presence of degradation. As is the flood so is the ebb. Let this faith depart, and the very words it spake and the things it made become false and hurtful. Then falls the church, the state, art, letters, life. The doctrine of the divine nature being forgotten, a sickness infects and dwarfs the constitution. Once man was all; now he is an appendage, a nuisance. And because the indwelling Supreme Spirit cannot wholly be got rid of, the doctrine of it suffers this perversion, that the divine nature is attributed to one or two persons, and denied to all the rest, and denied with fury. The doctrine of inspiration is lost; the base doctrine of the majority of voices usurps the place of the doctrine of the soul.

Miracles, prophecy, poetry, the ideal life, the holy life, exist as ancient history merely; they are not in the belief, nor in the aspiration of society; but, when suggested, seem ridiculous. Life is comic or pitiful as soon as the high ends of being fade out of sight, and man becomes near-sighted, and can only attend to what addresses the senses.

These general views, which, whilst they are general, none will contest, find abundant illustration in the history of religion, and especially in the history of the Christian church. In that, all of us have had our birth and nurture. The truth contained in that, you, my young friends, are now setting forth to teach. As the Cultus, or established worship of the civilized world, it has great historical interest for us. Of its blessed words, which have been the consolation of humanity, you need not that I should speak. I shall endeavor to discharge my duty to you on this occasion, by pointing out two errors in its administration, which daily appear more gross from the point of view we have just now taken.

Jesus Christ belonged to the true race of prophets. He saw with open eye the mystery of the soul. Drawn by its severe harmony, ravished with its beauty, he lived in it, and had his being there. Alone in all history he estimated the greatness of man. One man was true to what is in you and me. He saw that God incarnates himself in man, and evermore goes forth anew to take possession of his World. He said, in this jubilee of sublime emotion, "I am divine. Through me, God acts; through me, speaks. Would you see God, see me; or see thee, when thou also thinkest as I now think." But what a distortion did his doctrine and memory suffer in the same, in the next, and the following ages! There is no doctrine of the Reason which will bear to be taught by the Understanding. The understanding caught this high

chant from the poet's lips, and said, in the next age,
"This was Jehovah come down out of heaven. I will kill
you, if you say he was a man." The idioms of his language and the figures of his rhetoric have usurped the
place of his truth; and churches are not built on his
principles, but on his tropes. Christianity became a
Mythus, as the poetic teaching of Greece and of Egypt,
before. He spoke of miracles; for he felt that man's life
was a miracle, and all that man doth, and he knew that
this daily miracle shines as the character ascends. But
the word Miracle, as pronounced by Christian churches,
gives a false impression; it is Monster. It is not one with
the blowing clover and the falling rain.

He felt respect for Moses and the prophets, but no
unfit tenderness at postponing their initial revelations to
the hour and the man that now is: to the eternal revelation in the heart. Thus was he a true man. Having seen
that the law in us is commanding, he would not suffer
it to be commanded. Boldly, with hand, and heart, and
life, he declared it was God. Thus is he, as I think, the
only soul in history who has appreciated the worth of
man.

1. In this point of view we become sensible of the
first defect of historical Christianity. Historical Christianity has fallen into the error that corrupts all attempts
to communicate religion. As it appears to us, and as it
has appeared for ages, it is not the doctrine of the soul,
but an exaggeration of the personal, the positive, the
ritual. It has dwelt, it dwells, with noxious exaggeration
about the *person* of Jesus. The soul knows no persons.
It invites every man to expand to the full circle of the
universe, and will have no preferences but those of
spontaneous love. But by this eastern monarchy of a
Christianity, which indolence and fear have built, the
friend of man is made the injurer of man. The manner

in which his name is surrounded with expressions which
were once sallies of admiration and love, but are now
petrified into official titles, kills all generous sympathy
and liking. All who hear me, feel that the language that
describes Christ to Europe and America is not the style
of friendship and enthusiasm to a good and noble heart,
but is appropriated and formal—paints a demigod, as
the Orientals or the Greeks would describe Osiris or
Apollo. Accept the injurious impositions of our early
catechetical instruction, and even honesty and self-
denial were but splendid sins, if they did not wear the
Christian name. One would rather be

A pagan, suckled in a creed outworn,

than to be defrauded of his manly right in coming into
nature and finding not names and places, not land and
professions, but even virtue and truth foreclosed and
monopolized. You shall not be a man even. You shall
not own the world; you shall not dare and live after
the infinite Law that is in you, and in company with
the infinite Beauty which heaven and earth reflect to
you in all lovely forms; but you must subordinate your
nature to Christ's nature; you must accept our inter-
pretations, and take his portrait as the vulgar draw it.

That is always best which gives me to myself. The
sublime is excited in me by the great stoical doctrine,
Obey thyself. That which shows God in me, fortifies me.
That which shows God out of me, makes me a wart and
a wen. There is no longer a necessary reason for my
being. Already the long shadows of untimely oblivion
creep over me, and I shall decease forever.

The divine bards are the friends of my virtue, of my
intellect, of my strength. They admonish me that the
gleams which flash across my mind are not mine, but

God's; that they had the like, and were not disobedient to the heavenly vision. So I love them. Noble provocations go out from them, inviting me to resist evil; to subdue the world; and to Be. And thus, by his holy thoughts, Jesus serves us, and thus only. To aim to convert a man by miracles, is a profanation of the soul. A true conversion, a true Christ, is now, as always, to be made by the reception of beautiful sentiments. It is true that a great and rich soul, like his, falling among the simple, does so preponderate, that, as his did, it names the world. The world seems to them to exist for him, and they have not yet drunk so deeply of his sense as to see that only by coming again to themselves, or to God in themselves, can they grow forevermore. It is a low benefit to give me something; it is a high benefit to enable me to do somewhat of myself. The time is coming when all men will see that the gift of God to the soul is not a vaunting, overpowering, excluding sanctity, but a sweet, natural goodness, a goodness like thine and mine, and that so invites thine and mine to be and to grow.

The injustice of the vulgar tone of preaching is not less flagrant to Jesus than to the souls which it profanes. The preachers do not see that they make his gospel not glad, and shear him of the locks of beauty and the attributes of heaven. When I see a majestic Epaminondas, or Washington; when I see among my contemporaries a true orator, an upright judge, a dear friend; when I vibrate to the melody and fancy of a poem; I see beauty that is to be desired. And so lovely, and with yet more entire consent of my human being, sounds in my ear the severe music of the bards that have sung of the true God in all ages. Now do not degrade the life and dialogues of Christ out of the circle of this charm, by insulation and peculiarity. Let them lie as they befell, alive and warm, part of human life and of the landscape and of the cheerful day.

2. The second defect of the traditionary and limited way of using the mind of Christ, is a consequence of the first; this, namely; that the Moral Nature, that Law of laws whose revelations introduce greatness—yea, God himself—into the open soul, is not explored as the fountain of the established teaching in society. Men have come to speak of the revelation as somewhat long ago given and done, as if God were dead. The injury to faith throttles the preacher; and the goodliest of institutions becomes an uncertain and inarticulate voice.

It is very certain that it is the effect of conversation with the beauty of the soul, to beget a desire and need to impart to others the same knowledge and love. If utterance is denied, the thought lies like a burden on the man. Always the seer is a sayer. Somehow his dream is told; somehow he publishes it with solemn joy: sometimes with pencil on canvas, sometimes with chisel on stone, sometimes in towers and aisles of granite, his soul's worship is builded; sometimes in anthems of indefinite music; but clearest and most permanent, in words.

The man enamored of this excellency becomes its priest or poet. The office is coeval with the world. But observe the condition, the spiritual limitation of the office. The spirit only can teach. Not any profane man, not any sensual, not any liar, not any slave can teach, but only he can give, who has; he only can create, who is. The man on whom the soul descends, through whom the soul speaks, alone can teach. Courage, piety, love, wisdom, can teach; and every man can open his door to these angels, and they shall bring him the gift of tongues. But the man who aims to speak as books enable, as synods use, as the fashion guides, and as interest commands, babbles. Let him hush.

To this holy office you propose to devote yourselves. I wish you may feel your call in throbs of desire and hope. The office is the first in the world. It is of that reality that it cannot suffer the deduction of any false-hood. And it is my duty to say to you that the need was never greater of new revelation than now. From the views I have already expressed, you will infer the sad conviction, which I share, I believe, with numbers, of the universal decay and now almost death of faith in society. The soul is not preached. The Church seems to totter to its fall, almost all life extinct. On this occasion, any complaisance would be criminal which told you, whose hope and commission it is to preach the faith of Christ, that the faith of Christ is preached.

It is time that this ill-suppressed murmur of all thoughtful men against the famine of our churches—this moaning of the heart because it is bereaved of the con-solation, the hope, the grandeur that come alone out of the culture of the moral nature,—should be heard through the sleep of indolence, and over the din of routine. This great and perpetual office of the preacher is not discharged. Preaching is the expression of the moral sentiment in application to the duties of life. In how many churches, by how many prophets, tell me, is man made sensible that he is an infinite Soul; that the earth and heavens are passing into his mind; that he is drinking forever the soul of God? Where now sounds the persuasion, that by its very melody imparadises my heart, and so affirms its own origin in heaven? Where shall I hear words such as in elder ages drew men to leave all and follow—father and mother, house and land, wife and child? Where shall I hear these august laws of moral being so pronounced as to fill my ear, and I feel ennobled by the offer of my uttermost action and passion? The test of the true faith, certainly, should be its power to charm and command the soul, as the laws of nature control the activity of the hands, so commanding that we find pleasure and honor in obeying. The faith should blend with the light of rising and of setting suns, with the flying cloud, the singing bird, and the breath of flowers. But now the priest's Sabbath has lost the splendor of nature; it is unlovely; we are glad when it is done; we can make, we do make, even sitting in our pews, a far better, holier, sweeter, for ourselves.

Whenever the pulpit is usurped by a formalist, then is the worshipper defrauded and disconsolate. We shrink as soon as the prayers begin, which do not uplift, but smite and offend us. We are fain to wrap our cloaks about us, and secure, as best we can, a solitude that hears not. I once heard a preacher who sorely tempted me to say I would go to church no more. Men go, thought I, where they are wont to go, else had no soul entered the temple in the afternoon. A snow-storm was falling around us. The snow-storm was real, the preacher merely spectral, and the eye felt the sad contrast in looking at him, and then out of the window behind him into the beautiful meteor of the snow. He had lived in vain. He had no one word intimating that he had laughed or wept, was married or in love, had been commended, or cheated, or chagrined. If he had ever lived and acted, we were none the wiser for it. The capital secret of his profession, namely, to convert life into truth, he had not learned. Not one fact in all his experience had he yet imported into his doctrine. This man had ploughed and planted and talked and bought and sold; he had read books; he had eaten and drunken; his head aches, his heart throbs; he smiles and suffers; yet was there not a surmise, a hint, in all the discourse, that he had ever lived at all. Not a line did he draw out of real history. The true preacher can be known by this, that he deals out to the people his life—life passed through the fire of thought. But of the bad preacher, it could not be told from his sermon what age of the world he fell in; whether he had a father or a child; whether he was a freeholder or a pauper; whether he was a citizen or a countryman; or any other fact of his biography. It seemed strange that the people should come to church. It seemed as if their houses were very unentertaining, that they should prefer this thoughtless clamor. It shows that there is a commanding attraction in the moral senti-ment, that can lend a faint tint of light to dullness and ignorance coming in its name and place. The good hearer is sure he has been touched sometimes; is sure there is somewhat to be reached, and some word that can reach it. When he listens to these vain words, he comforts him-self by their relation to his remembrance of better hours, and so they clatter and echo unchallenged.

I am not ignorant that when we preach unworthily, it is not always quite in vain. There is a good ear, in some men, that draws supplies to virtue out of very in-different nutriment. There is poetic truth concealed in all the common-places of prayer and of sermons, and though foolishly spoken, they may be wisely heard; for each is some select expression that broke out in a mo-ment of piety from some stricken or jubilant soul, and its excellency made it remembered. The prayers and even the dogmas of our church are like the zodiac of Denderah and the astronomical monuments of the Hin-doos, wholly insulated from anything now extant in the life and business of the people. They mark the height to which the waters once rose. But this docility is a check upon the mischief from the good and devout. In a large portion of the community, the religious service gives rise to quite other thoughts and emotions. We need not chide the negligent servant. We are struck with pity, rather, at the swift retribution of his sloth. Alas for the unhappy man that is called to stand in the pulpit, and *not* give bread of life. Everything that befalls, accuses him. Would he ask contributions for the missions, foreign or domestic? Instantly his face is suffused with shame, to propose to his parish that they should send money a hundred or a thousand miles, to furnish such poor fare as they have at home and would do well to go the hundred or the thousand miles to escape. Would he urge people to a godly way of living—and can he ask a fellow-creature to come to Sabbath meetings, when he and they all know what is the poor uttermost they can hope for therein? Will he invite them privately to the Lord's Supper? He dares not. If no heart warm this rite, the hollow, dry, creaking formality is too plain than that he can face a man of wit and energy and put the invitation without terror. In the street, what has he to say to the bold village blasphemer? The village blasphemer sees fear in the face, form, and gait of the minister.

Let me not taint the sincerity of this plea by any oversight of the claims of good men. I know and honor the purity and strict conscience of numbers of the clergy. What life the public worship retains, it owes to the scattered company of pious men, who minister here and there in the churches, and who, sometimes accepting with too great tenderness the tenet of the elders, have not accepted from others, but from their own heart, the genuine impulses of virtue, and so still command our love and awe, to the sanctity of character. Moreover, the exceptions are not so much to be found in a few eminent preachers, as in the better hours, the truer inspirations of all—nay, in the sincere moments of every man. But, with whatever exception, it is still true that tradition characterizes the preaching of this country; that it comes out of the memory, and not out of the soul; that it aims at what is usual, and not at what is necessary and eternal; that thus historical Christianity destroys the power of preaching, by withdrawing it from the exploration of the moral nature of man; where the sublime is, where are the resources of astonishment and power. What a cruel injustice it is to that Law, the joy of the whole earth, which alone can make thought dear and rich; that Law whose fatal sureness the astronomical orbits poorly emulate—that it is travestied and depreciated, that it is behooted and behowled, and not a trait, not a word of it articulated. The pulpit in losing sight of this Law, loses its reason, and gropes after it knows not what. And for want of this culture the soul of the community is sick and faithless. It wants nothing so much as a stern, high, stoical, Christian discipline, to make it know itself and the divinity that speaks through it. Now man is ashamed of himself; he skulks and sneaks through the world, to be tolerated, to be pitied, and scarcely in a thousand years does any man dare to be wise and good, and so draw after him the tears and blessings of his kind.

Certainly there have been periods when, from the inactivity of the intellect on certain truths, a greater faith was possible in names and persons. The Puritans in England and America found in the Christ of the Catholic Church and in the dogmas inherited from Rome, scope for their austere piety and their longings for civil freedom. But their creed is passing away, and none arises in its room. I think no man can go with his thoughts about him into one of our churches, without feeling that what hold the public worship had on men is gone, or going. It has lost its grasp on the affection of the good and the fear of the bad. In the country, neighbor-

hoods, half parishes are *signing off*, to use the local term.
It is already beginning to indicate character and religion
to withdraw from the religious meetings. I have heard a
devout person, who prized the Sabbath, say in bitterness
of heart, "On Sundays, it seems wicked to go to church."
And the motive that holds the best there is now only a
hope and a waiting. What was once a mere circumstance, that the best and the worst men in the parish, the
poor and the rich, the learned and the ignorant, young
and old, should meet one day as fellows in one house, in
sign of an equal right in the soul, has come to be a paramount motive for going thither.

My friends, in these two errors, I think, I find the
causes of a decaying church and a wasting unbelief. And
what greater calamity can fall upon a nation than the
loss of worship? Then all things go to decay. Genius
leaves the temple to haunt the senate or the market.
Literature becomes frivolous. Science is cold. The eye
of youth is not lighted by the hope of other worlds, and
age is without honor. Society lives to trifles, and when
men die we do not mention them.

And now, my brothers, you will ask, What in these
desponding days can be done by us? The remedy is already declared in the ground of our complaint of the
Church. We have contrasted the Church with the Soul.
In the soul then let the redemption be sought. Wherever
a man comes, there comes revolution. The old is for
slaves. When a man comes, all books are legible, all
things transparent, all religions are forms. He is religious. Man is the wonder-worker. He is seen amid miracles. All men bless and curse. He saith yea and nay, only.
The stationariness of religion; the assumption that the
age of inspiration is past, that the Bible is closed; the
fear of degrading the character of Jesus by representing
him as a man—indicate with sufficient clearness the

falsehood of our theology. It is the office of a true
teacher to show us that God is, not was; that He speak-
eth, not spake. The true Christianity—a faith like
Christ's in the infinitude of man—is lost. None believeth
in the soul of man, but only in some man or person old
and departed. Ah me! no man goeth alone. All men go
in flocks to this saint or that poet, avoiding the God who
seeth in secret. They cannot see in secret; they love to
be blind in public. They think society wiser than their
soul, and know not that one soul, and their soul, is wiser
than the whole world. See how nations and races flit by
on the sea of time and leave no ripple to tell where they
floated or sunk, and one good soul shall make the name
of Moses, or of Zeno, or of Zoroaster, reverend forever.
None assayeth the stern ambition to be the Self of the
nation and of nature, but each would be an easy secondary to some Christian scheme, or sectarian connection, or some eminent man. Once leave your own knowledge of God, your own sentiment, and take secondary
knowledge, as St. Paul's, or George Fox's, or Swedenborg's, and you get wide from God with every year this
secondary form lasts, and if, as now, for centuries—the
chasm yawns to that breadth, that men can scarcely be
convinced there is in them anything divine.

Let me admonish you, first of all, to go alone; to refuse the good models, even those which are sacred in
the imagination of men, and dare to love God without
mediator or veil. Friends enough you shall find who
will hold up to your emulation Wesleys and Oberlins,
Saints and Prophets. Thank God for these good men,
but say, "I also am a man." Imitation cannot go above its
model. The imitator dooms himself to hopeless mediocrity. The inventor did it because it was natural to him,
and so in him it has a charm. In the imitator something

else is natural, and he bereaves himself of his own beauty, to come short of another man's.

Yourself a newborn bard of the Holy Ghost, cast behind you all conformity, and acquaint men at first hand with Deity. Look to it first and only, that fashion, custom, authority, pleasure, and money, are nothing to you —are not bandages over your eyes, that you cannot see —but live with the privilege of the immeasurable mind. Not too anxious to visit periodically all families and each family in your parish connection—when you meet one of these men or women, be to them a divine man; be to them thought and virtue; let their timid aspirations find in you a friend; let their trampled instincts be genially tempted out in your atmosphere; let their doubts know that you have doubted, and their wonder feel that you have wondered. By trusting your own heart, you shall gain more confidence in other men. For all our penny-wisdom, for all our soul-destroying slavery to habit, it is not to be doubted that all men have sublime thoughts; that all men value the few real hours of life; they love to be heard; they love to be caught up into the vision of principles. We mark with light in the memory the few interviews we have had, in the dreary years of routine and of sin, with souls that made our souls wiser; that spoke what we thought; that told us what we knew; that gave us leave to be what we inly were. Discharge to men the priestly office, and, present or absent, you shall be followed with their love as by an angel.

And, to this end, let us not aim at common degrees of merit. Can we not leave, to such as love it, the virtue that glitters for the commendation of society, and ourselves pierce the deep solitudes of absolute ability and worth? We easily come up to the standard of goodness in society. Society's praise can be cheaply secured, and almost all men are content with those easy merits; but the instant effect of conversing with God will be to put them away. There are persons who are not actors, not speakers, but influences; persons too great for fame, for display; who disdain eloquence; to whom all we call art and artist seems too nearly allied to show and by-ends, to the exaggeration of the finite and selfish, and loss of the universal. The orators, the poets, the commanders encroach on us only as fair women do, by our allowance and homage. Slight them by preoccupation of mind, slight them, as you can well afford to do, by high and universal aims, and they instantly feel that you have right, and that it is in lower places that they must shine. They also feel your right; for they with you are open to the influx of the all-knowing Spirit, which annihilates before its broad noon the little shades and gradations of intelligence in the compositions we call wiser and wisest.

In such high communion let us study the grand strokes of rectitude: a bold benevolence, an independence of friends, so that not the unjust wishes of those who love us shall impair our freedom, but we shall resist for truth's sake the freest flow of kindness, and appeal to sympathies far in advance; and—what is the highest form in which we know this beautiful element —a certain solidity of merit, that has nothing to do with opinion, and which is so essentially and manifestly virtue, that it is taken for granted that the right, the brave, the generous step will be taken by it, and nobody thinks of commending it. You would compliment a coxcomb doing a good act, but you would not praise an angel. The silence that accepts merit as the most natural thing in the world is the highest applause. Such souls, when they appear, are the Imperial Guard of Virtue, the perpetual reserve, the dictators of fortune. One needs not praise their courage—they are the heart and soul of nature. O my friends, there are resources in us on which we have not drawn. There are men who rise refreshed on hearing a threat; men to whom a crisis which intimidates and paralyzes the majority—demanding not the faculties of prudence and thrift, but comprehension, immovableness, the readiness of sacrifice—comes graceful and beloved as a bride. Napoleon said of Massena, that he was not himself until the battle began to go against him; then, when the dead began to fall in ranks around him, awoke his powers of combination, and he put on terror and victory as a robe. So it is in rugged crises, in unweariable endurance, and in aims which put sympathy out of question, that the angel is shown. But these are heights that we can scarce remember and look up to without contrition and shame. Let us thank God that such things exist.

And now let us do what we can to rekindle the smoldering, nigh-quenched fire on the altar. The evils of the church that now is are manifest. The question returns, What shall we do? I confess, all attempts to project and establish a Cultus with new rites and forms seem to me vain. Faith makes us, and not we it, and faith makes its own forms. All attempts to contrive a system are as cold as the new worship introduced by the French to the goddess of Reason—today, pasteboard and filigree, and ending tomorrow in madness and murder. Rather let the breath of new life be breathed by you through the forms already existing. For if once you are alive, you shall find they shall become plastic and new. The remedy to their deformity is first, soul, and second, soul, and evermore, soul. A whole popedom of forms one pulsation of virtue can uplift and vivify. Two inestimable advantages Christianity has given us; first the Sabbath, the jubilee of the whole world, whose light dawns welcome alike into the closet of the philosopher, into the garret of toil, and into prison-cells, and everywhere suggests, even to the vile, the dignity of spiritual being. Let it stand forevermore, a temple, which new love, new faith, new sight shall restore to more than its first splendor to mankind. And secondly, the institution of preaching—the speech of man to men—essentially the most flexible of all organs, of all forms. What hinders that now, everywhere, in pulpits, in lecture-rooms, in houses, in fields, wherever the invitation of men or your own occasions lead you, you speak the very truth, as your life and conscience teach it, and cheer the waiting, fainting hearts of men with new hope and new revelation?

I look for the hour when that supreme Beauty which ravished the souls of those Eastern men, and chiefly of those Hebrews, and through their lips spoke oracles to all time, shall speak in the West also. The Hebrew and Greek Scriptures contain immortal sentences, that have been bread of life to millions. But they have no epical integrity; are fragmentary; are not shown in their order to the intellect. I look for the new Teacher that shall follow so far those shining laws that he shall see them come full circle; shall see their rounding complete grace; shall see the world to be the mirror of the soul; shall see the identity of the law of gravitation with purity of heart; and shall show that the Ought, that Duty, is one thing with Science, with Beauty, and with Joy.

MAN THE REFORMER

A Lecture Read before the Mechanics' Apprentices' Library Association, Boston, January 25, 1841.

MR. PRESIDENT and Gentlemen, I wish to offer to your consideration some thoughts on the particular and general relations of man as a reformer. I shall assume that the aim of each young man in this association is the very highest that belongs to a rational mind. Let it be granted that our life, as we lead it, is common and mean; that some of those offices and functions for which we were mainly created are grown so rare in society that the memory of them is only kept alive in old books and in dim traditions; that prophets and poets, that beautiful and perfect men we are not now, no, nor have even seen such; that some sources of human instruction are almost unnamed and unknown among us; that the community in which we live will hardly bear to be told that every man should be open to ecstasy or a divine illumination, and his daily walk elevated by intercourse with the spiritual world. Grant all this, as we must, yet I suppose none of my auditors will deny that we ought to seek to establish ourselves in such disciplines and courses as will deserve that guidance and clearer communication with the spiritual nature. And further, I will not dissemble my hope that each person whom I address has felt his own call to cast aside all evil customs, timidities, and limitations, and to be in his place a free and helpful man, a reformer, a benefactor, not content to

69

slip along through the world like a footman or a spy, escaping by his nimbleness and apologies as many knocks as he can, but a brave and upright man, who must find or cut a straight road to everything excellent in the earth, and not only go honorably himself, but make it easier for all who follow him to go in honor and with benefit.

In the history of the world the doctrine of Reform had never such scope as at the present hour. Lutherans, Hernhutters, Jesuits, Monks, Quakers, Knox, Wesley, Swedenborg, Bentham, in their accusations of society, all respected something—church or state, literature or history, domestic usages, the market town, the dinner table, coined money. But now all these and all things else hear the trumpet, and must rush to judgment— Christianity, the laws, commerce, schools, the farm, the laboratory; and not a kingdom, town, statute, rite, calling, man, or woman, but is threatened by the new spirit.

What if some of the objections whereby our institutions are assailed are extreme and speculative, and the reformers tend to idealism? That only shows the extravagance of the abuses which have driven the mind into the opposite extreme. It is when your facts and persons grow unreal and fantastic by too much falsehood, that the scholar flies for refuge to the world of ideas, and aims to recruit and replenish nature from that source. Let ideas establish their legitimate sway again in society, let life be fair and poetic, and the scholars will gladly be lovers, citizens, and philanthropists.

It will afford no security from the new ideas, that the old nations, the laws of centuries, the property and institutions of a hundred cities, are built on other foundations. The demon of reform has a secret door into the heart of every law-maker, of every inhabitant of every city. The fact that a new thought and hope have dawned in your breast, should apprise you that in the same hour a new light broke in upon a thousand private hearts. That secret which you would fain keep—as soon as you go abroad, lo! there is one standing on the doorstep to tell you the same. There is not the most bronzed and sharpened money-catcher who does not, to your consternation almost, quail and shake the moment he hears a question prompted by the new ideas. We thought he had some semblance of ground to stand upon, that such as he at least would die hard; but he trembles and flees. Then the scholar says, "Cities and coaches shall never impose on me again; for behold every solitary dream of mine is rushing to fulfillment. That fancy I had, and hesitated to utter because you would laugh—the broker, the attorney, the market-man are saying the same thing. Had I waited a day longer to speak, I had been too late. Behold, State Street thinks, and Wall Street doubts, and begins to prophesy!"

It cannot be wondered at that this general inquest into abuses should arise in the bosom of society, when one considers the practical impediments that stand in the way of virtuous young men. The young man, on entering life, finds the way to lucrative employments blocked with abuses. The ways of trade are grown selfish to the borders of theft, and supple to the borders (if not beyond the borders) of fraud. The employments of commerce are not intrinsically unfit for a man, or less genial to his faculties; but these are now in their general course so vitiated by derelictions and abuses at which all connive, that it requires more vigor and resources than can be expected of every young man, to right himself in them; he is lost in them; he cannot move hand or foot in them. Has he genius and virtue? the less does he find them fit for him to grow in, and if he would thrive in them, he must sacrifice all the brilliant dreams of boy hood and youth as dreams; he must forget the prayers of his childhood and must take on him the harness of routine and obsequiousness. If not so minded, nothing is left him but to begin the world anew, as he does who puts the spade into the ground for food. We are all implicated of course in this charge; it is only necessary to ask a few questions as to the progress of the articles of commerce from the fields where they grew, to our houses, to become aware that we eat and drink and wear perjury and fraud in a hundred commodities. How many articles of daily consumption are furnished us from the West Indies; yet it is said that in the Spanish islands the venality of the officers of the government has passed into usage, and that no article passes into our ships which has not been fraudulently cheapened. In the Spanish islands, every agent or factor of the Americans, unless he be a consul, has taken oath that he is a Catholic, or has caused a priest to make that declaration for him. The abolitionist has shown us our dreadful debt to the southern Negro. In the island of Cuba, in addition to the ordinary abominations of slavery, it appears only men are bought for the plantations, and one dies in ten every year, of these miserable bachelors, to yield us sugar. I leave for those who have the knowledge the part of sifting the oaths of our custom-houses; I will not inquire into the oppression of the sailors; I will not pry into the usages of our retail trade. I content myself with the fact that the general system of our trade (apart from the blacker traits, which, I hope, are exceptions denounced and unshared by all reputable men), is a system of selfishness; is not dictated by the high sentiments of human nature; is not measured by the exact law of reciprocity, much less by the sentiments of love and heroism, but is a system of distrust, of concealment, of superior keenness, not of giving but of taking advantage. It is not that which a man delights to unlock to a noble friend; which he meditates on with joy and self-approval in his hour of love and aspiration; but rather what he then puts out of sight, only showing the brilliant result, and atoning for the manner of acquiring, by the manner of expending it. I do not charge the merchant or the manufacturer. The sins of our trade belong to no class, to no individual. One plucks, one distributes, one eats. Everybody partakes, everybody confesses—with cap and knee volunteers his confession, yet none feels himself accountable. He did not create the abuse; he cannot alter it. What is he? an obscure private person who must get his bread. That is the vice—that no one feels himself called to act for man, but only as a fraction of man. It happens therefore that all such ingenuous souls as feel within themselves the irrepressible strivings of a noble aim, who by the law of their nature must act simply, find these ways of trade unfit for them, and they come forth from it. Such cases are becoming more numerous every year.

But by coming out of trade you have not cleared yourself. The trail of the serpent reaches into all the lucrative professions and practices of man. Each has its own wrongs. Each finds a tender and very intelligent conscience a disqualification for success. Each requires of the practitioner a certain shutting of the eyes, a certain dapperness and compliance, an acceptance of customs, a sequestration from the sentiments of generosity and love, a compromise of private opinion and lofty integrity. Nay, the evil custom reaches into the whole institution of property, until our laws which establish and protect it seem not to be the issue of love and reason, but of selfishness. Suppose a man is so unhappy as to be born a saint, with keen perceptions but with the conscience and love of an angel, and he is to get his living in the world; he finds himself excluded from all lucrative works; he has no farm, and he cannot get one; for to earn money enough to buy one requires a sort of concentration toward money, which is the selling himself for a number of years, and to him the present hour is as sacred and inviolable as any future hour. Of course, whilst another man has no land, my title to mine, your title to yours, is at once vitiated. Inextricable seem to be the twinings and tendrils of this evil, and we all involve ourselves in it the deeper by forming connections, by wives and children, by benefits and debts.

Considerations of this kind have turned the attention of many philanthropic and intelligent persons to the claims of manual labor, as a part of the education of every young man. If the accumulated wealth of the past generation is thus tainted—no matter how much of it is offered to us—we must begin to consider if it were not the nobler part to renounce it, and to put ourselves into primary relations with the soil and nature, and abstaining from whatever is dishonest and unclean, to take each of us bravely his part, with his own hands, in the manual labor of the world.

But it is said, "What! will you give up the immense advantages reaped from the division of labor, and set every man to make his own shoes, bureau, knife, wagon, sails, and needle? This would be to put men back into barbarism by their own act." I see no instant prospect of a virtuous revolution; yet I confess I should not be pained at a change which threatened a loss of some of the luxuries or conveniences of society, if it proceeded from a preference of the agricultural life out of the belief that our primary duties as men could be better discharged in that calling. Who could regret to see a high conscience and a purer taste exercising a sensible effect on young men in their choice of occupation, and thinning the ranks of competition in the labors of commerce, of law, and of state? It is easy to see that the inconvenience would last but a short time. This would be great action, which always opens the eyes of men. When many persons shall have done this, when the majority shall admit the necessity of reform in all these institutions, their abuses will be redressed, and the way will be open again to the advantages which arise from the division of labor, and a man may select the fittest employment for his peculiar talent again, without compromise.

But quite apart from the emphasis which the times give to the doctrine that the manual labor of society ought to be shared among all the members, there are reasons proper to every individual why he should not be deprived of it. The use of manual labor is one which never grows obsolete, and which is inapplicable to no person. A man should have a farm or a mechanical craft for his culture. We must have a basis for our higher accomplishments, our delicate entertainments of poetry and philosophy, in the work of our hands. We must have an antagonism in the tough world for all the variety of our spiritual faculties, or they will not be born. Manual labor is the study of the external world. The advantage of riches remains with him who procured them, not with the heir. When I go into my garden with a spade, and dig a bed, I feel such an exhilaration and health that I discover that I have been defrauding myself all this time in letting others do for me what I should have done with my own hands. But not only health, but education is in the work. Is it possible that I, who get indefinite quantities of sugar, hominy, cotton, buckets, crockery-ware, and letter-paper, by simply signing my name once in three months to a check in favor of John Smith & Co. traders, get the fair share of exercise to my faculties by

that act which nature intended for me in making all
these far-fetched matters important to my comfort? It is
Smith himself, and his carriers, and dealers, and manufacturers; it is the sailor, the hidedrogher, the butcher,
the Negro, the hunter, and the planter, who have in-
tercepted the sugar of the sugar, and the cotton of the
cotton. They have got the education, I only the commodity. This were all very well if I were necessarily
absent, being detained by work of my own, like theirs,
work of the same faculties; then should I be sure of my
hands and feet; but now I feel some shame before my
wood-chopper, my ploughman, and my cook, for they
have some sort of self-sufficiency, they can contrive
without my aid to bring the day and year round, but I
depend on them, and have not earned by use a right to
my arms and feet.

Consider further the difference between the first and
second owner of property. Every species of property is
preyed on by its own enemies, as iron by rust; timber by
rot; cloth by moths; provisions by mold, putridity, or
vermin; money by thieves; an orchard by insects; a
planted field by weeds and the inroad of cattle; a stock
of cattle by hunger; a road by rain and frost; a bridge by
freshets. And whoever takes any of these things into his
possession, takes the charge of defending them from
this troop of enemies, or of keeping them in repair. A
man who supplies his own want, who builds a raft or a
boat to go a-fishing, finds it easy to calk it, or put in a
thole-pin, or mend the rudder. What he gets only as
fast as he wants for his own ends, does not embarrass
him, or take away his sleep with looking after. But when
he comes to give all the goods he has year after year
collected, in one estate to his son—house, orchard,
ploughed land, cattle, bridges, hardware. wooden-ware,
carpets, cloths, provisions, books, money—and cannot

give him the skill and experience which made or collected these, and the method and place they have in his own life, the son finds his hands full—not to use these things, but to look after them and defend them from their natural enemies. To him they are not means, but masters. Their enemies will not remit; rust, mold, vermin, rain, sun, freshet, fire, all seize their own, fill him with vexation, and he is converted from the owner into a watchman or a watch-dog to this magazine of old and new chattels. What a change! Instead of the masterly good humor and sense of power and fertility of resource in himself; instead of those strong and learned hands, those piercing and learned eyes, that supple body, and that mighty and prevailing heart which the father had, whom nature loved and feared, whom snow and rain, water and land, beast and fish seemed all to know and to serve—we have now a puny, protected person, guarded by walls and curtains, stoves and down beds, coaches, and men-servants and women-servants from the earth and the sky, and who, bred to depend on all these, is made anxious by all that endangers those possessions, and is forced to spend so much time in guarding them, that he has quite lost sight of their original use, namely, to help him to his ends—to the prosecution of his love; to the helping of his friend, to the worship of his God, to the enlargement of his knowledge, to the serving of his country, to the indulgence of his sentiment; and he is now what is called a rich man—the menial and runner of his riches.

Hence it happens that the whole interest of history lies in the fortunes of the poor. Knowledge, Virtue, Power are the victories of man over his necessities, his march to the dominion of the world. Every man ought to have this opportunity to conquer the world for himself. Only such persons interest us, Spartans, Romans, Saracens, English, Americans, who have stood in the jaws of need, and have by their own wit and might extricated themselves, and made man victorious.

I do not wish to overstate this doctrine of labor, or insist that every man should be a farmer, any more than that every man should be a lexicographer. In general one may say that the husbandman's is the oldest and most universal profession, and that where a man does not yet discover in himself any fitness for one work more than another, this may be preferred. But the doc· trine of the Farm is merely this, that every man ought to stand in primary relations with the work of the world; ought to do it himself, and not to suffer the accident of his having a purse in his pocket, or his having been bred to some dishonorable and injurious craft, to sever him from those duties; and for this reason, that labor is God's education; that he only is a sincere learner, he only can become a master, who learns the secrets of labor, and who, by real cunning extorts from nature its sceptre.

Neither would I shut my ears to the plea of the learned professions, of the poet, the priest, the law-giver, and men of study generally; namely, that in the experience of all men of that class, the amount of manual labor which is necessary to the maintenance of a family, indisposes and disqualifies for intellectual exertion. I know, it often, perhaps usually happens that where there is a fine organization, apt for poetry and philosophy, that individual finds himself compelled to wait on his thoughts; to waste several days that he may enhance and glorify one; and is better taught by a moderate and dainty exercise, such as rambling in the fields, rowing, skating, hunting, than by the downright drudgery of the farmer and the smith. I would not quite forget the venerable counsel of the Egyptian mysteries, which declared that "there were two pairs of eyes in man, and it is requisite that the pair which are beneath should be closed, when the pair that are above them perceive, and that when the pair above are closed, those which are beneath should be opened." Yet I will suggest that no separation from labor can be without some loss of power and of truth to the seer himself; that, I doubt not, the faults and vices of our literature and philosophy, their too great fineness, effeminacy, and melancholy, are attributable to the enervated and sickly habits of the literary class. Better that the book should not be quite so good, and the book-maker abler and better, and not himself often a ludicrous contrast to all that he has written.

But granting that for ends so sacred and dear some relaxation must be had, I think that if a man find in himself any strong bias to poetry, to art, to the contemplative life, drawing him to these things with a devotion incompatible with good husbandry, that man ought to reckon early with himself, and, respecting the compensations of the Universe, ought to ransom himself from the duties of economy by a certain rigor and privation in his habits. For privileges so rare and grand, let him not stint to pay a great tax. Let him be a cænobite, a pauper, and if need be, celibate also. Let him learn to eat his meals standing, and to relish the taste of fair water and black bread. He may leave to others the costly conveniences of housekeeping, and large hospitality, and the possession of works of art. Let him feel that genius is a hospitality, and that he who can create works of art needs not collect them. He must live in a chamber, and postpone his self-indulgence, forewarned and forearmed against that frequent misfortune of men of genius —the taste for luxury. This is the tragedy of genius—

attempting to drive along the ecliptic with one horse of the heavens and one horse of the earth, there is only discord and ruin and downfall to chariot and charioteer.

The duty that every man should assume his own vows, should call the institutions of society to account, and examine their fitness to him, gains in emphasis if we look at our modes of living. Is our housekeeping sacred and honorable? Does it raise and inspire us, or does it cripple us instead? I ought to be armed by every part and function of my household, by all my social function, by my economy, by my feasting, by my voting, by my traffic. Yet I am almost no party to any of these things. Custom does it for me, gives me no power therefrom, and runs me in debt to boot. We spend our incomes for paint and paper, for a hundred trifles, I know not what, and not for the things of a man. Our expense is almost all for conformity. It is for cake that we run in debt; it is not the intellect, not the heart, not beauty, not worship, that costs so much. Why needs any man be rich? Why must he have horses, fine garments, handsome apartments, access to public houses and places of amusement? Only for want of thought. Give his mind a new image, and he flees into a solitary garden or garret to enjoy it, and is richer with that dream than the fee of a county could make him. But we are first thoughtless, and then find that we are moneyless. We are first sensual, and then must be rich. We dare not trust our wit for making our house pleasant to our friend, and so we buy icecreams. He is accustomed to carpets, and we have not sufficient character to put floor cloths out of his mind whilst he stays in the house, and so we pile the floor with carpets. Let the house rather be a temple of the Furies of Lacedæmon, formidable and holy to all, which none but a Spartan may enter or so much as behold. As soon as there is faith, as soon as there is society, comfits and cushions will be left to slaves. Expense will be inventive and heroic. We shall eat hard and lie hard, we shall dwell like the ancient Romans in narrow tenements, whilst our public edifices, like theirs, will be worthy for their proportion of the landscape in which we set them, for conversation, for art, for music, for worship. We shall be rich to great purposes; poor only for selfish ones.

Now what help for these evils? How can the man who has learned but one art, procure all the conveniences of life honestly? Shall we say all we think? Perhaps with his own hands. Suppose he collects or makes them ill—yet he has learned their lesson. If he cannot do that? Then perhaps he can go without. Immense wisdom and riches are in that. It is better to go without, than to have them at too great a cost. Let us learn the meaning of economy. Economy is a high, humane office, a sacrament, when its aim is grand; when it is the prudence of simple tastes, when it is practised for freedom, or love, or devotion. Much of the economy which we see in houses is of a base origin, and is best kept out of sight. Parched corn eaten today, that I may have roast fowl to my dinner on Sunday, is a baseness; but parched corn and a house with one apartment, that I may be free of all perturbations, that I may be serene and docile to what the mind shall speak, and girt and road-ready for the lowest mission of knowledge or good will, is frugality for gods and heroes.

Can we not learn the lesson of self-help? Society is full of infirm people, who incessantly summon others to serve them. They contrive everywhere to exhaust for their single comfort the entire means and appliances of that luxury to which our invention has yet attained. Sofas, ottomans, stoves, wine, game-fowl, spices, perfumes, rides, the theater, entertainments—all these they want, they need, and whatever can be suggested more than these they crave also, as if it was the bread which should keep them from starving; and if they miss any one, they represent themselves as the most wronged and most wretched persons on earth. One must have been born and bred with them to know how to prepare a meal for their learned stomach. Meantime they never bestir themselves to serve another person; not they! they have a great deal more to do for themselves than they can possibly perform, nor do they once perceive the cruel joke of their lives, but the more odious they grow, the sharper is the tone of their complaining and craving. Can anything be so elegant as to have few wants and to serve them one's self, so as to have somewhat left to give, instead of being always prompt to grab? It is more elegant to answer one's own needs than to be richly served; inelegant perhaps it may look today, and to a few, but it is an elegance forever and to all.

I do not wish to be absurd and pedantic in reform. I do not wish to push my criticism on the state of things around me to that extravagant mark that shall compel me to suicide, or to an absolute isolation from the advantages of civil society. If we suddenly plant our foot and say—I will neither eat nor drink nor wear nor touch any food or fabric which I do not know to be innocent, or deal with any person whose whole manner of life is not clear and rational, we shall stand still. Whose is so? Not mine; not thine; not his. But I think we must clear ourselves each one by the interrogation, whether we have earned our bread today by the hearty contribution of our energies to the common benefit; and we must not cease to *tend* to the correction of flagrant wrongs, by laying one stone aright every day.

But the idea which now begins to agitate society has a wider scope than our daily employments, our households, and the institutions of property. We are to revise the whole of our social structure, the state, the school, religion, marriage, trade, science, and explore their foundations in our own nature; we are to see that the world not only fitted the former men, but fits us, and to clear ourselves of every usage which has not its roots in our own mind. What is a man born for but to be a Reformer, a Re-maker of what man has made; a renouncer of lies; a restorer of truth and good, imitating that great Nature which embosoms us all, and which sleeps no moment on an old past, but every hour repairs herself, yielding us every morning a new day, and with every pulsation a new life? Let him renounce everything which is not true to him, and put all his practices back on their first thoughts, and do nothing for which he has not the whole world for his reason. If there are inconveniences and what is called ruin in the way, because we have so enervated and maimed ourselves, yet it would be like dying of perfumes to sink in the effort to re-attach the deeds of every day to the holy and mysterious recesses of life.

The power which is at once spring and regulator in all efforts of reform is the conviction that there is an infinite worthiness in man, which will appear at the call of worth, and that all particular reforms are the removing of some impediment. Is it not the highest duty that man should be honored in us? I ought not to allow any man, because he has broad lands, to feel that he is rich in my presence. I ought to make him feel that I can do without his riches, that I cannot be bought— neither by comfort, neither by pride—and though I be utterly penniless, and receiving bread from him, that he is the poor man beside me. And if, at the same time, a woman or a child discovers a sentiment of piety, or a juster way of thinking than mine, I ought to confess it by my respect and obedience, though it go to alter my whole way of life.

The Americans have many virtues, but they have not Faith and Hope. I know no two words whose meaning is more lost sight of. We use these words as if they were as obsolete as Selah and Amen. And yet they have the broadest meaning, and the most cogent application to Boston in this year. The Americans have little faith. They rely on the power of a dollar; they are deaf to a sentiment. They think you may talk the north wind down as easily as raise society; and no class more faithless than the scholars or intellectual men. Now if I talk with a sincere wise man, and my friend, with a poet, with a conscientious youth who is still under the dominion of his own wild thoughts, and not yet harnessed in the team of society to drag with us all in the ruts of custom, I see at once how paltry is all this generation of unbelievers, and what a house of cards their institutions are, and I see what one brave man, what one great thought executed might effect. I see that the reason of the distrust of the practical man in all theory is his inability to perceive the means whereby we work. Look, he says, at the tools with which this world of yours is to be built. As we cannot make a planet, with atmosphere, rivers, and forests, by means of the best carpenters' or engineers' tools, with chemist's laboratory and smith's forge to boot—so neither can we ever construct that heavenly society you prate of out of foolish. sick, selfish men and women, such as we know them to be. But the believer not only beholds his heaven to be possible, but already to begin to exist—not by the men or materials the statesman uses, but by men transfigured and raised above themselves by the power of principles. To principles something else is possible that transcends all the power of expedients.

Every great and commanding moment in the annals of the world is the triumph of some enthusiasm. The victories of the Arabs after Mahomet, who, in a few years, from a small and mean beginning, established a larger empire than that of Rome, is an example. They did they knew not what. The naked Derar, horsed on an idea, was found an overmatch for a troop of Roman cavalry. The women fought like men, and conquered the Roman men. They were miserably equipped, miserably fed. They were Temperance troops. There was neither brandy nor flesh needed to feed them. They conquered Asia, and Africa, and Spain, on barley. The Caliph Omar's walking-stick struck more terror into those who saw it than another man's sword. His diet was barley bread; his sauce was salt; and oftentimes by way of abstinence he ate his bread without salt. His drink was water. His palace was built of mud; and when he left Medina to go to the conquest of Jerusalem, he rode on a red camel, with a wooden platter hanging at his saddle, with a bottle of water and two sacks, one holding barley, and the other dried fruits.

But there will dawn ere long on our politics, on our modes of living, a nobler morning than that Arabian faith, in the sentiment of love. This is the one remedy for all ills, the panacea of nature. We must be lovers, and at once the impossible becomes possible. Our age and history, for these thousand years, has not been the history of kindness, but of selfishness. Our distrust is very expensive. The money we spend for courts and prisons is very ill laid out. We make, by distrust, the thief, and burglar, and incendiary, and by our court and jail we keep him so. An acceptance of the sentiment of love throughout Christendom for a season would bring the felon and the outcast to our side in tears, with the devotion of his faculties to our service. See this wide society of laboring men and women. We allow ourselves to be served by them, we live apart from them, and meet

them without a salute in the streets. We do not greet
their talents, nor rejoice in their good fortune, nor foster
their hopes, nor in the assembly of the people vote for
what is dear to them. Thus we enact the part of the selfish noble and king from the foundation of the world.
See, this tree always bears one fruit. In every household,
the peace of a pair is poisoned by the malice, slyness,
indolence, and alienation of domestics. Let any two
matrons meet, and observe how soon their conversation
turns on the troubles from their *"help,"* as our phrase is.
In every knot of laborers the rich man does not feel himself among his friends—and at the polls he finds them
arrayed in a mass in distinct opposition to him. We complain that the politics of masses of the people are controlled by designing men, and led in opposition to
manifest justice and the common weal, and to their own
interest. But the people do not wish to be represented
or ruled by the ignorant and base. They only vote for
these, because they were asked with the voice and semblance of kindness. They will not vote for them long.
They inevitably prefer wit and probity. To use an Egyptian metaphor, it is not their will for any long time "to
raise the nails of wild beasts, and to depress the heads
of the sacred birds." Let our affection flow out to our
fellow; it would operate in a day the greatest of all revolutions. It is better to work on institutions by the sun
than by the wind. The State must consider the poor man,
and all voices must speak for him. Every child that is
born must have a just chance for his bread. Let the
amelioration in our laws of property proceed from the
concession of the rich, not from the grasping of the
poor. Let us begin by habitual imparting. Let us understand that the equitable rule is, that no one should take
more than his share, let him be ever so rich. Let me feel
that I am to be a lover. I am to see to it that the world is

the better for me, and to find my reward in the act
Love would put a new face on this weary old world in
which we dwell as pagans and enemies too long, and it
would warm the heart to see how fast the vain diplo-
macy of statesmen, the impotence of armies, and navies,
and lines of defence, would be superseded by this unarmed child. Love will creep where it cannot go, will
accomplish that by imperceptible methods—being its
own lever, fulcrum, and power—which force could
never achieve. Have you not seen in the woods, in a
late autumn morning, a poor fungus or mushroom—a
plant without any solidity, nay, that seemed nothing but
a soft mush or jelly—by its constant, total, and incon-
ceivably gentle pushing, manage to break its way up
through the frosty ground, and actually to lift a hard
crust on its head? It is the symbol of the power of kindness. The virtue of this principle in human society in
application to great interests is obsolete and forgotten.
Once or twice in history it has been tried in illustrious
instances, with signal success. This great, overgrown,
dead Christendom of ours still keeps alive at least the
name of a lover of mankind. But one day all men will be
lovers; and every calamity will be dissolved in the universal sunshine.

Will you suffer me to add one trait more to this portrait of man the reformer? The mediator between the
spiritual and the actual world should have a great pro-
spective prudence. An Arabian poet describes his hero
by saying,

> Sunshine was he
> In the winter day;
> And in the midsummer
> Coolness and shade.

He who would help himself and others should not be a
subject of irregular and interrupted impulses of virtue.

but a continent, persisting, immovable person—such as we have seen a few scattered up and down in time for the blessing of the world; men who have in the gravity of their nature a quality which answers to the fly-wheel in a mill, which distributes the motion equably over all the wheels and hinders it from falling unequally and suddenly in destructive shocks. It is better that joy should be spread over all the day in the form of strength, than that it should be concentrated into ecstasies, full of danger and followed by reactions. There is a sublime prudence which is the very highest that we know of man, which, believing in a vast future,—sure of more to come than is yet seen—postpones always the present hour to the whole life; postpones talent to genius, and special results to character. As the merchant gladly takes money from his income to add to his capital, so is the great man very willing to lose particular powers and talents, so that he gain in the elevation of his life. The opening of the spiritual senses disposes men ever to greater sacrifices, to leave their signal talents, their best means and skill of procuring a present success, their power and their fame—to cast all things behind, in the insatiable thirst for divine communications. A purer fame, a greater power rewards the sacrifice. It is the conversion of our harvest into seed. As the farmer casts into the ground the finest ears of his grain, the time will come when we too shall hold nothing back, but shall eagerly convert more than we now possess into means and powers, when we shall be willing to sow the sun and the moon for seeds.

THE CONSERVATIVE

A Lecture Delivered at the Masonic Temple, Boston,
December 9, 1841.

THE two parties which divide the state, the party of Conservatism and that of Innovation, are very old, and have disputed the possession of the world ever since it was made. This quarrel is the subject of civil history. The Conservative Party established the reverend hierarchies and monarchies of the most ancient world. The battle of patrician and plebeian, of parent state and colony, of old usage and accommodation to new facts, of the rich and the poor, reappears in all countries and times. The war rages not only in battle fields, in national councils and ecclesiastical synods, but agitates every man's bosom with opposing advantages every hour. On rolls the old world meantime, and now one, now the other gets the day, and still the fight renews itself as if for the first time, under new names and hot personalities.

Such an irreconcilable antagonism of course must have a correspondent depth of seat in the human constitution. It is the opposition of Past and Future, of Memory and Hope, of the Understanding and the Reason. It is the primal antagonism, the appearance in trifles of the two poles of nature.

There is a fragment of old fable which seems somehow to have been dropped from the current mythologies, which may deserve attention, as it appears to relate to this subject.

Saturn grew weary of sitting alone, or with none but the great Uranus or Heaven beholding him, and he created an oyster. Then he would act again, but he made nothing more, but went on creating the race of oysters. Then Uranus cried, "A new work, O Saturn! the old is not good again."

Saturn replied, "I fear. There is not only the alternative of making and not making, but also of unmaking. Seest thou the great sea, how it ebbs and flows? so is it with me; my power ebbs; and if I put forth my hands, I shall not do, but undo. Therefore I do what I have done; I hold what I have got; and so I resist Night and Chaos."

"O Saturn," replied Uranus, "thou canst not hold thine own but by making more. Thy oysters are barnacles and cockles, and with the next flowing of the tide they will be pebbles and sea-foam."

"I see," rejoins Saturn, "thou art in league with Night, thou art become an evil eye; thou spakest from love; now thy words smite me with hatred. I appeal to Fate, must there not be rest?"—"I appeal to Fate also," said Uranus, "must there not be motion?"—But Saturn was silent, and went on making oysters for a thousand years.

After that, the word of Uranus came into his mind like a ray of the sun, and he made Jupiter; and then he feared again; and nature froze, the things that were made went backward, and to save the world, Jupiter slew his father Saturn.

This may stand for the earliest account of a conversation on politics between a Conservative and a Radical which has come down to us. It is ever thus. It is the counteraction of the centripetal and the centrifugal forces. Innovation is the salient energy; Conservatism the pause on the last movement. "That which is was made by God," saith Conservatism. "He is leaving that, he is entering this other," rejoins Innovation.

There is always a certain meanness in the argument of Conservatism, joined with a certain superiority in its fact. It affirms because it holds. Its fingers clutch the fact, and it will not open its eyes to see a better fact. The castle which Conservatism is set to defend is the actual state of things, good and bad. The project of Innovation is the best possible state of things. Of course Conservatism always has the worst of the argument, is always apologizing, pleading a necessity, pleading that to change would be to deteriorate: it must saddle itself with the mountainous load of the violence and vice of society, must deny the possibility of good, deny ideas, and suspect and stone the prophet: whilst Innovation is always in the right, triumphant, attacking, and sure of final success. Conservatism stands on man's confessed limitations, Reform on his indisputable infinitude; Conservatism on circumstance, Liberalism on power; one goes to make an adroit member of the social frame, the other to postpone all things to the man himself; Conservatism is debonair and social, Reform is individual and imperious. We are reformers in spring and summer, in autumn and winter we stand by the old; reformers in the morning, conservers at night. Reform is affirmative, Conservatism negative; Conservatism goes for comfort, Reform for truth. Conservatism is more candid to behold another's worth; Reform more disposed to maintain and increase its own. Conservatism makes no poetry, breathes no prayer, has no invention; it is all memory. Reform has no gratitude, no prudence, no husbandry. It makes a great difference to your figure and to your thought whether your foot is advancing or receding. Conservatism never puts the foot forward; in the hour when it does that, it is not establishment, but reform. Conservatism tends to universal seeming and treachery, believes in a negative fate; believes that men's temper governs them; that for me it avails not to trust in principles, they will fail me, I must bend a little; it distrusts nature; it thinks there is a general law without a particular application—law for all that does not include anyone. Reform in its antagonism inclines to asinine resistance, to kick with hoofs; it runs to egotism and bloated self-conceit; it runs to a bodiless pretension, to unnatural refining and elevation which ends in hypocrisy and sensual reaction.

And so, whilst we do not go beyond general statements, it may be safely affirmed of these two metaphysical antagonists, that each is a good half, but an impossible whole. Each exposes the abuses of the other, but in a true society, in a true man, both must combine. Nature does not give the crown of its approbation, namely beauty, to any action or emblem or actor but to one which combines both these elements; not to the rock which resists the waves from age to age, nor to the wave which lashes incessantly the rock, but the superior beauty is with the oak which stands with its hundred arms against the storms of a century, and grows every year like a sapling; or the river which ever flowing, yet is found in the same bed from age to age; or, greatest of all, the man who has subsisted for years amid the changes of nature, yet has distanced himself, so that when you remember what he was, and see what he is, you say, What strides! what a disparity is here!

Throughout nature the past combines in every creature with the present. Each of the convolutions of the sea-shell, each node and spine marks one year of the fish's life; what was the mouth of the shell for one season, with the addition of new matter by the growth of the animal, becoming an ornamental node. The leaves and a shell of soft wood are all that the vegetation of this summer has made; but the solid columnar stem, which lifts that bank of foliage into the air, to draw the eye and to cool us with its shade, is the gift and legacy of dead and buried years.

In nature, each of these elements being always present, each theory has a natural support. As we take our stand on Necessity, or on Ethics, shall we go for the conservative, or for the reformer? If we read the world historically, we shall say, Of all the ages, the present hour and circumstance is the cumulative result; this is the best throw of the dice of nature that has yet been, or that is yet possible. If we see it from the side of Will, or the Moral Sentiment, we shall accuse the Past and the Present, and require the impossible of the Future.

But although this bi-fold fact lies thus united in real nature, and so united that no man can continue to exist in whom both these elements do not work, yet men are not philosophers, but are rather very foolish children, who, by reason of their partiality, see everything in the most absurd manner, and are the victims at all times of the nearest object. There is even no philosopher who is a philosopher at all times. Our experience, our perception is conditioned by the need to acquire in parts and in succession, that is, with every truth a certain falsehood. As this is the invariable method of our training, we must give it allowance, and suffer men to learn as they have done for six millenniums, a word at a time; to pair off into insane parties, and learn the amount of truth each knows by the denial of an equal amount of truth. For the present, then, to come at what sum is attainable to us, we must even hear the parties plead as parties.

That which is best about Conservatism, that which, though it cannot be expressed in detail, inspires reverence in all, is the Inevitable. There is the question not only what the conservative says for himself, but, why must he say it? What insurmountable fact binds him to that side? Here is the fact which men call Fate, and fate in dread degrees, fate behind fate, not to be disposed of by the consideration that the Conscience commands this or that, but necessitating the question whether the faculties of man will play him true in re-sisting the facts of universal experience. For although the commands of the Conscience are *essentially* absolute, they are *historically* limitary. Wisdom does not seek a literal rectitude, but a useful, that is a conditioned one, such a one as the faculties of man and the constitution of things will warrant. The reformer, the partisan, loses himself in driving to the utmost some specialty of right conduct, until his own nature and all nature resist him; but Wisdom attempts nothing enormous and dispropor-tioned to its powers, nothing which it cannot perform or nearly perform. We have all a certain intellection or presentiment of reform existing in the mind, which does not yet descend into the character, and those who throw themselves blindly on this lose themselves. Whatever they attempt in that direction fails, and reacts suicidally on the actor himself. This is the penalty of having tran-scended nature. For the existing world is not a dream, and cannot with impunity be treated as a dream; neither is it a disease; but it is the ground on which you stand, it is the mother of whom you were born. Reform converses with possibilities, perchance with impossibilities; but here is sacred fact. This also was true, or it could not be: it had life in it, or it could not have existed; it has life in it, or it could not continue. Your schemes may be feasible, or may not be, but this has the endorsement of nature and a long friendship and cohabitation with the powers of nature. This will stand until a better cast of the dice is made. The contest between the Future and the Past is one between Divinity entering and Divinity departing. You are welcome to try your experiments, and, if you can, to displace the actual order by that ideal republic you announce, for nothing but God will expel God. But plainly the burden of proof must lie with the projector. We hold to this, until you can demonstrate something better.

The system of property and law goes back for its origin to barbarous and sacred times; it is the fruit of the same mysterious cause as the mineral or animal world. There is a natural sentiment and prepossession in favor of age, of ancestors, of barbarous and aboriginal usages, which is a homage to the element of necessity and divinity which is in them. The respect for the old names of places, of mountains and streams, is universal. The Indian and barbarous name can never be supplanted without loss. The ancients tell us that the gods loved the Ethiopians for their stable customs; and the Egyptians and Chaldeans, whose origin could not be explored, passed among the junior tribes of Grecee and Italy for sacred nations.

Moreover, so deep is the foundation of the existing social system, that it leaves no one out of it. We may be partial, but Fate is not. All men have their root in it. You who quarrel with the arrangements of society, and are willing to embroil all, and risk the indisputable good that exists, for the chance of better, live, move, and have your being in this, and your deeds contradict your words every day. For as you cannot jump from the ground without using the resistance of the ground, nor put out the boat to sea without shoving from the shore, nor attain liberty without rejecting obligation, so you are under the necessity of using the Actual order of things, in order to disuse it; to live by it, whilst you wish to take away its life. The past has baked your loaf, and in the strength of its bread you would break up the oven. But you are betrayed by your own nature. You also are conservatives. However men please to style themselves, I see no other than a Conservative party. You are not only identical with us in your needs, but also in your methods and aims. You quarrel with my Conservatism, but it is to build up one of your own; it will have a new beginning, but the same course and end, the same trials, the same passions; among the lovers of the new I observe that there is a jealousy of the newest, and that the seceder from the seceder is as damnable as the pope himself.

On these and the like grounds of general statement, Conservatism plants itself without danger of being displaced. Especially before this *personal* appeal, the innovator must confess his weakness, must confess that no man is to be found good enough to be entitled to stand champion for the principle. But when this great tendency comes to practical encounters, and is challenged by young men, to whom it is no abstraction, but a fact of hunger, distress, and exclusion from opportunities, it must needs seem injurious. The youth, of course, is an innovator by the fact of his birth. There he stands, newly born on the planet, a universal beggar, with all the reason of things, one would say, on his side. In his first consideration how to feed, clothe, and warm himself, he is met by warnings on every hand that this thing and that thing have owners, and he must go elsewhere. Then he says, "If I am born in the earth, where is my part? have the goodness, gentlemen of this world, to show me my wood-lot, where I may fell my wood, my field where to plant my corn, my pleasant ground where to build my cabin."

"Touch any wood, or field, or house-lot, on your peril," cry all the gentlemen of this world; "but you may come and work in ours, for us, and we will give you a piece of bread."

"And what is that peril?"

"Knives and muskets, if we meet you in the act; imprisonment, if we find you afterward."

"And by what authority, kind gentlemen?"

"By our law."

"And your law—is it just?"

"As just for you as it was for us. We wrought for others under this law, and got our lands so."

"I repeat the question, Is your law just?"

"Not quite just, but necessary. Moreover, it is juster now than it was when we were born; we have made it milder and more equal."

"I will none of your law," returns the youth; "it encumbers me. I cannot understand, or so much as spare time to read that needless library of your laws. Nature has sufficiently provided me with rewards and sharp penalties, to bind me not to transgress. Like the Persian noble of old, I ask 'that I may neither command nor obey.' I do not wish to enter into your complex social system. I shall serve those whom I can, and they who can will serve me. I shall seek those whom I love, and shun those whom I love not, and what more can all your laws render me?"

With equal earnestness and good faith, replies to this plaintiff an upholder of the establishment, a man of many virtues:

"Your opposition is feather-brained and overfine. Young man, I have no skill to talk with you, but look at me; I have risen early and sat late, and toiled honestly and painfully for very many years. I never dreamed about methods; I laid my bones to, and drudged for the good I possess; it was not got by fraud, nor by luck, but by work, and you must show me a warrant like these stubborn facts in your own fidelity and labor, before I suffer you, on the faith of a few fine words, to ride into my estate, and claim to scatter it as your own."

"Now you touch the heart of the matter," replies the reformer. "To that fidelity and labor I pay homage. I am unworthy to arraign your manner of living, until I too have been tried. But I should be more unworthy if I did not tell you why I cannot walk in your steps. I find this vast network, which you call property, extended over the whole planet. I cannot occupy the bleakest crag of the White Hills or the Alleghany Range, but some man or corporation steps up to me to show me that it is his. Now, though I am very peaceable, and on my private account could well enough die, since it appears there was some mistake in my creation, and that I have been *missent* to this earth, where all the seats were already taken—yet I feel called upon in behalf of rational nature, which I represent, to declare to you my opinion that if the Earth is yours so also is it mine. All your aggregate existences are less to me a fact than is my own; as I am born to the Earth, so the Earth is given to me, what I want of it to till and to plant; nor could I, without pusillanimity, omit to claim so much. I must not only have a name to live, I must live. My genius leads me to build a different manner of life from any of yours. I cannot then spare you the whole world. I love you better. I must tell you the truth practically; and take that which you call yours. It is God's world and mine; yours as much as you want, mine as much as I want. Besides, I know your ways; I know the symptoms of the disease. To the end of your power you will serve this lie which cheats you. Your want is a gulf which the possession of the broad earth would not fill. Yonder sun in heaven you would pluck down from shining on the universe, and make him a property and privacy, if you could; and the moon and the north star you would quickly have occasion for in your closet and bed-chamber. What you do not want for use, you crave for ornament, and what your convenience could spare, your pride cannot."

On the other hand, precisely the defence which was set up for the British Constitution, namely that with all its admitted defects, rotten boroughs and monopolies, it worked well, and substantial justice was somehow done; the wisdom and the worth did get into parliament, and every interest did by right, or might, or sleight, get represented; the same defence is set up for the existing institutions. They are not the best; they are not just; and in respect to you, personally, O brave young man! they cannot be justified. They have, it is most true, left you no acre for your own, and no law but our law, to the ordaining of which you were no party. But they do answer the end, they are really friendly to the good, unfriendly to the bad; they second the industrious and the kind; they foster genius. They really have so much flexibility as to afford your talent and character, on the whole, the same chance of demonstration and success which they might have if there was no law and no property.

It is trivial and merely superstitious to say that nothing is given you, no outfit, no exhibition; for in this institution of *credit*, which is as universal as honesty and promise in the human countenance, always some neighbor stands ready to be bread and land and tools and stock to the young adventurer. And if in any one respect they have come short, see what ample retribution of good they have made. They have lost no time and spared no expense to collect libraries, museums, galleries, colleges, palaces, hospitals, observatories, cities. The ages have not been idle, nor kings slack, nor the rich niggardly. Have we not atoned for this small offence (which we could not help) of leaving you no right in the soil.

by this splendid indemnity of ancestral and national wealth? Would you have been born like a gipsy in a hedge, and preferred your freedom on a heath, and the range of a planet which had no shed or boscage to cover you from sun and wind—to this towered and citied world? to this world of Rome, and Memphis, and Constantinople, and Vienna, and Paris, and London, and New York? For thee Naples, Florence, and Venice; for thee the fair Mediterranean, the sunny Adriatic; for thee both Indies smile; for thee the hospitable North opens its heated palaces under the polar circle; for thee roads have been cut in every direction across the land, and fleets of floating palaces with every security for strength and provision for luxury, swim by sail and by steam through all the waters of this world. Every island for thee has a town; every town a hotel. Though thou wast born landless, yet to thy industry and thrift and small condescension to the established usage, scores of servants are swarming in every strange place with cap and knee to thy command; scores, nay hundreds and thousands, for thy wardrobe, thy table, thy chamber, thy library, thy leisure; and every whim is anticipated and served by the best ability of the whole population of each country. The king on the throne governs for thee, and the judge judges; the barrister pleads, the farmer tills, the joiner hammers, the postman rides. Is it not exaggerating a trifle to insist on a formal acknowledgment of your claims, when these substantial advantages have been secured to you? Now can your children be educated, your labor turned to their advantage, and its fruits secured to them after your death. It is frivolous to say you have no acre, because you have not a mathematically measured piece of land. Providence takes care that you shall have a place, that you are waited for, and come accredited; and as soon as you put your gift to use.

you shall have acre or acre's worth according to your exhibition of desert—acre, if you need land—acre's worth, if you prefer to draw, or carve, or make shoes or wheels, to the tilling of the soil.

Besides, it might temper your indignation at the supposed wrong which society has done you, to keep the question before you, how society got into this predicament? Who put things on this false basis? No single man, but all men. No man voluntarily and knowingly; but it is the result of that degree of culture there is in the planet. The order of things is as good as the character of the population permits. Consider it as the work of a great and beneficent and progressive necessity, which, from the first pulsation in the first animal life, up to the present high culture of the best nations, has advanced thus far. Thank the rude foster-mother though she has taught you a better wisdom than her own, and has set hopes in your heart which shall be history in the next ages. You are yourself the result of this manner of living, this foul compromise, this vituperated Sodom. It nourished you with care and love on its breast, as it had nourished many a lover of the right and many a poet, and prophet, and teacher of men. Is it so irremediably bad? Then again, if the mitigations are considered, do not all the mischiefs virtually vanish? The form is bad, but see you not how every personal character reacts on the form, and makes it new? A strong person makes the law and custom null before his own will. Then the principle of love and truth reappears in the strictest courts of fashion and property. Under the richest robes, in the darlings of the selectest circles of European or American aristocracy, the strong heart will beat with love of mankind, with impatience of accidental distinctions, with the desire to achieve its own fate and make every ornament it wears authentic and real.

Moreover, as we have already shown that there is no pure reformer, so it is to be considered that there is no pure conservative, no man who from the beginning to the end of his life maintains the defective institutions; but he who sets his face like a flint against every novelty, when approached in the confidence of conversation, in the presence of friendly and generous persons, has also his gracious and relenting moments, and espouses for the time the cause of man; and even if this be a short-lived emotion, yet the remembrance of it in private hours mitigates his selfishness and compliance with custom.

The Friar Bernard lamented in his cell on Mount Cenis the crimes of mankind, and rising one morning before day from his bed of moss and dry leaves, he gnawed his roots and berries, drank of the spring, and set forth to go to Rome to reform the corruption of mankind. On his way he encountered many travellers who greeted him courteously, and the cabins of the peasants and the castles of the lords supplied his few wants. When he came at last to Rome, his piety and good will easily introduced him to many families of the rich, and on the first day he saw and talked with gentle mothers with their babes at their breasts, who told him how much love they bore their children, and how they were perplexed in their daily walk lest they should fail in their duty to them. "What!" he said, "and this on rich embroidered carpets, on marble floors, with cunning sculpture, and carved wood, and rich pictures, and piles of books about you?"—"Look at our pictures and books," they said, "and we will tell you, good Father, how we spent the last evening. These are stories of godly children and holy families and romantic sacrifices made in old or in recent times by great and not mean persons; and last evening our family was collected and our husbands and brothers discoursed sadly on what we could save and give in the hard times." Then came in the men, and they said, "What cheer, brother? Does thy convent want gifts?" Then the Friar Bernard went home swiftly with other thoughts than he brought, saying, "This way of life is wrong, yet these Romans, whom I prayed God to destroy, are lovers, they are lovers; what can I do?"

The reformer concedes that these mitigations exist, and that if he proposed comfort, he should take sides with the establishment. Your words are excellent, but they do not tell the whole. Conservatism is affluent and openhanded, but there is a cunning juggle in riches. I observe that they take somewhat for everything they give. I look bigger, but am less; I have more clothes, but am not so warm; more armor, but less courage; more books, but less wit. What you say of your planted, builded and decorated world is true enough, and I gladly avail myself of its convenience; yet I have re- marked that what holds in particular, holds in general, that the plant Man does not require for his most glorious flowering this pomp of preparation and convenience, but the thoughts of some beggarly Homer who strolled, God knows when, in the infancy and barbarism of the old world; the gravity and sense of some slave Moses who leads away his fellow slaves from their masters; the contemplation of some Scythian Anacharsis; the erect, formidable valor of some Dorian townsmen in the town of Sparta; the vigor of Clovis the Frank, and Alfred the Saxon, and Alaric the Goth, and Mahomet, Ali and Omar the Arabians, Saladin the Curd, and Othman the Turk, sufficed to build what you call society on the spot and in the instant when the sound mind in a sound body ap- peared. Rich and fine is your dress, O Conservatism! your horses are of the best blood; your roads are well cut and well paved; your pantry is full of meats and your cellar of wines, and a very good state and condition are you for gentlemen and ladies to live under; but every one of these goods steals away a drop of my blood. I want the necessity of supplying my own wants. All this costly culture of yours is not necessary. Greatness does not need it. Yonder peasant, who sits neglected there in a corner, carries a whole revolution of man and nature in his head, which shall be a sacred history to some future ages. For man is the end of nature; nothing so easily organizes itself in every part of the universe as he; no moss, no lichen is so easily born; and he takes along with him and puts out from himself the whole apparatus of society and condition *extempore*, as an army encamps in a desert, and where all was just now blowing sand, creates a white city in an hour, a government, a market, a place for feasting, for conversation, and for love.

These considerations, urged by those whose characters and whose fortunes are yet to be formed, must needs command the sympathy of all reasonable persons. But beside that charity which should make all adult persons interested for the youth, and engage them to see that he has a free field and fair play on his entrance into life, we are bound to see that the society of which we compose a part, does not permit the formation or continuance of views and practices injurious to the honor and welfare of mankind. The objection to Conservatism, when embodied in a party, is that in its love of acts it hates principles; it lives in the senses, not in truth; it sacrifices to despair; it goes for availableness in its candidate, not for worth; and for expediency in its measures, and not for the right. Under pretence of allowing for friction, it makes so many additions and supplements to the machine of society that it will play smoothly and softly, but will no longer grind any grist.

The Conservative party in the universe concedes that the Radical would talk sufficiently to the purpose, if we were still in the Garden of Eden; he legislates for man as he ought to be; his theory is right, but he makes no allowance for friction; and this omission makes his whole doctrine false. The Idealist retorts that the Conservative falls into a far more noxious error in the other extreme. The Conservative assumes sickness as a necessity, and his social frame is a hospital, his total legislation is for the present distress, a universe in slippers and flannels, with bib and papspoon, swallowing pills and herb-tea. Sickness gets organized as well as health, the vice as well as the virtue. Now that a vicious system of trade has existed so long, it has stereotyped itself in the human generation, and misers are born. And now that sickness has got such a foothold, leprosy has grown cunning, has got into the ballot-box; the lepers outvote the clean; Society has resolved itself into a Hospital Committee, and all its laws are quarantine. If any man resist and set up a foolish hope he has entertained as good against the general despair, Society frowns on him, shuts him out of her opportunities, her granaries, her refectories, her water and bread, and will serve him a sexton's turn. Conservatism takes as low a view of every part of human action and passion. Its religion is just as bad; a lozenge for the sick; a dolorous tune to beguile the distemper; mitigations of pain by pillows and anodynes; always mitigations, never remedies; pardons for sin, funeral honors—never self-help, renovation, and virtue. Its social and political action has no better aim; to keep out wind and weather, to bring the week and year about, and make the world last our day; not to sit on the world and steer it; not to sink the memory of the past in the glory of a new and more excellent creation; a timid cobbler and patcher, it degrades whatever it touches. The cause of education is urged in this country with the utmost earnestness—on what ground? Why on this, that the people have the power, and if they are not instructed to sympathize with the intelligent, reading, trading, and governing class; inspired with a taste for the same competitions and prizes, they will upset the fair pageant of Judicature, and perhaps lay a hand on the sacred muniments of wealth itself, and new distribute the land. Religion is taught in the same spirit. The contractors who were building a road out of Baltimore, some years ago, found the Irish laborers quarrelsome and refractory to a degree that embarrassed the agents and seriously interrupted the progress of the work. The corporation were advised to call off the police and build a Catholic chapel, which they did; the priest presently restored order, and the work went on prosperously. Such hints, be sure, are too valuable to be lost. If you do not value the Sabbath, or other religious institutions, give yourself no concern about maintaining them. They have already acquired a market value as conservators of property; and if priest and church-member should fail, the chambers of commerce and the presidents of the banks, the very innholders and landlords of the county, would muster with fury to their support.

Of course, religion in such hands loses its essence. Instead of that reliance which the soul suggests, on the eternity of truth and duty, men are misled into a reliance on institutions, which, the moment they cease to be the instantaneous creations of the devout sentiment, are worthless. Religion among the low becomes low. As it loses its truth, it loses credit with the sagacious. They detect the falsehood of the preaching, but when they say so, all good citizens cry, Hush; do not weaken the State, do not take off the strait-jacket from dangerous persons. Every honest fellow must keep up the hoax the best he can; must patronize providence and piety, and wherever he sees anything that will keep men amused, schools or churches or poetry or picture-galleries or music, or what not, he must cry "Hist-a-boy," and urge the game on. What a compliment we pay to the good SPIRIT with our superserviceable zeal!

But not to balance reasons for and against the establishment any longer, and if it still be asked in this necessity of partial organization, which party on the whole has the highest claims on our sympathy—I bring it home to the private heart, where all such questions must have their final arbitrement. How will every strong and generous mind choose its ground—with the defenders of the old? or with the seekers of the new? Which is that state which promises to edify a great, brave, and beneficent man; to throw him on his resources, and tax the strength of his character? On which part will each of us find himself in the hour of health and of aspiration?

I understand well the respect of mankind for war, because that breaks up the Chinese stagnation of Society, and demonstrates the personal merits of all men. A state of war or anarchy, in which law has little force, is so far valuable that it puts every man on trial. The man of principle is known as such, and even in the fury of faction is respected. In the civil wars of France, Montaigne alone, among all the French gentry, kept his castle gates unbarred, and made his personal integrity as good at least as a regiment. The man of courage and resources is shown, and the effeminate and base person. Those who rise above war, and those who fall below it, it easily discriminates, as well as those who, accepting its rude conditions, keep their own head by their own sword.

But in peace and a commercial state we depend, not as we ought, on our knowledge and all men's knowledge that we are honest men, but we cowardly lean on the virtue of others. For it is always at last the virtue of some men in the society, which keeps the law in any reverence and power. Is there not something shameful that I should owe my peaceful occupancy of my house and field, not to the knowledge of my countrymen that I am useful, but to their respect for sundry other reputable persons, I know not whom, whose joint virtue still keeps the law in good odor?

It will never make any difference to a hero what the laws are. His greatness will shine and accomplish itself unto the end, whether they second him or not. If he have earned his bread by drudgery, and in the narrow and crooked ways which were all an evil law had left him, he will make it at least honorable by his expenditure. Of the past he will take no heed; for its wrongs he will not hold himself responsible: he will say, All the meanness of my progenitors shall not bereave me of the power to make this hour and company fair and fortunate. Whatsoever streams of power and commodity flow to me, shall of me acquire healing virtue, and become fountains of safety. Cannot I too descend a Redeemer into nature? Whosoever hereafter shall name my name, shall not record a malefactor but a benefactor in the earth. If there be power in good intention, in fidelity, and in toil, the north wind shall be purer, the stars in heaven shall glow with a kindlier beam, that I have lived. I am primarily engaged to myself to be a public servant of all the gods, to demonstrate to all men that there is intelligence and good will at the heart of things, and ever higher and yet higher leadings. These are my engagements; how can your law further or hinder me in what I shall do to men? On the other hand, these dispositions establish their relations to me. Wherever there is worth, I shall be greeted. Wherever there are men, are the objects of my study and love. Sooner or later all men will be my friends, and will testify in all methods the energy of their regard. I cannot thank your law for my protection. I protect it. It is not in its power to protect me. It is my business to make myself revered. I depend on my honor, my labor, and my dispositions for my place in the affections of mankind, and not on any conventions or parchments of yours.

But if I allow myself in derelictions and become idle and dissolute, I quickly come to love the protection of a strong law, because I feel no title in myself to my advantages. To the intemperate and covetous person no love flows; to him mankind would pay no rent, no dividend, if force were once relaxed; nay, if they could give their verdict, they would say that his self-indulgence and his oppression deserved punishment from Society, and not that rich board and lodging he now enjoys. The law acts then as a screen of his unworthiness, and makes him worse the longer it protects him.

In conclusion, to return from this alternation of partial views to the high platform of universal and necessary history, it is a happiness for mankind that Innovation has got on so far and has so free a field before it. The boldness of the hope men entertain transcends all former experience. It calms and cheers them with the picture of a simple and equal life of truth and piety. And this hope flowered on what tree? It was not imported from the stock of some celestial plant, but grew here on the wild crab of Conservatism. It is much that this old and vituperated system of things has borne so fair a child. It predicts that amidst a planet peopled with Conservatives, one Reformer may yet be born.

NEW ENGLAND REFORMERS

*A Lecture Read before the Society in Amory Hall,
on Sunday, March 3, 1844.*

WHOEVER has had opportunity of acquaintance with society in New England during the last twenty-five years, with those middle and with those leading sections that may constitute any just representation of the character and aim of the community, will have been struck with the great activity of thought and experimenting. His attention must be commanded by the signs that the Church, or religious party, is falling from the Church nominal, and is appearing in temperance and non-resistance societies; in movements of abolitionists and of socialists; and in very significant assemblies called Sabbath and Bible Conventions; composed of ultraists, of seekers, of all the soul of the soldiery of dissent, and meeting to call in question the authority of the Sabbath, of the priesthood, and of the Church. In these movements nothing was more remarkable than the discontent they begot in the movers. The spirit of protest and of detachment drove the members of these Conventions to bear testimony against the Church, and immediately afterwards to declare their discontent with these Conventions, their independence of their colleagues, and their impatience of the methods whereby they were working. They defied each other, like a congress of kings, each of whom had a realm to rule, and a way of his own that made concert unprofitable. What a fertility of projects for the salvation of the world! One apostle thought all men should go to farming, and another that no man should buy or sell, that the use of money was the cardinal evil; another that the mischief was in our diet, that we eat and drink damnation. These made unleavened bread, and were foes to the death to fermentation. It was in vain urged by the housewife that God made yeast, as well as dough, and loves fermentation just as dearly as he loves vegetation; that fermentation develops the saccharine element in the grain, and makes it more palatable and more digestible. No; they wish the pure wheat, and will die but it shall not ferment. Stop, dear nature, these incessant advances of thine; let us scotch these ever-rolling wheels! Others attacked the system of agriculture, the use of animal manures in farming, and the tyranny of man over brute nature; these abuses polluted his food. The ox must be taken from the plough and the horse from the cart, the hundred acres of the farm must be spaded, and the man must walk, wherever boats and locomotives will not carry him. Even the insect world was to be defended—that had been too long neglected, and a society for the protection of ground-worms, slugs, and mosquitos was to be incorporated without delay. With these appeared the adepts of homœopathy, of hydropathy, of mesmerism, of phrenology, and their wonderful theories of the Christian miracles! Others assailed particular vocations, as that of the lawyer, that of the merchant, of the manufacturer, of the clergyman, of the scholar. Others attacked the institution of marriage as the fountain of social evils. Others devoted themselves to the worrying of churches and meetings for public worship; and the fertile forms of antinomianism among the elder Puritans seemed to have their match in the plenty of the new harvest of reform.

With this din of opinion and debate there was a
keener scrutiny of institutions and domestic life than
any we had known; there was sincere protesting against
existing evils, and there were changes of employment
dictated by conscience. No doubt there was plentiful
vaporing, and cases of backsliding might occur. But in
each of these movements emerged a good result, a tendency to the adoption of simpler methods, and an assertion of the sufficiency of the private man. Thus it was
directly in the spirit and genius of the age, what happened in one instance when a church censured and
threatened to excommunicate one of its members on account of the somewhat hostile part to the church which
his conscience led him to take in the anti-slavery business; the threatened individual immediately excommuni-
cated the church, in a public and formal process. This
has been several times repeated: it was excellent when
it was done the first time, but of course loses all value
when it is copied. Every project in the history of reform,
no matter how violent and surprising, is good when it is
the dictate of a man's genius and constitution, but very
dull and suspicious when adopted from another. It is
right and beautiful in any man to say, "I will take this
coat, or this book, or this measure of corn of yours"—
in whom we see the act to be original, and to flow from
the whole spirit and faith of him; for then that taking
will have a giving as free and divine; but we are very
easily disposed to resist the same generosity of speech
when we miss originality and truth to character in it.

There was in all the practical activities of New
England for the last quarter of a century, a gradual with-
drawal of tender consciences from the social organizations. There is observable throughout, the contest
between mechanical and spiritual methods, but with a

steady tendency of the thoughtful and virtuous to a deeper belief and reliance on spiritual facts.

In politics for example it is easy to see the progress of dissent. The country is full of rebellion; the country is full of kings. Hands off! let there be no control and no interference in the administration of the affairs of this kingdom of me. Hence the growth of the doctrine and of the party of Free Trade, and the willingness to try that experiment, in the face of what appear incontestable facts. I confess, the motto of the Globe newspaper is so attractive to me that I can seldom find much appetite to read what is below it in its columns: "The world is governed too much." So the country is frequently affording solitary examples of resistance to the government, solitary nullifiers, who throw themselves on their reserved rights; nay, who have reserved all their rights; who reply to the assessor and to the clerk of court that they do not know the State, and embarrass the courts of law by non-juring and the commander-in-chief of the militia by non-resistance.

The same disposition to scrutiny and dissent appeared in civil, festive, neighborly, and domestic society. A restless, prying, conscientious criticism broke out in unexpected quarters. Who gave me the money with which I bought my coat? Why should professional labor and that of the counting-house be paid so disproportionately to the labor of the porter and woodsawyer? This whole business of Trade gives me to pause and think, as it constitutes false relations between men; inasmuch as I am prone to count myself relieved of any responsibility to behave well and nobly to that person whom I pay with money; whereas if I had not that commodity, I should be put on my good behavior in all companies, and man would be a benefactor to man, as being himself his only certificate that he had a right to those aids and services which each asked of the other. Am I not too protected a person? is there not a wide disparity between the lot of me and the lot of thee, my poor brother, my poor sister? Am I not defrauded of my best culture in the loss of those gymnastics which manual labor and the emergencies of poverty constitute? I find nothing healthful or exalting in the smooth conventions of society; I do not like the close air of saloons. I begin to suspect myself to be a prisoner, though treated with all this courtesy and luxury. I pay a destructive tax in my conformity.

The same insatiable criticism may be traced in the efforts for the reform of Education. The popular education has been taxed with a want of truth and nature. It was complained that an education to things was not given. We are students of words: we are shut up in schools, and colleges, and recitation-rooms, for ten or fifteen years, and come out at last with a bag of wind, a memory of words, and do not know a thing. We cannot use our hands, or our legs, or our eyes, or our arms. We do not know an edible root in the woods, we cannot tell our course by the stars, nor the hour of the day by the sun. It is well if we can swim and skate. We are afraid of a horse, of a cow, of a dog, of a snake, of a spider. The Roman rule was to teach a boy nothing that he could not learn standing. The old English rule was, "All summer in the field, and all winter in the study." And it seems as if a man should learn to plant, or to fish, or to hunt, that he might secure his subsistence at all events, and not be painful to his friends and fellow men. The lessons of science should be experimental also. The sight of a planet through a telescope is worth all the course on astronomy; the shock of the electric spark in the elbow outvalues all the theories; the taste of the nitrous oxide, the firing of an artificial volcano, are better than volumes of chemistry.

One of the traits of the new spirit is the inquisition it fixed on our scholastic devotion to the dead languages. The ancient languages, with great beauty of structure, contain wonderful remains of genius, which draw, and always will draw, certain likeminded men—Greek men, and Roman men—in all countries, to their study; but by a wonderful drowsiness of usage they had exacted the study of *all* men. Once (say two centuries ago), Latin and Greek had a strict relation to all the science and culture there was in Europe, and the Mathematics had a momentary importance at some era of activity in physical science. These things became stereotyped as *education,* as the manner of men is. But the Good Spirit never cared for the colleges, and though all men and boys were now drilled in Latin, Greek, and Mathematics, it had quite left these shells high and dry on the beach, and was now creating and feeding other matters at other ends of the world. But in a hundred high schools and colleges this warfare against common sense still goes on. Four, or six, or ten years, the pupil is parsing Greek and Latin, and as soon as he leaves the University, as it is ludicrously styled, he shuts those books for the last time. Some thousands of young men are graduated at our colleges in this country every year, and the persons who, at forty years, still read Greek, can all be counted on your hand. I never met with ten. Four or five persons I have seen who read Plato.

But is not this absurd, that the whole liberal talent of this country should be directed in its best years on studies which lead to nothing? What was the consequence? Some intelligent persons said or thought, "Is that Greek and Latin some spell to conjure with, and not words of reason? If the physician, the lawyer, the divine, never use it to come at their ends, I need never learn it to come at mine. Conjuring is gone out of fashion, and I will omit this conjugating, and go straight to affairs." So they jumped the Greek and Latin, and read law, medicine, or sermons, without it. To the astonishment of all, the self-made men took even ground at once with the oldest of the regular graduates, and in a few months the most conservative circles of Boston and New York had quite forgotten who of their gownsmen was college-bred, and who was not.

One tendency appears alike in the philosophical speculation and in the rudest democratical movements, through all the petulance and all the puerility, the wish, namely, to cast aside the superfluous and arrive at short methods; urged, as I suppose, by an intuition that the human spirit is equal to all emergencies, alone, and that man is more often injured than helped by the means he uses.

I conceive this gradual casting off of material aids, and the indication of growing trust in the private self-supplied powers of the individual, to be the affirmative principle of the recent philosophy, and that it is feeling its own profound truth and is reaching forward at this very hour to the happiest conclusions. I readily concede that in this, as in every period of intellectual activity, there has been a noise of denial and protest; much was to be resisted, much was to be got rid of by those who were reared in the old, before they could begin to affirm and to construct. Many a reformer perishes in his removal of rubbish; and that makes the offensiveness of the class. They are partial; they are not equal to the work they pretend. They lose their way; in the assault on the kingdom of darkness they expend all their energy on some accidental evil, and lose their sanity and power of benefit. It is of little moment that one or two or twenty errors of our social system be corrected, but of much that the man be in his senses.

The criticism and attack on institutions, which we have witnessed, has made one thing plain, that society gains nothing whilst a man, not himself renovated, attempts to renovate things around him: he has become tediously good in some particular but negligent or narrow in the rest; and hypocrisy and vanity are often the disgusting result.

It is handsomer to remain in the establishment better than the establishment, and conduct that in the best manner, than to make a sally against evil by some single improvement, without supporting it by a total regeneration. Do not be so vain of your one objection. Do you think there is only one? Alas! my good friend, there is no part of society or of life better than any other part. All our things are right and wrong together. The wave of evil washes all our institutions alike. Do you complain of our Marriage? Our marriage is no worse than our education, our diet, our trade, our social customs. Do you complain of the laws of Property? It is a pedantry to give such importance to them. Can we not play the game of life with these counters, as well as with those? in the institution of property, as well as out of it? Let into it the new and renewing principle of love, and property will be universality. No one gives the impression of superiority to the institution, which he must give who will reform it. It makes no difference what you say, you must make me feel that you are aloof from it; by your natural and supernatural advantages do easily see to the end of it—do see how man can do without it. Now all men are on one side. No man deserves to be heard against property. Only Love, only an Idea, is against property as we hold it.

I cannot afford to be irritable and captious, nor to

waste all my time in attacks. If I should go out of church whenever I hear a false sentiment I could never stay there five minutes. But why come out? the street is as false as the church, and when I get to my house, or to my manners, or to my speech, I have not got away from the lie. When we see an eager assailant of one of these wrongs, a special reformer, we feel like asking him, What right have you, sir, to your one virtue? Is virtue piecemeal? This is a jewel amidst the rags of a beggar.

In another way the right will be vindicated. In the midst of abuses, in the heart of cities, in the aisles of false churches, alike in one place and in another— wherever, namely, a just and heroic soul finds itself, there it will do what is next at hand, and by the new quality of character it shall put forth it shall abrogate that old condition, law or school in which it stands, before the law of its own mind.

If partiality was one fault of the movement party, the other defect was their reliance on Association. Doubts such as those I have intimated drove many good persons to agitate the questions of social reform. But the revolt against the spirit of commerce, the spirit of aristocracy, and the inveterate abuses of cities, did not appear possible to individuals; and to do battle against numbers they armed themselves with numbers, and against concert they relied on new concert.

Following or advancing beyond the ideas of St. Simon, of Fourier, and of Owen, three communities have already been formed in Massachusetts on kindred plans, and many more in the country at large. They aim to give every member a share in the manual labor, to give an equal reward to labor and to talent, and to unite a liberal culture with an education to labor. The scheme offers, by the economies of associated labor and expense, to make every member rich, on the same amount of property that, in separate families, would leave every member poor. These new associations are composed of men and women of superior talents and sentiments; yet it may easily be questioned whether such a community will draw, except in its beginnings, the able and the good; whether those who have energy will not prefer their chance of superiority and power in the world, to the humble certainties of the association; whether such a retreat does not promise to become an asylum to those who have tried and failed, rather than a field to the strong; and whether the members will not necessarily be fractions of men, because each finds that he cannot enter it without some compromise. Friendship and association are very fine things, and a grand phalanx of the best of the human race, banded for some catholic object; yes, excellent; but remember that no society can ever be so large as one man. He, in his friendship, in his natural and momentary associations, doubles or multiplies himself; but in the hour in which he mortgages himself to two or ten or twenty, he dwarfs himself below the stature of one.

But the men of less faith could not thus believe, and to such, concert appears the sole specific of strength. I have failed, and you have failed, but perhaps together we shall not fail. Our housekeeping is not satisfactory to us, but perhaps a phalanx, a community, might be. Many of us have differed in opinion, and we could find no man who could make the truth plain, but possibly a college, or an ecclesiastical council, might. I have not been able either to persuade my brother or to prevail on myself to disuse the traffic or the potation of brandy, but perhaps a pledge of total abstinence might effectually restrain us. The candidate my party votes for is not to be trusted with a dollar, but he will be honest in the Senate, for we can bring public opinion to bear on him. Thus concert was the specific in all cases. But concert is neither better nor worse, neither more nor less potent, than individual force. All the men in the world cannot make a statue walk and speak, cannot make a drop of blood, or a blade of grass, any more than one man can. But let there be one man, let there be truth in two men, in ten men, then is concert for the first time possible; because the force which moves the world is a new quality, and can never be furnished by adding whatever quantities of a different kind. What is the use of the concert of the false and the disunited? There can be no concert in two, where there is no concert in one. When the individual is not *individual,* but is dual; when his thoughts look one way and his actions another; when his faith is traversed by his habits; when his will, enlightened by reason, is warped by his sense; when with one hand he rows and with the other backs water, what concert can be?

I do not wonder at the interest these projects inspire. The world is awaking to the idea of union, and these experiments show what it is thinking of. It is and will be magic. Men will live and communicate, and plough, and reap, and govern, as by added ethereal power, when once they are united; as in a celebrated experiment, by expiration and respiration exactly together, four persons lift a heavy man from the ground by the little finger only, and without sense of weight. But this union must be inward, and not one of covenants, and is to be reached by a reverse of the methods they use. The union is only perfect when all the uniters are isolated. It is the union of friends who live in different streets or towns. Each man, if he attempts to join himself to others, is on all sides cramped and diminished of his proportion; and the stricter the union the smaller and the more pitiful he is. But leave him alone, to recognize in every hour and place the secret soul; he will go up and down doing the works of a true member, and, to the astonishment of all, the work will be done with concert, though no man spoke. Government will be adamantine without any governor. The union must be ideal in actual individualism.

I pass to the indication in some particulars of that faith in man, which the heart is preachnig to us in these days, and which engages the more regard, from the consideration that the speculations of one generation are the history of the next following.

In alluding just now to our system of education, I spoke of the deadness of its details. But it is open to graver criticism than the palsy of its members: it is a system of despair. The disease with which the human mind now labors is want of faith. Men do not believe in a power of education. We do not think we can speak to divine sentiments in man, and we do not try. We renounce all high aims. We believe that the defects of so many perverse and so many frivolous people who make up society, are organic, and society is a hospital of incurables. A man of good sense but of little faith, whose compassion seemed to lead him to church as often as he went there, said to me that "he liked to have concerts, and fairs, and churches, and other public amusements go on." I am afraid the remark is too honest, and comes from the same origin as the maxim of the tyrant, "If you would rule the world quietly, you must keep it amused." I notice too that the ground on which eminent public servants urge the claims of popular education is fear; "This country is filling up with thousands and millions of voters, and you must educate them to keep them from our throats." We do not believe that any education, any system of philosophy, any influence of genius, will ever give depth of insight to a superficial mind. Having settled ourselves into this infidelity, our skill is expended to procure alleviations, diversion, opiates. We adorn the victim with manual skill, his tongue with languages, his body with inoffensive and comely manners. So have we cunningly hid the tragedy of limitation and inner death we cannot avert. Is it strange that society should be devoured by a secret melancholy which breaks through all its smiles and all its gayety and games?

But even one step farther our infidelity has gone. It appears that some doubt is felt by good and wise men whether really the happiness and probity of men is increased by the culture of the mind in those disciplines to which we give the name of education. Unhappily too the doubt comes from scholars, from persons who have tried these methods. In their experience the scholar was not raised by the sacred thoughts amongst which he dwelt, but used them to selfish ends. He was a profane person, and became a showman, turning his gifts to a marketable use, and not to his own sustenance and growth. It was found that the intellect could be independently developed, that is, in separation from the man, as any single organ can be invigorated, and the result was monstrous. A canine appetite for knowledge was generated, which must still be fed but was never satisfied, and this knowledge, not being directed on action, never took the character of substantial, humane truth, blessing those whom it entered. It gave the scholar certain powers of expression, the power of speech, the power of poetry, of literary art, but it did not bring him to peace or to beneficence.

When the literary class betray a destitution of faith, it is not strange that society should be disheartened and sensualized by unbelief. What remedy? Life must be lived on a higher plane. We must go up to a higher platform, to which we are always invited to ascend;

there, the whole aspect of things changes. I resist the skepticism of our education and of our educated men. I do not believe that the differences of opinion and character in men are organic. I do not recognize, beside the class of the good and the wise, a permanent class of skeptics, or a class of conservatives, or of malignants, or of materialists. I do not believe in two classes. You remember the story of the poor woman who importuned King Philip of Macedon to grant her justice, which Philip refused: the woman exclaimed, "I appeal": the king, astonished, asked to whom she appealed: the woman replied, "From Philip drunk to Philip sober." The text will suit me very well. I believe not in two classes of men, but in man in two moods, in Philip drunk and Philip sober. I think, according to the good-hearted word of Plato, "Unwillingly the soul is deprived of truth." Iron conservative, miser, or thief, no man is but by a supposed necessity which he tolerates by shortness or torpidity of sight. The soul lets no man go without some visitations and holy days of a diviner presence. It would be easy to show, by a narrow scanning of any man's biography, that we are not so wedded to our paltry performances of every kind but that every man has at intervals the grace to scorn his performances, in comparing them with his belief of what he should do—that he puts himself on the side of his enemies, listening gladly to what they say of him, and accusing himself of the same things.

What is it men love in Genius, but its infinite hope, which degrades all it has done? Genius counts all its miracles poor and short. Its own idea it never executed. The Iliad, the Hamlet, the Doric column, the Roman arch, the Gothic minster, the German anthem, when they are ended, the master casts behind him. How sinks the song in the waves of melody which the universe pours over his soul! Before that gracious Infinite out of which he drew these few strokes, how mean they look, though the praises of the world attend them. From the triumphs of his art he turns with desire to this greater defeat. Let those admire who will. With silent joy he sees himself to be capable of a beauty that eclipses all which his hands have done; all which human hands have ever done.

Well, we are all the children of genius, the children of virtue—and feel their inspirations in our happier hours. Is not every man sometimes a radical in politics? Men are conservatives when they are least vigorous, or when they are most luxurious. They are conservatives after dinner, or before taking their rest; when they are sick, or aged: in the morning, or when their intellect or their conscience has been aroused; when they hear music, or when they read poetry, they are radicals. In the circle of the rankest Tories that could be collected in England, Old or New, let a powerful and stimulating intellect, a man of great heart and mind act on them, and very quickly these frozen conservators will yield to the friendly influence, these hopeless will begin to hope, these haters will begin to love, these immovable statues will begin to spin and revolve. I cannot help recalling the fine anecdote which Warton relates of Bishop Berkeley, when he was preparing to leave England with his plan of planting the gospel among the American savages. "Lord Bathurst told me that the members of the Scriblerus club being met at his house at dinner, they agreed to rally Berkeley, who was also his guest, on his scheme at Bermudas. Berkeley, having listened to the many lively things they had to say, begged to be heard in his turn, and displayed his plan with such an astonishing and animating force of eloquence and enthusiasm that they were struck dumb, and, after some pause, rose up all together with earnestness, exclaiming, 'Let us set out with him immediately.'" Men in all ways are better than they seem. They like flattery for the moment, but they know the truth for their own. It is a foolish cowardice which keeps us from trusting them and speaking to them rude truth. They resent your honesty for an instant, they will thank you for it always. What is it we heartily wish of each other? Is it to be pleased and flattered? No, but to be convicted and exposed, to be shamed out of our nonsense of all kinds, and made men of, instead of ghosts and phantoms. We are weary of gliding ghostlike through the world, which is itself so slight and unreal. We crave a sense of reality, though it come in strokes of pain. I explain so—by this manlike love of truth—those excesses and errors into which souls of great vigor, but not equal insight, often fall. They feel the poverty at the bottom of all the seeming affluence of the world. They know the speed with which they come straight through the thin masquerade, and conceive a disgust at the indigence of nature: Rousseau, Mirabeau, Charles Fox, Napoleon, Byron—and I could easily add names nearer home, of raging riders, who drive their steeds so hard, in the violence of living to forget its illusion: they would know the worst, and tread the floors of hell. The heroes of ancient and modern fame, Cimon, Themistocles, Alcibiades, Alexander, Cæsar, have treated life and fortune as a game to be well and skilfully played, but the stake not to be so valued but that any time it could be held as a trifle light as air, and thrown up. Cæsar, just before the battle of Pharsalia, discourses with the Egyptian priest concerning the fountains of the Nile, and offers to quit the army, the empire, and Cleopatra, if he will show him those mysterious sources.

The same magnanimity shows itself in our social relations, in the preference, namely, which each man gives to the society of superiors over that of his equals. All that a man has will he give for right relations with his mates. All that he has will he give for an erect demeanor in every company and on each occasion. He aims at such things as his neighbors prize, and gives his days and nights, his talents and his heart, to strike a good stroke, to acquit himself in all men's sight as a man. The consideration of an eminent citizen, of a noted merchant, of a man of mark in his profession; a naval and military honor, a general's commission, a marshal's baton, a ducal coronet, the laurel of poets, and, anyhow procured, the acknowledgment of eminent merit—have this lustre for each candidate that they enable him to walk erect and unashamed in the presence of some persons before whom he felt himself inferior. Having raised himself to this rank, having established his equality with class after class of those with whom he would live well, he still finds certain others before whom he cannot possess himself, because they have somewhat fairer, somewhat grander, somewhat purer, which extorts homage of him. Is his ambition pure? then will his laurels and his possessions seem worthless: instead of avoiding these men who make his fine gold dim, he will cast all behind him and seek their society only, woo and embrace this his humiliation and mortification, until he shall know why his eye sinks, his voice is husky, and his brilliant talents are paralyzed in this presence. He is sure that the soul which gives the lie to all things will tell none. His constitution will not mislead him. If it cannot carry itself as it ought, high and unmatchable in the presence of any man; if the secret oracles whose whisper makes the sweetness and dignity of his life do here withdraw and accompany him no longer—it is time to undervalue what he has valued, to dispossess himself of what he has acquired, and with Cæsar to take in his hand the army, the empire, and Cleopatra, and say, "All these will I relinquish, if you will show me the fountains of the Nile." Dear to us are those who love us; the swift moments we spend with them are a compensation for a great deal of misery; they enlarge our life—but dearer are those who reject us as unworthy, for they add another life: they build a heaven before us whereof we had not dreamed, and thereby supply to us new powers out of the recesses of the spirit, and urge us to new and unattempted performances.

As every man at heart wishes the best and not inferior society, wishes to be convicted of his error and to come to himself—so he wishes that the same healing should not stop in his thought, but should penetrate his will or active power. The selfish man suffers more from his selfishness than he from whom that selfishness withholds some important benefit. What he most wishes is to be lifted to some higher platform, that he may see beyond his present fear the trans-Alpine good, so that his fear, his coldness, his custom may be broken up like fragments of ice, melted and carried away in the great stream of good will. Do you ask my aid? I also wish to be a benefactor. I wish more to be a benefactor and servant than you wish to be served by me; and surely the greatest good fortune that could befall me is precisely to be so moved by you that I should say, "Take me and all mine, and use me and mine freely to your ends!" for I could not say it otherwise than because a great enlargement had come to my heart and mind, which made me superior to my fortunes. Here we are paralyzed with fear; we hold on to our little properties, house and land, office and money, for the bread which they have in our experience yielded us, although we confess that our being does not flow through them. We desire to be made great; we desire to be touched with that fire which shall command this ice to stream, and make our existence a benefit. If therefore we start objections to your project, O friend of the slave, or friend of the poor or of the race, understand well that it is because we wish to drive you to drive us into your measures. We wish to hear ourselves confuted. We are haunted with a belief that you have a secret which it would highliest advantage us to learn, and we would force you to impart it to us, though it should bring us to prison or to worse extremity.

Nothing shall warp me from the belief that every man is a lover of truth. There is no pure lie, no pure malignity in nature. The entertainment of the proposition of depravity is the last profligacy and profanation. There is no skepticism, no atheism but that. Could it be received into common belief, suicide would unpeople the planet. It has had a name to live in some dogmatic theology, but each man's innocence and his real liking of his neighbor have kept it a dead letter. I remember standing at the polls one day when the anger of the political contest gave a certain grimness to the faces of the independent electors, and a good man at my side, looking on the people, remarked, "I am satisfied that the largest part of these men, on either side, mean to vote right." I suppose considerate observers, looking at the masses of men in their blameless and in their equivocal actions, will assent, that in spite of selfishness and frivolity, the general purpose in the great number of persons is fidelity. The reason why anyone refuses his assent to your opinion, or his aid to your benevolent design, is in you: he refuses to accept you as a bringer of truth, because though you think you have it, he feels that you have it not. You have not given him the authentic sign.

If it were worth while to run into details this general doctrine of the latent but ever soliciting Spirit, it would be easy to adduce illustration in particulars of a man's equality to the Church, of his equality to the State, and of his equality to every other man. It is yet in all men's memory that, a few years ago, the liberal churches complained that the Calvinistic Church denied to them the name of Christian. I think the complaint was confession: a religious church would not complain. A religious man, like Behmen, Fox, or Swedenborg is not irritated by wanting the sanction of the Church, but the Church feels the accusation of his presence and belief.

It only needs that a just man should walk in our streets to make it appear how pitiful and inartificial a contrivance is our legislation. The man whose part is taken and who does not wait for society in anything, has a power which society cannot choose but feel. The familiar experiment called the hydrostatic paradox, in which a capillary column of water balances the ocean, is a symbol of the relation of one man to the whole family of men. The wise Dandamis, on hearing the lives of Socrates, Pythagoras and Diogenes read, "judged them to be great men every way, excepting that they were too much subjected to the reverence of the laws, which to second and authorize, true virtue must abate very much of its original vigor."

And as a man is equal to the Church and equal to the State, so he is equal to every other man. The disparities of power in men are superficial; and all frank and searching conversation, in which a man lays himself open to his brother, apprises each of their radical unity. When two persons sit and converse in a thoroughly good understanding, the remark is sure to be made, See how we have disputed about words! Let a clear, apprehensive mind, such as every man knows among his friends, converse with the most commanding poetic genius, I think it would appear that there was no inequality such as men fancy, between them; that a perfect understanding, a like receiving, a like perceiving, abolished differences; and the poet would confess that his creative imagination gave him no deep advantage, but only the superficial one that he could express himself and the other could not; that his advantage was a knack, which might impose on indolent men but could not impose on lovers of truth; for they know the tax of talent, or what a price of greatness the power of expression too often pays. I believe it is the conviction of the purest men that the net amount of man and man does not much vary. Each is incomparably superior to his companion in some faculty. His want of skill in other directions has added to his fitness for his own work. Each seems to have some compensation yielded to him by his infirmity, and every hindrance operates as a concentration of his force.

These and the like experiences intimate that man stands in strict connection with a higher fact never yet manifested. There is power over and behind us, and we are the channels of its communications. We seek to say thus and so, and over our head some spirit sits which contradicts what we say. We would persuade our fellow to this or that; another self within our eyes dissuades him. That which we keep back, this reveals. In vain we compose our faces and our words; it holds uncontrollable communication with the enemy, and he answers civilly to us, but believes the spirit. We exclaim, "There's a traitor in the house!" but at last it appears that he is the true man, and I am the traitor. This open channel to the highest life is the first and last reality, so subtle, so quiet, yet so tenacious, that although I have never expressed the truth, and although I have never heard the expression of it from any other, I know that the whole truth is here for me. What if I cannot answer your questions? I am not pained that I cannot frame a reply to the question, What is the operation we call Providence? There lies the unspoken thing, present, omnipresent. Every time we converse we seek to translate it into speech, but whether we hit or whether we miss, we have the fact. Every discourse is an approximate answer: but it is of small consequence that we do not get it into verbs and nouns, whilst it abides for contemplation forever.

If the auguries of the prophesying heart shall make themselves good in time, the man who shall be born, whose advent men and events prepare and foreshow, is one who shall enjoy his connection with a higher life, with the man within man; shall destroy distrust by his trust, shall use his native but forgotten methods, shall not take counsel of flesh and blood, but shall rely on the Law alive and beautiful which works over our heads and under our feet. Pitiless, it avails itself of our success when we obey it, and of our ruin when we contravene it. Men are all secret believers in it, else the word justice would have no meaning: they believe that the best is the true; that right is done at last; or chaos would come. It rewards actions after their nature, and not after the design of the agent. "Work," it saith to man, "in every hour, paid or unpaid, see only that thou work, and thou canst not escape the reward: whether thy work be fine or coarse, planting corn or writing epics, so only it be honest work, done to thine own approbation, it shall earn a reward to the senses as well as to the thought: no matter how often defeated, you are born to victory. The reward of a thing well done, is to have done it."

As soon as a man is wonted to look beyond surfaces, and to see how this high will prevails without an exception or an interval, he settles himself into serenity. He can already rely on the laws of gravity, that every stone will fall where it is due; the good globe is faithful, and carries us securely through the celestial spaces, anxious or resigned, we need not interfere to help it on: and he will learn one day the mild lesson they teach, that our own orbit is all our task, and we need not assist the administration of the universe. Do not be so impatient to set the town right concerning the unfounded pretensions and the false reputation of certain men of standing. They are laboring harder to set the town right concerning themselves, and will certainly succeed. Suppress for a few days your criticism on the insufficiency of this or that teacher or experimenter, and he will have demonstrated his insufficiency to all men's eyes. In like manner, let a man fall into the divine circuits, and he is enlarged. Obedience to his genius is the only liberating influence. We wish to escape from subjection and a sense of inferiority, and we make self-denying ordinances, we drink water, we eat grass, we refuse the laws, we go to jail: it is all in vain; only by obedience to his genius, only by the freest activity in the way constitutional to him, does an angel seem to arise before a man and lead him by the hand out of all the wards of the prison.

That which befits us, embosomed in beauty and wonder as we are, is cheerfulness and courage, and the endeavor to realize our aspirations. The life of man is the true romance, which when it is valiantly conducted will yield the imagination a higher joy than any fiction. All around us what powers are wrapped up under the coarse mattings of custom, and all wonder prevented. It is so wonderful to our neurologists that a man can see without his eyes, that it does not occur to them that it is just as wonderful that he should see with them; and that is ever the difference between the wise and the unwise: the latter wonders at what is unusual, the wise man wonders at the usual. Shall not the heart which has received so much, trust the Power by which it lives? May it not quit other leadings, and listen to the Soul that has guided it so gently and taught it so much, secure that the future will be worthy of the past?

The Ways of Life

EDITOR'S NOTE

PROGRAMS might be wild or wise, but meanwhile life went on and was itself. As Emerson grew in his own wisdom he became more and more absorbed in the fact, and the facts, of existence. The body of his work is analytical of things as he thought they were; it stands or falls by our consent to agree with his findings, or to recognize their pertinence. The final success of Emerson the writer is measured by the number of true things a reader hears him saying. There may be little method in his search, there may be no argument that he can clinch. But those who value him can point to a thousand isolated sentences in which he has spoken exciting truth. In such sentences he is both sensible and inspired. The combination is rare.

History, Manners, and *Politics* are three of the famous *Essays.* They are statements, as rich as Emerson could make them, of the way life arranges itself. *The Comic* and *The Tragic,* originally printed in the pages of *The Dial,* are attempts, sometimes more dutiful than successful, to complete the "theory of nature" which Emerson had committed himself to searching for. *Illusions,* which brings *The Conduct of Life* to its brilliant close, earned this from Carlyle: "You have grown older, more pungent, piercing; I never read from you before such lightning-gleams of meaning as are to be found here. The finale of all, that of 'Illusions' falling on us like snow-showers, but again of 'the gods sitting steadfast on their thrones' all the while—what a *Fiat Lux*

is there!" Carlyle as usual was possessed of a good ear.
Emerson's prose had never produced so high a music,
and never was to match it again.

Farming, from *Society and Solitude,* has the melancholy interest which attaches to any celebration of a life
that boasts less future than past. The farmers of Concord were precious symbols to Emerson of something
which he knew had now a rival: industrialism. He was
attracted to that too, but he clung to the older myth,
and into this essay he gathered its sentiments as nose-
gays are gathered, one flower at a time. *Education*
was put together after his death from a number of com-
mencement and other such addresses that he had made.
No subject ever interested him more. *Memory* is a lecture which he delivered at various times during the
period between 1857 and 1871. *Quotation and Originality* was first delivered as a lecture in 1859. Emerson's
memory was both good and bad—hence the fascination of the subject—but in quotation he was always an
artist, and it is interesting to hear him in defense of
the art.

HISTORY

There is no great and no small
To the Soul that maketh all:
And where it cometh, all things are;
And it cometh everywhere.

I am owner of the sphere,
Of the seven stars and the solar year,
Of Cæsar's hand, and Plato's brain,
Of Lord Christ's heart, and Shakespeare's strain.

THERE is one mind common to all individual men.
Every man is an inlet to the same and to all of the
same. He that is once admitted to the right of reason is
made a freeman of the whole estate. What Plato has
thought, he may think; what a saint has felt, he may
feel; what at any time has befallen any man, he can understand. Who hath access to this universal mind is a
party to all that is or can be done, for this is the only and
sovereign agent.

Of the works of this mind history is the record. Its
genius is illustrated by the entire series of days. Man is
explicable by nothing less than all his history. Without
hurry, without rest, the human spirit goes forth from the
beginning to embody every faculty, every thought, every
emotion which belongs to it, in appropriate events. But
the thought is always prior to the fact; all the facts of
history pre-exist in the mind as laws. Each law in turn
is made by circumstances predominant, and the limits
of nature give power to but one at a time. A man is the

whole encyclopedia of facts. The creation of a thousand
forests is in one acorn, and Egypt, Greece, Rome, Gaul,
Britain, America, lie folded already in the first man.
Epoch after epoch, camp, kingdom, empire, republic,
democracy, are merely the application of his manifold
spirit to the manifold world.

This human mind wrote history, and this must read it.
The Sphinx must solve her own riddle. If the whole of
history is in one man, it is all to be explained from individual experience. There is a relation between the hours
of our life and the centuries of time. As the air I breathe
is drawn from the great repositories of nature, as the
light on my book is yielded by a star a hundred millions
of miles distant, as the poise of my body depends on the
equilibrium of centrifugal and centripetal forces, so the
hours should be instructed by the ages and the ages explained by the hours. Of the universal mind each individual man is one more incarnation. All its properties
consist in him. Each new fact in his private experience
flashes a light on what great bodies of men have done,
and the crises of his life refer to national crises. Every
revolution was first a thought in one man's mind, and
when the same thought occurs to another man, it is the
key to that era. Every reform was once a private opinion,
and when it shall be a private opinion again it will solve
the problem of the age. The fact narrated must corre-
spond to something in me to be credible or intelligible.
We, as we read, must become Greeks, Romans, Turks,
priest and king, martyr and executioner; must fasten
these images to some reality in our secret experience, or
we shall learn nothing rightly. What befell Asdrubal or
Caesar Borgia is as much an illustration of the mind's
powers and depravations as what has befallen us. Each
new law and political movement has meaning for you.
Stand before each of its tablets and say, "Under this

mask did my Proteus nature hide itself." This remedies the defect of our too great nearness to ourselves. This throws our actions into perspective; and as crabs, goats, scorpions, the balance and the water pot lose their meanness when hung as signs in the zodiac, so I can see my own vices without heat in the distant persons of Solomon, Alcibiades, and Catiline.

It is the universal nature which gives worth to particular men and things. Human life, as containing this, is mysterious and inviolable, and we hedge it round with penalties and laws. All laws derive hence their ultimate reason; all express more or less distinctly some command of this supreme, illimitable essence. Property also holds of the soul, covers great spiritual facts, and instinctively we at first hold to it with swords and laws and wide and complex combinations. The obscure consciousness of this fact is the light of all our day, the claim of claims; the plea for education, for justice, for charity; the foundation of friendship and love and of the heroism and grandeur which belong to acts of self-reliance. It is remarkable that involuntarily we always read as superior beings. Universal history, the poets, the romancers, do not in their stateliest pictures—in the sacerdotal, the imperial palaces, in the triumphs of will or of genius—anywhere lose our ear, anywhere make us feel that we intrude, that this is for better men; but rather is it true that in their grandest strokes we feel most at home. All that Shakespeare says of the king, yonder slip of a boy that reads in the corner feels to be true of himself. We sympathize in the great moments of history, in the great discoveries, the great resistances, the great prosperities of men—because there law was enacted, the sea was searched, the land was found, or the blow was struck, *for us,* as we ourselves in that place would have done or applauded.

We have the same interest in condition and character.

We honor the rich because they have externally the freedom, power, and grace which we feel to be proper to
man, proper to us. So all that is said of the wise man by
Stoic or Oriental or modern essayist, describes to each
reader his own idea, describes his unattained but attainable self. All literature writes the character of the wise
man. Books, monuments, pictures, conversation, are portraits in which he finds the lineaments he is forming.
The silent and the eloquent praise him and accost him,
and he is stimulated wherever he moves, as by personal
allusions. A true aspirant therefore never needs look for
allusions personal and laudatory in discourse. He hears
the commendation, not of himself, but, more sweet, of
that character he seeks, in every word that is said concerning character, yea further in every fact and circumstance—in the running river and the rustling corn.
Praise is looked, homage tendered, love flows, from mute
nature, from the mountains and the lights of the firmament.

These hints, dropped as it were from sleep and night,
let us use in broad day. The student is to read history
actively and not passively; to esteem his own life the
text, and books the commentary. Thus compelled, the
Muse of history will utter oracles, as never to those who
do not respect themselves. I have no expectation that
any man will read history aright who thinks that what
was done in a remote age, by men whose names have
resounded far, has any deeper sense than what he is doing today.

The world exists for the education of each man. There
is no age or state of society or mode of action in history
to which there is not somewhat corresponding in his
life. Everything tends in a wonderful manner to abbrevi-
ate itself and yield its own virtue to him. He should see
that he can live all history in his own person. He must

sit solidly at home, and not suffer himself to be bullied
by kings or empires, but know that he is greater than all
the geography and all the government of the world; he
must transfer the point of view from which history is
commonly read, from Rome and Athens and London, to
himself, and not deny his conviction that he is the court,
and if England or Egypt have anything to say to him he
will try the case; if not, let them forever be silent. He
must attain and maintain that lofty sight where facts
yield their secret sense, and poetry and annals are alike.
The instinct of the mind, the purpose of nature, betrays
itself in the use we make of the signal narrations of history. Time dissipates to shining ether the solid angularity
of facts. No anchor, no cable, no fences avail to keep a
fact a fact. Babylon, Troy, Tyre, Palestine, and even
early Rome are passing already into fiction. The Garden
of Eden, the sun standing still in Gibeon, is poetry
thenceforward to all nations. Who cares what the fact
was, when we have made a constellation of it to hang
in heaven an immortal sign? London and Paris and New
York must go the same way. "What is history," said
Napoleon, "but a fable agreed upon?" This life of ours
is stuck round with Egypt, Greece, Gaul, England, War,
Colonization, Church, Court and Commerce, as with so
many flowers and wild ornaments grave and gay. I will
not make more account of them. I believe in Eternity.
I can find Greece, Asia, Italy, Spain and the Islands—
the genius and creative principle of each and of all eras,
in my own mind.

We are always coming up with the emphatic facts of
history in our private experience and verifying them
here. All history becomes subjective; in other words
there is properly no history, only biography. Every mind
must know the whole lesson for itself—must go over the
whole ground. What it does not see, what it does not

live, it will not know. What the former age has epito-
mized into a formula or rule for manipular convenience,
it will lose all the good of verifying for itself, by means
of the wall of that rule. Somewhere, sometime, it will
demand and find compensation for that loss, by doing
the work itself. Ferguson discovered many things in
astronomy which had long been known. The better for
him.

History must be this or it is nothing. Every law which
the state enacts indicates a fact in human nature; that
is all. We must in ourselves see the necessary reason of
every fact—see how it could and must be. So stand before every public and private work; before an oration of
Burke, before a victory of Napoleon, before a martyrdom
of Sir Thomas More, of Sidney, of Marmaduke Robinson; before a French Reign of Terror, and a Salem
hanging of witches; before a fanatic Revival and the
Animal Magnetism in Paris, or in Providence. We assume that we under like influence should be alike affected, and should achieve the like; and we aim to
master intellectually the steps and reach the same height
or the same degradation that our fellow, our proxy has
done.

All inquiry into antiquity, all curiosity respecting the
Pyramids, the excavated cities, Stonehenge, the Ohio
Circles, Mexico, Memphis—is the desire to do away this
wild, savage, and preposterous There or Then, and introduce in its place the Here and the Now. Belzoni digs
and measures in the mummy-pits and pyramids of
Thebes until he can see the end of the difference between the monstrous work and himself. When he has
satisfied himself, in general and in detail, that it was
made by such a person as he, so armed and so motived,
and to ends to which he himself should also have
worked, the problem is solved; his thought lives along

the whole line of temples and sphinxes and catacombs, passes through them all with satisfaction, and they live again to the mind, or are *now*.

A Gothic cathedral affirms that it was done by us and not done by us. Surely it was by man, but we find it not in our man. But we apply ourselves to the history of its production. We put ourselves into the place and state of the builder. We remember the forest-dwellers, the first temples, the adherence to the first type, and the decoration of it as the wealth of the nation increased; the value which is given to wood by carving led to the carving over the whole mountain of stone of a cathedral. When we have gone through this process, and added thereto the Catholic Church, its cross, its music, its processions, its Saints' days and image-worship, we have as it were been the man that made the minster; we have seen how it could and must be. We have the sufficient reason.

The difference between men is in their principle of association. Some men classify objects by color and size and other accidents of appearance; others by intrinsic likeness, or by the relation of cause and effect. The progress of the intellect is to the clearer vision of causes, which neglects surface differences. To the poet, to the philosopher, to the saint, all things are friendly and sacred, all events profitable, all days holy, all men divine. For the eye is fastened on the life, and slights the circumstance. Every chemical substance, every plant, every animal in its growth, teaches the unity of cause, the variety of appearance.

Upborne and surrounded as we are by this all-creating nature, soft and fluid as a cloud or the air, why should we be such hard pedants, and magnify a few forms? Why should we make account of time, or of magnitude, or of figure? The soul knows them not, and genius, obeying its law, knows how to play with them as a young child plays with graybeards and in churches. Genius studies the causal thought, and far back in the womb of things sees the rays parting from one orb, that diverge, ere they fall, by infinite diameters. Genius watches the monad through all his masks as he performs the metempsychosis of nature. Genius detects through the fly, through the caterpillar, through the grub, through the egg, the constant individual; through countless individuals the fixed species; through many species the genus; through all genera the steadfast type; through all the kingdoms of organized life the eternal unity. Nature is a mutable cloud which is always and never the same. She casts the same thought into troops of forms, as a poet makes twenty fables with one moral. Through the bruteness and toughness of matter, a subtle spirit bends all things to its own will. The adamant streams into soft but precise form before it, and whilst I look at it its outline and texture are changed again. Nothing is so fleeting as form; yet never does it quite deny itself. In man we still trace the remains or hints of all that we esteem badges of servitude in the lower races; yet in him they enhance his nobleness and grace; as Io, in Aeschylus, transformed to a cow, offends the imagination; but how changed when as Isis in Egypt she meets Osiris-Jove, a beautiful woman with nothing of the metamorphosis left but the lunar horns as the splendid ornament of her brows!

The identity of history is equally intrinsic, the diversity equally obvious. There is, at the surface, infinite variety of things; at the center there is simplicity of cause. How many are the acts of one man in which we recognize the same character! Observe the sources of our information in respect to the Greek genius. We have the *civil history* of that people, as Herodotus, Thucydides, Xenophon, and Plutarch have given it; a very sufficient account of what manner of persons they were and what they did. We have the same national mind expressed for us again in their *literature*, in epic and lyric poems, drama, and philosophy; a very complete form. Then we have it once more in their *architecture*, a beauty as of temperance itself, limited to the straight line and the square—a builded geometry. Then we have it once again in *sculpture*, the "tongue on the balance of expression," a multitude of forms in the utmost freedom of action and never transgressing the ideal serenity; like votaries performing some religious dance before the gods, and, though in convulsive pain or mortal combat, never daring to break the figure and decorum of their dance. Thus of the genius of one remarkable people we have a fourfold representation: and to the senses what more unlike than an ode of Pindar, a marble centaur, the peristyle of the Parthenon, and the last actions of Phocion?

Everyone must have observed faces and forms which, without any resembling feature, make a like impression on the beholder. A particular picture or copy of verses, if it do not awaken the same train of images, will yet superinduce the same sentiment as some wild mountain walk, although the resemblance is nowise obvious to the senses, but is occult and out of the reach of the understanding. Nature is an endless combination and repetition of a very few laws. She hums the old well-known air through innumerable variations.

Nature is full of a sublime family likeness throughout her works, and delights in startling us with resemblances in the most unexpected quarters. I have seen the head of an old sachem of the forest which at once reminded the eye of a bald mountain summit, and the furrows of the brow suggested the strata of the rock. There are men whose manners have the same essential splendor as the simple and awful sculpture on the friezes of the Parthenon and the remains of the earliest Greek art. And there are compositions of the same strain to be found in the books of all ages. What is Guido's "Rospigliosi Aurora" but a morning thought, as the horses in it are only a morning cloud? If anyone will but take pains to observe the variety of actions to which he is equally inclined in certain moods of mind, and those to which he is averse, he will see how deep is the chain of affinity.

A painter told me that nobody could draw a tree without in some sort becoming a tree; or draw a child by studying the outlines of its form merely—but, by watching for a time his motions and plays, the painter enters into his nature and can then draw him at will in every attitude. So Roos "entered into the inmost nature of a sheep." I knew a draughtsman employed in a public survey who found that he could not sketch the rocks until their geological structure was first explained to him. In a certain state of thought is the common origin of very diverse works. It is the spirit and not the fact that is identical. By a deeper apprehension, and not primarily by a painful acquisition of many manual skills, the artist attains the power of awakening other souls to a given activity.

It has been said that "common souls pay with what they do, nobler souls with that which they are." And why? Because a profound nature awakens in us by its actions and words, by its very looks and manners, the same power and beauty that a gallery of sculpture or of pictures addresses.

Civil and natural history, the history of art and of literature, must be explained from individual history, or must remain words. There is nothing but is related to us, nothing that does not interest us—kingdom, college, tree, horse, or iron shoe—the roots of all things are in

man. Santa Croce and the Dome of St. Peter's are lame
copies after a divine model. Strasburg Cathedral is a
material counterpart of the soul of Erwin of Steinbach.
The true poem is the poet's mind; the true ship is the
ship-builder. In the man, could we lay him open, we
should see the reason for the last flourish and tendril of
his work; as every spine and tint in the sea-shell pre-
exist in the secreting organs of the fish. The whole of
heraldry and of chivalry is in courtesy. A man of fine
manners shall pronounce your name with all the ornament that titles of nobility could ever add.

The trivial experience of every day is always verifying
some old prediction to us and converting into things the
words and signs which we had heard and seen without
heed. A lady with whom I was riding in the forest said
to me that the woods always seemed to her *to wait*, as
if the genii who inhabit them suspended their deeds
until the wayfarer had passed onward; a thought which
poetry has celebrated in the dance of the fairies, which
breaks off on the approach of human feet. The man who
has seen the rising moon break out of the clouds at midnight, has been present like an archangel at the creation
of light and of the world. I remember one summer day
in the fields my companion pointed out to me a broad
cloud, which might extend a quarter of a mile parallel
to the horizon, quite accurately in the form of a cherub
as painted over churches—a round block in the center,
which it was easy to animate with eyes and mouth, supported on either side by wide-stretched symmetrical
wings. What appears once in the atmosphere may appear
often, and it was undoubtedly the archetype of that
familiar ornament. I have seen in the sky a chain of
summer lightning which at once showed to me that the
Greeks drew from nature when they painted the thun-
derbolt in the hand of Jove. I have seen a snow-drift

along the sides of the stone wall which obviously gave the idea of the common architectural scroll to abut a tower.

By surrounding ourselves with the original circumstances we invent anew the orders and the ornaments of architecture, as we see how each people merely decorated its primitive abodes. The Doric temple preserves the semblance of the wooden cabin in which the Dorian dwelt. The Chinese pagoda is plainly a Tartar tent. The Indian and Egyptian temples still betray the mounds and subterranean houses of their forefathers. "The custom of making houses and tombs in the living rock," says Heeren in his *Researches on the Ethiopians,* "determined very naturally the principal character of the Nubian Egyptian architecture to the colossal form which it assumed. In these caverns, already prepared by nature, the eye was accustomed to dwell on huge shapes and masses, so that when art came to the assistance of nature it could not move on a small scale without degrading itself. What would statues of the usual size, or neat porches and wings have been, associated with those gigantic halls before which only Colossi could sit as watchmen or lean on the pillars of the interior?"

The Gothic church plainly originated in a rude adaptation of the forest trees, with all their boughs, to a festal or solemn arcade; as the bands about the cleft pillars still indicate the green withes that tied them. No one can walk in a road cut through pine woods, without being struck with the architectural appearance of the grove, especially in winter, when the barrenness of all other trees shows the low arch of the Saxons. In the woods in a winter afternoon one will see as readily the origin of the stained-glass window, with which the Gothic cathedrals are adorned, in the colors of the western sky seen through the bare and crossing branches of the forest. Nor can any lover of nature enter the old piles of Oxford and the English cathedrals, without feeling that the forest overpowered the mind of the builder, and that his chisel, his saw and plane still reproduced its ferns, its spikes of flowers, its locust, elm, oak, pine, fir and spruce.

The Gothic cathedral is a blossoming in stone subdued by the insatiable demand of harmony in man. The mountain of granite blooms into an eternal flower, with the lightness and delicate finish as well as the aerial proportions and perspective of vegetable beauty.

In like manner all public facts are to be individualized, all private facts are to be generalized. Then at once History becomes fluid and true, and Biography deep and sublime. As the Persian imitated in the slender shafts and capitals of his architecture the stem and flower of the lotus and palm, so the Persian court in its magnificent era never gave over the nomadism of its barbarous tribes, but traveled from Ecbatana, where the spring was spent, to Susa in summer and to Babylon for the winter.

In the early history of Asia and Africa, nomadism and agriculture are the two antagonist facts. The geography of Asia and of Africa necessitated a nomadic life. But the nomads were the terror of all those whom the soil or the advantages of a market had induced to build towns. Agriculture therefore was a religious injunction, because of the perils of the state from nomadism. And in these late and civil countries of England and America these propensities still fight out the old battle, in the nation and in the individual. The nomads of Africa were constrained to wander, by the attacks of the gad-fly, which drives the cattle mad, and so compels the tribe to emigrate in the rainy season and to drive off the cattle to the higher sandy regions. The nomads of Asia follow the pasturage from month to month. In America and Europe the nomadism is of trade and curiosity; a progress, certainly, from the gad-fly of Astaboras to the Anglo- and Italo-mania of Boston Bay. Sacred cities, to which a periodical religious pilgrimage was enjoined, or stringent laws and customs tending to invigorate the national bond, were the check on the old rovers; and the cumulative values of long residence are the restraints on the itinerancy of the present day. The antagonism of the two tendencies is not less active in individuals, as the love of adventure or the love of repose happens to predominate. A man of rude health and flowing spirits has the faculty of rapid domestication, lives in his wagon and roams through all latitudes as easily as a Calmuc. At sea, or in the forest, or in the snow, he sleeps as warm, dines with as good appetite, and associates as happily as beside his own chimneys. Or perhaps his facility is deeper seated, in the increased range of his faculties of observation, which yield him points of interest wherever fresh objects meet his eyes. The pastoral nations were needy and hungry to desperation; and this intellectual nomadism, in its excess, bankrupts the mind through the dissipation of power on a miscellany of objects. The home-keeping wit, on the other hand, is that continence or content which finds all the elements of life in its own soil; and which has its own perils of monotony and deterioration, if not stimulated by foreign infusions.

Everything the individual sees without him corresponds to his states of mind, and everything is in turn intelligible to him, as his onward thinking leads him into the truth to which that fact or series belongs.

The primeval world—the Fore-World, as the Germans say—I can dive to it in myself as well as grope for it with researching fingers in catacombs, libraries, and the broken reliefs and torsos of ruined villas.

What is the foundation of that interest all men feel in Greek history, letters, art and poetry, in all its periods from the Heroic or Homeric age down to the domestic life of the Athenians and Spartans, four or five centuries later? What but this, that every man passes personally through a Grecian period. The Grecian state is the era of the bodily nature, the perfection of the senses—of the spiritual nature unfolded in strict unity with the body. In it existed those human forms which supplied the sculptor with his models of Hercules, Phœbus, and Jove; not like the forms abounding in the streets of modern cities, wherein the face is a confused blur of features, but composed of incorrupt, sharply defined and symmetrical features, whose eye-sockets are so formed that it would be impossible for such eyes to squint and take furtive glances on this side and on that, but they must turn the whole head. The manners of that period are plain and fierce. The reverence exhibited is for personal qualities; courage, address, self-command, justice, strength, swiftness, a loud voice, a broad chest. Luxury and elegance are not known. A sparse population and want make every man his own valet, cook, butcher and soldier, and the habit of supplying his own needs educates the body to wonderful performances. Such are the Agamemnon and Diomed of Homer, and not far different is the picture Xenophon gives of himself and his compatriots in the *Retreat of the Ten Thousand*. "After the army had crossed the river Teleboas in Armenia, there fell much snow, and the troops lay miserably on the ground covered with it. But Xenophon arose naked, and taking an axe, began to split wood; whereupon others rose and did the like." Throughout his army exists a boundless liberty of speech. They quarrel for plunder, they wrangle with the generals on each new order, and Xenophon is as sharp-tongued as any and sharper-tongued than most, and so gives as good as he gets. Who does not see that this is a gang of great boys, with such a code of honor and such lax discipline as great boys have?

The costly charm of the ancient tragedy, and indeed of all the old literature, is that the persons speak simply —speak as persons who have great good sense without knowing it, before yet the reflective habit has become the predominant habit of the mind. Our admiration of the antique is not admiration of the old, but of the natural. The Greeks are not reflective, but perfect in their senses and in their health, with the finest physical organization in the world. Adults acted with the simplicity and grace of children. They made vases, tragedies and statues, such as healthy senses should—that is, in good taste. Such things have continued to be made in all ages, and are now, wherever a healthy physique exists; but, as a class, from their superior organization, they have surpassed all. They combine the energy of manhood with the engaging unconsciousness of childhood. The attraction of these manners is that they belong to man, and are known to every man in virtue of his being once a child; besides that there are always individuals who retain these characteristics. A person of childlike genius and inborn energy is still a Greek, and revives our love of the Muse of Hellas. I admire the love of nature in the *Philoctetes*. In reading those fine apostrophes to sleep, to the stars, rocks, mountains and waves, I feel time passing away as an ebbing sea. I feel the eternity of man, the identity of his thought. The Greek had it seems the same fellow-beings as I. The sun and moon, water and fire, met his heart precisely as they meet mine. Then the vaunted distinction between Greek and English, between Classic and Romantic schools, seems superficial and pedantic. When a thought of Plato becomes a thought to me—when a truth that fired the soul of Pindar fires mine, time is no more. When I feel that we two meet in a perception, that our two souls are tinged with the same hue, and do as it were run into one, why should I measure degrees of latitude, why should I count Egyptian years?

The student interprets the age of chivalry by his own age of chivalry, and the days of maritime adventure and circumnavigation by quite parallel miniature experiences of his own. To the sacred history of the world he has the same key. When the voice of a prophet out of the deeps of antiquity merely echoes to him a sentiment of his infancy, a prayer of his youth, he then pierces to the truth through all the confusion of tradition and the caricature of institutions.

Rare, extravagant spirits come by us at intervals, who disclose to us new facts in nature. I see that men of God have from time to time walked among men and made their commission felt in the heart and soul of the commonest hearer. Hence evidently the tripod, the priest, the priestess inspired by the divine afflatus.

Jesus astonishes and overpowers sensual people. They cannot unite him to history, or reconcile him with themselves. As they come to revere their intuitions and aspire to live holily, their own piety explains every fact, every word.

How easily these old worships of Moses, of Zoroaster, of Menu, of Socrates, domesticate themselves in the mind. I cannot find any antiquity in them. They are mine as much as theirs.

I have seen the first monks and anchorets, without crossing seas or centuries. More than once some individual has appeared to me with such negligence of labor and such commanding contemplation, a haughty beneficiary begging in the name of God, as made good to the nineteenth century Simeon the Stylite, the Thebais, and the first Capuchins.

The priestcraft of the East and West, of the Magian, Brahmin, Druid, and Inca, is expounded in the individual's private life. The cramping influence of a hard formalist on a young child, in repressing his spirits and courage, paralyzing the understanding, and that without producing indignation, but only fear and obedience, and even much sympathy with the tyranny—is a familiar fact, explained to the child when he becomes a man, only by seeing that the oppressor of his youth is himself a child tyrannized over by those names and words and forms of whose influence he was merely the organ to the youth. The fact teaches him how Belus was worshipped and how the Pyramids were built, better than the discovery by Champollion of the names of all the workmen and the cost of every tile. He finds Assyria and the Mounds of Cholula at his door, and himself has laid the courses.

Again, in that protest which each considerate person makes against the superstition of his times, he repeats step for step the part of old reformers, and in the search after truth finds, like them, new perils to virtue. He learns again what moral vigor is needed to supply the girdle of a superstition. A great licentiousness treads on the heels of a reformation. How many times in the history of the world has the Luther of the day had to lament the decay of piety in his own household! "Doctor," said his wife to Martin Luther, one day, "how is it that whilst subject to papacy we prayed so often and with such fervor, whilst now we pray with the utmost coldness and very seldom?"

The advancing man discovers how deep a property he has in literature—in all fable as well as in all history. He finds that the poet was no odd fellow who described strange and impossible situations, but that universal man wrote by his pen a confession true for one and true for all. His own secret biography he finds in lines wonderfully intelligible to him, dotted down before he was born. One after another he comes up in his private adventures with every fable of Aesop, of Homer, of Hafiz, of Ariosto, of Chaucer, of Scott, and verifies them with his own head and hands.

The beautiful fables of the Greeks, being proper creations of the imagination and not of the fancy, are universal verities. What a range of meanings and what perpetual pertinence has the story of Prometheus! Beside its primary value as the first chapter of the history of Europe (the mythology thinly veiling authentic facts, the invention of the mechanic arts and the migration of colonies), it gives the history of religion, with some closeness to the faith of later ages. Prometheus is the Jesus of the old mythology. He is the friend of man; stands between the unjust "justice" of the Eternal Father and the race of mortals, and readily suffers all things on their account. But where it departs from the Calvinistic Christianity and exhibits him as the defier of Jove, it represents a state of mind which readily appears wherever the doctrine of Theism is taught in a crude, objective form, and which seems the self-defence of man against this untruth, namely a discontent with the believed fact that a God exists, and a feeling that the obligation of reverence is onerous. It would steal if it could the fire of the Creator, and live apart from him and independent of him. The *Prometheus Vinctus* is the romance of skepticism. Not less true to all time are the details of that stately apologue. Apollo kept the flocks of Admetus, said the poets. When the gods come among men, they are not known. Jesus was not; Socrates and Shakespeare were not. Antaeus was suffocated by the gripe of Hercules, but every time he touched his mother earth his strength was renewed. Man is the broken giant, and in all his weakness both his body and his mind are invigorated by habits of conversation with nature. The power of music, the power of poetry, to unfix and as it were clap wings to solid nature, interprets the riddle of Orpheus. The philosophical perception of identity through endless mutations of form makes him know the Proteus. What else am I who laughed or wept yesterday, who slept last night like a corpse, and this morning stood and ran? And what see I on any side but the transmigrations of Proteus? I can symbolize my thought by using the name of any creature, of any fact, because every creature is man agent or patient. Tantalus is but a name for you and me. Tantalus means the impossibility of drinking the waters of thought which are always gleaming and waving within sight of the soul. The transmigration of souls is no fable. I would it were; but men and women are only half human. Every animal of the barnyard, the field and the forest, of the earth and of the waters that are under the earth, has contrived to get a footing and to leave the print of its features and form in some one or other of these upright, heaven-facing speakers. Ah! brother, stop the ebb of thy soul—ebbing downward into the forms into whose habits thou hast now for many years slid. As near and proper to us is also that old fable of the Sphinx, who was said to sit in the roadside and put riddles to every passenger. If the man could not answer, she swallowed him alive. If he could solve the riddle, the Sphinx was slain. What is our life but an endless flight of winged facts or events? In splendid variety these changes come, all putting questions to the human spirit. Those men who cannot answer by a superior wisdom these facts or questions of time, serve them. Facts encumber them, tyrannize over them, and make the men of routine, the men of *sense,* in whom a literal obedience to facts has extinguished every spark of that light by which man is truly man. But if the man is true to his better instincts or sentiments, and refuses the dominion of facts, as one that comes of a higher race; remains fast by the soul and sees the principle, then the facts fall aptly and supplely into their places; they know their master, and the meanest of them glorifies him.

See in Goethe's "Helena" the same desire that every word should be a thing. These figures, he would say, these Chirons, Griffins, Phorkyas, Helen and Leda, are somewhat, and do exert a specific influence on the mind. So far then are they eternal entities, as real today as in the first Olympiad. Much revolving them he writes out freely his humor, and gives them body to his own imagination. And although that poem be as vague and fantastic as a dream, yet is it much more attractive than the more regular dramatic pieces of the same author, for the reason that it operates a wonderful relief to the mind from the routine of customary images—awakens the reader's invention and fancy by the wild freedom of the design, and by the unceasing succession of brisk shocks of surprise.

The universal nature, too strong for the petty nature of the bard, sits on his neck and writes through his hand; so that when he seems to vent a mere caprice and wild romance, the issue is an exact allegory. Hence Plato said that "poets utter great and wise things which they do not themselves understand." All the fictions of the Middle Age explain themselves as a masked or frolic expression of that which in grave earnest the mind of that period toiled to achieve. Magic and all that is ascribed to it is a deep presentiment of the powers of science. The shoes of swiftness, the sword of sharpness, the power of subduing the elements, of using the secret virtues of minerals, of understanding the voices of birds, are the obscure efforts of the mind in a right direction. The preternatural prowess of the hero, the gift of perpetual youth, and the like, are alike the endeavor of the human spirit "to bend the shows of things to the desires of the mind."

In "Perceforest" and "Amadis de Gaul" a garland and a rose bloom on the head of her who is faithful, and fade on the brow of the inconstant. In the story of the *Boy and the Mantle* even a mature reader may be surprised with a glow of virtuous pleasure at the triumph of the gentle Genelas; and indeed all the postulates of elfin annals—that the fairies do not like to be named; that their gifts are capricious and not to be trusted; that who seeks a treasure must not speak; and the like—I find true in Concord, however they might be in Cornwall or Bretagne.

Is it otherwise in the newest romance? I read the *Bride of Lammermoor.* Sir William Ashton is a mask for a vulgar temptation, Ravenswood Castle a fine name for proud poverty, and the foreign mission of state only a Bunyan disguise for honest industry. We may all shoot a wild bull that would toss the good and beautiful, by fighting down the unjust and sensual. Lucy Ashton is another name for fidelity, which is always beautiful and always liable to calamity in this world.

But along with the civil and metaphysical history of man, another history goes daily forward—that of the external world—in which he is not less strictly implicated. He is the compend of time; he is also the correlative of nature. His power consists in the multitude of

his affinities, in the fact that his life is intertwined with
the whole chain of organic and inorganic being. In old
Rome the public roads beginning at the Forum proceeded north, south, east, west, to the center of every
province of the empire, making each market-town of
Persia, Spain and Britain pervious to the soldiers of the
capital: so out of the human heart go as it were highways to the heart of every object in nature, to reduce it
under the dominion of man. A man is a bundle of relations, a knot of roots, whose flower and fruitage is the
world. His faculties refer to natures out of him and predict the world he is to inhabit, as the fins of the fish foreshow that water exists, or the wings of an eagle in the
egg presuppose air. He cannot live without a world.
Put Napoleon in an island prison, let his faculties find
no men to act on, no Alps to climb, no stake to play for,
and he would beat the air, and appear stupid. Transport
him to large countries, dense population, complex interests and antagonist power, and you shall see that the
man Napoleon, bounded that is by such a profile and
outline, is not the virtual Napoleon. This is but Talbot's
shadow—

> His substance is not here.
> For what you see is but the smallest part
> And least proportion of humanity;
> But were the whole frame here,
> It is of such a spacious, lofty pitch,
> Your roof were not sufficient to contain it.
>
> HENRY VI

Columbus needs a planet to shape his course upon.
Newton and Laplace need myriads of age and thick-
strewn celestial areas. One may say a gravitating solar
system is already prophesied in the nature of Newton's
mind. Not less does the brain of Davy or of Gay-Lussac,
from childhood exploring the affinities and repulsions
of particles, anticipate the laws of organization. Does

not the eye of the human embryo predict the light? the ear of Handel predict the witchcraft of harmonic sound? Do not the constructive fingers of Watt, Fulton, Whittemore, Arkwright, predict the fusible, hard, and temperable texture of metals, the properties of stone, water, and wood? Do not the lovely attributes of the maiden child predict the refinements and decorations of civil society? Here also we are reminded of the action of man on man. A mind might ponder its thoughts for ages and not gain so much self-knowledge as the passion of love shall teach it in a day. Who knows himself before he has been thrilled with indignation at an outrage, or has heard an eloquent tongue, or has shared the throb of thousands in a national exultation or alarm? No man can antedate his experience, or guess what faculty or feeling a new object shall unlock, any more than he can draw today the face of a person whom he shall see tomorrow for the first time.

I will not now go behind the general statement to explore the reason of this correspondency. Let it suffice that in the light of these two facts, namely, that the mind is One, and that nature is its correlative, history is to be read and written.

Thus in all ways does the soul concentrate and reproduce its treasures for each pupil. He too shall pass through the whole cycle of experience. He shall collect into a focus the rays of nature. History no longer shall be a dull book. It shall walk incarnate in every just and wise man. You shall not tell me by languages and titles a catalogue of the volumes you have read. You shall make me feel what periods you have lived. A man shall be the Temple of Fame. He shall walk, as the poets have described that goddess, in a robe painted all over with wonderful events and experiences—his own form and features by their exalted intelligence shall be that variegated vest. I shall find in him the Fore-World; in his childhood the Age of Gold, the Apples of Knowledge, the Argonautic Expedition, the calling of Abraham, the building of the Temple, the Advent of Christ, Dark Ages, the Revival of Letters, the Reformation, the discovery of new lands, the opening of new sciences and new regions in man. He shall be the priest of Pan, and bring with him into humble cottages the blessing of the morning stars, and all the recorded benefits of heaven and earth.

Is there somewhat overweening in this claim? Then I reject all I have written, for what is the use of pretending to know what we know not? But it is the fault of our rhetoric that we cannot strongly state one fact without seeming to belie some other. I hold our actual knowledge very cheap. Hear the rats in the wall, see the lizard on the fence, the fungus under foot, the lichen on the log. What do I know sympathetically, morally, of either of these worlds of life? As old as the Caucasian man—perhaps older—these creatures have kept their counsel beside him, and there is no record of any word or sign that has passed from one to the other. What connection do the books show between the fifty or sixty chemical elements and the historical eras? Nay, what does history yet record of the metaphysical annals of man? What light does it shed on those mysteries which we hide under the names Death and Immortality? Yet every history should be written in a wisdom which divined the range of our affinities and looked at facts as symbols. I am ashamed to see what a shallow village tale our so-called History is. How many times we must say Rome, and Paris, and Constantinople! What does Rome know of rat and lizard? What are Olympiads and Consulates to these neighboring systems of being? Nay, what food or experience or succor have they for the Esquimaux seal-hunter, for the Kanàka in his canoe, for the fisherman, the stevedore, the porter?

Broader and deeper we must write our annals—from an ethical reformation, from an influx of the ever new, ever sanative conscience—if we would trulier express our central and wide-related nature, instead of this old chronology of selfishness and pride to which we have too long lent our eyes. Already that day exists for us, shines in on us at unawares, but the path of science and of letters is not the way into nature. The idiot, the Indian, the child and unschooled farmer's boy stand nearer to the light by which nature is to be read, than the dissector or the antiquary.

MANNERS

HALF the world, it is said, knows not how the other half live. Our exploring expedition saw the Fiji islanders getting their dinner off human bones; and they are said to eat their own wives and children. The husbandry of the modern inhabitants of Gournou (west of old Thebes) is philosophical to a fault. To set up their housekeeping nothing is requisite but two or three earthen pots, a stone to grind meal, and a mat which is the bed. The house, namely a tomb, is ready without rent or taxes. No rain can pass through the roof, and there is no door, for there is no want of one, as there is nothing to lose. If the house do not please them, they walk out and enter another, as there are several hundreds at their command. "It is somewhat singular," adds Belzoni, to whom we owe this account, "to talk of happiness among people who live in sepulchres, among the corpses and rags of an ancient nation which they know nothing of." In the deserts of Borgoo the rock-Tibboos still dwell in caves, like cliff-swallows, and the language of these Negroes is compared by their neighbors to the shrieking of bats and to the whistling of birds. Again, the Bornoos have no proper names; individuals are called after their height, thickness, or other accidental quality, and have nicknames merely. But the salt, the dates, the ivory, and the gold, for which these horrible regions are visited, find their way into countries where the purchaser and consumer can hardly be ranked in one race with these cannibals and man-stealers; countries where man serves himself with metals, wood, stone, glass, gum, cotton, silk, and wool; honors himself with architecture; writes laws, and contrives to execute his will through the hands of many nations; and, especially, establishes a select society, running through all the countries of intelligent men, a self-constituted aristocracy, or fraternity of the best, which, without written law or exact usage of any kind, perpetuates itself, colonizes every new-planted island and adopts and makes its own whatever personal beauty or extraordinary native endowment anywhere appears.

What fact more conspicuous in modern history than the creation of the gentleman? Chivalry is that, and loyalty is that, and, in English literature half the drama, and all the novels, from Sir Philip Sidney to Sir Walter Scott, paint this figure. The word *gentleman,* which, like the word Christian, must hereafter characterize the present and the few preceding centuries by the importance attached to it, is a homage to personal and incommunicable properties. Frivolous and fantastic additions have got associated with the name, but the steady interest of mankind in it must be attributed to the valuable properties which it designates. An element which unites all the most forcible persons of every country, makes them intelligible and agreeable to each other, and is somewhat so precise that it is at once felt if an individual lack the masonic sign—cannot be any casual product, but must be an average result of the character and faculties universally found in men. It seems a certain permanent average; as the atmosphere is a permanent composition, whilst so many gases are combined only to be decompounded. *Comme il faut,* is the Frenchman's description of good society: *as we must be.* It is a spontaneous fruit of talents and feelings of precisely that class who have most vigor, who take the lead in the world of this hour, and though far from pure, far from constituting the gladdest and highest tone of human feeling, it is as good as the whole society permits it to be. It is made of the spirit, more than of the talent of men, and is a compound result into which every great force enters as an ingredient, namely virtue, wit, beauty, wealth, and power.

There is something equivocal in all the words in use to express the excellence of manners and social cultivation, because the quantities are fluxional, and the last effect is assumed by the senses as the cause. The word *gentleman* has not any correlative abstract to express the quality. *Gentility* is mean, and *gentilesse* is obsolete. But we must keep alive in the vernacular the distinction between *fashion,* a word of narrow and often sinister meaning, and the heroic character which *the gentleman* imports. The usual words, however, must be respected; they will be found to contain the root of the matter. The point of distinction in all this class of names, as courtesy, chivalry, fashion, and the like, is that the flower and fruit, not the grain of the tree, are contemplated. It is beauty which is the aim this time, and not

worth. The result is now in question, although our words
intimate well enough the popular feeling that the ap·
pearance supposes a substance. The gentleman is a man
of truth, lord of his own actions, and expressing that
lordship in his behavior; not in any manner dependent
and servile, either on persons, or opinions, or possessions. Beyond this fact of truth and real force, the word
denotes good-nature or benevolence: manhood first, and
then gentleness. The popular notion certainly adds a
condition of ease and fortune; but that is a natural result of personal force and love, that they should possess
and dispense the goods of the world. In times of violence, every eminent person must fall in with many
opportunities to approve his stoutness and worth; therefore every man's name that emerged at all from the mass
in the feudal ages, rattles in our ear like a flourish of
trumpets. But personal force never goes out of fashion.
That is still paramount today, and in the moving crowd
of good society the men of valor and reality are known
and rise to their natural place. The competition is transferred from war to politics and trade, but the personal
force appears readily enough in these new arenas.

Power first, or no leading class. In politics and in
trade, bruisers and pirates are of better promise than
talkers and clerks. God knows that all sorts of gentlemen
knock at the door; but whenever used in strictness and
with any emphasis, the name will be found to point at
original energy. It describes a man standing in his own
right and working after untaught methods. In a good
lord there must first be a good animal, at least to the
extent of yielding the incomparable advantage of animal
spirits. The ruling class must have more, but they must
have these, giving in every company the sense of power,
which makes things easy to be done which daunt the
wise. The society of the energetic class, in their friendly

and festive meetings, is full of courage and of attempts which intimidate the pale scholar. The courage which girls exhibit is like a battle of Lundy's Lane, or a sea-fight. The intellect relies on memory to make some supplies to face these extemporaneous squadrons. But memory is a base mendicant with basket and badge, in the presence of these sudden masters. The rulers of society must be up to the work of the world, and equal to their versatile office: men of the right Caesarian pattern, who have great range of affinity. I am far from believing the timid maxim of Lord Falkland ("that for ceremony there must go two to it; since a bold fellow will go through the cunningest forms"), and am of opinion that the gentleman is the bold fellow whose forms are not to be broken through; and only that plenteous nature is rightful master which is the complement of whatever person it converses with. My gentleman gives the law where he is; he will outpray saints in chapel, outgeneral veterans in the field, and outshine all courtesy in the hall. He is good company for pirates and good with academicians; so that it is useless to fortify yourself against him; he has the private entrance to all minds, and I could as easily exclude myself, as him. The famous gentlemen of Asia and Europe have been of this strong type; Saladin, Sapor, the Cid, Julius Caesar, Scipio, Alexander, Pericles, and the lordliest personages. They sat very carelessly in their chairs, and were too excellent themselves to value any condition at a high rate.

A plentiful fortune is reckoned necessary, in the popular judgment, to the completion of this man of the world; and it is a material deputy which walks through the dance which the first has led. Money is not essential, but this wide affinity is, which transcends the habits of clique and caste and makes itself felt by men of all classes. If the aristocrat is only valid in fashionable circles and not with truckmen, he will never be a leader in fashion; and if the man of the people cannot speak on equal terms with the gentleman, so that the gentleman shall perceive that he is already really of his own order, he is not to be feared. Diogenes, Socrates, and Epaminondas are gentlemen of the best blood who have chosen the condition of poverty when that of wealth was equally open to them. I use these old names, but the men I speak of are my contemporaries. Fortune will not supply to every generation one of these well-appointed knights, but every collection of men furnishes some example of the class; and the politics of this country, and the trade of every town, are controlled by these hardy and irresponsible doers, who have invention to take the lead, and a broad sympathy which puts them in fellowship with crowds, and makes their action popular.

The manners of this class are observed and caught with devotion by men of taste. The association of these masters with each other and with men intelligent of their merits, is mutually agreeable and stimulating. The good forms, the happiest expressions of each, are repeated and adopted. By swift consent everything superfluous is dropped, everything graceful is renewed. Fine manners show themselves formidable to the uncultivated man. They are a subtler science of defence to parry and intimidate; but once matched by the skill of the other party, they drop the point of the sword—points and fences disappear, and the youth finds himself in a more transparent atmosphere, wherein life is a less troublesome game, and not a misunderstanding rises between the players. Manners aim to facilitate life, to get rid of impediments and bring the man pure to energize. They aid our dealing and conversation as a railway aids traveling, by getting rid of all avoidable obstructions of the road and leaving nothing to be conquered but pure space. These forms very soon become fixed, and a fine sense of propriety is cultivated with the more heed that it becomes a badge of social and civil distinctions. Thus grows up Fashion, an equivocal semblance, the most puissant, the most fantastic and frivolous, the most feared and followed, and which morals and violence assault in vain.

There exists a strict relation between the class of power and the exclusive and polished circles. The last are always filled or filling from the first. The strong men usually give some allowance even to the petulances of fashion, for that affinity they find in it. Napoleon, child of the revolution, destroyer of the old noblesse, never ceased to court the Faubourg St. Germain; doubtless with the feeling that fashion is a homage to men of his stamp. Fashion, though in a strange way, represents all manly virtue. It is virtue gone to seed: it is a kind of posthumous honor. It does not often caress the great, but the children of the great: it is a hall of the Past. It usually sets its face against the great of this hour. Great men are not commonly in its halls; they are absent in the field: they are working, not triumphing. Fashion is made up of their children; of those who through the value and virtue of somebody, have acquired lustre to their name, marks of distinction, means of cultivation and generosity, and in their physical organization a certain health and excellence which secure to them, if not the highest power to work, yet high power to enjoy. The class of power, the working heroes, the Cortez, the Nelson, the Napoleon, see that this is the festivity and permanent celebration of such as they; that fashion is funded talent; is Mexico, Marengo, and Trafalgar beaten out thin; that the brilliant names of fashion run back to just such busy names as their own, fifty or sixty years ago. They are the sowers, their sons shall be the reapers, and *their* sons, in the ordinary course of things, must yield the possession of the harvest to new competitors with keener eyes and stronger frames. The city is recruited from the country. In the year 1805, it is said, every legitimate monarch in Europe was imbecile. The city would have died out, rotted, and exploded, long ago, but that it was reinforced from the fields. It is only country which came to town day before yesterday that is city and court today.

Aristocracy and fashion are certain inevitable results. These mutual selections are indestructible. If they provoke anger in the least favored class, and the excluded majority revenge themselves on the excluding minority by the strong hand and kill them, at once a new class finds itself at the top, as certainly as cream rises in a bowl of milk: and if the people should destroy class after class, until two men only were left, one of these would be the leader and would be involuntarily served and copied by the other. You may keep this minority out of sight and out of mind, but it is tenacious of life, and is one of the estates of the realm. I am the more struck with this tenacity, when I see its work. It respects the administration of such unimportant matters, that we should not look for any durability in its rule. We sometimes meet men under some strong moral influence, as a patriotic, a literary, a religious movement, and feel that the moral sentiment rules man and nature. We think all other distinctions and ties will be slight and fugitive, this of caste or fashion for example; yet come from year to year and see how permanent that is, in this Boston or New York life of man, where too it has not the least countenance from the law of the land. Not in Egypt or in India a firmer or more impassable line. Here are associations whose ties go over and under and through it, a meeting of merchants, a military corps, a college class, a fire-club, a professional association, a political, a religious convention—the persons seem to draw inseparably near; yet, that assembly once dispersed, its members will not in the year meet again. Each returns to his degree in the scale of good society, porcelain remains porcelain, and earthen earthen. The objects of fashion may be frivolous, or fashion may be objectless, but the nature of this union and selection can be neither frivolous nor accidental. Each man's rank in that perfect graduation depends on some symmetry in his structure or some agreement in his structure to the symmetry of society. Its doors unbar instantaneously to a natural claim of their own kind. A natural gentleman finds his way in, and will keep the oldest patrician out who has lost his intrinsic rank. Fashion understands itself; good breeding and personal superiority of whatever country readily fraternize with those of every other. The chiefs of savage tribes have distinguished themselves in London and Paris by the purity of their tournure.

To say what good of fashion we can, it rests on reality, and hates nothing so much as pretenders; to exclude and mystify pretenders and send them into everlasting "Coventry," is its delight. We contemn in turn every other gift of men of the world; but the habit even in little and the least matters of not appealing to any but our own sense of propriety, constitutes the foundation of all chivalry. There is almost no kind of self-reliance, so it be sane and proportioned, which fashion does not occasionally adopt and give it the freedom of its salons. A sainted soul is always elegant, and, if it will, passes unchallenged into the most guarded ring. But so will Jock the teamster pass, in some crisis that brings him thither, and find favor, as long as his head is not giddy with the new circumstance, and the iron shoes do not wish to dance in waltzes and cotillions. For there is nothing settled in manners, but the laws of behavior yield to the energy of the individual. The maiden at her first ball, the countryman at a city dinner, believes that there is a ritual according to which every act and compliment must be performed, or the failing party must be cast out of this presence. Later they learn that good sense and character make their own forms every moment, and speak or abstain, take wine or refuse it, stay or go, sit in a chair or sprawl with children on the floor, or stand on their head, or what else soever, in a new and aboriginal way; and that strong will is always in fashion, let who will be unfashionable. All that fashion demands is composure and self-content. A circle of men perfectly well bred would be a company of sensible persons in which every man's native manners and character appeared. If the fashionist have not this quality, he is nothing. We are such lovers of self-reliance that we excuse in a man many sins if he will show us a complete satisfaction in his position, which asks no leave to be, of mine, or any man's good opinion. But any deference to some eminent man or woman of the world forfeits all privilege of nobility. He is an underling: I have nothing to do with him; I will speak with his master. A man should not go where he cannot carry his whole sphere or society with him—not bodily, the whole circle of his friends, but atmospherically. He should preserve in a new company the same attitude of mind and reality of relation which his daily associates draw him to, else he is shorn of his best beams, and will be an orphan in the merriest club. "If you could see Vich Ian Vohr with his tail on!——" But Vich Ian Vohr must always carry his belongings in some fashion, if not added as honor, then severed as disgrace.

There will always be in society certain persons who are mercuries of its approbation, and whose glance will at any time determine for the curious their standing in the world. These are the chamberlains of the lesser gods. Accept their coldness as an omen of grace with the loftier deities, and allow them all their privilege. They are clear in their office, nor could they be thus formidable without their own merits. But do not measure the importance of this class by their pretension, or imagine that a fop can be the dispenser of honor and shame. They pass also at their just rate; for how can they otherwise, in circles which exist as a sort of herald's office for the sifting of character?

As the first thing man requires of man is reality, so that appears in all the forms of society. We pointedly, and by name, introduce the parties to each other. Know you before all heaven and earth, that this is Andrew, and this is Gregory—they look each other in the eye; they grasp each other's hand, to identify and signalize each other. It is a great satisfaction. A gentleman never dodges; his eyes look straight forward, and he assures the other party, first of all, that he has been met. For what is it that we seek, in so many visits and hospitalities? Is it your draperies, pictures, and decorations? Or do we not insatiably ask, Was a man in the house? I may easily go into a great household where there is much substance, excellent provision for comfort, luxury, and taste, and yet not encounter there any Amphitryon who shall subordinate these appendages. I may go into a cottage, and find a farmer who feels that he is the man I have come to see, and fronts me accordingly. It was therefore a very natural point of old feudal etiquette that a gentleman who received a visit, though it were of his sovereign, should not leave his roof, but should wait his arrival at the door of his house. No house, though it were the Tuileries or the Escurial, is good for anything without a master. And yet we are not often gratified by this hospitality. Everybody we know surrounds himself with a fine house, fine books, conservatory, gardens, equipage and all manner of toys, as screens to interpose between himself and his guest. Does it not seem as if man was of a very sly, elusive nature, and dreaded nothing so much as a full rencontre front to front with his fellow? It were unmerciful, I know, quite to abolish the use of these screens, which are of eminent convenience, whether the guest is too great or too little. We call together many friends who keep each other in play, or by luxuries and ornaments we amuse the young people, and guard our retirement. Or if perchance a searching realist comes to our gate, before whose eye we have no care to stand, then again we run to our curtain, and hide ourselves as Adam at the voice of the Lord God in the garden. Cardinal Caprara, the Pope's legate at Paris, defended himself from the glances of Napoleon by an immense pair of green spectacles. Napoleon remarked them, and speedily managed to rally them off: and yet Napoleon, in his turn, was not great enough, with eight hundred thousand troops at his back, to face a pair of freeborn eyes, but fenced himself with etiquette and within triple barriers of reserve; and, as all the world knows from Madame de Staël, was wont, when he found himself observed, to discharge his face of all expression. But emperors and rich men are by no means the most skilful masters of good manners. No rent-roll nor army-list can dignify skulking and dissimulation; and the first point of courtesy must always be truth, as really all the forms of good breeding point that way.

I have just been reading, in Mr. Hazlitt's translation, Montaigne's account of his journey into Italy, and am struck with nothing more agreeably than the self-respecting fashions of the time. His arrival in each place, the arrival of a gentleman of France, is an event of some consequence. Wherever he goes he pays a visit to whatever prince or gentleman of note resides upon his road, as a duty to himself and to civilization. When he leaves any house in which he has lodged for a few weeks, he causes his arms to be painted and hung up as a perpetual sign to the house, as was the custom of gentlemen.

The complement of this graceful self-respect, and that of all the points of good breeding I most require and insist upon, is deference. I like that every chair should be a throne, and hold a king. I prefer a tendency to stateliness to an excess of fellowship. Let the incommunicable objects of nature and the metaphysical isolation of man teach us independence. Let us not be too much acquainted. I would have a man enter his house through a hall filled with heroic and sacred sculptures, that he might not want the hint of tranquility and self-poise. We should meet each morning as from foreign countries, and, spending the day together, should depart at night, as into foreign countries. In all things I would have the island of a man inviolate. Let us sit apart as the gods, talking from peak to peak all round Olympus. No degree of affection need invade this religion. This is myrrh and rosemary to keep the other sweet. Lovers should guard their strangeness. If they forgive too much, all slides into confusion and meanness. It is easy to push this deference to a Chinese etiquette; but coolness and absence of heat and haste indicate fine qualities. A gentleman makes no noise; a lady is serene. Proportionate is our disgust at those invaders who fill a studious house with blast and running, to secure some paltry convenience. Not less I dislike a low sympathy of each with his neighbor's needs. Must we have a good understanding with one another's palates? as foolish people who have lived long together know when each wants salt or sugar. I pray my companion, if he wishes for bread, to ask me for bread, and if he wishes for sassafras or arsenic, to ask me for them, and not to hold out his plate as if I knew already. Every natural function can be dignified by deliberation and privacy. Let us leave hurry to slaves. The compliments and ceremonies of our breeding should recall, however remotely, the grandeur of our destiny.

The flower of courtesy does not very well bide handling, but if we dare to open another leaf and explore what parts go to its conformation, we shall find also an intellectual quality. To the leaders of men, the brain as well as the flesh and the heart must furnish a proportion. Defect in manners is usually the defect of fine perceptions. Men are too coarsely made for the delicacy of beautiful carriage and customs. It is not quite sufficient to good breeding, a union of kindness and independence. We imperatively require a perception of, and a homage to beauty in our companions. Other virtues are in request in the field and workyard, but a certain degree of taste is not to be spared in those we sit with. I could better eat with one who did not respect the truth or the laws than with a sloven and unpresentable person. Moral qualities rule the world, but at short distances the senses are despotic. The same discrimination of fit and fair runs out, if with less rigor, into all parts of life. The average spirit of the energetic class is good sense, acting under certain limitations and to certain ends. It entertains every natural gift. Social in its nature, it respects everything which tends to unite men. It delights in measure. The love of beauty is mainly the love of measure of proportion. The person who screams, or uses the superlative degree, or converses with heat, puts whole drawing-rooms to flight. If you wish to be loved, love measure. You must have genius or a prodigious usefulness if you will hide the want of measure. This perception comes in to polish and perfect the parts of the social instrument. Society will pardon much to genius and special gifts, but, being in its nature a convention, it loves what is conventional, or what belongs to coming together. That makes the good and bad of manners, namely what helps or hinders fellowship. For fashion is not good sense absolute, but relative; not good sense private, but good sense entertaining company. It hates corners and sharp points of character, hates quarrelsome, egotistical, solitary, and gloomy people; hates whatever can interfere with total blending of parties; whilst it values all peculiarities as in the highest degree refreshing, which can consist with good fellowship. And besides the general infusion of wit to heighten civility, the direct splendor of intellectual power is ever welcome in fine society as the costliest addition to its rule and its credit.

The dry light must shine in to adorn our festival, but it must be tempered and shaded, or that will also offend. Accuracy is essential to beauty, and quick perceptions to politeness, but not too quick perceptions. One may be too punctual and too precise. He must leave the omniscience of business at the door, when he comes into the palace of beauty. Society loves creole natures, and sleepy languishing manners, so that they cover sense, grace and good will: the air of drowsy strength, which disarms criticism; perhaps because such a person seems to reserve himself for the best of the game, and not spend himself on surfaces; an ignoring eye, which does not see the annoyances, shifts, and inconveniences that cloud the brow and smother the voice of the sensitive.

Therefore besides personal force and so much perception as constitutes unerring taste, society demands in its patrician class another element already intimated, which it significantly terms good nature—expressing all degrees of generosity, from the lowest willingness and faculty to oblige, up to the heights of magnanimity and love. Insight we must have, or we shall run against one another and miss the way to our food; but intellect is selfish and barren. The secret of success in society is a certain heartiness and sympathy. A man who is not happy in the company cannot find any word in his memory that will fit the occasion. All his information is a little impertinent. A man who is happy there, finds in every turn of the conversation equally lucky occasions for the introduction of that which he has to say. The favorites of society, and what it calls *whole souls,* are able men and of more spirit than wit, who have no uncomfortable egotism, but who exactly fill the hour and the company; contented and contenting, at a marriage or a funeral, a ball or a jury, a water-party or a shooting-match. England, which is rich in gentlemen, furnished, in the beginning of the present century, a good model of that genius which the world loves, in Mr. Fox, who added to his great abilities the most social disposition and real love of men. Parliamentary history has few better passages than the debate in which Burke and Fox separated in the House of Commons; when Fox urged on his old friend the claims of old friendship with such tenderness that the house was moved to tears. Another anecdote is so close to my matter, that I must hazard the story. A tradesman who had long dunned him for a note of three hundred guineas, found him one day counting gold, and demanded payment—"No," said Fox, "I owe this money to Sheridan; it is a debt of honor; if an accident should happen to me, he has nothing to show." "Then," said the creditor, "I change my debt into a debt of honor," and tore the note in pieces. Fox thanked the man for his confidence and paid him, saying, "his debt was of older standing, and Sheridan must wait." Lover of liberty, friend of the Hindu, friend of the African slave, he possessed a great personal popularity; and Napoleon said of him on the occasion of his visit to Paris, in 1805, "Mr. Fox will always hold the first place in an assembly at the Tuileries."

We may easily seem ridiculous in our eulogy of courtesy, whenever we insist on benevolence as its foundation. The painted phantasm Fashion rises to cast a species of derision on what we say. But I will neither be driven from some allowance to Fashion as a symbolic institution, nor from the belief that love is the basis of courtesy. We must obtain *that,* if we can; but by all means we must affirm *this.* Life owes much of its spirit to these sharp contrasts. Fashion, which affects to be honor, is often, in all men's experience, only a ballroom-code. Yet so long as it is the highest circle in the imagination of the best heads on the planet, there is something necessary and excellent in it; for it is not to be supposed that men have agreed to be the dupes of anything preposterous; and the respect which these mysteries inspire in the most rude and sylvan characters, and the curiosity with which details of high life are read, betray the universality of the love of cultivated manners. I know that a comic disparity would be felt, if we should enter the acknowledged "first circles" and apply these terrific standards of justice, beauty, and benefit to the individuals actually found there. Monarchs and heroes, sages and lovers, these gallants are not. Fashion has many classes and many rules of probation and admission, and not the best alone. There is not only the right of conquest, which genius pretends—the individual demonstrating his natural aristocracy best of the best— but less claims will pass for the time; for Fashion loves lions, and points like Circe to her horned company. This gentleman is this afternoon arrived from Denmark; and that is my Lord Ride, who came yesterday from

Baghdad; here is Captain Friese, from Cape Turnagain;
and Captain Symmes, from the interior of the earth; and
Monsieur Jovaire, who came down this morning in a
balloon; Mr. Hobnail, the reformer; and Reverend Jul
Bat, who has converted the whole torrid zone in his
Sunday school; and Signor Torre del Greco, who extinguished Vesuvius by pouring into it the Bay of Naples;
Spahi, the Persian ambassador; and Tul Wil Shan, the
exiled nabob of Nepaul, whose saddle is the new moon.
—But these are monsters of one day, and tomorrow will
be dismissed to their holes and dens; for in these rooms
every chair is waited for. The artist, the scholar, and, in
general, the clergy, win their way up into these places
and get represented here, somewhat on this footing of
conquest. Another mode is to pass through all the degrees, spending a year and a day in St. Michael's Square,
being steeped in Cologne water, and perfumed, and
dined, and introduced, and properly grounded in all the
biography and politics and anecdotes of the boudoirs.

Yet these fineries may have grace and wit. Let there
be grotesque sculpture about the gates and offices of
temples. Let the creed and commandments even have
the saucy homage of parody. The forms of politeness universally express benevolence in superlative degrees.
What if they are in the mouths of selfish men, and used
as means of selfishness? What if the false gentleman
almost bows the true out of the world? What if the false
gentleman contrives so to address his companion as
civilly to exclude all others from his discourse, and also
to make them feel excluded? Real service will not lose
its nobleness. All generosity is not merely French and
sentimental; nor is it to be concealed that living blood
and a passion of kindness does at last distinguish God's
gentleman from Fashion's. The epitaph of Sir Jenkin
Grout is not wholly unintelligible to the present age:

"Here lies Sir Jenkin Grout, who loved his friend and persuaded his enemy: what his mouth ate, his hand paid for: what his servants robbed, he restored: if a woman gave him pleasure, he supported her in pain: he never forgot his children; and whoso touched his finger, drew after it his whole body." Even the line of heroes is not utterly extinct. There is still ever some admirable person in plain clothes, standing on the wharf, who jumps in to rescue a drowning man; there is still some absurd inventor of charities; some guide and comforter of run-away slaves; some friend of Poland; some Philhellene; some fanatic who plants shade trees for the second and third generation, and orchards when he is grown old; some well-concealed piety; some just man happy in an ill fame; some youth ashamed of the favors of fortune and impatiently casting them on other shoulders. And these are the centers of society, on which it returns for fresh impulses. These are the creators of Fashion, which is an attempt to organize beauty of behavior. The beautiful and the generous are, in the theory, the doctors and apostles of this church: Scipio, and the Cid, and Sir Philip Sidney, and Washington, and every pure and valiant heart who worshipped Beauty by word and by deed. The persons who constitute the natural aristocracy are not found in the actual aristocracy, or only on its edge; as the chemical energy of the spectrum is found to be greatest just outside of the spectrum. Yet that is the infirmity of the seneschals, who do not know their sovereign when he appears. The theory of society sup-poses the existence and sovereignty of these. It divines afar off their coming. It says with the elder gods—

> As Heaven and Earth are fairer far
> Than Chaos and blank Darkness, though once chiefs;
> And as we show beyond that Heaven and Earth,
> In form and shape compact and beautiful;

So, on our heels a fresh perfection treads;
A power, more strong in beauty, born of us,
And fated to excel us, as we pass
In glory that old Darkness:
—————————for, 't is the eternal law,
That first in beauty shall be first in might.

Therefore, within the ethical circle of good society
there is a narrower and higher circle, concentration of its
light, and flower of courtesy, to which there is always a
tacit appeal of pride and reference, as to its inner and
imperial court; the parliament of love and chivalry. And
this is constituted of those persons in whom heroic dispositions are native; with the love of beauty, the delight
in society, and the power to embellish the passing day.
If the individuals who compose the purest circles of
aristocracy in Europe, the guarded blood of centuries,
should pass in review, in such manner as that we could
at leisure and critically inspect their behavior, we might
find no gentleman and no lady; for although excellent
specimens of courtesy and high breeding would gratify
us in the assemblage, in the particulars we should
detect offence. Because elegance comes of no breeding,
but of birth. There must be romance of character, or the
most fastidious exclusion of impertinencies will not avail.
It must be genius which takes that direction: it must be
not courteous, but courtesy. High behavior is as rare in
fiction as it is in fact. Scott is praised for the fidelity with
which he painted the demeanor and conversation of the
superior classes. Certainly, kings and queens, nobles and
great ladies, had some right to complain of the absurdity that had been put in their mouths before the days
of Waverley; but neither does Scott's dialogue bear
criticism. His lords brave each other in smart epigram-
matic speeches, but the dialogue is in costume, and does
not please on the second reading: it is not warm with

life. In Shakespeare alone the speakers do not strut and bridle, the dialogue is easily great, and he adds to so many titles that of being the best-bred man in England and in Christendom. Once or twice in a lifetime we are permitted to enjoy the charm of noble manners, in the presence of a man or woman who have no bar in their nature, but whose character emanates freely in their word and gesture. A beautiful form is better than a beautiful face; a beautiful behavior is better than a beautiful form: it gives a higher pleasure than statues or pictures; it is the finest of the fine arts. A man is but a little thing in the midst of the objects of nature, yet, by the moral quality radiating from his countenance he may abolish all considerations of magnitude, and in his manners equal the majesty of the world. I have seen an individual whose manners, though wholly within the conventions of elegant society, were never learned there, but were original and commanding and held out protection and prosperity; one who did not need the aid of a court-suit, but carried the holiday in his eye; who exhilarated the fancy by flinging wide the doors of new modes of existence; who shook off the captivity of etiquette, with happy, spirited bearing, good natured and free as Robin Hood; yet with the port of an emperor, if need be—calm, serious, and fit to stand the gaze of millions.

The open air and the fields, the street and public chambers are the places where Man executes his will; let him yield or divide the sceptre at the door of the house. Woman, with her instinct of behavior, instantly detects in man a love of trifles, any coldness or imbecility, or, in short, any want of that large, flowing, and magnanimous deportment which is indispensable as an exterior in the hall. Our American institutions have been friendly to her, and at this moment I esteem it a chief felicity of this country, that it excels in women. A certain awkward consciousness of inferiority in the men may give rise to the new chivalry in behalf of Woman's Rights. Certainly let her be as much better placed in the laws and in social forms as the most zealous reformer can ask, but I confide so entirely in her inspiring and musical nature, that I believe only herself can show us how she shall be served. The wonderful generosity of her sentiments raises her at times into heroical and godlike regions, and verifies the pictures of Minerva, Juno, or Polymnia; and by the firmness with which she treads her upward path, she convinces the coarsest calculators that another road exists than that which their feet know. But besides those who make good in our imagination the place of muses and of Delphic Sibyls, are there not women who fill our vase with wine and roses to the brim, so that the wine runs over and fills the house with perfume; who inspire us with courtesy; who unloose our tongues and we speak; who anoint our eyes and we see? We say things we never thought to have said; for once, our walls of habitual reserve vanished and left us at large; we were children playing with children in a wide field of flowers. Steep us, we cried, in these influences, for days, for weeks, and we shall be sunny poets and will write out in many-colored words the romance that you are. Was it Hafiz or Firdousi that said of his Persian Lilla, She was an elemental force, and astonished me by her amount of life, when I saw her day after day radiating, every instant, redundant joy and grace on all around her? She was a solvent powerful to reconcile all heterogeneous persons into one society: like air or water, an element of such a great range of affinities that it combines readily with a thousand substances. Where she is present all others will be more than they are wont. She was a unit and whole, so that whatsoever she did, became her. She had too much sympathy and desire to please, than that you could say her manners were marked with dignity, yet no princess could surpass her clear and erect demeanor on each occasion. She did not study the Persian grammar, nor the books of the seven poets, but all the poems of the seven seemed to be written upon her. For though the bias of her nature was not to thought, but to sympathy, yet was she so perfect in her own nature as to meet intellectual persons by the fulness of her heart, warming them by her sentiments; believing, as she did, that by dealing nobly with all, all would show themselves noble.

I know that this Byzantine pile of chivalry or Fashion, which seems so fair and picturesque to those who look at the contemporary facts for science or for entertainment, is not equally pleasant to all spectators. The constitution of our society makes it a giant's castle to the ambitious youth who have not found their names enrolled in its Golden Book, and whom it has excluded from its coveted honors and privileges. They have yet to learn that its seeming grandeur is shadowy and relative: it is great by their allowance; its proudest gates will fly open at the approach of their courage and virtue. For the present distress, however, of those who are predisposed to suffer from the tyrannies of this caprice, there are easy remedies. To remove your residence a couple of miles, or at most four, will commonly relieve the most extreme susceptibility. For the advantages which fashion values are plants which thrive in very confined localities, in a few streets namely. Out of this precinct they go for nothing; are of no use in the farm, in the forest, in the market, in war, in the nuptial society, in the literary or scientific circle, at sea, in friendship, in the heaven of thought or virtue.

But we have lingered long enough in these painted courts. The worth of the thing signified must vindicate our taste for the emblem. Everything that is called fashion and courtesy humbles itself before the cause and fountain of honor, creator of titles and dignities, namely the heart of love. This is the royal blood, this the fire, which, in all countries and contingencies, will work after its kind and conquer and expand all that approaches it. This gives new meanings to every fact. This impoverishes the rich, suffering no grandeur but its own. What *is* rich? Are you rich enough to help anybody? to succor the unfashionable and the eccentric? rich enough to make the Canadian in his wagon, the itinerant with his consul's paper which commends him "To the charitable," the swarthy Italian with his few broken words of English, the lame pauper hunted by overseers from town to town, even the poor insane or besotted wreck of man or woman, feel the noble exception of your presence and your house from the general bleakness and stoniness; to make such feel that they were greeted with a voice which made them both remember and hope? What is vulgar but to refuse the claim on acute and conclusive reasons? What is gentle, but to allow it, and give their heart and yours one holiday from the national caution? Without the rich heart, wealth is an ugly beggar. The King of Schiraz could not afford to be so bountiful as the poor Osman who dwelt at his gate. Osman had a humanity so broad and deep that although his speech was so bold and free with the Koran as to disgust all the dervishes, yet was there never a poor outcast, eccentric, or insane man, some fool who had cut off his beard, or who had been mutilated under a vow, or had a pet madness in his brain, but fled at once to him; that great heart lay there so sunny and hospitable in the center of the country, that it seemed as if the instinct of all sufferers drew them to his side. And the madness which he harbored he did not share. Is not this to be rich? this only to be rightly rich?

But I shall hear without pain that I play the courtier very ill, and talk of that which I do not well understand. It is easy to see that what is called by distinction society and fashion has good laws as well as bad, has much that is necessary, and much that is absurd. Too good for banning, and too bad for blessing, it reminds us of a tradition of the pagan mythology, in any attempt to settle its character. "I overheard Jove, one day," said Silenus, "talking of destroying the earth; he said it had failed; they were all rogues and vixens, who went from bad to worse, as fast as the days succeeded each other. Minerva said she hoped not; they were only ridiculous little creatures, with this odd circumstance, that they had a blur, or indeterminate aspect, seen far or seen near; if you called them bad, they would appear so; if you called them good, they would appear so; and there was no one person or action among them which would not puzzle her owl, much more all Olympus, to know whether it was fundamentally bad or good."

POLITICS

Gold and iron are good
To buy iron and gold;
All earth's fleece and food
For their like are sold.
Boded Merlin wise,
Proved Napoleon great—
Nor kind nor coinage buys

Aught above its rate.
Fear, Craft, and Avarice
Cannot rear a State.
Out of dust to build
What is more than dust—
Walls Amphion piled
Phoebus stablish must.
When the Muses nine
With the Virtues meet,
Find to their design
An Atlantic seat,
By green orchard boughs
Fended from the heat,
Where the statesman ploughs
Furrow for the wheat;
When the Church is social worth,
When the state-house is the hearth,
Then the perfect State is come,
The republican at home.

I N DEALING with the State we ought to remember
that its institutions are not aboriginal, though they
existed before we were born; that they are not superior
to the citizen; that every one of them was once the act
of a single man; every law and usage was a man's expedient to meet a particular case; that they all are
imitable, all alterable; we may make as good, we may
make better. Society is an illusion to the young citizen.
It lies before him in rigid repose, with certain names,
men and institutions rooted like oak trees to the center,
round which all arrange themselves the best they can.
But the old statesman knows that society is fluid; there
are no such roots and centers, but any particle may suddenly become the center of the movement and compel
the system to gyrate round it; as every man of strong
will, like Pisistratus or Cromwell, does for a time, and
every man of truth, like Plato or Paul, does forever. But
politics rest on necessary foundations, and cannot be

treated with levity. Republics abound in young civilians who believe that the laws make the city, that grave modifications of the policy and modes of living and employments of the population, that commerce, education, and religion, may be voted in or out; and that any measure, though it were absurd, may be imposed on a people if only you can get sufficient voices to make it a law. But the wise know that foolish legislation is a rope of sand which perishes in the twisting; that the State must follow and not lead the character and progress of the citizen; the strongest usurper is quickly got rid of; and they only who build on Ideas, build for eternity; and that the form of government which prevails is the expression of what cultivation exists in the population which permits it. The law is only a memorandum. We are superstitious, and esteem the statute somewhat: so much life as it has in the character of living men is its force. The statute stands there to say, Yesterday we agreed so and so, but how feel ye this article today? Our statute is a currency which we stamp with our own portrait: it soon becomes unrecognizable, and in process of time will return to the mint. Nature is not democratic, nor limited-monarchical, but despotic, and will not be fooled or abated of any jot of her authority by the protest of her sons; and as fast as the public mind is opened to more intelligence, the code is seen to be brute and stammering. It speaks not articulately, and must be made to. Meantime the education of the general mind never stops. The reveries of the true and simple are prophetic. What the tender poetic youth dreams, and prays, and paints today, but shuns the ridicule of saying aloud, shall presently be the resolutions of public bodies; then shall be carried as grievance and bill of rights through conflict and war, and then shall be triumphant law and establishment for a hundred years, until it gives place in turn to new prayers and pictures. The history of the State sketches in coarse outline the progress of thought, and follows at a distance the delicacy of culture and of aspiration.

The theory of politics which has possessed the mind of men, and which they have expressed the best they could in their laws and in their revolutions, considers persons and property as the two objects for whose protection government exists. Of persons, all have equal rights, in virtue of being identical in nature. This interest of course with its whole power demands a democracy. Whilst the rights of all as persons are equal, in virtue of their access to reason, their rights in property are very unequal. One man owns his clothes, and another owns a county. This accident, depending primarily on the skill and virtue of the parties, of which there is every degree, and secondarily on patrimony, falls unequally, and its rights of course are unequal. Personal rights, universally the same, demand a government framed on the ratio of the census; property demands a government framed on the ratio of owners and of owning. Laban, who has flocks and herds, wishes them looked after by an officer on the frontiers, lest the Midianites shall drive them off; and pays a tax to that end. Jacob has no flocks or herds and no fear of the Midianites, and pays no tax to the officer. It seemed fit that Laban and Jacob should have equal rights to elect the officer who is to defend their persons, but that Laban and not Jacob should elect the officer who is to guard the sheep and cattle. And if question arise whether additional officers or watch-towers should be provided, must not Laban and Isaac, and those who must sell part of their herds to buy protection for the rest, judge better of this, and with more right, than Jacob, who, because he is a youth and a traveler, eats their bread and not his own?

In the earliest society the proprietors made their own wealth, and so long as it comes to the owners in the direct way, no other opinion would arise in any equitable community than that property should make the law for property, and persons the law for persons.

But property passes through donation or inheritance to those who do not create it. Gift, in one case, makes it as really the new owner's, as labor made it the first owner's: in the other case, of patrimony, the law makes an ownership which will be valid in each man's view according to the estimate which he sets on the public tranquility.

It was not however found easy to embody the readily admitted principle that property should make law for property, and persons for persons; since persons and property mixed themselves in every transaction. At last it seemed settled that the rightful distinction was that the proprietors should have more elective franchise than non-proprietors, on the Spartan principle of "calling that which is just, equal; not that which is equal, just."

That principle no longer looks so self-evident as it appeared in former times, partly because doubts have arisen whether too much weight had not been allowed in the laws to property, and such a structure given to our usages as allowed the rich to encroach on the poor, and to keep them poor; but mainly because there is an instinctive sense, however obscure and yet inarticulate, that the whole constitution of property, on its present tenures, is injurious, and its influence on persons deteriorating and degrading; that truly the only interest for the consideration of the State is persons; that property will always follow persons; that the highest end of government is the culture of men; and that if men can be educated, the institutions will share their improvement and the moral sentiment will write the law of the land.

If it be not easy to settle the equity of this question, the peril is less when we take note of our natural defences. We are kept by better guards than the vigilance of such magistrates as we commonly elect. Society always consists in greatest part of young and foolish persons. The old, who have seen through the hypocrisy of courts and statesmen, die and leave no wisdom to their sons. They believe their own newspaper, as their fathers did at their age. With such an ignorant and deceivable majority, States would soon run to ruin, but that there are limitations beyond which the folly and ambition of governors cannot go. Things have their laws, as well as men; and things refuse to be trifled with. Property will be protected. Corn will not grow unless it is planted and manured; but the farmer will not plant or hoe it unless the chances are a hundred to one that he will cut and harvest it. Under any forms, persons and property must and will have their just sway. They exert their power, as steadily as matter its attraction. Cover up a pound of earth never so cunningly, divide and subdivide it; melt it to liquid, convert it to gas; it will always weigh a pound; it will always attract and resist other matter by the full virtue of one pound weight—and the attributes of a person, his wit and his moral energy, will exercise, under any law or extinguishing tyranny, their proper force—if not overtly, then covertly; if not for the law, then against it; if not wholesomely, then poisonously; with right, or by might.

The boundaries of personal influence it is impossible to fix, as persons are organs of moral or supernatural force. Under the dominion of an idea which possesses the minds of multitudes, as civil freedom, or the religious sentiment, the powers of persons are no longer subjects of calculation. A nation of men unanimously bent on freedom or conquest can easily confound the arithmetic of statists, and achieve extravagant actions, out of all proportion to their means; as the Greeks, the Saracens, the Swiss, the Americans, and the French have done.

In like manner to every particle of property belongs its own attraction. A cent is the representative of a certain quantity of corn or other commodity. Its value is in the necessities of the animal man. It is so much warmth, so much bread, so much water, so much land. The law may do what it will with the owner of property; its just power will still attach to the cent. The law may in a mad freak say that all shall have power except the owners of property; they shall have no vote. Nevertheless, by a higher law, the property will, year after year, write every statute that respects property. The non-proprietor will be the scribe of the proprietor. What the owners wish to do, the whole power of property will do, either through the law or else in defiance of it. Of course I speak of all the property, not merely of the great estates. When the rich are outvoted, as frequently happens, it is the joint treasury of the poor which exceeds their accumulations. Every man owns something, if it is only a cow, or a wheel-barrow, or his arms, and so has that property to dispose of.

The same necessity which secures the rights of person and property against the malignity or folly of the magistrate, determines the form and methods of governing, which are proper to each nation and to its habit of thought, and nowise transferable to other states of society. In this country we are very vain of our political institutions, which are singular in this, that they sprung, within the memory of living men, from the character and condition of the people, which they still express with sufficient fidelity—and we ostentatiously prefer them to any other in history. They are not better, but only fitter for us. We may be wise in asserting the advantage in modern times of the democratic form, but to other states of society, in which religion consecrated the monarchical, that and not this was expedient. Democracy is better for us, because the religious sentiment of the present time accords better with it. Born democrats, we are nowise qualified to judge of monarchy, which, to our fathers living in the monarchical idea, was also relatively right. But our institutions, though in coincidence with the spirit of the age, have not any exemption from the practical defects which have discredited other forms. Every actual State is corrupt. Good men must not obey the laws too well. What satire on government can equal the severity of censure conveyed in the word *politic*, which now for ages has signified *cunning*, intimating that the State is a trick?

The same benign necessity and the same practical abuse appear in the parties, into which each State divides itself, of opponents and defenders of the administration of the government. Parties are also founded on instincts, and have better guides to their own humble aims than the sagacity of their leaders. They have nothing perverse in their origin, but rudely mark some real and lasting relation. We might as wisely reprove the east wind or the frost, as a political party, whose members, for the most part, could give no account of their position, but stand for the defence of those interests in which they find themselves. Our quarrel with them begins when they quit this deep natural ground at the bidding of some leader, and obeying personal considerations, throw themselves into the maintenance and defence of points nowise belonging to their system. A party is perpetually corrupted by personality. Whilst we absolve the association from dishonesty, we cannot extend the same charity to their leaders. They reap the rewards of the docility and zeal of the masses which they direct. Ordinarily our parties are parties of circumstance, and not of principle; as the planting interest in conflict with the commercial; the party of capitalists and that of operatives: parties which are identical in their moral character, and which can easily change ground with each other in the support of many of their measures. Parties of principle, as, religious sects, or the party of free-trade, of universal suffrage, of abolition of slavery, of abolition of capital punishment—degenerate into personalities, or would inspire enthusiasm. The vice of our leading parties in this country (which may be cited as a fair specimen of these societies of opinion) is that they do not plant themselves on the deep and necessary grounds to which they are respectively entitled, but lash themselves to fury in the carrying of some local and momentary measure, nowise useful to the commonwealth. Of the two great parties which at this hour almost share the nation between them, I should say that one has the best cause, and the other contains the best men. The philosopher, the poet, or the religious man, will of course wish to cast his vote with the democrat, for free-trade, for wide suffrage, for the abolition of legal cruelties in the penal code, and for facilitating in every manner the access of the young and the poor to the sources of wealth and power. But he can rarely accept the persons whom the so-called popular party propose to him as representatives of these liberalities. They have not at heart the ends which give to the name of democracy what hope and virtue are in it. The spirit of our American radicalism is destructive and aimless: it is not loving; it has no ulterior and divine ends, but is destructive only out of hatred and selfishness. On the other side, the conservative party, composed of the most moderate, able, and cultivated part of the population, is timid, and merely defensive of property. It vindicates no right, it aspires to no real good, it brands no crime, it proposes no generous policy; it does not build, nor write, nor cherish the arts, nor foster religion, nor establish schools, nor encourage science, nor emancipate the slave, nor befriend the poor, or the Indian, or the immigrant. From neither party, when in power, has the world any benefit to expect in science, art, or humanity, at all commensurate with the resources of the nation.

I do not for these defects despair of our republic. We are not at the mercy of any waves of chance. In the strife of ferocious parties, human nature always finds itself cherished; as the children of the convicts at Botany Bay are found to have as healthy a moral sentiment as other children. Citizens of feudal states are alarmed at our democratic institutions lapsing into anarchy, and the older and more cautious among ourselves are learning from Europeans to look with some terror at our turbulent freedom. It is said that in our license of construing the Constitution, and in the despotism of public opinion, we have no anchor; and one foreign observer thinks he has found the safeguard in the sanctity of Marriage among us; and another thinks he has found it in our Calvinism. Fisher Ames expressed the popular security more wisely, when he compared a monarchy and a republic, saying that a monarchy is a merchantman, which sails well, but will sometimes strike on a rock and go to the bottom; whilst a republic is a raft, which would never sink, but then your feet are always in water. No forms can have any dangerous importance whilst we are befriended by the laws of things. It makes no difference how many tons weight of atmosphere presses on our heads, so long as the same pressure resists it within the lungs. Augment the mass a thousandfold, it cannot begin to crush us, as long as reaction is equal to action. The fact of two poles, of two forces, centripetal and centrif-

ugal, is universal, and each force by its own activity
develops the other. Wild liberty develops iron conscience. Want of liberty, by strengthening law and decorum, stupefies conscience. "Lynch-law" prevails only
where there is greater hardihood and self-subsistency in
the leaders. A mob cannot be a permanency; everybody's
interest requires that it should not exist, and only justice
satisfies all.

We must trust infinitely to the beneficent necessity
which shines through all laws. Human nature expresses
itself in them as characteristically as in statues, or songs,
or railroads; and an abstract of the codes of nations
would be a transcript of the common conscience.
Governments have their origin in the moral identity of
men. Reason for one is seen to be reason for another,
and for every other. There is a middle measure which
satisfies all parties, be they never so many or so resolute
for their own. Every man finds a sanction for his simplest
claims and deeds, in decisions of his own mind, which
he calls Truth and Holiness. In these decisions all the
citizens find a perfect agreement, and only in these; not
in what is good to eat, good to wear, good use of time, or
what amount of land or of public aid each is entitled to
claim. This truth and justice men presently endeavor to
make application of to the measuring of land, the appor-
tionment of service, the protection of life and property.
Their first endeavors, no doubt, are very awkward. Yet
absolute right is the first governor; or, every government
is an impure theocracy. The idea after which each community is aiming to make and mend its law, is the will of
the wise man. The wise man it cannot find in nature,
and it makes awkward but earnest efforts to secure his
government by contrivance; as by causing the entire
people to give their voices on every measure; or by a
double choice to get the representation of the whole; or

by a selection of the best citizens; or to secure the advantages of efficiency and internal peace by confiding the government to one, who may himself select his agents. All forms of government symbolize an immortal government, common to all dynasties and independent of numbers, perfect where two men exist, perfect where there is only one man.

Every man's nature is a sufficient advertisement to him of the character of his fellows. My right and my wrong is their right and their wrong. Whilst I do what is fit for me, and abstain from what is unfit, my neighbor and I shall often agree in our means, and work together for a time to one end. But whenever I find my dominion over myself not sufficient for me, and undertake the direction of him also, I overstep the truth, and come into false relations to him. I may have so much more skill or strength than he that he cannot express adequately his sense of wrong, but it is a lie, and hurts like a lie both him and me. Love and nature cannot maintain the assumption; it must be executed by a practical lie, namely by force. This undertaking for another is the blunder which stands in colossal ugliness in the governments of the world. It is the same thing in numbers, as in a pair, only not quite so intelligible. I can see well enough a great difference between my setting myself down to a self-control, and my going to make somebody else act after my views; but when a quarter of the human race assume to tell me what I must do, I may be too much disturbed by the circumstances to see so clearly the absurdity of their command. Therefore all public ends look vague and quixotic beside private ones. For any laws but those which men make for themselves, are laughable. If I put myself in the place of my child, and we stand in one thought and see that things are thus or thus, that perception is law for him and me. We are both there, both act. But if, without carrying him into the thought, I look over into his plot, and, guessing how it is with him, ordain this or that, he will never obey me. This is the history of governments—one man does something which is to bind another. A man who cannot be acquainted with me, taxes me; looking from afar at me ordains that a part of my labor shall go to this or that whimsical end—not as I, but as he happens to fancy. Behold the consequence. Of all debts men are least willing to pay the taxes. What a satire is this on government! Everywhere they think they get their money's worth, except for these.

Hence the less government we have the better, the fewer laws, and the less confided power. The antidote to this abuse of formal Government is the influence of private character, the growth of the Individual; the appearance of the principal to supersede the proxy; the appearance of the wise man; of whom the existing government is, it must be owned, but a shabby imitation. That which all things tend to educe; which freedom, cultivation, intercourse, revolutions, go to form and deliver, is character; that is the end of Nature, to reach unto this coronation of her king. To educate the wise man the State exists, and with the appearance of the wise man the State expires. The appearance of character makes the State unnecessary. The wise man is the State. He needs no army, fort, or navy—he loves men too well; no bribe, or feast, or palace, to draw friends to him; no vantage ground, no favorable circumstance. He needs no library, for he has not done thinking; no church, for he is a prophet; no statute book, for he has the law-giver; no money, for he is value; no road, for he is at home where he is; no experience, for the life of the creator shoots through him, and looks from his eyes. He has no personal friends, for he who has the spell to draw the prayer and piety of all men unto him needs not husband and educate a few to share with him a select and poetic life. His relation to men is angelic; his memory is myrrh to them; his presence, frankincense and flowers.

We think our civilization near its meridian, but we are yet only at the cock-crowing and the morning star. In our barbarous society the influence of character is in its infancy. As a political power, as the rightful lord who is to tumble all rulers from their chairs, its presence is hardly yet suspected. Malthus and Ricardo quite omit it; the Annual Register is silent; in the Conversations' Lexicon it is not set down; the President's Message, the Queen's Speech, have not mentioned it; and yet it is never nothing. Every thought which genius and piety throw into the world, alters the world. The gladiators in the lists of power feel, through all their frocks of force and simulation, the presence of worth. I think the very strife of trade and ambition is confession of this divinity; and successes in those fields are the poor amends, the fig-leaf with which the shamed soul attempts to hide its nakedness. I find the like unwilling homage in all quarters. It is because we know how much is due from us that we are impatient to show some petty talent as a substitute for worth. We are haunted by a conscience of this right to grandeur of character, and are false to it. But each of us has some talent, can do somewhat useful, or graceful, or formidable, or amusing, or lucrative. That we do, as an apology to others and to ourselves for not reaching the mark of a good and equal life. But it does not satisfy us, whilst we thrust it on the notice of our companions. It may throw dust in their eyes, but does not smooth our own brow, or give us the tranquility of the strong when we walk abroad. We do penance as we go. Our talent is a sort of expiation, and we are constrained to reflect on our splendid moment with a certain humiliation, as somewhat too fine, and not as one act of many acts, a fair expression of our permanent energy. Most persons of ability meet in society with a kind of tacit appeal. Each seems to say, "I am not all here." Senators and presidents have climbed so high with pain enough, not because they think the place specially agreeable, but as an apology for real worth, and to vindicate their manhood in our eyes. This conspicuous chair is their compensation to themselves for being of a poor, cold, hard nature. They must do what they can. Like one class of forest animals, they have nothing but a prehensile tail; climb they must, or crawl. If a man found himself so rich-natured that he could enter into strict relations with the best persons and make life serene around him by the dignity and sweetness of his behavior, could he afford to circumvent the favor of the caucus and the press, and covet relations so hollow and pompous as those of a politician? Surely nobody would be a charlatan who could afford to be sincere.

The tendencies of the times favor the idea of self-government, and leave the individual, for all code, to the rewards and penalties of his own constitution; which work with more energy than we believe whilst we depend on artificial restraints. The movement in this direction has been very marked in modern history. Much has been blind and discreditable, but the nature of the revolution is not affected by the vices of the revolters; for this is a purely moral force. It was never adopted by any party in history, neither can be. It separates the individual from all party, and unites him at the same time to the race. It promises a recognition of higher rights than those of personal freedom, or the security of property. A man has a right to be employed, to be trusted, to be loved, to be revered. The power of love, as the basis of a State, has never been tried. We must not imagine that all things are lapsing into confusion if every tender protestant be not compelled to bear his part in certain social conventions; nor doubt that roads can be built, letters carried, and the fruit of labor secured, when the government of force is at an end. Are our methods now so excellent that all competition is hopeless? could not a nation of friends even devise better ways? On the other hand, let not the most conservative and timid fear anything from a premature surrender of the bayonet and the system of force. For, according to the order of nature, which is quite superior to our will, it stands thus; there will always be a government of force where men are selfish; and when they are pure enough to abjure the code of force they will be wise enough to see how these public ends of the post-office, of the highway, of commerce and the exchange of property, of museums and libraries, of institutions of art and science can be answered.

We live in a very low state of the world, and pay unwilling tribute to governments founded on force. There is not, among the most religious and instructed men of the most religious and civil nations, a reliance on the moral sentiment and a sufficient belief in the unity of things, to persuade them that society can be maintained without artificial restraints, as well as the solar system; or that the private citizen might be reasonable and a good neighbor, without the hint of a jail or a confiscation. What is strange too, there never was in any man sufficient faith in the power of rectitude to inspire him with the broad design of renovating the State on the principle of right and love. All those who have pretended this design have been partial reformers, and have admitted in some manner the supremacy of the bad State. I do not call to mind a single human being who has steadily denied the authority of the laws, on the simple ground of his own moral nature. Such designs, full of genius and full of faith as they are, are not entertained except avowedly as air-pictures. If the individual who exhibits them dare to think them practicable, he disgusts scholars and churchmen; and men of talent and women of superior sentiments cannot hide their contempt. Not the less does nature continue to fill the heart of youth with suggestions of this enthusiasm, and there are now men—if indeed I can speak in the plural number—more exactly, I will say, I have just been conversing with one man, to whom no weight of adverse experience will make it for a moment appear impossible that thousands of human beings might exercise towards each other the grandest and simplest sentiments, as well as a knot of friends, or a pair of lovers.

THE COMIC

A TASTE for fun is all but universal in our species, which is the only joker in nature. The rocks, the plants, the beasts, the birds, neither do anything ridiculous, nor betray a perception of anything absurd done in their presence. And as the lower nature does not jest, neither does the highest. The Reason pronounces its omniscient yea and nay, but meddles never with degrees or fractions; and it is in comparing fractions with essential integers or wholes that laughter begins.

Aristotle's definition of the ridiculous is, "what is out of time and place, without danger." If there be pain and danger, it becomes tragic; if not, comic. I confess, this definition, though by an admirable definer, does not satisfy me, does not say all we know.

The essence of all jokes, of all comedy, seems to be an honest or well-intended halfness; a non-performance of what is pretended to be performed, at the same time that one is giving loud pledges of performance. The balking of the intellect, the frustrated expectation, the break of continuity in the intellect, is comedy; and it announces itself physically in the pleasant spasms we call laughter.

With the trifling exception of the stratagems of a few beasts and birds, there is no seeming, no halfness in nature, until the appearance of man. Unconscious creatures do the whole will of wisdom. An oak or a chestnut undertakes no function it cannot execute; or if there be phenomena in botany which we call abortions, the abortion is also a function of nature, and assumes to the intellect the like completeness with the further function to which in different circumstances it had attained. The same rule holds true of the animals. Their activity is marked by unerring good sense. But man, through his access to Reason, is capable of the perception of a whole and a part. Reason is the whole, and whatsoever is not that is a part. The whole of nature is agreeable to the whole of thought, or to the Reason; but separate any part of nature and attempt to look at it as a whole by itself, and the feeling of the ridiculous begins. The perpetual game of humor is to look with considerate good nature at every object in existence, *aloof*, as a man might look at a mouse, comparing it with the eternal Whole; enjoying the figure which each self-satisfied particular creature cuts in the unrespecting All, and dismissing it with a benison. Separate any object, as a particular bodily man, a horse, a turnip, a flour-barrel, an umbrella, from the connection of things, and contemplate it alone, standing there in absolute nature, it becomes at once comic; no useful, no respectable qualities can rescue it from the ludicrous.

In virtue of man's access to Reason, or the Whole, the human form is a pledge of wholeness, suggests to our imagination the perfection of truth or goodness, and exposes by contrast any halfness or imperfection. We have a primary association between perfectness and this form. But the facts that occur when actual men enter do not make good this anticipation; a discrepancy which is at once detected by the intellect, and the outward sign is the muscular irritation of laughter.

Reason does not joke, and men of reason do not; a prophet, in whom the moral sentiment predominates, or a philosopher, in whom the love of truth predominates, these do not joke, but they bring the standard, the ideal whole, exposing all actual defect; and hence the best of all jokes is the sympathetic contemplation of things by the understanding from the philosopher's point of view. There is no joke so true and deep in actual life as when some pure idealist goes up and down among the institutions of society, attended by a man who knows the world, and who, sympathizing with the philosopher's scrutiny, sympathizes also with the confusion and indignation of the detected, skulking institutions. His perception of disparity, his eye wandering perpetually from the rule to the crooked, lying, thieving fact, makes the eyes run over with laughter.

This is the radical joke of life and then of literature. The presence of the ideal of right and of truth in all action makes the yawning delinquencies of practice remorseful to the conscience, tragic to the interest, but droll to the intellect. The activity of our sympathies may for a time hinder our perceiving the fact intellectually, and so deriving mirth from it; but all falsehoods, all vices seen at sufficient distance, seen from the point where our moral sympathies do not interfere, become ludicrous. The comedy is in the intellect's perception of discrepancy. And whilst the presence of the ideal discovers the difference, the comedy is enhanced whenever that ideal is embodied visibly in a man. Thus Falstaff, in Shakespeare, is a character of the broadest comedy, giving himself unreservedly to his senses, coolly ignoring the Reason, whilst he invokes its name, pretending to patriotism and to parental virtues, not with any intent to deceive, but only to make the fun perfect by enjoying the confusion betwixt reason and the negation of reason —in other words, the rank rascaldom he is calling by its name. Prince Hal stands by, as the acute understanding, who sees the Right, and sympathizes with it, and in the heyday of youth feels also the full attractions of pleasure, and is thus eminently qualified to enjoy the joke. At the same time he is to that degree under the Reason that it does not amuse him as much as it amuses another spectator.

If the essence of the Comic be the contrast in the intellect between the idea and the false performance, there is good reason why we should be affected by the exposure. We have no deeper interest than our integrity, and that we should be made aware by joke and by stroke of any lie we entertain. Besides, a perception of the Comic seems to be a balance-wheel in our metaphysical structure. It appears to be an essential element in a fine character. Wherever the intellect is constructive, it will be found. We feel the absence of it as a defect in the noblest and most oracular soul. The perception of the Comic is a tie of sympathy with other men, a pledge of sanity, and a protection from those perverse tendencies and gloomy insanities in which fine intellects sometimes lose themselves. A rogue alive to the ludicrous is still convertible. If that sense is lost, his fellow-men can do little for him.

It is true the sensibility to the ludicrous may run into excess. Men celebrate their perception of halfness and a latent lie by the peculiar explosions of laughter. So painfully susceptible are some men to these impressions, that if a man of wit come into the room where they are, it seems to take them out of themselves with violent convulsions of the face and sides, and obstreperous roarings of the throat. How often and with what unfeigned compassion we have seen such a person receiving like a willing martyr the whispers into his ear of a man of wit. The victim who has just received the discharge, if in a solemn company, has the air very much of a stout vessel which has just shipped a heavy sea; and though it does not split it, the poor bark is for the moment critically staggered. The peace of society and the decorum of tables seem to require that next to a notable wit should always be posted a phlegmatic bolt-upright man, able to stand without movement of muscle whole broadsides of this Greek fire. It is a true shaft of Apollo, and traverses the universe, and unless it encounter a mystic or a dumpish soul, goes everywhere heralded and harbingered by smiles and greetings. Wit makes its own welcome, and levels all distinctions. No dignity, no learning, no force of character, can make any stand against good wit. It is like ice, on which no beauty of form, no majesty of carriage can plead any immunity—they must walk gingerly, according to the laws of ice, or down they must go, dignity and all. "Dost thou think, because thou art virtuous, there shall be no more cakes and ale?" Plutarch happily expresses the value of the jest as a legitimate weapon of the philosopher. "Men cannot exercise their rhetoric unless they speak, but their philosophy even whilst they are silent or jest merrily; for as it is the highest degree of injustice not to be just and yet seem so, so it is the top of wisdom to philosophize yet not appear to do it, and in mirth to do the same with those that are serious and seem in earnest; for as in Euripides, the Bacchae, though unprovided of iron weapons, and unarmed, wounded their invaders with the boughs of trees which they carried, thus the very jests and merry talk of true philosophers move those that are not altogether insensible, and unusually reform."

In all the parts of life, the occasion of laughter is some seeming, some keeping of the word to the ear and eye, whilst it is broken to the soul. Thus, as the religious sentiment is the most vital and sublime of all our sentiments, and capable of the most prodigious effects, so is it abhorrent to our whole nature, when, in the absence of the sentiment, the act or word or officer volunteers to stand in its stead. To the sympathies this is shocking, and occasions grief. But to the intellect the lack of the sentiment gives no pain; it compares incessantly the sublime idea with the bloated nothing which pretends to be it, and the sense of the disproportion is comedy. And as the religious sentiment is the most real and earnest thing in nature, being a mere rapture, and excluding, when it appears, all other considerations, the vitiating this is the greatest lie. Therefore, the oldest gibe of literature is the ridicule of false religion. This is the joke of jokes. In religion, the sentiment is all; the ritual or ceremony indifferent. But the inertia of men inclines them, when the sentiment sleeps, to imitate that thing it did; it goes through the ceremony omitting only the will, makes the mistake of the wig for the head, the clothes for the man. The older the mistake and the more overgrown the particular form is, the more ridiculous to the intellect. Captain John Smith, the discoverer of New England, was not wanting in humor. The Society in London which had contributed their means to convert the savages, hoping doubtless to see the Keokuks, Black Hawks, Roaring Thunders, and Tustanuggees of that day converted into church-wardens and deacons at least, pestered the gallant rover with frequent solicitations out of England touching the conversion of the Indians, and the enlargement of the Church. Smith, in his perplexity how to satisfy the Society, sent out a party into the swamp, caught an Indian, and sent him home in the first ship to London, telling the Society they might convert one themselves.

The satire reaches its climax when the actual Church is set in direct contradiction to the dictates of the religious sentiment, as in the sketch of our Puritan politics in *Hudibras*—

> Our brethren of New England use
> Choice malefactors to excuse,
> And hang the guiltless in their stead,
> Of whom the churches have less need;
> As lately happened, in a town
> Where lived a cobbler, and but one,
> That out of doctrine could cut use,
> And mend men's lives as well as shoes.
> This precious brother having slain,
> In times of peace, an Indian,
> Not out of malice, but mere zeal
> (Because he was an infidel),
> The mighty Tottipottymoy
> Sent to our elders an envoy,
> Complaining loudly of the breach
> Of league held forth by Brother Patch,
> Against the articles in force
> Between both churches, his and ours,
> For which he craved the saints to render
> Into his hands, or hang the offender;
> But they, maturely having weighed
> They had no more but him o' th' trade
> (A man that served them in the double

Capacity to teach and cobble),
Resolved to spare him; yet to do
The Indian Hoghan Moghan too
Impartial justice, in his stead did
Hang an old weaver that was bedrid.

In science the jest at pedantry is analogous to that in religion which lies against superstition. A classification or nomenclature used by the scholar only as a memorandum of his last lesson in the laws of nature, and confessedly a makeshift, a bivouac for a night, and implying a march and a conquest tomorrow—becomes through indolence a barrack and a prison, in which the man sits down immovably, and wishes to detain others. The physiologist Camper humorously confesses the effect of his studies in dislocating his ordinary associations. "I have been employed," he says, "six months on the *Cetacea;* I understand the osteology of the head of all these monsters, and have made the combination with the human head so well that everybody now appears to me narwhale, porpoise, or marsouins. Women, the prettiest in society, and those whom I find less comely, they are all either narwhales or porpoises to my eyes." I chanced the other day to fall in with an odd illustration of the remark I had heard, that the laws of disease are as beautiful as the laws of health; I was hastening to visit an old and honored friend, who, I was informed, was in a dying condition, when I met his physician, who accosted me in great spirits, with joy sparkling in his eyes. "And how is my friend, the reverend Doctor?" I inquired. "O, I saw him this morning; it is the most correct apoplexy I have ever seen: face and hands livid, breathing stertorous, all the symptoms perfect." And he rubbed his hands with delight, for in the country we cannot find every day a case that agrees with the diagnosis of the books. I think there is malice in a very trifling story which goes about, and which I should not take any notice of, did I not suspect it to contain some satire upon my brothers of the Natural History Society. It is of a boy who was learning his alphabet. "That letter is A," said the teacher; "A," drawled the boy. "That is B," said the teacher; "B," drawled the boy, and so on. "That is W," said the teacher. "The devil!" exclaimed the boy, "is that W?"

The pedantry of literature belongs to the same category. In both cases there is a lie, when the mind, seizing a classification to help it to a sincerer knowledge of the fact, stops in the classification; or learning languages and reading books to the end of a better acquaintance with man, stops in the languages and books; in both the learner seems to be wise, and is not.

The same falsehood, the same confusion of the sympathies because a pretension is not made good, points the perpetual satire against poverty, since, according to Latin poetry and English doggerel,

> Poverty does nothing worse
> Than to make man ridiculous.

In this instance the halfness lies in the pretension of the parties to some consideration on account of their condition. If the man is not ashamed of his poverty, there is no joke. The poorest man who stands on his manhood destroys the jest. The poverty of the saint, of the rapt philosopher, of the naked Indian, is not comic. The lie is in the surrender of the man to his appearance; as if a man should neglect himself and treat his shadow on the wall with marks of infinite respect. It affects us oddly, as to see things turned upside down, or to see a man in a high wind run after his hat, which is always droll. The relation of the parties is inverted—hat being for the moment master, the by-standers cheering the hat. The multiplication of artificial wants and expenses in civilized life, and the exaggeration of all trifling forms, present innumerable occasions for this discrepancy to expose itself. Such is the story told of the painter Astley, who, going out of Rome one day with a party for a ramble in the Campagna and the weather proving hot, refused to take off his coat when his companions threw off theirs, but sweltered on; which, exciting remark, his comrades playfully forced off his coat, and behold on the back of his waistcoat a gay cascade was thundering down the rocks with foam and rainbow, very refreshing in so sultry a day—a picture of his own, with which the poor painter had been fain to repair the shortcomings of his wardrobe. The same astonishment of the intellect at the disappearance of the man out of nature, through some superstition of his house or equipage, as if truth and virtue should be bowed out of creation by the clothes they wore, is the secret of all the fun that circulates concerning eminent fops and fashionists, and, in like manner, of the gay Rameau of Diderot, who believes in nothing but hunger, and that the sole end of art, virtue, and poetry is to put something for mastication between the upper and lower mandibles.

Alike in all these cases and in the instance of cowardice or fear of any sort, from the loss of life to the loss of spoons, the majesty of man is violated. He whom all things should serve, serves some one of his own tools. In fine pictures the head sheds on the limbs the expression of the face. In Raphael's "Angel driving Heliodorus from the Temple," the crest of the helmet is so remarkable, that but for the extraordinary energy of the face, it would draw the eye too much; but the countenance of the celestial messenger subordinates it, and we see it not. In poor pictures the limbs and trunk degrade the face. So among the women in the street, you shall see one whose bonnet and dress are one thing, and the lady herself quite another, wearing withal an expression of meek submission to her bonnet and dress; and another whose dress obeys and heightens the expression of her form.

More food for the Comic is afforded whenever the personal appearance, the face, form, and manners, are subjects of thought with the man himself. No fashion is the best fashion for those matters which will take care of themselves. This is the butt of those jokes of the Paris drawing-rooms, which Napoleon reckoned so formidable, and which are copiously recounted in the French Mémoires. A lady of high rank, but of lean figure, had given the Countess Dulauloy the nickname of "Le Grenadier tricolore," in allusion to her tall figure, as well as to her republican opinions; the Countess retaliated by calling Madame "the Venus of the Père-Lachaise," a compliment to her skeleton which did not fail to circulate. "Lord C.," said the Countess of Gordon, "O, he is a perfect comb, all teeth and back." The Persians have a pleasant story of Tamerlane which relates to the same particulars: "Timur was an ugly man; he had a blind eye and a lame foot. One day when Chodscha was with him, Timur scratched his head, since the hour of the barber was come, and commanded that the barber should be called. Whilst he was shaven, the barber gave him a looking-glass in his hand. Timur saw himself in the mirror and found his face quite too ugly. Therefore he began to weep; Chodscha also set himself to weep, and so they wept for two hours. On this, some courtiers began to comfort Timur, and entertained him with strange stories in order to make him forget all about it. Timur ceased weeping, but Chodscha ceased not, but began now first to weep amain, and in good earnest. At last said Timur to Chodscha, 'Hearken! I have looked in the mirror, and seen myself ugly. Thereat I grieved, because, although I am Caliph, and have also much wealth, and many wives, yet still I am so ugly; therefore have I wept. But thou, why weepest thou without ceasing?' Chodscha answered, 'If thou hast only seen thy face once, and at once seeing hast not been able to contain thyself, but hast wept, what should we do—we who see thy face every day and night? If we weep not, who should weep? Therefore have I wept.' Timur almost split his sides with laughing."

Politics also furnish the same mark for satire. What is nobler than the expansive sentiment of patriotism, which would find brothers in a whole nation? But when this enthusiasm is perceived to end in the very intelligible maxims of trade, so much for so much, the intellect feels again the half-man. Or what is fitter than that we should espouse and carry a principle against all opposition? But when the men appear who ask our votes as representatives of this ideal, we are sadly out of countenance.

But there is no end to this analysis. We do nothing that is not laughable whenever we quit our spontaneous sentiment. All our plans, managements, houses, poems, if compared with the wisdom and love which man represents, are equally imperfect and ridiculous. But we cannot afford to part with any advantages. We must learn by laughter, as well as by tears and terrors; explore the whole of nature, the farce and buffoonery in the yard below, as well as the lessons of poets and philosophers upstairs in the hall, and get the rest and refreshment of the shaking of the sides. But the Comic also has its own speedy limits. Mirth quickly becomes intemperate, and the man would soon die of inanition, as some persons have been tickled to death. The same scourge whips the joker and the enjoyer of the joke. When Carlini was convulsing Naples with laughter, a patient

waited on a physician in that city, to obtain some remedy for excessive melancholy, which was rapidly con-
suming his life. The physician endeavored to cheer his
spirits, and advised him to go to the theater and see Carlini. He replied, "I am Carlini."

THE TRAGIC

HE HAS seen but half the universe who never has
been shown the house of Pain. As the salt sea covers more than two-thirds of the surface of the globe, so
sorrow encroaches in man on felicity. The conversation
of men is a mixture of regrets and apprehensions. I do
not know but the prevalent hue of things to the eye of
leisure is melancholy. In the dark hours, our existence
seems to be a defensive war, a struggle against the encroaching All, which threatens surely to engulf us soon,
and is impatient of our short reprieve. How slender the
possession that yet remains to us; how faint the anima-
tion! how the spirit seems already to contract its domain,
retiring within narrower walls by the loss of memory,
leaving its planted fields to erasure and annihilation. Already our own thoughts and words have an alien sound.
There is a simultaneous diminution of memory and hope.
Projects that once we laughed and leapt to execute, find
us now sleepy and preparing to lie down in the snow.
And in the serene hours we have no courage to spare.
We cannot afford to let go any advantages. The riches of
body or of mind which we do not need today, are the
reserved fund against the calamity that may arrive tomorrow. It is usually agreed that some nations have a

more sombre temperament, and one would say that history gave no record of any society in which despondency came so readily to heart as we see it and feel it in ours. Melancholy cleaves to the English mind in both hemispheres as closely as to the strings of an Aeolian harp. Men and women at thirty years, and even earlier, have lost all spring and vivacity, and if they fail in their first enterprises they throw up the game. But whether we and those who are next to us are more or less vulnerable, no theory of life can have any right which leaves out of account the values of vice, pain, disease, poverty, insecurity, disunion, fear and death.

What are the conspicuous tragic elements in human nature? The bitterest tragic element in life to be derived from an intellectual source is the belief in a brute Fate or Destiny; the belief that the order of nature and events is controlled by a law not adapted to man, nor man to that, but which holds on its way to the end, serving him if his wishes chance to lie in the same course, crushing him if his wishes lie contrary to it, and heedless whether it serves or crushes him. This is the terrible meaning that lies at the foundation of the old Greek tragedy, and makes the Oedipus and Antigone and Orestes objects of such hopeless commiseration. They must perish, and there is no over-god to stop or to mollify this hideous enginery that grinds or thunders, and snatches them up into its terrific system. The same idea makes the paralyzing terror with which the East Indian mythology haunts the imagination. The same thought is the predestination of the Turk. And universally, in uneducated and unreflecting persons on whom too the religious sentiment exerts little force, we discover traits of the same superstition: "If you balk water you will be drowned the next time"; "if you count ten stars you will fall down dead"; "if you spill the salt"; "if your fork sticks upright in the floor"; "if you say the Lord's prayer backwards"—and so on, a several penalty, nowise grounded in the nature of the thing, but on an arbitrary will. But this terror of contravening an unascertained and unascertainable will, cannot co-exist with reflection: it disappears with civilization, and can no more be reproduced than the fear of ghosts after childhood. It is discriminated from the doctrine of Philosophical Necessity herein: that the last is an Optimism, and therefore the suffering individual finds his good consulted in the good of all, of which he is a part. But in destiny, it is not the good of the whole or the *best will* that is enacted, but only *one particular will*. Destiny properly is not a will at all, but an immense whim; and this the only ground of terror and despair in the rational mind, and of tragedy in literature. Hence the antique tragedy, which was founded on this faith, can never be reproduced.

After reason and faith have introduced a better public and private tradition, the tragic element is somewhat circumscribed. There must always remain, however, the hindrance of our private satisfaction by the laws of the world. The law which establishes nature and the human race, continually thwarts the will of ignorant individuals, and this in the particulars of disease, want, insecurity and disunion.

But the essence of tragedy does not seem to me to lie in any list of particular evils. After we have enumerated famine, fever, inaptitude, mutilation, rack, madness and loss of friends, we have not yet included the proper tragic element, which is Terror, and which does not respect definite evils but indefinite; an ominous spirit which haunts the afternoon and the night, idleness and solitude.

A low, haggard sprite sits by our side, "casting the fashion of uncertain evils"—a sinister presentiment, a power of the imagination to dislocate things orderly and cheerful and show them in startling array. Hark! what sounds on the night wind, the cry of Murder in that friendly house; see these marks of stamping feet, of hidden riot. The whisper overheard, the detected glance, the glare of malignity, ungrounded fears, suspicions, half-knowledge and mistakes, darken the brow and chill the heart of men. And accordingly it is natures not clear, not of quick and steady perceptions, but imperfect characters from which somewhat is hidden that all others see, who suffer most from these causes. In those persons who move the profoundest pity, tragedy seems to consist in temperament, not in events. There are people who have an appetite for grief, pleasure is not strong enough and they crave pain, mithridatic stomachs which must be fed on poisoned bread, natures so doomed that no prosperity can soothe their ragged and dishevelled desolation. They mis-hear and mis-behold, they suspect and dread. They handle every nettle and ivy in the hedge, and tread on every snake in the meadow.

> Come bad chance,
> And we add to it our strength,
> And we teach it art and length,
> Itself o'er us to advance.

Frankly, then, it is necessary to say that all sorrow dwells in a low region. It is superficial; for the most part fantastic, or in the appearance and not in things. Tragedy is in the eye of the observer, and not in the heart of the sufferer. It looks like an insupportable load under which earth moans aloud. But analyze it; it is not I, it is not you, it is always another person who is tormented. If a man says, Lo! I suffer—it is apparent that he suffers not, for grief is dumb. It is so distributed as not to destroy. That which would rend you falls on tougher

textures. That which seems intolerable reproach or be-
reavement, does not take from the accused or bereaved
man or woman appetite or sleep. Some men are above
grief, and some below it. Few are capable of love. In
phlegmatic natures calamity is unaffecting, in shallow
natures it is rhetorical. Tragedy must be somewhat
which I can respect. A querulous habit is not tragedy. A
panic such as frequently in ancient or savage nations
put a troop or an army to flight without an enemy; a
fear of ghosts; a terror of freezing to death that seizes a
man in a winter midnight on the moors; a fright at uncertain sounds heard by a family at night in the cellar
or on the stairs—are terrors that make the knees knock
and the teeth clatter, but are no tragedy, any more than
seasickness, which may also destroy life. It is full of illusion. As it comes, it has its support. The most exposed
classes, soldiers, sailors, paupers, are nowise destitute of
animal spirits. The spirit is true to itself, and finds its
own support in any condition, learns to live in what is
called calamity as easily as in what is called felicity; as
the frailest glass-bell will support a weight of a thousand pounds of water at the bottom of a river or sea, if
filled with the same.

A man should not commit his tranquility to things,
but should keep as much as possible the reins in his own
hands, rarely giving way to extreme emotion of joy or
grief. It is observed that the earliest works of the art of
sculpture are countenances of sublime tranquility. The
Egyptian sphinxes, which sit today as they sat when the
Greek came and saw them and departed, and when the
Roman came and saw them and departed, and as they
will still sit when the Turk, the Frenchman and the
Englishman, who visit them now, shall have passed by
—"with their stony eyes fixed on the East and on the
Nile," have countenances expressive of complacency and

repose, an expression of health, deserving their longevity, and verifying the primeval sentence of history on the permanency of that people, "Their strength is to sit still." To this architectural stability of the human form, the Greek genius added an ideal beauty, without disturbing the seals of serenity; permitting no violence of mirth, or wrath, or suffering. This was true to human nature. For, in life, actions are few, opinions even few, prayers few; loves, hatreds, or any emissions of the soul. All that life demands of us through the greater part of the day, is an equilibrium, a readiness, open eyes and ears, and free hands. Society asks this, and truth, and love, and the genius of our life. There is a fire in some men which demands an outlet in some rude action; they betray their impatience of quiet by an irregular Catalinarian gait; by irregular, faltering, disturbed speech, too emphatic for the occasion. They treat trifles with a tragic air. This is not beautiful. Could they not lay a rod or two of stone wall, and work off this superabundant irritability? When two strangers meet in the highway, what each demands of the other is that the aspect should show a firm mind, ready for any event of good or ill, prepared alike to give death or to give life, as the emergency of the next moment may require. We must walk as guests in nature; not impassioned, but cool and disengaged. A man should try Time, and his face should wear the expression of a just judge, who has nowise made up his opinion, who fears nothing, and even hopes nothing, but who puts nature and fortune on their merits: he will hear the case out, and then decide. For all melancholy, as all passion, belongs to the exterior life. Whilst a man is not grounded in the divine life by his proper roots, he clings by some tendrils of affection to society—mayhap to what is best and greatest in it, and in calm times it will not appear that he is adrift and not moored; but let any shock take place in society, any revolution of custom, of law, of opinion, and at once his type of permanence is shaken. The disorder of his neighbors appears to him universal disorder; chaos is come again. But in truth he was already a driving wreck, before the wind arose which only revealed to him his vagabond state. If a man is centered, men and events appear to him a fair image or reflection of that which he knoweth beforehand in himself. If any perversity or profligacy break out in society, he will join with others to avert the mischief, but it will not arouse resentment or fear, because he discerns its impassable limits. He sees already in the ebullition of sin the simultaneous redress.

Particular reliefs also, fit themselves to human calamities; for the world will be in equilibrium, and hates all manner of exaggeration.

Time, the consoler, Time, the rich carrier of all changes, dries the freshest tears by obtruding new figures, new costumes, new roads, on our eye, new voices on our ear. As the west wind lifts up again the heads of the wheat which were bent down and lodged in the storm, and combs out the matted and dishevelled grass as it lay in night-locks on the ground, so we let in time as a drying wind into the seed-field of thoughts which are dark and wet and low bent. Time restores to them temper and elasticity. How fast we forget the blow that threatened to cripple us. Nature will not sit still; the faculties will do somewhat; new hopes spring, new affections twine and the broken is whole again.

Time consoles, but Temperament resists the impression of pain. Nature proportions her defence to the assault. Our human being is wonderfully plastic; if it cannot win this satisfaction here, it makes itself amends by running out there and winning that. It is like a stream of water, which if dammed up on one bank, overruns the other, and flows equally at its own convenience over sand, or mud, or marble. Most suffering is only apparent. We fancy it is torture; the patient has his own compensations. A tender American girl doubts of Divine Providence whilst she reads the horrors of "the middle passage"; and they are bad enough at the mildest; but to such as she these crucifixions do not come: they come to the obtuse and barbarous, to whom they are not horrid, but only a little worse than the old sufferings. They exchange a cannibal war for the stench of the hold. They have gratifications which would be none to the civilized girl. The market-man never damned the lady because she had not paid her bill, but the stout Irishwoman has to take that once a month. She however never feels weakness in her back because of the slave-trade. This self-adapting strength is especially seen in disease. "It is my duty," says Sir Charles Bell, "to visit certain wards of the hospital where there is no patient admitted but with that complaint which most fills the imagination with the idea of insupportable pain and certain death. Yet these wards are not the least remarkable for the composure and cheerfulness of their inmates. The individual who suffers has a mysterious counterbalance to that condition, which, to us who look upon her, appears to be attended with no alleviating circumstance." Analogous supplies are made to those individuals whose character leads them to vast exertions of body and mind. Napoleon said to one of his friends at St. Helena, "Nature seems to have calculated that I should have great reverses to endure, for she has given me a temperament like a block of marble. Thunder cannot move it; the shaft merely glides along. The great events of my life have slipped over me without making any demand on my moral or physical nature."

The intellect is a consoler, which delights in detach-

ing or putting an interval between a man and his fortune, and so converts the sufferer into a spectator and
his pain into poetry. It yields the joys of conversation, of
letters and of science. Hence also the torments of life
become tuneful tragedy, solemn and soft with music,
and garnished with rich dark pictures. But higher still
than the activities of art, the intellect in its purity and
the moral sense in its purity are not distinguished from
each other, and both ravish us into a region whereinto
these passionate clouds of sorrow cannot rise.

ILLUSIONS

Flow, flow the waves hated,
Accursed, adored,
The waves of mutation:
No anchorage is.
Sleep is not, death is not;
Who seem to die live.
House you were born in,
Friends of your springtime,
Old man and young maid,
Day's toil and its guerdon,
They are all vanishing,
Fleeing to fables,
Cannot be moored.
See the stars through them,
Through treacherous marbles.
Know, the stars yonder,
The stars everlasting,
Are fugitive also,
And emulate, vaulted,
The lambent heat-lightning.
And fire-fly's flight.

When thou dost return
On the wave's circulation,
Beholding the shimmer,
The wild dissipation,
And, out of endeavor
To change and to flow
The gas become solid,
And phantoms and nothings
Return to be things,
And endless imbroglio
Is law and the world—
Then first shalt thou know,
That in the wild turmoil,
Horsed on the Proteus,
Thou ridest to power,
And to endurance.

SOME years ago, in company with an agreeable party, I spent a long summer day in exploring the Mammoth Cave in Kentucky. We traversed, through spacious galleries affording a solid masonry foundation for the town and county overhead, the six or eight black miles from the mouth of the cavern to the innermost recess which tourists visit,—a niche or grotto made of one seamless stalactite, and called, I believe, Serena's Bower. I lost the light of one day. I saw high domes and bottomless pits; heard the voice of unseen waterfalls; paddled three-quarters of a mile in the deep Echo River, whose waters are peopled with the blind fish; crossed the streams "Lethe" and "Styx"; plied with music and guns the echoes in these alarming galleries; saw every form of stalagmite and stalactite in the sculptured and fretted chambers—icicle, orange-flower, acanthus, grapes, and snowball. We shot Bengal lights into the vaults and groins of the sparry cathedrals and examined all the masterpieces which the four combined engineers, water, limestone, gravitation and time could make in the dark.

The mysteries and scenery of the cave had the same dignity that belongs to all natural objects, and which shames the fine things to which we foppishly compare them. I remarked especially the mimetic habit with which Nature, on new instruments, hums her old tunes, making night to mimic day, and chemistry to ape vegetation. But I then took notice and still chiefly remember that the best thing which the cave had to offer was an illusion. On arriving at what is called the "Star-Chamber," our lamps were taken from us by the guide and extinguished or put aside, and, on looking upwards, I saw or seemed to see the night heaven thick with stars glimmering more or less brightly over our heads, and even what seemed a comet flaming among them. All the party were touched with astonishment and pleasure. Our musical friends sung with much feeling a pretty song, "The stars are in the quiet sky," etc., and I sat down on the rocky floor to enjoy the serene picture. Some crystal specks in the black ceiling high overhead, reflecting the light of a half-hid lamp, yielded this magnificent effect.

I own I did not like the cave so well for eking out its sublimities with this theatrical trick. But I have had many experiences like it, before and since; and we must be content to be pleased without too curiously analyzing the occasions. Our conversation with Nature is not just what it seems. The cloud-rack, the sunrise and sunset glories, rainbows and Northern Lights are not quite so spheral as our childhood thought them, and the part our organization plays in them is too large. The senses interfere everywhere and mix their own structure with all they report of. Once we fancied the earth a plane, and stationary. In admiring the sunset we do not yet deduct the rounding, coordinating, pictorial powers of the eye.

The same interference from our organization creates the most of our pleasure and pain. Our first mistake is the belief that the circumstance gives the joy which we give to the circumstance. Life is an ecstasy. Life is sweet as nitrous oxide; and the fisherman dripping all day over a cold pond, the switchman at the railway intersection, the farmer in the field, the Negro in the rice-swamp, the fop in the street, the hunter in the woods, the barrister with the jury, the belle at the ball, all ascribe a certain pleasure to their employment, which they themselves give it. Health and appetite impart the sweetness to sugar, bread, and meat. We fancy that our civilization has got on far, but we still come back to our primers.

We live by our imaginations, by our admirations, by our sentiments. The child walks amid heaps of illusions, which he does not like to have disturbed. The boy, how sweet to him is his fancy! how dear the story of barons and battles! What a hero he is, whilst he feeds on his heroes! What a debt is his to imaginative books! He has no better friend or influence than Scott, Shakespeare, Plutarch, and Homer. The man lives to other objects, but who dare affirm that they are more real? Even the prose of the streets is full of refractions. In the life of the dreariest alderman, fancy enters into all details and colors them with rosy hue. He imitates the air and actions of people whom he admires, and is raised in his own eyes. He pays a debt quicker to a rich man than to a poor man. He wishes the bow and compliment of some leader in the state or in society; weighs what he says; perhaps he never comes nearer to him for that, but dies at last better contented for this amusement of his eyes and his fancy.

The world rolls, the din of life is never hushed. In London, in Paris, in Boston, in San Francisco, the carnival, the masquerade is at its height. Nobody drops his domino. The unities, the fictions of the piece it would be an impertinence to break. The chapter of fascinations

is very long. Great is paint; nay, God is the painter; and
we rightly accuse the critic who destroys too many illusions. Society does not love its unmaskers. It was wittily
if somewhat bitterly said by D'Alembert, "qu'un état de
vapeur était un état très fâcheux, parcequ'il nous faisait
voir les choses comme elles sont." I find men victims of
illusion in all parts of life. Children, youths, adults and
old men, all are led by one bawble or another. Yoganidra, the goddess of illusion, Proteus, or Momus, or
Gylfi's Mocking—for the Power has many names—is
stronger than the Titans, stronger than Apollo. Few have
overheard the gods or surprised their secret. Life is a
succession of lessons which must be lived to be understood. All is riddle, and the key to a riddle is another
riddle. There are as many pillows of illusion as flakes in
a snow-storm. We wake from one dream into another
dream. The toys to be sure are various, and are graduated in refinement to the quality of the dupe. The intellectual man requires a fine bait; the sots are easily
amused. But everybody is drugged with his own frenzy,
and the pageant marches at all hours, with music and
banner and badge.

Amid the joyous troop who give in to the charivari,
comes now and then a sad-eyed boy whose eyes lack
the requisite refractions to clothe the show in due glory,
and who is afflicted with a tendency to trace home the
glittering miscellany of fruits and flowers to one root.
Science is a search after identity, and the scientific whim
is lurking in all corners. At the State Fair a friend of
mine complained that all the varieties of fancy pears in
our orchards seem to have been selected by somebody
who had a whim for a particular kind of pear, and only
cultivated such as had that perfume; they were all alike.
And I remember the quarrel of another youth with the
confectioners, that when he racked his wit to choose the

best comfits in the shops, in all the endless varieties of
sweetmeat he could find only three flavors, or two. What
then? Pears and cakes are good for something; and because you unluckily have an eye or nose too keen, why
need you spoil the comfort which the rest of us find in
them? I knew a humorist who in a good deal of rattle
had a grain or two of sense. He shocked the company by
maintaining that the attributes of God were two—power
and risibility, and that it was the duty of every pious
man to keep up the comedy. And I have known gentlemen of great stake in the community, but whose sympathies were cold—presidents of colleges and governors
and senators—who held themselves bound to sign every
temperance pledge, and act with Bible societies and missions and peace-makers, and cry *Hist-a-boy!* to every
good dog. We must not carry comity too far, but we all
have kind impulses in this direction. When the boys
come into my yard for leave to gather horse-chestnuts,
I own I enter into Nature's game, and affect to grant
the permission reluctantly, fearing that any moment they
will find out the imposture of that showy chaff. But this
tenderness is quite unnecessary; the enchantments are
laid on very thick. Their young life is thatched with
them. Bare and grim to tears is the lot of the children in
the hovel I saw yesterday; yet not the less they hung it
round with frippery romance, like the children of the
happiest fortune, and talked of "the dear cottage where
so many joyful hours had flown." Well, this thatching of
hovels is the custom of the country. Women, more than
all, are the element and kingdom of illusion. Being
fascinated, they fascinate. They see through Claude-
Lorraines. And how dare any one, if he could, pluck
away the *coulisses*, stage effects and ceremonies, by
which they live? Too pathetic, too pitiable, is the region
of affection, and its atmosphere always liable to *mirage*.

We are not very much to blame for our bad marriages. We live amid hallucinations; and this especial trap is laid to trip up our feet with, and all are tripped up first or last. But the mighty Mother who had been so sly with us, as if she felt that she owed us some indemnity, insinuates into the Pandora-box of marriage some deep and serious benefits and some great joys. We find a delight in the beauty and happiness of children that makes the heart too big for the body. In the worst-assorted connections there is ever some mixture of true marriage. Teague and his jade get some just relations of mutual respect, kindly observation, and fostering of each other; learn something, and would carry themselves wiselier if they were now to begin.

'Tis fine for us to point at one or another fine madman, as if there were any exempts. The scholar in his library is none. I, who have all my life heard any number of orations and debates, read poems and miscellaneous books, conversed with many geniuses, am still the victim of any new page; and if Marmaduke, or Hugh, or Moosehead, or any other, invent a new style or mythology, I fancy that the world will be all brave and right if dressed in these colors, which I had not thought of. Then at once I will daub with this new paint; but it will not stick. 'Tis like the cement which the peddler sells at the door; he makes broken crockery hold with it, but you can never buy of him a bit of the cement which will make it hold when he is gone.

Men who make themselves felt in the world avail themselves of a certain fate in their constitution which they know how to use. But they never deeply interest us unless they lift a corner of the curtain, or betray, never so slightly, their penetration of what is behind it. 'Tis the charm of practical men that outside of their practicality are a certain poetry and play, as if they led the good horse Power by the Bridle, and preferred to walk, though they can ride so fiercely. Bonaparte is intellectual, as well as Caesar; and the best soldiers, sea-captains and railway men have a gentleness when off duty, a good-natured admission that there are illusions, and who shall say that he is not their sport? We stigmatize the cast-iron fellows who cannot so detach themselves, as "dragon-ridden," "thunder-stricken," and "fools of fate," with whatever powers endowed.

Since our tuition is through emblems and indirections, it is well to know that there is method in it, a fixed scale and rank above rank in the phantasms. We begin low with coarse masks and rise to the most subtle and beautiful. The red men told Columbus "they had an herb which took away fatigue"; but he found the illusion of "arriving from the east at the Indies" more composing to his lofty spirit than any tobacco. Is not our faith in the impenetrability of matter more sedative than narcotics? You play with jackstraws, balls, bowls, horse and gun, estates and politics; but there are finer games before you. Is not time a pretty toy? Life will show you masks that are worth all your carnivals. Yonder mountain must migrate into your mind. The fine star-dust and nebulous blur in Orion, "the portentous year of Mizar and Alcor," must come down and be dealt with in your household thought. What if you shall come to discern that the play and playground of all this pompous history are radiations from yourself, and that the sun borrows his beams? What terrible questions we are learning to ask! The former men believed in magic, by which temples, cities, and men were swallowed up, and all trace of them gone. We are coming on the secret of a magic which sweeps out of men's minds all vestige of theism and beliefs which they and their fathers held and were framed upon.

There are deceptions of the senses, deceptions of the

passions, and the structural, beneficent illusions of sentiment and of the intellect. There is the illusion of love,
which attributes to the beloved person all which that
person shares with his or her family, sex, age, or condition, nay, with the human mind itself. 'Tis these which
the lover loves, and Anna Matilda gets the credit of
them. As if one shut up always in a tower, with one
window through which the face of heaven and earth
could be seen, should fancy that all the marvels he beheld belonged to that window. There is the illusion of
time, which is very deep; who has disposed of it? or
come to the conviction that what seems the *succession*
of thought is only the distribution of wholes into causal
series? The intellect sees that every atom carries the
whole of Nature; that the mind opens to omnipotence;
that, in the endless striving and ascents, the metamorphosis is entire, so that the soul doth not know itself in
its own act when that act is perfected. There is illusion
that shall deceive even the elect. There is illusion that
shall deceive even the performer of the miracle. Though
he make his body, he denies that he makes it. Though
the world exist from thought, thought is daunted in presence of the world. One after the other we accept the
mental laws, still resisting those which follow, which
however must be accepted. But all our concessions only
compel us to new profusion. And what avails it that
science has come to treat space and time as simply forms
of thought, and the material world as hypothetical, and
withal our pretension of *property* and even of self-hood
are fading with the rest, if, at last, even our thoughts are
not finalities, but the incessant flowing and ascension
reach these also, and each thought which yesterday
was a finality, today is yielding to a larger generalization?

With such volatile elements to work in, 'tis no wonder if our estimates are loose and floating. We must work and affirm, but we have no guess of the value of what we say or do. The cloud is now as big as your hand, and now it covers a county. That story of Thor, who was set to drain the drinking-horn in Asgard and to wrestle with the old woman and to run with the runner Lok, and presently found that he had been drinking up the sea, and wrestling with Time, and racing with Thought, describes us, who are contending, amid these seeming trifles, with the supreme energies of Nature. We fancy we have fallen into bad company and squalid condition, low debts, shoe bills, broken glass to pay for, pots to buy, butcher's meat, sugar, milk, and coal. "Set me some great task, ye gods! and I will show my spirit." "Not so," says the good Heaven; "plod and plough, vamp your old coats and hats, weave a shoestring; great affairs and the best wine by and by." Well, 'tis all phantasm; and if we weave a yard of tape in all humility and as well as we can, long hereafter we shall see it was no cotton tape at all but some galaxy which we braided, and that the threads were Time and Nature.

We cannot write the order of the variable winds. How can we penetrate the law of our shifting moods and susceptibility? Yet they differ as all and nothing. Instead of the firmament of yesterday, which our eyes require, it is today an eggshell which coops us in; we cannot even see what or where our stars of destiny are. From day to day the capital facts of human life are hidden from our eyes. Suddenly the mist rolls up and reveals them, and we think how much good time is gone that might have been saved had any hint of these things been shown. A sudden rise in the road shows us the system of mountains, and all the summits, which have been just as near us all the year, but quite out of mind. But these alternations are not without their order, and we are parties to our various fortune. If life seem a succession of dreams, yet poetic justice is done in dreams also. The visions of good men are good; it is the undisciplined will that is whipped with bad thoughts and bad fortunes. When we break the laws, we lose our hold on the central reality. Like sick men in hospitals, we change only from bed to bed, from one folly to another; and it cannot signify much what becomes of such castaways, wailing, stupid, comatose creatures, lifted from bed to bed, from the nothing of life to the nothing of death.

In this kingdom of illusions we grope eagerly for stays and foundations. There is none but a strict and faithful dealing at home and a severe barring out of all duplicity or illusion there. Whatever games are played with us, we must play no games with ourselves, but deal in our privacy with the last honesty and truth. I look upon the simple and childish virtues of veracity and honesty as the root of all that is sublime in character. Speak as you think, be what you are, pay your debts of all kinds. I prefer to be owned as sound and solvent, and my word as good as my bond, and to be what cannot be skipped, or dissipated, or undermined, to all the *éclat* in the universe. This reality is the foundation of friendship, religion, poetry, and art. At the top or at the bottom of all illusions, I set the cheat which still leads us to work and live for appearances; in spite of our conviction, in all sane hours, that it is what we really are that avails, with friends, with strangers, and with fate or fortune.

One would think from the talk of men that riches and poverty were a great matter; and our civilization mainly respects it. But the Indians say that they do not think the white man, with his brow of care, always toiling, afraid of heat and cold, and keeping withindoors, has any advantage of them. The permanent interest of every man is never to be in a false position, but to have the

weight of Nature to back him in all that he does. Riches
and poverty are a thick or thin costume; and our life—
the life of all of us—identical. For we transcend the
circumstance continually and taste the real quality of
existence; as in our employments, which only differ in
the manipulations but express the same laws; or in our
thoughts, which wear no silks and taste no ice creams.
We see God face to face every hour, and know the savor
of Nature.

The early Greek philosophers Heraclitus and Xenoph-
anes measured their force on this problem of identity.
Diogenes of Apollonia said that unless the atoms were
made of one stuff, they could never blend and act with
one another. But the Hindus, in their sacred writings,
express the liveliest feeling, both of the essential identity
and of that illusion which they conceive variety to be.
"The notions, 'I am,' and 'This is Mine,' which influence
mankind, are but delusions of the mother of the world.
Dispel, O Lord of all creatures! the conceit of knowledge
which proceeds from ignorance." And the beatitude of
man they hold to lie in being freed from fascination.

The intellect is stimulated by the statement of truth
in a trope, and the will by clothing the laws of life in
illusions. But the unities of Truth and of Right are not
broken by the disguise. There need never be any confusion in these. In a crowded life of many parts and performers, on a stage of nations, or in the obscurest hamlet
in Maine or California, the same elements offer the same
choices to each newcomer, and, according to his election, he fixes his fortune in absolute Nature. It would
be hard to put more mental and moral philosophy than
the Persians have thrown into a sentence—

> Fooled thou must be, though wisest of the wise:
> Then be the fool of virtue, not of vice.

There is no chance and no anarchy in the universe. All is system and gradation. Every god is there sitting in his sphere. The young mortal enters the hall of the firmament; there is he alone with them alone, they pouring on him benedictions and gifts, and beckoning him up to their thrones. On the instant, and incessantly, fall snowstorms of illusions. He fancies himself in a vast crowd which sways this way and that and whose movement and doings he must obey: he fancies himself poor, orphaned, insignificant. The mad crowd drives hither and thither, now furiously commanding this thing to be done, now that. What is he that he should resist their will, and think or act for himself? Every moment new changes and new showers of deceptions to baffle and distract him. And when, by and by, for an instant, the air clears and the cloud lifts a little, there are the gods still sitting around him on their thrones—they alone with him alone.

FARMING

THE GLORY of the farmer is that, in the division of labors, it is his part to create. All trade rests at last on his primitive activity. He stands close to nature; he obtains from the earth the bread and the meat. The food which was not, he causes to be. The first farmer was the first man, and all historic nobility rests on possession and use of land. Men do not like hard work, but every man has an exceptional respect for tillage, and a feeling that this is the original calling of his race, that he himself is only excused from it by some circumstance which made him delegate it for a time to other hands.

If he have not some skill which recommends him to the farmer, some product for which the farmer will give him corn, he must himself return into his due place among the planters. And the profession has in all eyes its ancient charm, as standing nearest to God, the first cause.

Then the beauty of nature, the tranquility and innocence of the countryman, his independence, and his pleasing arts—the care of bees, of poultry, of sheep, of cows, the dairy, the care of hay, of fruits, orchards and forests, and the reaction of these on the workman, in giving him a strength and plain dignity like the face and manners of nature—all men acknowledge. All men keep the farm in reserve as an asylum where, in case of mischance, to hide their poverty—or a solitude, if they do not succeed in society. And who knows how many glances of remorse are turned this way from the bankrupts of trade, from mortified pleaders in courts and senates, or from the victims of idleness and pleasure? Poisoned by town life and town vices, the sufferer resolves: "Well, my children, whom I have injured, shall go back to the land, to be recruited and cured by that which should have been my nursery, and now shall be their hospital."

The farmer's office is precise and important, but you must not try to paint him in rose-color; you cannot make pretty compliments to fate and gravitation, whose minister he is. He represents the necessities. It is the beauty of the great economy of the world that makes his comeliness. He bends to the order of the seasons, the weather, the soils and crops, as the sails of a ship bend to the wind. He represents continuous hard labor, year in, year out, and small gains. He is a slow person, timed to nature, and not to city watches. He takes the pace of seasons, plants, and chemistry. Nature never hurries: atom by atom, little by little, she achieves her work. The lesson one learns in fishing, yachting, hunting, or planting, is the manners of Nature; patience with the delays of wind and sun, delays of the seasons, bad weather, excess or lack of water—patience with the slowness of our feet, with the parsimony of our strength, with the largeness of sea and land we must traverse, etc. The farmer times himself to Nature, and acquires that livelong patience which belongs to her. Slow, narrow man, his rule is that the earth shall feed and clothe him; and he must wait for his crop to grow. His entertainments, his liberties and his spending must be on a farmer's scale, and not on a merchant's. It were as false for farmers to use a wholesale and massy expense, as for states to use a minute economy. But if thus pinched on one side, he has compensatory advantages. He is permanent, clings to his land as the rocks do. In the town where I live, farms remain in the same families for seven and eight generations; and most of the first settlers (in 1635), should they reappear on the farms today, would find their own blood and names still in possession. And the like fact holds in the surrounding towns.

This hard work will always be done by one kind of man; not by scheming speculators, nor by soldiers, nor professors, nor readers of Tennyson; but by men of endurance—deep-chested, long-winded, tough, slow and sure, and timely. The farmer has a great health, and the appetite of health, and means to his end; he has broad lands for his home, wood to burn great fires, plenty of plain food; his milk at least is unwatered; and for sleep, he has cheaper and better and more of it than citizens.

He has grave trusts confided to him. In the great household of Nature, the farmer stands at the door of the bread-room, and weighs to each his loaf. It is for him to say whether men shall marry or not. Early marriages and the number of births are indissolubly connected with abundance of food; or, as Burke said, "Man breeds at the mouth." Then he is the Board of Quarantine. The farmer is a hoarded capital of health, as the farm is the capital of wealth; and it is from him that the health and power, moral and intellectual, of the cities came. The city is always recruited from the country. The men in cities who are the centers of energy, the driving-wheels of trade, politics, or practical arts, and the women of beauty and genius, are the children or grandchildren of farmers, and are spending the energies which their fathers' hardy, silent life accumulated in frosty furrows, in poverty, necessity, and darkness.

He is the continuous benefactor. He who digs a well, constructs a stone fountain, plants a grove of trees by the roadside, plants an orchard, builds a durable house, reclaims a swamp, or so much as puts a stone seat by the wayside, makes the land so far lovely and desirable, makes a fortune which he cannot carry away with him, but which is useful to his country long afterwards. The man that works at home helps society at large with somewhat more of certainty than he who devotes himself to charities. If it be true that, not by votes of political parties but by the eternal laws of political economy, slaves are driven out of a slave State as fast as it is surrounded by free States, then the true abolitionist is the farmer, who, heedless of laws and constitutions, stands all day in the field, investing his labor in the land, and making a product with which no forced labor can compete.

We commonly say that the rich man can speak the truth, can afford honesty, can afford independence of opinion and action—and that is the theory of nobility. But it is the rich man in a true sense, that is to say, not the man of large income and large expenditure, but solely the man whose outlay is less than his income and is steadily kept so.

In English factories, the boy that watches the loom, to tie the thread when the wheel stops to indicate that a thread is broken, is called a *minder*. And in this great factory of our Copernican globe, shifting its slides, rotating its constellations, times, and tides, bringing now the day of planting, then of watering, then of weeding, then of reaping, then of curing and storing—the farmer is the *minder*. His machine is of colossal proportions; the diameter of the water-wheel, the arms of the levers, the power of the battery, are out of all mechanic measure; and it takes him long to understand its parts and its working. This pump never "sucks"; these screws are never loose; this machine is never out of gear; the vat and piston, wheels and tires, never wear out, but are self-repairing.

Who are the farmer's servants? Not the Irish, nor the coolies, but Geology and Chemistry, the quarry of the air, the water of the brook, the lightning of the cloud, the castings of the worm, the plough of the frost. Long before he was born, the sun of ages decomposed the rocks, mellowed his land, soaked it with light and heat, covered it with vegetable film, then with forests, and accumulated the sphagnum whose decays made the peat of his meadow.

Science has shown the great circles in which nature works; the manner in which marine plants balance the marine animals, as the land plants supply the oxygen which the animals consume, and the animals the carbon which the plants absorb. These activities are incessant. Nature works on a method of *all for each and each for all*. The strain that is made on one point bears on every arch and foundation of the structure. There is a perfect solidarity. You cannot detach an atom from its holdings, or strip off from it the electricity, gravitation, chemic affinity, or the relation to light and heat, and leave the atom bare. No, it brings with it its universal ties.

Nature, like a cautious testator, ties up her estate so as not to bestow it all on one generation, but has a fore-looking tenderness and equal regard to the next and the next, and the fourth and the fortieth age. There lie the inexhaustible magazines. The eternal rocks, as we call them, have held their oxygen or lime undiminished, en-tire, as it was. No particle of oxygen can rust or wear, but has the same energy as on the first morning. The good rocks, those patient waiters, say to him: "We have the sacred power as we received it. We have not failed of our trust, and now—when in our immense day the hour is at last struck—take the gas we have hoarded, mingle it with water, and let it be free to grow in plants and animals and obey the thought of man."

The earth works for him; the earth is a machine which yields almost gratuitous service to every application of intellect. Every plant is a manufacturer of soil. In the stomach of the plant development begins. The tree can draw on the whole air, the whole earth, on all the rolling main. The plant is all suction-pipe—imbibing from the ground by its root, from the air by its leaves, with all its might.

The air works for him. The atmosphere, a sharp sol-vent, drinks the essence and spirit of every solid on the globe—a menstruum which melts the mountains into it. Air is matter subdued by heat. As the sea is the grand receptacle of all rivers, so the air is the receptacle from which all things spring, and into which they all return. The invisible and creeping air takes form and solid mass. Our senses are skeptics, and believe only the impression of the moment, and do not believe the chemical fact that these huge mountain-chains are made up of gases and rolling wind. But Nature is as subtle as she is strong. She turns her capital day by day; deals never with dead, but ever with quick subjects. All things are flowing, even those that seem immovable. The adamant is always passing into smoke. The plants imbibe the materials which they want from the air and the ground. They burn, that is, exhale and decompose their own bodies into the air and earth again. The animal burns, or undergoes the like perpetual consumption. The earth burns, the mountains burn and decompose, slower, but incessantly. It is almost inevitable to push the generalization up into higher parts of nature, rank over rank into sentient beings. Nations burn with internal fire of thought and affection, which wastes while it works. We shall find finer combustion and finer fuel. Intellect is a fire: rash and pitiless it melts this wonderful bone-house which is called man. Genius even, as it is the greatest good, is the greatest harm. Whilst all thus burns—the universe in a blaze kindled from the torch of the sun—it needs a perpetual tempering, a phlegm, a sleep, atmospheres of azote, deluges of water, to check the fury of the conflagration; a hoarding to check the spending, a centripetence equal to the centrifugence; and this is invariably supplied.

The railroad dirt-cars are good excavators, but there is no porter like Gravitation, who will bring down any weights which man cannot carry, and if he wants aid, knows where to find his fellow laborers. Water works in masses, and sets its irresistible shoulder to your mills or your ships, or transports vast boulders of rock in its iceberg a thousand miles. But its far greater power depends on its talent of becoming little, and entering the smallest holes and pores. By this agency, carrying in solution elements needful to every plant, the vegetable world exists.

But as I said, we must not paint the farmer in rose-color. Whilst these grand energies have wrought for him and made his task possible, he is habitually engaged in small economies, and is taught the power that lurks in petty things. Great is the force of a few simple arrangements; for instance, the powers of a fence. On the prairie you wander a hundred miles and hardly find a stick or a stone. At rare intervals a thin oak-opening has been spared, and every such section has been long occupied. But the farmer manages to procure wood from far, puts up a rail fence, and at once the seeds sprout and the oaks rise. It was only browsing and fire which had kept them down. Plant fruit trees by the roadside, and their fruit will never be allowed to ripen. Draw a pine fence about them, and for fifty years they mature for the owner their delicate fruit. There is a great deal of enchantment in a chestnut rail or picketed pine boards.

Nature suggests every economcal expedient some where on a great scale. Set out a pine tree, and it dies in the first year, or lives a poor spindle. But Nature drops a pine-cone in Mariposa, and it lives fifteen centuries, grows three or four hundred feet high, and thirty in diameter—grows in a grove of giants, like a colonnade of Thebes. Ask the tree how it was done. It did not grow on a ridge, but in a basin, where it found deep soil, cold enough and dry enough for the pine; defended itself from the sun by growing in groves, and from the wind by the walls of the mountain. The roots that shot deepest, and the stems of happiest exposure, drew the nourishment from the rest, until the less thrifty perished and manured the soil for the stronger, and the mammoth Sequoias rose to their enormous proportions. The traveler who saw them remembered his orchard at home, where every year, in the destroying wind, his forlorn trees pined like suffering virtue. In September, when the

pears hang heaviest and are taking from the sun their
gay colors, comes usually a gusty day which shakes the
whole garden and throws down the heaviest fruit in
bruised heaps. The planter took the hint of the Sequoias,
built a high wall, or—better—surrounded the orchard
with a nursery of birches and evergreens. Thus he had
the mountain basin in miniature; and his pears grew to
the size of melons, and the vines beneath them ran an
eighth of a mile. But this shelter creates a new climate.
The wall that keeps off the strong wind keeps off the
cold wind. The high wall reflecting the heat back on the
soil gives that acre a quadruple share of sunshine—

> Enclosing in the garden square
> A dead and standing pool of air,

and makes a little Cuba within it, whilst all without is
Labrador.

The chemist comes to his aid every year by following
out some new hint drawn from nature, and now affirms
that this dreary space occupied by the farmer is needless; he will concentrate his kitchen-garden into a box
of one or two rods square, will take the roots into his
laboratory; the vines and stalks and stems may go
sprawling about in the fields outside, he will attend to
the roots in his tub, gorge them with food that is good
for them. The smaller his garden, the better he can feed
it, and the larger the crop. As he nursed his Thanksgiv-
ing turkeys on bread and milk, so he will pamper his
peaches and grapes on the viands they like best. If they
have an appetite for potash, or salt, or iron, or ground
bones, or even now and then for a dead hog, he will
indulge them. They keep the secret well, and never tell
on your table whence they drew their sunset complexion
or their delicate flavors.

See what the farmer accomplishes by a cart-load of

tiles: he alters the climate by letting off water which kept the land cold through constant evaporation, and allows the warm rain to bring down into the roots the temperature of the air and of the surface-soil; and he deepens the soil, since the discharge of this standing water allows the roots of his plants to penetrate below the surface to the subsoil, and accelerates the ripening of the crop. The town of Concord is one of the oldest towns in this country, far on now in its third century. The selectmen have once in every five years perambulated the boundaries, and yet, in this very year, a large quantity of land has been discovered and added to the town without a murmur of complaint from any quarter. By drainage we went down to a subsoil we did not know, and have found there is a Concord under old Concord, which we are now getting the best crops from; a Middlesex under Middlesex; and, in fine, that Massachusetts has a basement story more valuable and that promises to pay a better rent than all the superstructure. But these tiles have acquired by association a new interest. These tiles are political economists, confuters of Malthus and Ricardo; they are so many Young Americans announcing a better era—more bread. They drain the land, make it sweet and friable; have made English Chat Moss a garden, and will now do as much for the Dismal Swamp. But beyond this benefit they are the text of better opinions and better auguries for mankind.

There has been a nightmare bred in England of indigestion and spleen among landlords and loomlords, namely, the dogma that men breed too fast for the powers of the soil; that men multiply in a geometrical ratio, whilst corn multiplies only in an arithmetical; and hence that, the more prosperous we are, the faster we approach these frightful limits: nay, the plight of every new generation is worse than of the foregoing, because the first comers take up the best lands; the next, the second best; and each succeeding wave of population is driven to poorer, so that the land is ever yielding less returns to enlarging hosts of eaters. Henry Carey of Philadelphia replied: "Not so, Mr. Malthus, but just the opposite of so is the fact."

The first planter, the savage, without helpers, without tools, looking chiefly to safety from his enemy—man or beast—takes poor land. The better lands are loaded with timber, which he cannot clear; they need drainage, which he cannot attempt. He cannot plough, or fell trees, or drain the rich swamp. He is a poor creature; he scratches with a sharp stick, lives in a cave or a hutch, has no road but the trail of the moose or bear; he lives on their flesh when he can kill one, on roots and fruits when he cannot. He falls, and is lame; he coughs, he has a stitch in his side, he has a fever and chills; when he is hungry, he cannot always kill and eat a bear—chances of war—sometimes the bear eats him. 'Tis long before he digs or plants at all, and then only a patch. Later he learns that his planting is better than hunting; that the earth works faster for him than he can work for himself —works for him when he is asleep, when it rains, when heat overcomes him. The sunstroke which knocks him down brings his corn up. As his family thrive, and other planters come up around him, he begins to fell trees and clear good land; and when, by and by, there is more skill, and tools and roads, the new generations are strong enough to open the lowlands, where the wash of mountains has accumulated the best soil, which yield a hundredfold the former crops. The last lands are the best lands. It needs science and great numbers to cultivate the best lands, and in the best manner. Thus true political economy is not mean, but liberal, and on the pattern of the sun and sky. Population increases in the ratio of morality; credit exists in the ratio of morality.

Meantime we cannot enumerate the incidents and agents of the farm without reverting to their influence on the farmer. He carries out this cumulative preparation of means to their last effect. This crust of soil which ages have refined he refines again for the feeding of a civil and instructed people. The great elements with which he deals cannot leave him unaffected, or unconscious of his ministry; but their influence somewhat resembles that which the same Nature has on the child —of subduing and silencing him. We see the farmer with pleasure and respect when we think what powers and utilities are so meekly worn. He knows every secret of labor; he changes the face of the landscape. Put him on a new planet and he would know where to begin; yet there is no arrogance in his bearing, but a perfect gentleness. The farmer stands well on the world. Plain in manners as in dress, he would not shine in palaces; he is absolutely unknown and inadmissible therein; living or dying, he never shall be heard of in them; yet the drawing-room heroes put down beside him would shrivel in his presence; he solid and unexpressive, they expressed to gold-leaf. But he stands well on the world—as Adam did, as an Indian does, as Homer's heroes, Agamemnon or Achilles, do. He is a person whom a poet of any clime —Milton, Firdusi, or Cervantes—would appreciate as being really a piece of the old Nature, comparable to sun and moon, rainbow and flood; because he is, as all natural persons are, representative of Nature as much as these.

That uncorrupted behavior which we admire in animals and in young children belongs to him, to the hunter, the sailor—the man who lives in the presence of Nature. Cities force growth and make men talkative and entertaining, but they make them artificial. What possesses interest for us is the *naturel* of each, his constitutional excellence. This is forever a surprise, engaging and lovely; we cannot be satiated with knowing it, and about it; and it is this which the conversation with Nature cherishes and guards.

EDUCATION

A NEW degree of intellectual power seems cheap at any price. The use of the world is that man may learn its laws. And the human race have wisely signified their sense of this, by calling wealth, means— Man being the end. Language is always wise.

Therefore I praise New England because it is the country in the world where is the freest expenditure for education. We have already taken, at the planting of the Colonies (for aught I know for the first time in the world), the initial step, which for its importance might have been resisted as the most radical of revolutions, thus deciding at the start the destiny of this country— this, namely, that the poor man, whom the law does not allow to take an ear of corn when starving, nor a pair of shoes for his freezing feet, is allowed to put his hand into the pocket of the rich, and say, You shall educate me, not as you will, but as I will: not alone in the elements, but, by further provision, in the languages, in sciences, in the useful and in elegant arts. The child shall be taken up by the State, and taught, at the public cost, the rudiments of knowledge, and, at last, the ripest results of art and science.

Humanly speaking, the school, the college, society, make the difference between men. All the fairy tales of Aladdin or the invisible Gyges or the talisman that opens kings' palaces or the enchanted halls underground or in the sea, are only fictions to indicate the one miracle of intellectual enlargement. When a man stupid becomes a man inspired, when one and the same man passes out of the torpid into the perceiving state, leaves the din of trifles, the stupor of the senses, to enter into the quasi-omniscience of high thought—up and down, around, all limits disappear. No horizon shuts down. He sees things in their causes, all facts in their connection.

One of the problems of history is the beginning of civilization. The animals that accompany and serve man make no progress as races. Those called domestic are capable of learning of man a few tricks of utility or amusement, but they cannot communicate the skill to their race. Each individual must be taught anew. The trained dog cannot train another dog. And Man himself in many races retains almost the unteachableness of the beast. For a thousand years the islands and forests of a great part of the world have been filled with savages who made no steps of advance in art or skill beyond the necessity of being fed and warmed. Certain nations with a better brain and usually in more temperate climates have made such progress as to compare with these as these compare with the bear and the wolf.

Victory over things is the office of man. Of course, until it is accomplished, it is the war and insult of things over him. His continual tendency, his great danger, is to overlook the fact that the world is only his teacher, and the nature of sun and moon, plant and animal only

means of arousing his interior activity. Enamored of
their beauty, comforted by their convenience, he seeks
them as ends, and fast loses sight of the fact that they
have worse than no values, that they become noxious,
when he becomes their slave.

This apparatus of wants and faculties, this craving
body, whose organs ask all the elements and all the
functions of Nature for their satisfaction, educate the
wondrous creature which they satisfy with light, with
heat, with water, with wood, with bread, with wool. The
necessities imposed by this most irritable and all-related
texture have taught Man hunting, pasturage, agriculture,
commerce, weaving, joining, masonry, geometry, astronomy. Here is a world pierced and belted with natural
laws, and fenced and planted with civil partitions and
properties, which all put new restraints on the young inhabitant. He too must come into this magic circle of
relations, and know health and sickness, the fear of injury, the desire of external good, the charm of riches, the
charm of power. The household is a school of power.
There, within the door, learn the tragi-comedy of human
life. Here is the sincere thing, the wondrous composition
for which day and night go round. In that routine are
the sacred relations, the passions that bind and sever.
Here is poverty and all the wisdom its hated necessities
can teach, here labor drudges, here affections glow, here
the secrets of character are told, the guards of man, the
guards of woman, the compensations which, like angels
of justice, pay every debt: the opium of custom, whereof
all drink and many go mad. Here is Economy, and Glee,
and Hospitality, and Ceremony, and Frankness, and
Calamity, and Death, and Hope.

Every one has a trust of power—every man, every
boy a jurisdiction, whether it be over a cow or a rood of
a potato-field, or a fleet of ships, or the laws of a state.

And what activity the desire of power inspires! What toils it sustains! How it sharpens the perceptions and stores the memory with facts. Thus a man may well spend many years of life in trade. It is a constant teaching of the laws of matter and of mind. No dollar of property can be created without some direct communication with nature, and of course some acquisition of knowledge and practical force. It is a constant contest with the active faculties of men, a study of the issues of one and another course of action, an accumulation of power, and, if the higher faculties of the individual be from time to time quickened, he will gain wisdom and virtue from his business.

As every wind draws music out of the Aeolian harp, so doth every object in Nature draw music out of his mind. Is it not true that every landscape I behold, every friend I meet, every act I perform, every pain I suffer, leaves me a different being from that they found me? That poverty, love, authority, anger, sickness, sorrow, success, all work actively upon our being and unlock for us the concealed faculties of the mind? Whatever private or petty ends are frustrated, this end is always answered. Whatever the man does, or whatever befalls him, opens another chamber in his soul—that is, he has got a new feeling, a new thought, a new organ. Do we not see how amazingly for this end man is fitted to the world?

What leads him to science? Why does he track in the midnight heaven a pure spark, a luminous patch wandering from age to age, but because he acquires thereby a majestic sense of power; learning that in his own constitution he can set the shining maze in order, and finding and carrying their law in his mind, can, as it were, see his simple idea realized up yonder in giddy distances and frightful periods of duration. If Newton come and first of men perceive that not alone certain bodies fall to the ground at a certain rate, but that all bodies in the Universe, the universe of bodies, fall always, and at one rate; that every atom in nature draws to every other atom—he extends the power of his mind not only over every cubic atom of his native planet, but he reports the condition of millions of worlds which his eye never saw. And what is the charm which every ore, every new plant, every new fact touching winds, clouds, ocean currents, the secrets of chemical composition and decomposition possess for Humboldt? What but that much revolving of similar facts in his mind has shown him that always the mind contains in its transparent chambers the means of classifying the most refractory phenomena, of depriving them of all casual and chaotic aspect, and subordinating them to a bright reason of its own, and so giving to man a sort of property—yea, the very highest property in every district and particle of the globe.

By the permanence of Nature, minds are trained alike, and made intelligible to each other. In our condition are the roots of language and communication, and these instructions we never exhaust.

In some sort the end of life is that the man should take up the universe into himself, or out of that quarry leave nothing unrepresented. Yonder mountain must migrate into his mind. Yonder magnificent astronomy he is at last to import, fetching away moon, and planet, solstice, period, comet and binal star, by comprehending their relation and law. Instead of the timid stripling he was, he is to be the stalwart Archimedes, Pythagoras, Columbus, Newton, of the physic, metaphysic and ethics of the design of the world.

For truly the population of the globe has its origin in the aims which their existence is to serve; and so with every portion of them. The truth takes flesh in forms that can express it; and thus in history an idea always overhangs, like the moon, and rules the tide which rises simultaneously in all the souls of a generation.

Whilst thus the world exists for the mind; whilst thus the man is ever invited inward into shining realms of knowledge and power by the shows of the world, which interpret to him the infinitude of his own consciousness —it becomes the office of a just education to awaken him to the knowledge of this fact.

We learn nothing rightly until we learn the symbolical character of life. Day creeps after day, each full of facts, dull, strange, despised things, that we cannot enough despise—call heavy, prosaic, and desert. The time we seek to kill: the attention it is elegant to divert from things around us. And presently the aroused intellect finds gold and gems in one of these scorned facts—then finds that the day of facts is a rock of diamonds; that a fact is an Epiphany of God.

We have our theory of life, our religion, our philosophy; and the event of each moment, the shower, the steamboat disaster, the passing of a beautiful face, the apoplexy of our neighbor, are all tests to try our theory, the approximate result we call truth, and reveal its defects. If I have renounced the search of truth, if I have come into the port of some pretending dogmatism, some new church or old church, some Schelling or Cousin, I have died to all use of these new events that are born out of prolific time into multitude of life every hour. I am as a bankrupt to whom brilliant opportunities offer in vain. He has just foreclosed his freedom, tied his hands, locked himself up and given the key to another to keep.

When I see the doors by which God enters into the mind; that there is no sot or fop, ruffian or pedant into whom thoughts do not enter by passages which the individual never left open, I can expect any revolution in character. "I have hope," said the great Leibnitz, "that society may be reformed, when I see how much education may be reformed."

It is ominous, a presumption of crime, that this word Education has so cold, so hopeless a sound. A treatise on education, a convention for education, a lecture, a system, affects us with slight paralysis and a certain yawning of the jaws. We are not encouraged when the law touches it with its fingers. Education should be as broad as man. Whatever elements are in him that should foster and demonstrate. If he be dexterous, his tuition should make it appear; if he be capable of dividing men by the trenchant sword of his thought, education should unsheathe and sharpen it; if he is one to cement society by his all-reconciling affinities, oh! hasten their action! If he is jovial, if he is mercurial, if he is great-hearted, a cunning artificer, a strong commander, a potent ally, ingenious, useful, elegant, witty, prophet, diviner—society has need of all these. The imagination must be addressed. Why always coast on the surface and never open the interior of nature, not by science, which is surface still, but by poetry? Is not the Vast an element of the mind? Yet what teaching, what book of this day appeals to the Vast?

Our culture has truckled to the times—to the senses. It is not manworthy. If the vast and the spiritual are omitted, so are the practical and the moral. It does not make us brave or free. We teach boys to be such men as we are. We do not teach them to aspire to be all they can. We do not give them a training as if we believed in their noble nature. We scarce educate their bodies. We do not train the eye and the hand. We exercise their understandings to the apprehension and comparison of some facts, to a skill in numbers, in words; we aim to make accountants, attorneys, engineers; but not to make able, earnest, great-hearted men. The great object of Education should be commensurate with the object of life. It should be a moral one; to teach self-trust: to inspire the youthful man with an interest in himself; with a curiosity touching his own nature; to acquaint him with the resources of his mind, and to teach him that there is all his strength, and to inflame him with a piety towards the Grand Mind in which he lives. Thus would education conspire with the Divine Providence. A man is a little thing whilst he works by and for himself, but, when he gives voice to the rules of love and justice, is godlike, his word is current in all countries; and all men, though his enemies, are made his friends and obey it as their own.

In affirming that the moral nature of man is the predominant element and should therefore be mainly consulted in the arrangements of a school, I am very far from wishing that it should swallow up all the other instincts and faculties of man. It should be enthroned in his mind, but if it monopolize the man he is not yet sound, he does not yet know his wealth. He is in danger of becoming merely devout, and wearisome through the monotony of his thought. It is not less necessary that the intellectual and the active faculties should be nourished and matured. Let us apply to this subject the light of the same torch by which we have looked at all the phenomena of the time; the infinitude, namely, of every man. Everything teaches that.

One fact constitutes all my satisfaction, inspires all my trust, *viz.*, this perpetual youth, which, as long as there is any good in us, we cannot get rid of. It is very certain that the coming age and the departing age seldom understand each other. The old man thinks the young man has no distinct purpose, for he could never get anything intelligible and earnest out of him. Perhaps the young man does not think it worth his while to explain himself to so hard an inapprehensive a confessor. Let him be led up with a long-sighted forbearance, and let not the sallies of his petulance or folly be checked with disgust or indignation or despair.

I call our system a system of despair, and I find all the correction, all the revolution that is needed and that the best spirits of this age promise, in one word, in Hope. Nature, when she sends a new mind into the world, fills it beforehand with a desire for that which she wishes it to know and do. Let us wait and see what is this new creation, of what new organ the great Spirit had need when it incarnated this new Will. A new Adam in the garden, he is to name all the beasts in the field, all the gods in the sky. And jealous provision seems to have been made in his constitution that you shall not invade and contaminate him with the worn weeds of your language and opinions. The charm of life is this variety of genius, these contrasts and flavors by which Heaven has modulated the identity of truth, and there is a perpetual hankering to violate this individuality, to warp his ways of thinking and behavior to resemble or reflect your thinking and behavior. A low self-love in the parent desires that his child should repeat his character and fortune; an expectation which the child, if justice is done him, will nobly disappoint. By working on the theory that this resemblance exists, we shall do what in us lies to defeat his proper promise and produce the ordinary and mediocre. I suffer whenever I see that common sight of a parent or senior imposing his opinion and way of thinking and being on a young soul to which they are totally unfit. Cannot we let people be themselves, and enjoy life in their own way? You are trying to make that man another *you*. One's enough.

Or we sacrifice the genius of the pupil, the unknown possibilities of his nature, to a neat and safe uniformity, as the Turks whitewash the costly mosaics of ancient art which the Greeks left on their temple walls. Rather let us have men whose manhood is only the continuation of their boyhood, natural characters still; such are able and fertile for heroic action; and not that sad spectacle with which we are too familiar, educated eyes in uneducated bodies.

I like boys, the masters of the playground and of the street—boys, who have the same liberal ticket of admission to all shops, factories, armories, town-meetings, caucuses, mobs, target-shootings, as flies have; quite unsuspected, coming in as naturally as the janitor —known to have no money in their pockets, and themselves not suspecting the value of this poverty; putting nobody on his guard, but seeing the inside of the show —hearing all the asides. There are no secrets from them, they know everything that befalls in the fire-company, the merits of every engine and of every man at the brakes, how to work it, and are swift to try their hand at every part; so too the merits of every locomotive on the rails, and will coax the engineer to let them ride with him and pull the handles when it goes to the engine-house. They are there only for fun, and not knowing that they are at school, in the court-house, or the cattle-show, quite as much and more than they were, an hour ago, in the arithmetic class.

They know truth from counterfeit as quick as the chemist does. They detect weakness in your eye and behavior a week before you open your mouth, and have given you the benefit of their opinion quick as a wink. They make no mistakes, have no pedantry, but entire belief on experience. Their elections at baseball or cricket are founded on merit, and are right. They don't pass for swimmers until they can swim, nor for stroke-oar until they can row: and I desire to be saved from their contempt. If I can pass with them, I can manage well enough with their fathers.

Everybody delights in the energy with which boys deal and talk with each other; the mixture of fun and earnest, reproach and coaxing, love and wrath, with which the game is played—the good-natured yet defiant independence of a leading boy's behavior in the school-yard. How we envy in later life the happy youths to whom their boisterous games and rough exercise furnish the precise element which frames and sets off their school and college tasks, and teaches them, when least they think it, the use and meaning of these. In their fun and extreme freak they hit on the topmost sense of Horace. The young giant, brown from his hunting tramp, tells his story well, interlarded with lucky allusions to Homer, to Virgil, to college songs, to Walter Scott; and Jove and Achilles, partridge and trout, opera and binomial theorem, Caesar in Gaul, Sherman in Savannah, and hazing in Holworthy, dance through the narrative in merry confusion, yet the logic is good. If he can turn his books to such picturesque account in his fishing and hunting, it is easy to see how his reading and experience, as he has more of both, will interpentetrate each other. And every one desires that this pure vigor of action and wealth of narrative, cheered with so much humor and street rhetoric, should be carried into the habit of the young man, purged of its uproar and rudeness, but with all its vivacity entire. His hunting and campings-out have given him an indispensable base: I wish to add a taste for good company through his impatience of bad. That stormy genius of his needs a little direction to games, charades, verses of society, song, and a correspondence year by year with his wisest and best friends. Friendship is an order of nobility; from its revelations we come more worthily into nature. Society he must have or he is poor indeed; he gladly enters a school which forbids conceit, affectation, emphasis and dullness, and requires of each only the flower of his nature and experience; requires good will, beauty, wit, and select information; teaches by practice the law of conversation, namely, to hear as well as to speak.

Meantime, if circumstances do not permit the high social advantages, solitude has also its lessons. The obscure youth learns there the practice instead of the literature of his virtues; and, because of the disturbing effect of passion and sense, which by a multitude of trifles impede the mind's eye from the quiet search of that fine horizon-line which truth keeps—the way to knowledge and power has ever been an escape from too much engagement with affairs and possessions; a way, not through plenty and superfluity, but by denial and renunciation, into solitude and privation; and, the more is taken away, the more real and inevitable wealth of being is made known to us. The solitary knows the essence of the thought, the scholar in society only its fair face. There is no want of example of great men, great benefactors, who have been monks and hermits in habit. The bias of mind is sometimes irresistible in that direction. The man is, as it were, born deaf and dumb, and dedicated to a narrow and lonely life. Let him study the art of solitude, yield as gracefully as he can to his destiny. Why cannot he get the good of his doom, and if it is from eternity a settled fact that he and society shall be nothing to each other, why need he blush so, and make wry faces to keep up a freshman's seat in the fine world? Heaven often protects valuable souls charged with great secrets, great ideas, by long shutting them up with their own thoughts. And the most genial and amiable of men must alternate society with solitude, and learn its severe lessons.

There comes the period of the imagination to each, a later youth; the power of beauty, the power of books, of poetry. Culture makes his books realities to him, their characters more brilliant, more effective on his mind, than his actual mates. Do not spare to put novels into the hands of young people as an occasional holiday and experiment; but, above all, good poetry in all kinds, epic, tragedy, lyric. If we can touch the imagination, we serve them, they will never forget it. Let him read *Tom Brown at Rugby*, read *Tom Brown at Oxford*,—better yet, read *Hodson's Life*—Hodson who took prisoner the King of Delhi. They teach the same truth—a trust, against all appearances, against all privations, in your own worth, and not in tricks, plotting, or patronage.

I believe that our own experience instructs us that the secret of Education lies in respecting the pupil. It is not for you to choose what he shall know, what he shall do. It is chosen and foreordained, and he only holds the key to his own secret. By your tampering and thwarting and too much governing he may be hindered from his end and kept out of his own. Respect the child. Wait and see the new product of Nature. Nature loves analogies, but not repetitions. Respect the child. Be not too much his parent. Trespass not on his solitude.

But I hear the outcry which replies to this suggestion—Would you verily throw up the reins of public and private discipline; would you leave the young child to the mad career of his own passions and whimsies, and call this anarchy a respect for the child's nature? I answer—Respect the child, respect him to the end, but also respect yourself. Be the companion of his thought, the friend of his friendship, the lover of his virtue—but no kinsman of his sin. Let him find you so true to yourself that you are the irreconcilable hater of his vice and the imperturbable slighter of his trifling.

The two points in a boy's training are, to keep his *naturel* and train off all but that—to keep his *naturel*, but stop off his uproar, fooling and horseplay—keep his nature and arm it with knowledge in the very direction in which it points. Here are the two capital facts, Genius and Drill. The first is the inspiration in the well-born healthy child, the new perception he has of nature. Somewhat he sees in forms or hears in music or apprehends in mathematics, or believes practicable in mechanics or possible in political society, which no one else sees or hears or believes. This is the perpetual romance of new life, the invasion of God into the old dead world, when he sends into quiet houses a young soul with a thought which is not met, looking for something which is not there, but which ought to be there: the thought is dim but it is sure, and he casts about restless for means and masters to verify it; he makes wild attempts to explain himself and invoke the aid and consent of the bystanders. Baffled for want of language and methods to convey his meaning, not yet clear to himself, he conceives that though not in this house or town, yet in some other house or town is the wise master who can put him in possession of the rules and instruments to execute his will. Happy this child with a bias, with a thought which entrances him, leads him, now into deserts now into cities, the fool of an idea. Let him follow it in good and in evil report, in good or bad company; it will justify itself; it will lead him at last into the illustrious society of the lovers of truth.

In London, in a private company, I became acquainted with a gentleman, Sir Charles Fellowes, who, being at Xanthus, in the Aegean Sea, had seen a Turk point with his staff to some carved work on the corner of a stone almost buried in the soil. Fellowes scraped away the dirt, was struck with the beauty of the sculptured ornaments, and, looking about him, observed more blocks and fragments like this. He returned to the spot, procured laborers and uncovered many blocks. He went back to England, bought a Greek grammar and learned the language; he read history and studied ancient art to explain his stones; he interested Gibson the sculptor; he invoked the assistance of the English Government; he called in the succor of Sir Humphry Davy to analyze the pigments; of experts in coins, of scholars and connoisseurs; and at last in his third visit brought home to England such statues and marble reliefs and such careful plans that he was able to reconstruct, in the British Museum where it now stands, the perfect model of the Ionic trophy-monument, fifty years older than the Parthenon of Athens, and which had been destroyed by earthquakes, then by iconoclast Christians, then by savage Turks. But mark that in the task he had achieved an excellent education, and become associated with distinguished scholars whom he had interested in his pursuit; in short, had formed a college for himself; the enthusiast had found the master, the masters, whom he sought. Always genius seeks genius, desires nothing so much as to be a pupil and to find those who can lend it aid to perfect itself.

Nor are the two elements, enthusiasm and drill, incompatible. Accuracy is essential to beauty. The very definition of the intellect is Aristotle's: "that by which we know terms or boundaries." Give a boy accurate perceptions. Teach him the difference between the similar and the same. Make him call things by their right names. Pardon in him no blunder. Then he will give you solid satisfaction as long as he lives. It is better to teach the child arithmetic and Latin grammar than rhetoric or moral philosophy, because they require exactitude of performance; it is made certain that the lesson is mastered, and that power of performance is worth more than the knowledge. He can learn anything which is important to him now that the power to learn is secured: as mechanics say, when one has learned the use of tools, it is easy to work at a new craft.

Letter by letter, syllable by syllable, the child learns to read, and in good time can convey to all the domestic circle the sense of Shakespeare. By many steps each just as short, the stammering boy and the hesitating collegian, in the school debate, in college clubs, in mock court, comes at last to full, secure, triumphant unfolding of his thought in the popular assembly, with a fullness of power that makes all the steps forgotten.

But this function of opening and feeding the human mind is not to be fulfilled by any mechanical or military method; is not to be trusted to any skill less large than Nature itself. You must not neglect the form, but you must secure the essentials. It is curious how perverse and intermeddling we are, and what vast pains and cost we incur to do wrong. Whilst we all know in our own experience and apply natural methods in our own business —in education our common sense fails us, and we are continually trying costly machinery against nature, in patent schools and academies and in great colleges and universities.

The natural method forever confutes our experiments, and we must still come back to it. The whole theory of the school is on the nurse's or mother's knee. The child is as hot to learn as the mother is to impart. There is mutual delight. The joy of our childhood in hearing beautiful stories from some skilful aunt who loves to tell them, must be repeated in youth. The boy wishes to learn to skate, to coast, to catch a fish in the brook, to hit a mark with a snowball or a stone; and a boy a little older is just as well pleased to teach him these sciences. Not less delightful is the mutual pleasure of teaching and learning the secret of algebra, or of chemistry, or of good reading and good recitation of poetry or of prose, or of chosen facts in history or in biography.

Nature provided for the communication of thought, by planting with it in the receiving mind a fury to impart it. 'Tis so in every art, in every science. One burns to tell the new fact, the other burns to hear it. See how far a young doctor will ride or walk to witness a new surgical operation. I have seen a carriage-maker's shop emptied of all its workmen into the street, to scrutinize a new pattern from New York. So in literature, the young man who has taste for poetry, for fine images, for noble thoughts, is insatiable for this nourishment, and forgets all the world for the more learned friend—who finds equal joy in dealing out his treasures.

Happy the natural college thus self-instituted around every natural teacher; the young men of Athens around Socrates; of Alexandria around Plotinus; of Paris around Abelard; of Germany around Fichte, or Niebuhr, or Goethe: in short the natural sphere of every leading mind. But the moment this is organized, difficulties begin. The college was to be the nurse and home of genius; but, though every young man is born with some determination in his nature, and is a potential genius; is at last to be one; it is, in the most, obstructed and delayed, and, whatever they may hereafter be, their senses are now opened in advance of their minds. They are more sensual than intellectual. Appetite and indolence they have, but no enthusiasm. These come in numbers to the college: few geniuses: and the teaching comes to be arranged for these many, and not for those few. Hence the instruction seems to require skilful tutors, of accurate and systematic mind, rather than ardent and inventive masters. Besides, the youth of genius are eccentric, won't drill, are irritable, uncertain, explosive, solitary, not men of the world, not good for every-day association. You have to work for large classes instead of individuals; you must lower your flag and reef your sails to wait for the dull sailors; you grow departmental, routinary, military almost with your discipline and college police. But what doth such a school to form a great and heroic character? What abiding Hope can it inspire? What Reformer will it nurse? What poet will it breed to sing to the human race? What discoverer of Nature's laws will it prompt to enrich us by disclosing in the mind the statute which all matter must obey? What fiery soul will it send out to warm a nation with his charity? What tranquil mind will it have fortified to walk with meekness in private and obscure duties, to wait and to suffer? Is it not manifest that our academic institutions should have a wider scope; that they should not be timid and keep the ruts of the last generation, but that wise men thinking for themselves and heartily seeking the good of mankind, and counting the cost of innovation, should dare to arouse the young to a just and heroic life; that the moral nature should be addressed in the school-room, and children should be treated as the high-born candidates of truth and virtue?

So to regard the young child, the young man, requires, no doubt, rare patience: a patience that nothing but faith in the remedial forces of the soul can give. You see his sensualism; you see his want of those tastes and perceptions which make the power and safety of your character. Very likely. But he has something else. If he has his own vice, he has its correlative virtue. Every mind should be allowed to make its own statement in action, and its balance will appear. In these judgments one needs that foresight which was attributed to an eminent reformer, of whom it was said "his patience could see in the bud of the aloe the blossom at the end of a hundred years." Alas for the cripple Practice when it seeks to come up with the bird Theory, which flies before it. Try your design on the best school. The scholars are of all ages and temperaments and capacities. It is difficult to class them, some are too young, some are slow, some perverse. Each requires so much consideration, that the morning hope of the teacher, of a day of love and progress, is often closed at evening by despair. Each single case, the more it is considered, shows more to be done; and the strict conditions of the hours, on one side, and the number of tasks, on the other. Whatever becomes of our method, the conditions stand fast—six hours, and thirty, fifty, or a hundred and fifty pupils. Something must be done, and done speedily, and in this distress the wisest are tempted to adopt violent means, to proclaim martial law, corporal punishment, mechanical arrangement, bribes, spies, wrath, main strength and ignorance, in lieu of that wise genial providential influence they had hoped, and yet hope at some future day to adopt. Of course the devotion to details reacts injuriously on the teacher. He cannot indulge his genius, he cannot delight in personal relations with young friends, when his eye is always on the clock, and twenty classes are to be dealt with before the day is done. Besides, how can he please himself with genius, and foster modest virtue? A sure proportion of rogue and dunce finds its way into every school and requires a cruel share of time, and the gentle teacher, who wished to be a Providence to youth, is grown a martinet, sore with suspicions; knows as much vice as the judge of a police court, and his love of learning is lost in the routine of grammars and books of elements.

A rule is so easy that it does not need a man to apply it; an automaton, a machine, can be made to keep a school so. It facilitates labor and thought so much that there is always the temptation in large schools to omit the endless task of meeting the wants of each single mind, and to govern by steam. But it is at frightful cost. Our modes of Education aim to expedite, to save labor; to do for masses what cannot be done for masses, what must be done reverently, one by one: say rather, the whole world is needed for the tuition of each pupil. The advantages of this system of emulation and display are so prompt and obvious, it is such a time-saver, it is so energetic on slow and on bad natures, and is of so easy application, needing no sage or poet, but any tutor or schoolmaster in his first term can apply it—that it is not strange that this calomel of culture should be a popular medicine. On the other hand, total abstinence from this drug, and the adoption of simple discipline and the following of nature, involves at once immense claims on the time, the thoughts, on the life of the teacher. It requires time, use, insight, event, all the great lessons and assistances of God; and only to think of using it implies character and profoundness; to enter on this course of discipline is to be good and great. It is precisely analogous to the difference between the use of corporal punishment and the methods of love. It is so easy to bestow on a bad boy a blow, overpower him, and get obedience without words, that in this world of hurry and distraction, who can wait for the returns of reason and the conquest of self; in the uncertainty too whether that will ever come? And yet the familiar observation of the universal compensations might suggest the fear that so summary a stop of a bad humor was more jeopardous than its continuance.

Now the correction of this quack practice is to import into Education the wisdom of life. Leave this military hurry and adopt the pace of Nature. Her secret is patience. Do you know how the naturalist learns all the secrets of the forest, of plants, of birds, of beasts, of reptiles, of fishes, of the rivers and the sea? When he goes into the woods the birds fly before him and he finds none; when he goes to the river bank, the fish and the reptile swim away and leave him alone. His secret is patience; he sits down, and sits still; he is a statue; he is a log. These creatures have no value for their time, and he must put as low a rate on his. By dint of obstinate sitting still, reptile, fish, bird and beast, which all wish to return to their haunts, begin to return. He sits still; if they approach, he remains passive as the stone he sits upon. They lose their fear. They have curiosity too about him. By and by the curiosity masters the fear, and they come swimming, creeping and flying towards him; and as he is still immovable, they not only resume their haunts and their ordinary labors and manners, show themselves to him in their work-day trim, but also volunteer some degree of advances towards fellowship and good understanding with a biped who behaves so civilly and well. Can you not baffle the impatience and passion of the child by your tranquility? Can you not wait for him, as Nature and Providence do? Can you not keep for his mind and ways, for his secret, the same curiosity you give to the squirrel, snake, rabbit, and the sheldrake and the deer? He has a secret; wonderful methods in him; he is—every child—a new style of man; give him time and opportunity. Talk of Columbus and Newton! I tell you the child just born in yonder hovel is the beginning of a revolution as great as theirs. But you must have the believing and prophetic eye. Have the self-command you wish to inspire. Your teaching and discipline must have the reserve and taciturnity of Nature. Teach them to hold their tongues by holding your own. Say little; do not snarl; do not chide; but govern by the eye. See what they need, and that the right thing is done.

I confess myself utterly at a loss in suggesting particular reforms in our ways of teaching. No discretion that can be lodged with a school-committee, with the overseers or visitors of an academy, of a college, can at all avail to reach these difficulties and perplexities, but they solve themselves when we leave institutions and address individuals. The will, the male power, organizes, imposes its own thought and wish on others, and makes that military eye which controls boys as it controls men; admirable in its results, a fortune to him who has it, and only dangerous when it leads the workman to overvalue and overuse it and precludes him from finer means. Sympathy, the female force—which they must use who have not the first—deficient in instant control and the breaking down of resistance, is more subtle and lasting and creative. I advise teachers to cherish mother-wit. I assume that you will keep the grammar, reading, writing and arithmetic in order; 'tis easy and of course you will. But smuggle in a little contraband wit, fancy, imagination, thought. If you have a taste which you have suppressed because it is not shared by those about you, tell them that. Set this law up, whatever becomes of the rules of the school: they must not whisper, much less talk; but if one of the young people says a wise thing, greet it, and let all the children clap their hands. They shall have no book but school-books in the room; but if one has brought in a Plutarch or Shakespeare or Don Quixote or Goldsmith or any other good book, and understands what he reads, put him at once at the head of the class. Nobody shall be disorderly, or leave his desk without permission, but if a boy runs from his bench, or a girl, because the fire falls, or to check some injury that a little dastard is inflicting behind his desk on some helpless sufferer, take away the medal from the head of the class and give it on the instant to the brave rescuer. If a child happens to show that he knows any fact about astronomy, or plants, or birds, or rocks, or history, that interests him and you, hush all the classes and encourage him to tell it so that all may hear. Then you have made your school-room like the world. Of course you will insist on modesty in the children, and respect to their teachers, but if the boy stops you in your speech, cries out that you are wrong and sets you right, hug him!

To whatsoever upright mind, to whatsoever beating heart I speak, to you it is committed to educate men. By simple living, by an illimitable soul, you inspire, you correct, you instruct, you raise, you embellish all. By your own act you teach the beholder how to do the practicable. According to the depth from which you draw your life, such is the depth not only of your strenuous effort, but of your manners and presence.

The beautiful nature of the world has here blended your happiness with your power. Work straight on in absolute duty, and you lend an arm and an encouragement to all the youth of the universe. Consent yourself to be an organ of your highest thought, and lo! suddenly you put all men in your debt, and are the fountain of an energy that goes pulsing on with waves of benefit to the borders of society, to the circumference of things.

MEMORY

MEMORY is a primary and fundamental faculty, without which none other can work; the cement, the bitumen, the matrix in which the other faculties are imbedded; or it is the thread on which the beads of man are strung, making the personal identity which is necessary to moral action. Without it all life and thought were an unrelated succession. As gravity holds matter from flying off into space, so memory gives stability to knowledge; it is the cohesion which keeps things from falling into a lump, or flowing in waves.

We like longevity, we like signs of riches and extent of nature in an individual. And most of all we like a great memory. The lowest life remembers. The sparrow, the ant, the worm, have the same memory as we. If you bar their path, or offer them somewhat disagreeable to their senses, they make one or two trials, and then once for all avoid it.

Every machine must be perfect of its sort. It is essential to a locomotive that it can reverse its movement, and run backward and forward with equal celerity. The builder of the mind found it not less needful that it should have retroaction, and command its past act and deed. Perception, though it were immense and could pierce through the universe, was not sufficient.

Memory performs the impossible for man by the strength of his divine arms; holds together past and present, beholding both, existing in both, abides in the flowing, and gives continuity and dignity to human life. It holds us to our family, to our friends. Hereby a home is possible; hereby only a new fact has value.

Opportunities of investment are useful only to those who have capital. Any piece of knowledge I acquire today, a fact that falls under my eyes, a book I read, a piece of news I hear, has a value at this moment exactly proportioned to my skill to deal with it. Tomorrow, when I know more, I recall that piece of knowledge and use it better.

The Past has a new value every moment to the active mind, through the incessant purification and better method of its memory. Once it joined its facts by color and form and sensuous relations. Some fact that had a childish significance to your childhood and was a type in the nursery, when riper intelligence recalls it means more and serves you better as an illustration; and perhaps in your age has new meaning. What was an isolated, unrelated belief or conjecture, our later experience instructs us how to place in just connection with other views which confirm and expand it. The old whim or perception was an augury of a broader insight, at which we arrive later with securer conviction. This is the companion, this the tutor, the poet, the library, with which you travel. It does not lie, cannot be corrupted, reports to you not what you wish but what really befell. You say, "I can never think of some act of neglect, of selfishness, or of passion without pain." Well, that is as it should be. That is the police of the Universe: the angels are set to punish you, so long as you are capable of such crime. But in the history of character the day comes when you are incapable of such crime. Then you suffer no more, you look on it as heaven looks on it, with wonder at the deed, and with applause at the pain it has cost you.

Memory is not a pocket, but a living instructor, with a prophetic sense of the values which he guards; a guardian angel set there within you to record your life, and by recording to animate you to uplift it. It is a scripture written day by day from the birth of the man; all its records full of meanings which open as he lives on, explaining each other, explaining the world to him and expanding their sense as he advances, until it shall become the whole law of nature and life.

As every creature is furnished with teeth to seize and eat, and with stomach to digest its food, so the memory is furnished with a perfect apparatus. There is no book like the memory, none with such a good index, and that of every kind, alphabetic, systematic, arranged by names of persons, by colors, tastes, smells, shapes, likeness, unlikeness, by all sorts of mysterious hooks and eyes to catch and hold, and contrivances for giving a hint.

The memory collects and re-collects. We figure it as if the mind were a kind of looking-glass, which being carried through the street of time receives on its clear plate every image that passes; only with this difference that our plate is iodized so that every image sinks into it, and is held there. But in addition to this property it has one more, this, namely, that of all the million images that are imprinted, the very one we want reappears in the center of the plate in the moment when we want it.

We can tell much about it, but you must not ask us what it is. On seeing a face I am aware that I have seen it before, or that I have not seen it before. On hearing a fact told I am aware that I knew it already. You say the first words of the old song, and I finish the line and the stanza. But where I have them, or what becomes of them when I am not thinking of them for months and years, that they should lie so still, as if they did not exist, and yet so nigh that they come on the instant when they are called for, never any man was so sharp-sighted, or could turn himself inside out quick enough to find.

'Tis because of the believed incompatibility of the affirmative and advancing attitude of the mind with tenacious acts of recollection that people are often reproached with living in their memory. Late in life we live by memory, and in our solstices or periods of stagnation; as the starved camel in the desert lives on his humps. Memory was called by the schoolmen *vespertina cognitio*, evening knowledge, in distinction from the command of the future which we have by the knowledge of causes, and which they called *matutina cognitio*, or morning knowledge.

Am I asked whether the thoughts clothe themselves in words? I answer, Yes, always; but they are apt to be instantly forgotten. Never was truer fable than that of the Sibyl's writing on leaves which the wind scatters. The difference between men is that in one the memory with inconceivable swiftness flies after and re-collects the flying leaves—flies on wing as fast as that mysterious whirlwind, and the envious Fate is baffled.

This command of old facts, the clear beholding at will of what is best in our experience, is our splendid privilege. "He who calls what is vanished back again into being enjoys a bliss like that of creating," says Niebuhr. The memory plays a great part in settling the intellectual rank of men. We estimate a man by how much he remembers. A seneschal of Parnassus is Mnemosyne. This power will alone make a man remarkable; and it is found in all good wits. Therefore the poets represented the Muses as the daughters of Memory, for the power exists in some marked and eminent degree in men of an ideal determination. Quintilian reckoned it the measure of genius. *"Tantum ingenii quantum memoriae."*

We are told that Boileau having recited to Daguesseau one day an epistle or satire he had just been composing, Daguesseau tranquilly told him he knew it already, and in proof set himself to recite it from end to end. Boileau, astonished, was much distressed until he perceived that it was only a feat of memory.

The mind disposes all its experience after its affection and to its ruling end; one man by puns and one by cause and effect, one to heroic benefit and one to wrath and animal desire. This is the high difference, the quality of the association by which a man remembers. In the minds of most men memory is nothing but a farm-book or a pocket-diary. On such a day I paid my note; on the next day the cow calved; on the next I cut my finger; on the next the banks suspended payment. But another man's memory is the history of science and art and civility and thought; and still another deals with laws and perceptions that are the theory of the world.

This thread or order of remembering, this classification, distributes men, one remembering by shop-rule or interest; one by passion; one by trifling external marks, as dress or money. And one rarely takes an interest in how the facts really stand, in the order of cause and effect, without self-reference. This is an intellectual man. Nature interests him; a plant, a fish, time, space, mind, being, in their own method and law. Napoleon was such, and that saves him.

But this mysterious power that binds our life together has its own vagaries and interruptions. It sometimes occurs that memory has a personality of its own, and volunteers or refuses its informations at its will, not at mine. One sometimes asks himself, Is it possible that it is only a visitor, not a resident? Is it some old aunt who goes in and out of the house, and occasionally recites anecdotes of old times and persons which I recognize as having heard before, and she being gone again I search in vain for any trace of the anecdotes?

We can help ourselves to the *modus* of mental processes only by coarse material experiences. A knife with a good spring, a forceps whose lips accurately meet and match, a steel-trap, a loom, a watch, the teeth or jaws of which fit and play perfectly, as compared with the same tools when badly put together, describe to us the difference between a person of quick and strong perception, like Franklin or Swift or Webster or Richard Owen, and a heavy man who witnesses the same facts or shares experiences like theirs. 'Tis like the impression made by the same stamp in sand or in wax. The way in which Burke or Sheridan or Webster or any orator surprises us is by his always having a sharp tool that fits the present use. He has an old story, an odd circumstance, that illustrates the point he is now proving, and is better than an argument. The more he is heated, the wider he sees; he seems to remember all he ever knew; thus certifying us that he is in the habit of seeing better than other people; that what his mind grasps it does not let go. 'Tis the bull-dog bite; you must cut off the head to loosen the teeth.

We hate this fatal shortness of Memory, these docked men whom we behold. We gathered up what a rolling snow-ball as we came along—much of it professedly for the future, as capital stock of knowledge. Where is it now? Look behind you. I cannot see that your train is any longer than it was in childhood. The facts of the last two or three days or weeks are all you have with you— the reading of the last month's books. Your conversation, action, your face and manners report of no more, of no greater wealth of mind. Alas! you have lost something for everything you have gained, and cannot grow. Only so much iron will the load-stone draw; it gains new particles all the way as you move it, but one falls off for every one that adheres.

As there is strength in the wild horse which is never regained when he is once broken by training, and as there is a sound sleep of children and of savages, profound as the hibernation of bears, which never visits the eyes of civil gentlemen and ladies, so there is a wild memory in children and youth which makes what is early learned impossible to forget; and perhaps in the beginning of the world it had most vigor. Plato deplores writing as a barbarous invention which would weaken the memory by disuse. The Rhapsodists in Athens it seems could recite at once any passage of Homer that was desired.

If writing weakens the memory, we may say as much and more of printing. What is the newspaper but a sponge or invention for oblivion? the rule being that for every fact added to the memory, one is crowded out, and that only what the affection animates can be remembered.

The mind has a better secret in generalization than merely adding units to its list of facts. The reason of the short memory is shallow thought. As deep as the thought, so great is the attraction. An act of the understanding will marshal and concatenate a few facts; a principle of the reason will thrill and magnetize and redistribute the whole world.

But defect of memory is not always want of genius. By no means. It is sometimes owing to excellence of genius. Thus men of great presence of mind who are always equal to the occasion do not need to rely on what they have stored for use, but can think in this moment as well and deeply as in any past moment, and if they cannot remember the rule they can make one. Indeed it is remarked that inventive men have bad memories. Sir

Isaac Newton was embarrassed when the conversation turned on his discoveries and results; he could not recall them; but if he was asked why things were so or so he could find the reason on the spot.

A man would think twice about learning a new science or reading a new paragraph, if he believed the magnetism was only a constant amount, and that he lost a word or a thought for every word he gained. But the experience is not quite so bad. In reading a foreign language, every new word mastered is a lamp lighting up related words and so assisting the memory. Apprehension of the whole sentence aids to fix the precise meaning of a particular word, and what familiarity has been acquired with the genius of the language and the writer helps in fixing the exact meaning of the sentence. So is it with every fact in a new science: they are mutually explaining, and each one adds transparency to the whole mass.

The damages of forgetting are more than compensated by the large values which new thoughts and knowledge give to what we already know. If new impressions sometimes efface old ones, yet we steadily gain insight; and because all nature has one law and meaning —part corresponding to part—all we have known aids us continually to the knowledge of the rest of nature. Thus, all the facts in this chest of memory are property at interest. And who shall set a boundary to this mounting value? Shall we not on higher stages of being remember and understand our early history better?

They say in Architecture, "An arch never sleeps"; I say, the Past will not sleep, it works still. With every new fact a ray of light shoots up from the long buried years. Who can judge the new book? He who has read many books. Who, the new assertion? He who has heard many the like. Who, the new man? He that has seen men. The experienced and cultivated man is lodged in a hall hung with pictures which every new day retouches, and to which every step in the march of the soul adds a more sublime perspective.

We learn early that there is great disparity of value between our experiences; some thoughts perish in the using. Some days are bright with thought and sentiment, and we live a year in a day. Yet these best days are not always those which memory can retain. This water once spilled cannot be gathered. There are more inventions in the thoughts of one happy day than ages could execute, and I suppose I speak the sense of most thoughtful men when I say, I would rather have a perfect recollection of all I have thought and felt in a day or a week of high activity than read all the books that have been published in a century.

The memory is one of the compensations which Nature grants to those who have used their days well; when age and calamity have bereaved them of their limbs or organs, then they retreat on mental faculty and concentrate on that. The poet, the philosopher, lamed, old, blind, sick, yet disputing the ground inch by inch against fortune, finds a strength against the wrecks and decays sometimes more invulnerable than the heyday of youth and talent.

I value the praise of Memory. And how does Memory praise? By holding fast the best. A thought takes its true rank in the memory by surviving other thoughts that were once preferred. Plato remembered Anaxagoras by one of his sayings. If we recall our own favorites we shall usually find that it is for one crowning act or thought that we hold them dear.

Have you not found memory an apotheosis or deification? The poor, short lone fact dies at the birth. Memory catches it up into her heaven, and bathes it in immortal waters. Then a thousand times over it lives and acts again, each time transfigured, ennobled. In solitude, in darkness, we tread over again the sunny walks of youth; confined now in populous streets you behold again the green fields, the shadows of the gray birches; by the solitary river hear again the joyful voices of early companions, and vibrate anew to the tenderness and dainty music of the poetry your boyhood fed upon. At this hour the stream is still flowing, though you hear it not; the plants are still drinking their accustomed life and repaying it with their beautiful forms. But you need not wander thither. It flows for you, and they grow for you, in the returning images of former summers. In low or bad company you fold yourself in your cloak, withdraw yourself entirely from all the doleful circumstance, recall and surround yourself with the best associates and the fairest hours of your life—

Passing sweet are the domains of tender memory.

You may perish out of your senses, but not out of your memory or imagination.

The memory has a fine art of sifting out the pain and keeping all the joy. The spring days when the bluebird arrives have usually only few hours of fine temperature, are sour and unlovely; but when late in autumn we hear rarely a bluebird's notes they are sweet by reminding us of the spring. Well, it is so with other tricks of memory. Of the most romantic fact the memory is more romantic; and this power of sinking the pain of any experience and of recalling the saddest with tranquility, and even with a wise pleasure, is familiar. The memory is as the affection. Sampson Reed says, "The true way to store the memory is to develop the affections." A *souvenir* is a token of love. *Remember me* means, Do not cease to love me. We remember those things which we love and those things which we hate. The memory of all men is robust on the subject of a debt due to them, or of an insult inflicted on them. "They can remember," as Johnson said, "who kicked them last."

Every artist is alive on the subject of his art. The Persians say, "A real singer will never forget the song he has once learned." Michael Angelo, after having once seen a work of any other artist, would remember it so perfectly that if it pleased him to make use of any portion thereof, he could do so, but in such a manner that none could perceive it.

We remember what we understand, and we understand best what we like; for this doubles our power of attention, and makes it our own. Captain John Brown, of Ossawatomie, said he had in Ohio three thousand sheep on his farm, and could tell a strange sheep in his flock as soon as he saw its face. One of my neighbors, a grazier, told me that he should know again every cow, ox, or steer that he ever saw. Abel Lawton knew every horse that went up and down through Concord to the towns in the county. And in higher examples each man's memory is in the line of his action.

Nature trains us on to see illusions and prodigies with no more wonder than our toast and omelet at breakfast. Talk of memory and cite me these fine examples of Grotius and Daguesseau, and I think how awful is that power and what privilege and tyranny it must confer. Then I come to a bright schoolgirl who remembers all she hears, carries thousands of nursery rhymes and all the poetry in all the readers, hymn books, and pictorial ballads in her mind; and 'tis a mere drug. She carries it so carelessly, it seems like the profusion of hair on the shock heads of all the village boys and village dogs; it grows like grass. 'Tis a bushel-basket memory of all unchosen knowledge, heaped together in a huge hamper, without method, yet securely held, and ready to come at call; so that an old scholar, who knows what to do with a memory, is full of wonder and pity that this magical force should be squandered on such frippery.

He is a skilful doctor who can give me a recipe for the cure of a bad memory. And yet we have some hints from experience on this subject. And first, *health*. It is found that we remember best when the head is clear, when we are thoroughly awake. When the body is in a quiescent state in the absence of the passions, in the moderation of food, it yields itself a willing medium to the intellect. For the true river Lethe is the body of man, with its belly and uproar of appetite and mountains of indigestion and bad humors and quality of darkness. And for this reason, and observing some mysterious continuity of mental operation during sleep or when our will is suspended, 'tis an old rule of scholars, that which Fuller records, "'Tis best knocking in the nail overnight and clinching it next morning." Only I should give extension to this rule and say Yes, drive the nail this week and clinch it the next, and drive it this year and clinch it the next.

But Fate also is an artist. We forget also according to beautiful laws. Thoreau said, "Of what significance are the things you can forget. A little thought is sexton to all the world."

We must be severe with ourselves, and what we wish to keep we must once thoroughly possess. Then the thing seen will no longer be what it was, a mere sensuous object before the eye or ear, but a reminder of its law, a possession for the intellect. Then we relieve ourselves of all task in the matter, we put the *onus* of being remembered on the object, instead of on our will. We shall do as we do with all our studies, prize the fact or the name of the person by that predominance it takes in our mind after near acquaintance. I have several times forgotten the name of Flamsteed, never that of Newton; and can drop easily many poets out of the Elizabethan chronology, but not Shakespeare.

We forget rapidly what should be forgotten. The *universal* sense of fables and anecdotes is marked by our tendency to forget name and date and geography. "How in the right are children," said Margaret Fuller, "to forget name and date and place."

You cannot overstate our debt to the past, but has the present no claim? This past memory is the baggage, but where is the troop? The divine gift is not the old but the new. The divine is the instant life that receives and uses, the life that can well bury the old in the omnipotency with which it makes all things new.

The acceleration of mental process is equivalent to the lengthening of life. If a great many thoughts pass through your mind you will believe a long time has elapsed, many hours or days. In dreams a rush of many thoughts, of seeming experiences, of spending hours and going through a great variety of actions and companies, and when we start up and look at the watch, instead of a long night we are surprised to find it was a short nap. The opium-eater says, "I sometimes seemed to have lived seventy or a hundred years in one night." You know what is told of the experience of some persons who have been recovered from drowning. They relate that their whole life's history seemed to pass before them in review. They remembered in a moment all that they ever did.

If we occupy ourselves long on this wonderful faculty, and see the natural helps of it in the mind, and the way in which new knowledge calls upon old knowledge— new giving undreamed-of value to old; everywhere relation and suggestion, so that what one had painfully held by strained attention and recapitulation now falls into place and is clamped and locked by inevitable connection as a planet in its orbit (every other orb, or the law or system of which it is a part, being a perpetual reminder)—we cannot fail to draw thence a sublime hint that thus there must be an endless increase in the power of memory only through its use; that there must be a proportion between the power of memory and the amount of knowables; and since the Universe opens to us, the reach of the memory must be as large.

With every broader generalization which the mind makes, with every deeper insight, its retrospect is also wider. With every new insight into the duty or fact of today we come into new possession of the past.

When we live by principles instead of traditions, by obedience to the law of the mind instead of by passion, the Great Mind will enter into us, not as now in fragments and detached thoughts, but the light of today will shine backward and forward.

Memory is a presumption of a possession of the future. Now we are halves, we see the past but not the future, but in that day will the hemisphere complete itself and foresight be as perfect as aftersight.

QUOTATION
AND ORIGINALITY

WHOEVER looks at the insect world, at flies, aphides, gnats, and innumerable parasites, and even at the infant mammals, must have remarked the extreme content they take in suction, which constitutes the main business of their life. If we go into a library or news-room, we see the same function on a higher plane, performed with like ardor, with equal impatience of interruption, indicating the sweetness of the act. In the highest civilization the book is still the highest delight. He who has once known its satisfactions is provided with a resource against calamity. Like Plato's disciple who has perceived a truth, "he is preserved from harm until another period." In every man's memory, with the hours when life culminated are usually associated certain books which met his views. Of a large and powerful class we might ask with confidence, What is the event they most desire? what gift? What but the book that shall come, which they have sought through all libraries, through all languages, that shall be to their mature eyes what many a tinsel-covered toy pamphlet was to their childhood, and shall speak to the imagination? Our high respect for a well-read man is praise enough of literature. If we encountered a man of rare intellect, we should ask him what books he read. We expect a great man to be a good reader; or in proportion to the spontaneous power should be the assimilating power. And though such are a more difficult and exacting class, they are not less eager. "He that borrows the aid of an equal understanding," said Burke, "doubles his own; he that uses that of a superior elevates his own to the stature of that he contemplates."

We prize books, and they prize them most who are themselves wise. Our debt to tradition through reading and conversation is so massive, our protest or private addition so rare and insignificant—and this commonly on the ground of other reading or hearing—that, in a large sense, one would say there is no pure originality. All minds quote. Old and new make the warp and woof of every moment. There is no thread that is not a twist of these two strands. By necessity, by proclivity, and by delight, we all quote. We quote not only books and proverbs, but arts, sciences, religion, customs, and laws; nay, we quote temples and houses, tables and chairs by imitation. The Patent-Office Commissioner knows that all machines in use have been invented and re-invented over and over; that the mariner's compass, the boat, the pendulum, glass, movable types, the kaleidoscope, the railway, the power-loom, etc., have been many times found and lost, from Egypt, China, and Pompeii down; and if we have arts which Rome wanted, so also Rome had arts which we have lost; that the invention of yesterday of making wood indestructible by means of vapor of coal-oil or paraffine was suggested by the Egyptian method which has preserved its mummy-cases four thousand years.

The highest statement of new philosophy complacently caps itself with some prophetic maxim from the oldest learning. There is something mortifying in this perpetual circle. This extreme economy argues a very small capital of invention. The stream of affection flows broad and strong; the practical activity is a river of supply; but the dearth of design accuses the penury of intellect. How few thoughts! In a hundred years, millions of men and not a hundred lines of poetry, not a theory of philosophy that offers a solution of the great problems, not an art of education that fulfills the conditions. In this delay and vacancy of thought we must make the best amends we can by seeking the wisdom of others to fill the time.

If we confine ourselves to literature, 'tis easy to see that the debt is immense to past thought. None escapes it. The originals are not original. There is imitation, model, and suggestion, to the very archangels, if we knew their history. The first book tyrannizes over the second. Read Tasso, and you think of Virgil; read Virgil, and you think of Homer; and Milton forces you to reflect how narrow are the limits of human invention. The "Paradise Lost" had never existed but for these precursors; and if we find in India or Arabia a book out of our horizon of thought and tradition, we are soon taught by new researches in its native country to discover its foregoers, and its latent, but real connection with our own Bibles.

Read in Plato and you shall find Christian dogmas, and not only so, but stumble on our evangelical phrases. Hegel pre-exists in Proclus, and, long before, in Heraclitus and Parmenides. Whoso knows Plutarch, Lucian, Rabelais, Montaigne and Bayle will have a key to many supposed originalities. Rabelais is the source of many a proverb, story, and jest, derived from him into all modern languages; and if we knew Rabelais's reading we should see the rill of the Rabelais river. Swedenborg, Behmen, Spinoza, will appear original to uninstructed and to thoughtless persons: their originality will disappear to such as are either well-read or thoughtful; for scholars will recognize their dogmas as reappearing in men of a similar intellectual elevation throughout history. Albert, the "wonderful doctor," St. Buonaventura, the "seraphic doctor," Thomas Aquinas, the "angelic doctor" of the thirteenth century, whose books made the sufficient culture of these ages, Dante absorbed, and he survives for us. "Renard the Fox," a German poem of the thirteenth century, was long supposed to be the original work, until Grimm found fragments of another original a century older. M. Le Grand showed that in the old *fabliaux* were the originals of the tales of Molière, La Fontaine, Boccaccio, and of Voltaire.

Mythology is no man's work; but, what we daily observe in regard to the *bon-mots* that circulate in society

—that every talker helps a story in repeating it, until, at last, from the slenderest filament of fact a good fable is constructed—the same growth befalls mythology: the legend is tossed from believer to poet, from poet to believer, everybody adding a grace or dropping a fault or rounding the form, until it gets an ideal truth.

Religious literature, the psalms and liturgies of churches, are of course of this slow growth—a fagot of selections gathered through ages, leaving the worse and saving the better, until it is at last the work of the whole communion of worshippers. The Bible itself is like an old Cremona; it has been played upon by the devotion of thousands of years until every word and particle is public and tunable. And whatever undue reverence may have been claimed for it by the prestige of philonic inspiration, the stronger tendency we are describing is likely to undo. What divines had assumed as the distinctive revelations of Christianity, theologic criticism has matched by exact parallelisms from the Stoics and poets of Greece and Rome. Later, when Confucius and the Indian scriptures were made known, no claim to monopoly of ethical wisdom could be thought of; and the surprising results of the new researches into the history of Egypt have opened to us the deep debt of the churches of Rome and England to the Egyptian hierology.

The borrowing is often honest enough, and comes of magnanimity and stoutness. A great man quotes bravely, and will not draw on his invention when his memory serves him with a word as good. What he quotes, he fills with his own voice and humor, and the whole cyclopedia of his table-talk is presently believed to be his own. Thirty years ago, when Mr. Webster at the bar or in the Senate filled the eyes and minds of young men, you

might often hear cited as Mr. Webster's three rules:
first, never to do today what he could defer till tomorrow; secondly, never to do himself what he could make
another do for him; and, thirdly, never to pay any debt
today. Well, they are none the worse for being already
told, in the last generation, of Sheridan; and we find in
Grimm's *Mémoires* that Sheridan got them from the
witty D'Argenson; who, no doubt, if we could consult
him, could tell of whom he first heard them told. In our
own college days we remember hearing other pieces of
Mr. Webster's advice to students—among others, this:
that, when he opened a new book, he turned to the table
of contents, took a pen, and sketched a sheet of matters
and topics, what he knew and what he thought, before
he read the book. But we find in Southey's *Commonplace Book* this said of the Earl of Strafford: "I learned
one rule of him," says Sir G. Radcliffe, "which I think
worthy to be remembered. When he met with a well-
penned oration or tract upon any subject, he framed a
speech upon the same argument, inventing and dispos-
ing what seemed fit to be said upon that subject, before
he read the book; then, reading, compared his own with
the author's, and noted his own defects and the author's
art and fulness; whereby he drew all that ran in the
author more strictly, and might better judge of his own
wants to supply them." I remember to have heard Mr.
Samuel Rogers, in London, relate, among other anecdotes of the Duke of Wellington, that a lady having expressed in his presence a passionate wish to witness a
great victory, he replied: "Madam, there is nothing so
dreadful as a great victory—excepting a great defeat."
But this speech is also D'Argenson's, and is reported by
Grimm. So the sarcasm attributed to Baron Alderson
upon Brougham, "What a wonderful versatile mind has

Brougham! he knows politics, Greek, history, science; if he only knew a little of law, he would know a little of everything." You may find the original of this gibe in Grimm, who says that Louis XVI, going out of chapel after hearing a sermon from the Abbé Maury, said, "*Si l'Abbé nous avait parlé un peu de religion, il nous aurait parlé de tout.*" A pleasantry which ran through all the newspapers a few years since, taxing the eccentricities of a gifted family connection in New England, was only a theft of Lady Mary Wortley Montagu's *mot* of a hundred years ago, that "the world was made up of men and women and Herveys."

Many of the historical proverbs have a doubtful paternity. Columbus's egg is claimed for Brunelleschi. Rabelais's dying words, "I am going to see the great Perhaps" (*le grand Peut-être*), only repeats the "IF" inscribed on the portal of the temple at Delphi. Goethe's favorite phrase, "the open secret," translates Aristotle's answer to Alexander, "These books are published and not published." Madame de Staël's "Architecture is frozen music" is borrowed from Goethe's "dumb music," which is Vitruvius's rule, that "the architect must not only understand drawing, but music." Wordsworth's hero acting "on the plan which pleased his childish thought," is Schiller's "Tell him to reverence the dreams of his youth," and earlier, Bacon's "*Consilia juventutis plus divinitatis habent.*"

In romantic literature examples of this vamping abound. The fine verse in the old Scotch ballad of "The Drowned Lovers,"

> Thou art roaring ower loud, Clyde water.
>   Thy streams are ower strang;
> Make me thy wrack when I come back,
>   But spare me when I gang,

is a translation of Martial's epigram on Hero and Leander, where the prayer of Leander is the same—

> Parcite dum propero, mergite dum redeo.

Hafiz furnished Burns with the song of "John Barleycorn," and furnished Moore with the original of the piece,

> When in death I shall calm recline
> Oh, bear my heart to my mistress dear, etc.

There are many fables which, as they are found in every language, and betray no sign of being borrowed, are said to be agreeable to the human mind. Such are *The Seven Sleepers, Gyges's Ring, The Travelling Cloak, The Wandering Jew, The Pied Piper, Jack and his Beanstalk,* the *Lady Diving in the Lake and Rising in the Cave,* whose omnipresence only indicates how easily a good story crosses all frontiers. The popular incident of Baron Munchausen, who hung his bugle up by the kitchen fire and the frozen tune thawed out, is found in Greece in Plato's time. Antiphanes, one of Plato's friends, laughingly compared his writings to a city where the words froze in the air as soon as they were pronounced, and the next summer, when they were warmed and melted by the sun, the people heard what had been spoken in the winter. It is only within this century that England and America discovered that their nursery-tales were old German and Scandinavian stories; and now it appears that they came from India, and are the property of all the nations descended from the Aryan race, and have been warbled and babbled between nurses and children for unknown thousands of years.

If we observe the tenacity with which nations cling

to their first types of costume, of architecture, of tools and methods in tillage, and of decoration—if we learn how old are the patterns of our shawls, the capitals of our columns, the fret, the beads, and other ornaments on our walls, the alternate lotus-bud and leaf-stem of our iron fences—we shall think very well of the first men, or ill of the latest.

Now shall we say that only the first men were well alive, and the existing generation is invalided and degenerate? Is all literature eavesdropping, and all art Chinese imitation? our life a custom, and our body borrowed, like a beggar's dinner, from a hundred charities? A more subtle and severe criticism might suggest that some dislocation has befallen the race; that men are off their center; that multitudes of men do not live with Nature, but behold it as exiles. People go out to look at sunrises and sunsets who do not recognize their own, quietly and happily, but know that it is foreign to them. As they do by books, so they *quote* the sunset and the star, and do not make them theirs. Worse yet, they live as foreigners in the world of truth, and quote thoughts, and thus disown them. Quotation confesses inferiority. In opening a new book we often discover, from the unguarded devotion with which the writer gives his motto or text, all we have to expect from him. If Lord Bacon appears already in the preface, I go and read the *Instauration* instead of the new book.

The mischief is quickly punished in general and in particular. Admirable mimics have nothing of their own. In every kind of parasite, when Nature has finished an aphis, a teredo, or a vampire bat—an excellent sucking-pipe to tap another animal, or a mistletoe or dodder among plants—the self-supplying organs wither and dwindle, as being superfluous. In common prudence there is an early limit to this leaning on an original. In literature, quotation is good only when the writer whom I follow goes my way, and, being better mounted than I, gives me a cast, as we say; but if I like the gay equipage so well as to go out of my road, I had better have gone afoot.

But it is necessary to remember there are certain considerations which go far to qualify a reproach too grave. This vast mental indebtedness has every variety that pecuniary debt has—every variety of merit. The capitalist of either kind is as hungry to lend as the consumer to borrow; and the transaction no more indicates intellectual turpitude in the borrower than the simple fact of debt involves bankruptcy. On the contrary, in far the greater number of cases the transaction is honorable to both. Can we not help ourselves as discreetly by the force of two in literature? Certainly it only needs two well placed and well tempered for cooperation, to get somewhat far transcending any private enterprise! Shall we converse as spies? Our very abstaining to repeat and credit the fine remark of our friend is thievish. Each man of thought is surrounded by wiser men than he, if they cannot write as well. Cannot he and they combine? Cannot they sink their jealousies in God's love, and call their poem Beaumont and Fletcher, or the Theban Phalanx's? The city will for nine days or nine years make differences and sinister comparisons: there is a new and more excellent public that will bless the friends. Nay, it is an inevitable fruit of our social nature. The child quotes his father, and the man quotes his friend. Each man is a hero and an oracle to somebody, and to that person whatever he says has an enhanced value. Whatever we think and say is wonderfully better for our spirits and trust, in another mouth. There is none so eminent and wise but he knows minds whose opinion confirms or qualifies his own, and men of extraordinary genius acquire an almost absolute ascendant over their nearest companions. The Comte de Crillon said one day to M. d'Allonville, with French vivacity, "If the universe and I professed one opinion and M. Necker expressed a contrary one, I should be at once convinced that the universe and I were mistaken."

Original power is usually accompanied with assimilating power, and we value in Coleridge his excellent knowledge and quotations perhaps as much, possibly more, than his original suggestions. If an author give us just distinctions, inspiring lessons, or imaginative poetry, it is not so important to us whose they are. If we are fired and guided by these, we know him as a benefactor, and shall return to him as long as he serves us so well. We may like well to know what is Plato's and what is Montesquieu's or Goethe's part, and what thought was always dear to the writer himself; but the worth of the sentences consists in their radiancy and equal aptitude to all intelligence. They fit all our facts like a charm. We respect ourselves the more that we know them.

Next to the originator of a good sentence is the first quoter of it. Many will read the book before one thinks of quoting a passage. As soon as he has done this, that line will be quoted east and west. Then there are great ways of borrowing. Genius borrows nobly. When Shakespeare is charged with debts to his authors, Landor replies: "Yet he was more original than his originals. He breathed upon dead bodies and brought them into life." And we must thank Karl Ottfried Müller for the just remark, "Poesy, drawing within its circle all that is glorious and inspiring, gave itself but little concern as to where its flowers originally grew." So Voltaire usually imitated, but with such superiority that Dubuc said: "He is like the false Amphitryon; although the stranger, it is always he who has the air of being master of the house." Wordsworth, as soon as he heard a good thing, caught it up, meditated upon it, and very soon reproduced it in his conversation and writing. If De Quincey said, "That is what I told you," he replied, "No: that is mine—mine, and not yours." On the whole, we like the valor of it. 'Tis on Marmontel's principle, "I pounce on what is mine, wherever I find it"; and on Bacon's broader rule, "I take all knowledge to be my province." It betrays the consciousness that truth is the property of no individual, but is the treasure of all men. And inasmuch as any writer has ascended to a just view of man's condition, he has adopted this tone. In so far as the receiver's aim is on life, and not on literature, will be his indifference to the source. The nobler the truth or sentiment, the less imports the question of authorship. It never troubles the simple seeker from whom he derived such or such a sentiment. Whoever expresses to us a just thought makes ridiculous the pains of the critic who should tell him where such a word had been said before. "It is no more according to Plato than according to me." Truth is always present: it only needs to lift the iron lids of the mind's eye to read its oracles. But the moment there is the purpose of display, the fraud is exposed. In fact, it is as difficult to appropriate the thoughts of others, as it is to invent. Always some steep transition, some sudden alteration of temperature, or of point of view, betrays the foreign interpolation.

There is, besides, a new charm in such intellectual works as, passing through long time, have had a multitude of authors and improvers. We admire that poetry which no man wrote—no poet less than the genius of humanity itself—which is to be read in a mythology, in the effect of a fixed or national style of pictures, of sculptures, or drama, or cities, or sciences, on us. Such a poem also is language. Every word in the language has once been used happily. The ear, caught by that felicity, retains it, and it is used again and again, as if the charm belonged to the word and not to the life of thought which so enforced it. These profane uses, of course, kill it, and it is avoided. But a quick wit can at any time reinforce it, and it comes into vogue again. Then people quote so differently: one finding only what is gaudy and popular; another, the heart of the author, the report of his select and happiest hour; and the reader sometimes giving more to the citation than he owes to it. Most of the classical citations you shall hear or read in the current journals or speeches were not drawn from the originals, but from previous quotations in English books; and you can easily pronounce, from the use and relevancy of the sentence, whether it had not done duty many times before—whether your jewel was got from the mine or from an auctioneer. We are as much informed of a writer's genius by what he selects as by what he originates. We read the quotation with his eyes, and find a new and fervent sense; as a passage from one of the poets, well recited, borrows new interest from the rendering. As the journals say, "the italics are ours." The profit of books is according to the sensibility of the reader. The profoundest thought or passion sleeps as in a mine until an equal mind and heart finds and publishes it. The passages of Shakespeare that we most prize were never quoted until within this century; and Milton's prose, and Burke, even, have their best fame within it. Every one, too, remembers his friends by their favorite poetry or other reading.

Observe also that a writer appears to more advantage in the pages of another book than in his own. In his own he waits as a candidate for your approbation; in another's he is a lawgiver.

Then another's thoughts have a certain advantage

with us simply because they are another's. There is an illusion in a new phrase. A man hears a fine sentence out of Swedenborg, and wonders at the wisdom, and is very merry at heart that he has now got so fine a thing. Translate it out of the new words into his own usual phrase, and he will wonder again at his own simplicity, such tricks do fine words play with us.

It is curious what new interest an old author acquires by official canonization in Tiraboschi, or Dr. Johnson, or Von Hammer-Purgstall, or Hallam, or other historian of literature. Their registration of his book, or citation of a passage, carries the sentimental value of a college diploma. Hallam, though never profound, is a fair mind, able to appreciate poetry unless it becomes deep, being always blind and deaf to imaginative and analogy-loving souls, like the Platonists, like Giordano Bruno, like Donne, Herbert, Crashaw, and Vaughan; and Hallam cites a sentence from Bacon or Sidney, and distinguishes a lyric of Edwards or Vaux, and straightway it commends itself to us as if it had received the Isthmian crown.

It is a familiar expedient of brilliant writers, and not less of witty talkers, the device of ascribing their own sentence to an imaginary person, in order to give it weight—as Cicero, Cowley, Swift, Landor, and Carlyle have done. And Cardinal de Retz, at a critical moment in the Parliament of Paris, described himself in an extemporary Latin sentence, which he pretended to quote from a classic author, and which told admirably well. It is a curious reflex effect of this enhancement of our thought by citing it from another, that many men can write better under a mask than for themselves; as Chatterton in archaic ballad, Le Sage in Spanish costume, Macpherson as "Ossian"; and, I doubt not, many a young barrister in chambers in London, who forges good thunder for the *Times*, but never works as well under his own name. This is a sort of dramatizing talent; as it is not rare to find great powers of recitation, without the least original eloquence—or people who copy drawings with admirable skill, but are incapable of any design.

In hours of high mental activity we sometimes do the book too much honor, reading out of it better things than the author wrote—reading, as we say, between the lines. You have had the like experience in conversation: the wit was in what you heard, not in what the speakers said. Our best thought came from others. We heard in their words a deeper sense than the speakers put into them, and could express ourselves in other people's phrases to finer purpose than they knew. In Moore's *Diary*, Mr. Hallam is reported as mentioning at dinner one of his friends who had said, "I don't know how it is, a thing that falls flat from me seems quite an excellent joke when given at second-hand by Sheridan. I never like my own *bon-mots* until he adopts them." Dumont was exalted by being used by Mirabeau, by Bentham, and by Sir Philip Francis, who, again, was less than his own "Junius"; and James Hogg (except in his poems "Kilmeny" and "The Witch of Fife") is but a third-rate author, owing his fame to his effigy colossalized through the lens of John Wilson—who, again, writes better under the domino of "Christopher North" than in his proper clothes. The bold theory of Delia Bacon, that Shakespeare's plays were written by a society of wits— by Sir Walter Raleigh, Lord Bacon, and others around the Earl of Southampton—had plainly for her the charm of the superior meaning they would acquire when read under this light; this idea of the authorship controlling our appreciation of the works themselves. We once knew a man overjoyed at the notice of his pamphlet in a leading newspaper. What range he gave his imagination! Who could have written it? Was it not Colonel Carbine, or Senator Tonitrus, or, at the least, Professor Maximilian? Yes, he could detect in the style that fine Roman hand. How it seemed the very voice of the refined and discerning public, inviting merit at last to consent to fame, and come up and take place in the reserved and authentic chairs! He carried the journal with haste to the sympathizing Cousin Matilda, who is so proud of all we do. But what dismay when the good Matilda, pleased with his pleasure, confessed she had written the criticism, and carried it with her own hands to the post-office! "Mr. Wordsworth," said Charles Lamb, "allow me to introduce to you my only admirer."

Swedenborg threw a formidable theory into the world, that every soul existed in a society of souls, from which all its thoughts passed into it, as the blood of the mother circulates in her unborn child; and he noticed that, when in his bed, alternately sleeping and waking— sleeping, he was surrounded by persons disputing and offering opinions on the one side and on the other side of a proposition; waking, the like suggestions occurred for and against the proposition as his own thoughts; sleeping again, he saw and heard the speakers as before: and this as often as he slept or waked. And if we expand the image, does it not look as if we men were thinking and talking out of an enormous antiquity, as if we stood, not in a coterie of prompters that filled a sitting-room, but in a circle of intelligences that reached through all thinkers, poets, inventors, and wits, men and women, English, German, Celt, Aryan, Ninevite, Copt—back to the first geometer, bard, mason, carpenter, planter, shepherd—back to the first Negro, who, with more health or better perception, gave a shriller sound or name for the thing he saw and dealt with? Our benefactors are as many as the children who invented speech, word by word. Language is a city to the building of which every human being brought a stone; yet he is no more to be credited with the grand result than the acaleph which adds a cell to the coral reef which is the basis of the continent.

Πάντα ῥεῖ: all things are in flux. It is inevitable that you are indebted to the past. You are fed and formed by it. The old forest is decomposed for the composition of the new forest. The old animals have given their bodies to the earth to furnish through chemistry the forming race, and every individual is only a momentary fixation of what was yesterday another's, is today his, and will belong to a third tomorrow. So it is in thought. Our knowledge is the amassed thought and experience of innumerable minds: our language, our science, our religion, our opinions, our fancies we inherited. Our country, customs, laws, our ambitions, and our notions of fit and fair—all these we never made, we found them ready-made; we but quote them. Goethe frankly said, "What would remain to me if this art of appropriation were derogatory to genius? Every one of my writings has been furnished to me by a thousand different persons, a thousand things; wise and foolish have brought me, without suspecting it, the offering of their thoughts, faculties, and experience. My work is an aggregation of beings taken from the whole of nature; it bears the name of Goethe."

But there remains the indefeasible persistency of the individual to be himself. One leaf, one blade of grass, one meridian, does not resemble another. Every mind is different; and the more it is unfolded, the more pronounced is that difference. He must draw the elements into him for food, and, if they be granite and silex, will prefer them cooked by sun and rain, by time and art, to his hand. But, however received, these elements pass into the substance of his constitution. will be assimilated, and tend always to form, not a partisan, but a possessor of truth. To all that can be said of the preponderance of the Past, the single word Genius is a sufficient reply. The divine resides in the new. The divine never quotes, but is, and creates. The profound apprehension of the Present is Genius, which makes the Past forgotten. Genius believes its faintest presentiment against the testimony of all history; for it knows that facts are not ultimates, but that a state of mind is the ancestor of everything. And what is Originality? It is being, being one's self, and reporting accurately what we see and are. Genius is in the first instance, sensibility, the capacity of receiving just impressions from the external world, and the power of coordinating these after the laws of thought. It implies Will, or original force, for their right distribution and expression. If to this the sentiment of piety be added, if the thinker feels that the thought most strictly his own is not his own, and recognizes the perpetual suggestion of the Supreme Intellect, the oldest thoughts become new and fertile whilst he speaks them.

Originals never lose their value. There is always in them a style and weight of speech, which the immanence of the oracle bestowed, and which cannot be counterfeited. Hence the permanence of the high poets. Plato, Cicero, and Plutarch cite the poets in the manner in which Scripture is quoted in our churches. A phrase or a single word is adduced, with honoring emphasis, from Pindar, Hesiod, or Euripides, as precluding all argument, because thus had they said: importing that the bard spoke not his own, but the words of some god. True poets have always ascended to this lofty platform, and met this expectation. Shakespeare, Milton, Wordsworth, were very conscious of their responsibilities. When a man thinks happily, he finds no foot-track in the field he traverses. All spontaneous thought is irrespective of all else. Pindar uses this haughty defiance, as if it were impossible to find his sources: "There are many swift darts within my quiver, which have a voice for those with understanding; but to the crowd they need interpreters. He is gifted with genius who knoweth much by natural talent."

Our pleasure in seeing each mind take the subject to which it has a proper right is seen in mere fitness in time. He that comes second must needs quote him that comes first. The earliest describers of savage life, as Captain Cook's account of the Society Islands, or Alexander Henry's travels among our Indian tribes, have a charm of truth and just point of view. Landsmen and sailors freshly come from the most civilized countries, and with no false expectation, no sentimentality yet about wild life, healthily receive and report what they saw—seeing what they must, and using no choice; and no man suspects the superior merit of the description, until Chateaubriand, or Moore, or Campbell, or Byron, or the artists, arrive, and mix so much art with their picture that the incomparable advantage of the first narrative appears. For the same reason we dislike that the poet should choose an antique or far-fetched subject for his muse, as if he avowed want of insight. The great deal always with the nearest. Only as braveries of too prodigal power can we pardon it, when the life of genius is so redundant that out of petulance it flings its fire into some old mummy, and, lo! it walks and blushes again here in the street.

We cannot overstate our debt to the Past, but the moment has the supreme claim. The Past is for us; but the sole terms on which it can become ours are its subordination to the Present. Only an inventor knows how to borrow, and every man is or should be an inventor.

We must not tamper with the organic motion of the soul. 'Tis certain that thought has its own proper motion, and the hints which flash from it, the words overheard at unawares by the free mind, are trustworthy and fertile when obeyed and not perverted to low and selfish account. This vast memory is only raw material. The divine gift is ever the instant life, which receives and uses and creates, and can well bury the old in the omnipotency with which Nature decomposes all her harvest for re-composition.

Poems

Poems

EDITOR'S NOTE

EMERSON'S poetry, like that of most poets, gains by selection. But the selection has already taken place, nor was there any obstacle to its doing so. The best of Emerson's poetry sings out at once.

> I like a church; I like a cowl;
> I love a prophet of the soul;
> And on my heart monastic aisles
> Fall like sweet strains, or pensive smiles;
> Yet not for all his faith can see
> Would I that cowlèd churchman be.

From that point on, that point so personal and so crisply musical, there is no further question. The music comes again, or else it does not. Emerson seems not always to have known when he genuinely had it. But the reader knows, and delights himself often enough with a note unique in poetry.

Emerson is master of the short, nervous couplet, of the gnomic rhythm. But he is also master of the long line; witness "The Rhodora," "Days," and certain portions of "Wood-Notes," particularly those which have been assumed to celebrate Thoreau, though it is possible that they were written before Emerson had become acquainted with Thoreau's habits and genius as a naturalist.

> He trode the unplanted forest floor, whereon
> The all-seeing sun for ages hath not shone.

There at any rate is Emerson's ideal naturalist, and there is no reason why he should not be everybody else's.

Emerson's ideas reappear in the poems—unless this is where they started—but the poems are more than ideas. "Give All To Love," for example, approaches its subject by a route as much older than Emerson as Plato is; but the peculiar power of the statement here made comes from Emerson's ability to feel as well as think it, and to drive a rhythm through it—

> Friends, kindred, days,
> Estate, good-fame,
> Plans, credit and the Muse—

which carries his own sense of urgency, his own absoluteness of conviction. The idea is remembered for the way it sounded.

"Threnody," which laments the son whom Emerson lost in 1842 at the age of five, is not surpassed by any poem of its kind, particularly in its first two sections. "Brahma," which first appears in the journal for 1856, is the best fruit of Emerson's Oriental reading, though its idea is by no means strange to his native thought. As incantation it is complete; nothing needs to be added, and nothing could be taken away. "Concord Hymn" is of another order, and a familiar one; but it is not inferior.

EACH AND ALL

Little thinks, in the field, yon red-cloaked clown
Of thee from the hill-top looking down;
The heifer that lows in the upland farm,
Far-heard, lows not thine ear to charm;
The sexton, tolling his bell at noon,
Deems not that great Napoleon
Stops his horse, and lists with delight,
Whilst his files sweep round yon Alpine height;
Nor knowest thou what argument
Thy life to thy neighbor's creed has lent.
All are needed by each one;
Nothing is fair or good alone.
I thought the sparrow's note from heaven,
Singing at dawn on the alder bough;
I brought him home, in his nest, at even;
He sings the song, but it cheers not now,
For I did not bring home the river and sky;
He sang to my ear—they sang to my eye.
The delicate shells lay on the shore;
The bubbles of the latest wave
Fresh pearls to their enamel gave,
And the bellowing of the savage sea
Greeted their safe escape to me.
I wiped away the weeds and foam,
I fetched my sea-born treasures home;
But the poor, unsightly, noisome things
Had left their beauty on the shore
With the sun and the sand and the wild uproar.

The lover watched his graceful maid,
As 'mid the virgin train she strayed,
Nor knew her beauty's best attire
Was woven still by the snow-white choir.
At last she came to his hermitage,
Like the bird from the woodlands to the cage;
The gay enchantment was undone,
A gentle wife, but fairy none.
Then I said, "I covet truth;
Beauty is unripe childhood's cheat;
I leave it behind with the games of youth":
As I spoke, beneath my feet
The ground-pine curled its pretty wreath,
Running over the club-moss burrs;
I inhaled the violet's breath;
Around me stood the oaks and firs;
Pine-cones and acorns lay on the ground;
Over me soared the eternal sky,
Full of light and of deity;
Again I saw, again I heard,
The rolling river, the morning bird;
Beauty through my senses stole;
I yielded myself to the perfect whole.

THE PROBLEM

I like a church; I like a cowl;
I love a prophet of the soul;
And on my heart monastic aisles
Fall like sweet strains, or pensive smiles:

Yet not for all his faith can see
Would I that cowlèd churchman be.

Why should the vest on him allure,
Which I could not on me endure?
Not from a vain or shallow thought
His awful Jove young Phidias brought;
Never from lips of cunning fell
The thrilling Delphic oracle;
Out from the heart of nature rolled
The burdens of the Bible old;
The litanies of nations came,
Like the volcano's tongue of flame,
Up from the burning core below,
The canticles of love and woe:
The hand that rounded Peter's dome
And groined the aisles of Christian Rome
Wrought in a sad sincerity;
Himself from God he could not free;
He builded better than he knew;
The conscious stone to beauty grew.

Know'st thou what wove yon woodbird's nest
Of leaves, and feathers from her breast?
Or how the fish outbuilt her shell,
Painting with morn each annual cell?
Or how the sacred pine tree adds
To her old leaves new myriads?
Such and so grew these holy piles,
Whilst love and terror laid the tiles.
Earth proudly wears the Parthenon,
As the best gem upon her zone,
And Morning opes with haste her lids
To gaze upon the Pyramids;

O'er England's abbeys bends the sky,
As on its friends, with kindred eye;
For out of Thought's interior sphere
These wonders rose to upper air;
And Nature gladly gave them place,
Adopted them into her race,
And granted them an equal date
With Andes and with Ararat.

These temples grew as grows the grass;
Art might obey, but not surpass.
The passive Master lent his hand
To the vast soul that o'er him planned;
And the same power that reared the shrine
Bestrode the tribes that knelt within.
Ever the fiery Pentecost
Girds with one flame the countless host,
Trances the heart through chanting choirs,
And through the priest the mind inspires.
The word unto the prophet spoken
Was writ on tables yet unbroken;
The word by seers or sibyls told,
In groves of oak, or fanes of gold,
Still floats upon the morning wind,
Still whispers to the willing mind.
One accent of the Holy Ghost
The heedless world hath never lost.
I know what say the fathers wise,
The Book itself before me lies,
Old *Chrysostom,* best Augustine,
And he who blent both in his line,
The younger *Golden Lips* or mines,
Taylor, the Shakespeare of divines.
His words are music in my ear,
I see his cowlèd portrait dear;

And yet, for all his faith could see,
I would not the good bishop be.

HAMATREYA

Bulkeley, Hunt, Willard, Hosmer, Meriam, Flint,
Possessed the land which rendered to their toil
Hay, corn, roots, hemp, flax, apples, wool and wood.
Each of these landlords walked amidst his farm,
Saying, " 'Tis mine, my children's and my name's.
How sweet the west wind sounds in my own trees!
How graceful climb those shadows on my hill!
I fancy these pure waters and the flags
Know me, as does my dog: we sympathize;
And, I affirm, my actions smack of the soil."

Where are these men? Asleep beneath their grounds:
And strangers, fond as they, their furrows plough.
Earth laughs in flowers, to see her boastful boys
Earth-proud, proud of the earth which is not theirs;
Who steer the plough, but cannot steer their feet
Clear of the grave.

They added ridge to valley, brook to pond,
And sighed for all that bounded their domain;
"This suits me for a pasture; that's my park;
We must have clay, lime, gravel, granite-ledge,
And misty lowland, where to go for peat.
The land is well—lies fairly to the south.
'Tis good, when you have crossed the sea and back,
To find the sitfast acres where you left them."

Ah! the hot owner sees not Death, who adds
Him to his land, a lump of mold the more.
Hear what the Earth says:

EARTH-SONG

"Mine and yours;
Mine, not yours.
Earth endures;
Stars abide—
Shine down in the old sea;
Old are the shores;
But where are old men?
I who have seen much,
Such have I never seen.

"The lawyer's deed
Ran sure,
In tail,
To them, and to their heirs
Who shall succeed,
Without fail,
Forevermore.

"Here is the land,
Shaggy with wood,
With its old valley,
Mound and flood.
But the heritors?
Fled like the flood's foam.
The lawyer, and the laws,
And the kingdom,
Clean swept herefrom.

"They called me theirs,
Who so controlled me;
Yet every one
Wished to stay, and is gone,
How am I theirs,
If they cannot hold me,
But I hold them?"

When I heard the Earth-song,
I was no longer brave;
My avarice cooled
Like lust in the chill of the grave.

THE RHODORA

ON BEING ASKED, WHENCE IS
THE FLOWER?

In May, when sea-winds pierced our solitudes,
I found the fresh Rhodora in the woods,
Spreading its leafless blooms in a damp nook,
To please the desert and the sluggish brook.
The purple petals, fallen in the pool,
Made the black water with their beauty gay;
Here might the red-bird come his plumes to cool,
And court the flower that cheapens his array.
Rhodora! if the sages ask thee why
This charm is wasted on the earth and sky,
Tell them, dear, that if eyes were made for seeing,
Then Beauty is its own excuse for being:

Why thou wert there, O rival of the rose!
I never thought to ask, I never knew:
But, in my simple ignorance, suppose
The self-same Power that brought me there brought you.

THE SNOW-STORM

Announced by all the trumpets of the sky,
Arrives the snow, and, driving o'er the fields,
Seems nowhere to alight: the whited air
Hides hills and woods, the river, and the heaven,
And veils the farm-house at the garden's end.
The sled and traveler stopped, the courier's feet
Delayed, all friends shut out, the housemates sit
Around the radiant fireplace, enclosed
In a tumultuous privacy of storm.

Come see the north wind's masonry.
Out of an unseen quarry evermore
Furnished with tile, the fierce artificer
Curves his white bastions with projected roof
Round every windward stake, or tree, or door.
Speeding, the myriad-handed, his wild work
So fanciful, so savage, nought cares he
For number or proportion. Mockingly,
On coop or kennel he hangs Parian wreaths;
A swan-like form invests the hidden thorn;
Fills up the farmer's lane from wall to wall,

Maugre the farmer's sighs; and at the gate
A tapering turret overtops the work.

And when his hours are numbered, and the world
Is all his own, retiring, as he were not,
Leaves, when the sun appears, astonished Art
To mimic in slow structures, stone by stone,
Built in an age, the mad wind's night-work,
The frolic architecture of the snow.

WOODNOTES: I

1

When the pine tosses its cones
To the song of its waterfall tones,
Who speeds to the woodland walks?
To birds and trees who talks?
Caesar of his leafy Rome,
There the poet is at home.
He goes to the river-side,
Not hook nor line hath he;
He stands in the meadows wide,
Nor gun nor scythe to see.
Sure some god his eye enchants:
What he knows nobody wants.
In the wood he travels glad,
Without better fortune had,
Melancholy without bad.
Knowledge this man prizes best
Seems fantastic to the rest:
Pondering shadows, colors, clouds,
Grass-buds and caterpillar-shrouds,
Boughs on which the wild bees settle,

Tints that spot the violet's petal,
Why Nature loves the number five,
And why the star-form she repeats:
Lover of all things alive,
Wonderer at all he meets,
Wonderer chiefly at himself,
Who can tell him what he is?
Or how meet in human elf
Coming and past eternities?

2

And such I knew, a forest seer,
A minstrel of the natural year,
Foreteller of the vernal ides,
Wise harbinger of spheres and tides,
A lover true, who knew by heart
Each joy the mountain dales impart;
It seemed that Nature could not raise
A plant in any secret place,
In quaking bog, on snowy hill,
Beneath the grass that shades the rill,
Under the snow, between the rocks,
In damp fields known to bird and fox.
But he would come in the very hour
It opened in its virgin bower,
As if a sunbeam showed the place,
And tell its long-descended race.
It seemed as if the breezes brought him
It seemed as if the sparrows taught him
As if by secret sight he knew
Where, in far fields, the orchis grew.
Many haps fall in the field
Seldom seen by wishful eyes;

But all her shows did Nature yield,
To please and win this pilgrim wise.
He saw the partridge drum in the woods;
He heard the woodcock's evening hymn;
He found the tawny thrushes' broods;
And the shy hawk did wait for him;
What others did at distance hear,
And guessed within the thicket's gloom,
Was shown to this philosopher,
And at his bidding seemed to come.

3

In unploughed Maine he sought the lumberers' gang
Where from a hundred lakes young rivers sprang;
He trode the unplanted forest floor, whereon
The all-seeing sun for ages hath not shone;
Where feeds the moose, and walks the surly bear,
And up the tall mast runs the woodpecker.
He saw beneath dim aisles, in odorous beds,
The slight Linnaea hang its twin-born heads,
And blessed the monument of the man of flowers,
Which breathes his sweet fame through the northern
    bowers.
He heard, when in the grove, at intervals,
With sudden roar the aged pine tree falls,
One crash, the death-hymn of the perfect tree,
Declares the close of its green century.
Low lies the plant to whose creation went
Sweet influence from every element;
Whose living towers the years conspired to build,
Whose giddy top the morning loved to gild.
Through these green tents, by eldest Nature dressed,
He roamed, content alike with man and beast.

Where darkness found him he lay glad at night;
There the red morning touched him with its light.
Three moons his great heart him a hermit made,
So long he roved at will the boundless shade.
The timid it concerns to ask their way,
And fear what foe in caves and swamps can stray,
To make no step until the event is known,
And ills to come as evils past bemoan.
Not so the wise; no coward watch he keeps
To spy what danger on his pathway creeps;
Go where he will, the wise man is at home,
His hearth the earth—his hall the azure dome;
Where his clear spirit leads him, there's his road,
By God's own light illumined and foreshowed.

4

'Twas one of the charmed days
When the genius of God doth flow,
The wind may alter twenty ways,
A tempest cannot blow;
It may blow north, it still is warm;
Or south, it still is clear;
Or east, it smells like a clover-farm;
Or west, no thunder fear.
The musing peasant lowly great
Beside the forest water sate;
The rope-like pine roots crosswise grown
Composed the network of his throne;
The wide lake, edged with sand and grass,
Was burnished to a floor of glass,
Painted with shadows green and proud
Of the tree and of the cloud.
He was the heart of all the scene;

On him the sun looked more serene;
To hill and cloud his face was known,
It seemed the likeness of their own;
They knew by secret sympathy
The public child of earth and sky.
"You ask," he said, "what guide
Me through trackless thickets led,
Through thick-stemmed woodlands rough and wide.
I found the water's bed.
The watercourses were my guide;
I traveled grateful by their side,
Or through their channel dry;
They led me through the thicket damp,
Through brake and fern, the beavers' camp,
Through beds of granite cut my road,
And their resistless friendship showed:
The falling waters led me,
The foodful waters fed me,
And brought me to the lowest land,
Unerring to the ocean sand.
The moss upon the forest bark
Was pole-star when the night was dark;
The purple berries in the wood
Supplied me necessary food;
For Nature ever faithful is
To such as trust her faithfulness.
When the forest shall mislead me,
When the night and morning lie,
When sea and land refuse to feed me,
'Twill be time enough to die;
Then will yet my mother yield
A pillow in her greenest field,
Nor the June flowers scorn to cover
The clay of their departed lover."

ODE

INSCRIBED TO W. H. CHANNING

Though loath to grieve
The evil time's sole patriot,
I cannot leave
My honied thought
For the priest's cant,
Or statesman's rant.

If I refuse
My study for their politique,
Which at the best is trick,
The angry Muse
Puts confusion in my brain.

But who is he that prates
Of the culture of mankind,
Of better arts and life?
Go, blindworm, go,
Behold the famous States
Harrying Mexico
With rifle and with knife!

Or who, with accent bolder,
Dare praise the freedom-loving mountaineer?
I found by thee, O rushing Contoocook!
And in thy valleys, Agiochook!
The jackals of the Negro-holder.

The God who made New Hampshire
Taunted the lofty land
With little men;
Small bat and wren
House in the oak:
If earth-fire cleave
The upheaved land, and bury the folk,
The southern crocodile would grieve.
Virtue palters; Right is hence;
Freedom praised, but hid;
Funeral eloquence
Rattles the coffin-lid.

What boots thy zeal,
O glowing friend,
That would indignant rend
The northland from the south?
Wherefore? to what good end?
Boston Bay and Bunker Hill
Would serve things still;
Things are of the snake.

The horseman serves the horse,
The neatherd serves the neat,
The merchant serves the purse,
The eater serves his meat;
'Tis the day of the chattel,
Web to weave, and corn to grind;
Things are in the saddle,
And ride mankind.

There are two laws discrete,
Not reconciled,
Law for man, and law for thing;
The last builds town and fleet,

But it runs wild,
And doth the man unking.

'Tis fit the forest fall,
The steep be graded,
The mountain tunnelled,
The sand shaded,
The orchard planted,
The glebe tilled,
The prairie granted,
The steamer built.

Let man serve law for man;
Live for friendship, live for love,
For truth's and harmony's behoof;
The state may follow how it can,
As Olympus follows Jove.

Yet do not I implore
The wrinkled shopman to my sounding woods,
Nor bid the unwilling senator
Ask votes of thrushes in the solitudes.
Every one to his chosen work;
Foolish hands may mix and mar;
Wise and sure the issues are.
Round they roll till dark is light,
Sex to sex, and even to odd;
The over-god
Who marries Right to Might,
Who peoples, unpeoples,
He who exterminates
Races by stronger races,
Black by white faces,
Knows to bring honey
Out of the lion;

Grafts gentlest scion
On pirate and Turk.

The Cossack eats Poland,
Like stolen fruit;
Her last noble is ruined,
Her last poet mute:
Straight, into double band
The victors divide;
Half for freedom strike and stand;
The astonished Muse finds thousands at her side.

GIVE ALL TO LOVE

Give all to love;
Obey thy heart;
Friends, kindred, days,
Estate, good-fame,
Plans, credit and the Muse,
Nothing refuse.

'Tis a brave master;
Let it have scope:
Follow it utterly,
Hope beyond hope:
High and more high
It dives into noon,
With wing unspent,
Untold intent;
But it is a god,

Knows its own path
And the outlets of the sky.

It was never for the mean;
It requireth courage stout.
Souls above doubt,
Valor unbending,
It will reward,
They shall return
More than they were,
And ever ascending.

Leave all for love;
Yet, hear me, yet,
One word more thy heart behoved,
One pulse more of firm endeavor,
Keep thee today,
Tomorrow, forever,
Free as an Arab
Of thy beloved.

Cling with life to the maid;
But when the surprise,
First vague shadow of surmise
Flits across her bosom young,
Of a joy apart from thee,
Free be she, fancy-free;
Nor thou detain her vesture's hem,
Nor the palest rose she flung
From her summer diadem.

Though thou loved her as thyself,
As a self of purer clay,
Though her parting dims the day,
Stealing grace from all alive;

Heartily know,
When half-gods go,
The gods arrive.

MERLIN

I

Thy trivial harp will never please
Or fill my craving ear;
Its chords should ring as blows the breeze,
Free, peremptory, clear.
No jingling serenader's art,
Nor tinkle of piano strings,
Can make the wild blood start
In its mystic springs.
The kingly bard
Must smite the chords rudely and hard,
As with hammer or with mace;
That they may render back
Artful thunder, which conveys
Secrets of the solar track,
Sparks of the supersolar blaze.
Merlin's blows are strokes of fate,
Chiming with the forest tone,
When boughs buffet boughs in the wood;
Chiming with the gasp and moan
Of the ice-imprisoned flood;
With the pulse of manly hearts;
With the voice of orators;
With the din of city arts;

With the cannonade of wars;
With the marches of the brave;
And prayers of might from martyrs' cave.

Great is the art,
Great be the manners, of the bard.
He shall not his brain encumber
With the coil of rhythm and number;
But, leaving rule and pale forethought,
He shall aye climb
For his rhyme.
"Pass in, pass in," the angels say,
"In to the upper doors,
Nor count compartments of the floors,
But mount to paradise
By the stairway of surprise."

Blameless master of the games,
King of sport that never shames,
He shall daily joy dispense
Hid in song's sweet influence.
Forms more cheerly live and go,
What time the subtle mind
Sings aloud the tune whereto
Their pulses beat,
And march their feet,
And their members are combined.

By Sybarites beguiled,
He shall no task decline;
Merlin's mighty line
Extremes of nature reconciled,
Bereaved a tyrant of his will,
And made the lion mild.
Songs can the tempest still,

Scattered on the stormy air,
Mold the year to fair increase,
And bring in poetic peace.

He shall not seek to weave,
In weak, unhappy times,
Efficacious rhymes;
Wait his returning strength.
Bird that from the nadir's floor
To the zenith's top can soar,
The soaring orbit of the muse exceeds that
    journey's length.
Nor profane affect to hit
Or compass that, by meddling wit,
Which only the propitious mind
Publishes when 'tis inclined.
There are open hours
When the God's will sallies free,
And the dull idiot might see
The flowing fortunes of a thousand years;
Sudden, at unawares,
Self-moved, fly to the doors,
Nor sword of angels could reveal
What they conceal.

II

The rhyme of the poet
Modulates the king's affairs;
Balance-loving Nature
Made all things in pairs.
To every foot its antipode;
Each color with its counter glowed;
To every tone beat answering tones,

Higher or graver;
Flavor gladly blends with flavor;
Leaf answers leaf upon the bough;
And match the paired cotyledons.
Hands to hands, and feet to feet,
In one body grooms and brides;
Eldest rite, two married sides
In every mortal meet.
Light's far furnace shines,
Smelting balls and bars,
Forging double stars,
Glittering twins and trines.
The animals are sick with love,
Lovesick with rhyme;
Each with all propitious Time
Into chorus wove.
Like the dancers' ordered band,
Thoughts come also hand in hand;
In equal couples mated,
Or else alternated;
Adding by their mutual gage,
One to other, health and age.
Solitary fancies go
Short-lived wandering to and fro,
Most like to bachelors,
Or an ungiven maid,
Not ancestors,
With no posterity to make the lie afraid,
Or keep truth undecayed.
Perfect-paired as eagle's wings,
Justice is the rhyme of things;
Trade and counting use
The self-same tuneful muse;
And Nemesis,
Who with even matches odd,

Who athwart space redresses
The partial wrong,
Fills the just period,
And finishes the song.

Subtle rhymes, with ruin rife,
Murmur in the house of life,
Sung by the Sisters as they spin;
In perfect time and measure they
Build and unbuild our echoing clay.
As the two twilights of the day
Fold us music-drunken in.

BACCHUS

Bring me wine, but wine which never grew
In the belly of the grape,
Or grew on vine whose tap-roots, reaching through
Under the Andes to the Cape,
Suffer no savor of the earth to scape.

Let its grapes the morn salute
From a nocturnal root,
Which feels the acrid juice
Of Styx and Erebus;
And turns the woe of Night,
By its own craft, to a more rich delight.

We buy ashes for bread;
We buy diluted wine;
Give me of the true,

Whose ample leaves and tendrils curled
Among the silver hills of heaven
Draw everlasting dew;
Wine of wine,
Blood of the world,
Form of forms, and mold of statures,
That I intoxicated,
And by the draught assimilated,
May float at pleasure through all natures;
The bird-language rightly spell,
And that which roses say so well.

Wine that is shed
Like the torrents of the sun
Up the horizon walls,
Or like the Atlantic streams, which run
When the South Sea calls.

Water and bread,
Food which needs no transmuting,
Rainbow-flowering, wisdom-fruiting,
Wine which is already man,
Food which teach and reason can.

Wine which Music is,
Music and wine are one,
That I, drinking this,
Shall hear far Chaos talk with me;
Kings unborn shall walk with me;
And the poor grass shall plot and plan
What it will do when it is man.
Quickened so, will I unlock
Every crypt of every rock.

I thank the joyful juice
For all I know;
Winds of remembering
Of the ancient being blow,
And seeming-solid walls of use
Open and flow.

Pour, Bacchus! the remembering wine;
Retrieve the loss of me and mine!
Vine for vine be antidote,
And the grape requite the lote!
Haste to cure the old despair,
Reason in Nature's lotus drenched,
The memory of ages quenched;
Give them again to shine;
Let wine repair what this undid;
And where the infection slid,
A dazzling memory revive;
Refresh the faded tints,
Recut the aged prints,
And write my old adventures with the pen
Which on the first day drew,
Upon the tablets blue,
The dancing Pleiads and eternal men.

THRENODY

The South wind brings
Life, sunshine and desire,
And on every mount and meadow
Breathes aromatic fire;

But over the dead he has no power,
The lost, the lost, he cannot restore;
And, looking over the hills, I mourn
The darling who shall not return.

I see my empty house,
I see my trees repair their boughs;
And he, the wondrous child,
Whose silver warble wild
Outvalued every pulsing sound
Within the air's cerulean round,
The hyacinthine boy, for whom
Morn well might break and April bloom,
The gracious boy, who did adorn
The world whereinto he was born,
And by his countenance repay
The favor of the loving Day,
Has disappeared from the Day's eye;
Far and wide she cannot find him;
My hopes pursue, they cannot bind him.
Returned this day, the South wind searches,
And finds young pines and budding birches;
But finds not the budding man;
Nature, who lost, cannot remake him;
Fate let him fall, Fate can't retake him;
Nature, Fate, men, him seek in vain.

And whither now, my truant wise and sweet,
O, whither tend thy feet?
I had the right, few days ago,
Thy steps to watch, thy place to know:
How have I forfeited the right?
Hast thou forgot me in a new delight?
I hearken for thy household cheer,
O eloquent child!

Whose voice, an equal messenger,
Conveyed thy meaning mild.
What though the pains and joys
Whereof it spoke were toys
Fitting his age and ken,
Yet fairest dames and bearded men,
Who heard the sweet request,
So gentle, wise and grave,
Bended with joy to his behest
And let the world's affairs go by,
A while to share his cordial game,
Or mend his wicker wagon-frame,
Still plotting how their hungry ear
That winsome voice again might hear;
For his lips could well pronounce
Words that were persuasions.

Gentlest guardians marked serene
His early hope, his liberal mien;
Took counsel from his guiding eyes
To make this wisdom earthly wise.
Ah, vainly do these eyes recall
The school-march, each day's festival,
When every morn my bosom glowed
To watch the convoy on the road;
The babe in willow wagon closed,
With rolling eyes and face composed;
With children forward and behind,
Like Cupids studiously inclined;
And he the chieftain paced beside,
The center of the troop allied,
With sunny face of sweet repose,
To guard the babe from fancied foes.
The little captain innocent
Took the eye with him as he went,

Each village senior paused to scan
And speak the lovely caravan.
From the window I look out
To mark thy beautiful parade,
Stately marching in cap and coat
To some tune by fairies played;
A music heard by thee alone
To works as noble led thee on.

Now Love and Pride, alas! in vain,
Up and down their glances strain.
The painted sled stands where it stood;
The kennel by the corded wood;
His gathered sticks to stanch the wall
Of the snow-tower, when snow should fall;
The ominous hole he dug in the sand,
And childhood's castles built or planned:
His daily haunts I well discern,
The poultry-yard, the shed, the barn,
And every inch of garden ground
Paced by the blessed feet around,
From the roadside to the brook
Whereinto he loved to look.
Step the meek fowls where erst they ranged;
The wintry garden lies unchanged;
The brook into the stream runs on;
But the deep-eyed boy is gone.

On that shaded day,
Dark with more clouds than tempests are,
When thou didst yield thy innocent breath
In birdlike heavings unto death,
Night came, and Nature had not thee;
I said, "We are mates in misery."
The morrow dawned with needless glow;

Each snowbird chirped, each fowl must crow;
Each tramper started; but the feet
Of the most beautiful and sweet
Of human youth had left the hill
And garden—they were bound and still.
There's not a sparrow or a wren,
There's not a blade of autumn grain,
Which the four seasons do not tend
And tides of life and increase lend;
And every chick of every bird,
And weed and rock-moss is preferred.
O ostrich-like forgetfulness!
O loss of larger in the less!
Was there no star that could be sent,
No watcher in the firmament,
No angel from the countless host
That loiters round the crystal coast,
Could stoop to heal that only child,
Nature's sweet marvel undefiled,
And keep the blossom of the earth,
Which all her harvests were not worth?

Not mine—I never called thee mine,
But Nature's heir—if I repine,
And seeing rashly torn and moved
Not what I made, but what I loved,
Grow early old with grief that thou
Must to the wastes of Nature go,
'Tis because a general hope
Was quenched, and all must doubt and grope.
For flattering planets seemed to say
This child should ills of ages stay,
By wondrous tongue, and guided pen,
Bring the flown Muses back to men.
Perchance not he but Nature ailed,

The world and not the infant failed.
It was not ripe yet to sustain
A genius of so fine a strain,
Who gazed upon the sun and moon
As if he came unto his own,
And, pregnant with his grander thought,
Brought the old order into doubt.
His beauty once their beauty tried;
They could not feed him, and he died,
And wandered backward as in scorn,
To wait an eon to be born.
Ill day which made this beauty waste,
Plight broken, this high face defaced!
Some went and came about the dead;
And some in books of solace read;
Some to their friends the tidings say;
Some went to write, some went to pray;
One tarried here, there hurried one
But their heart abode with none.
Covetous death bereaved us all,
To aggrandize one funeral.

The eager fate which carried thee
Took the largest part of me:
For this losing is true dying;
This is lordly man's down-lying,
This his slow but sure reclining,
Star by star his world resigning.

O child of paradise,
Boy who made dear his father's home,
In whose deep eyes
Men read the welfare of the times to come,
I am too much bereft.
The world dishonored thou hast left.

O truth's and nature's costly lie!
O trusted broken prophecy!
O richest fortune sourly crossed!
Born for the future, to the future lost!

The deep Heart answered, "Weepest thou?
Worthier cause for passion wild
If I had not taken the child.
And deemest thou as those who pore,
With aged eyes, short way before,
Think'st Beauty vanished from the coast
Of matter, and thy darling lost?
Taught he not thee—the man of eld,
Whose eyes within his eyes beheld
Heaven's numerous hierarchy span
The mystic gulf from God to man?
To be alone wilt thou begin
When worlds of lovers hem thee in?
Tomorrow, when the masks shall fall
That dizen Nature's carnival,
The pure shall see by their own will,
Which overflowing Love shall fill,
'Tis not within the force of fate
The fate-conjoined to separate.
But thou, my votary, weepest thou?
I gave thee sight—where is it now?
I taught thy heart beyond the reach
Of ritual, bible, or of speech;
Wrote in thy mind's transparent table,
As far as the incommunicable;
Taught thee each private sign to raise
Lit by the supersolar blaze.
Past utterance, and past belief,
And past the blasphemy of grief,
The mysteries of Nature's heart;

And though no Muse can these impart,
Throb thine with Nature's throbbing breast,
And all is clear from east to west.

"I came to thee as to a friend;
Dearest, to thee I did not send
Tutors, but a joyful eye,
Innocence that matched the sky,
Lovely locks, a form of wonder,
Laughter rich as woodland thunder,
That thou might'st entertain apart
The richest flowering of all art:
And, as the great all-loving Day
Through smallest chambers takes its way,
That thou might'st break thy daily bread
With prophet, savior and head;
That thou might'st cherish for thine own
The riches of sweet Mary's Son,
Boy-Rabbi, Israel's paragon.
And thoughtest thou such guest
Would in thy hall take up his rest?
Would rushing life forget her laws,
Fate's glowing revolution pause?
High omens ask diviner guess;
Not to be conned to tediousness.
And know my higher gifts unbind
The zone that girds the incarnate mind.
When the scanty shores are full
With Thought's perilous, whirling pool;
When frail Nature can no more,
Then the Spirit strikes the hour:
My servant Death, with solving rite,
Pours finite into infinite.
Wilt thou freeze love's tidal flow,
Whose streams through nature circling go?

Nail the wild star to its track
On the half-climbed zodiac?
Light is light which radiates,
Blood is blood which circulates,
Life is life which generates,
And many-seeming life is one,
Wilt thou transfix and make it none?
Its onward force too starkly pent
In figure, bone, and lineament?
Wilt thou, uncalled, interrogate,
Talker! the unreplying Fate?
Nor see the genius of the whole
Ascendant in the private soul,
Beckon it when to go and come,
Self-announced its hour of doom?
Fair the soul's recess and shrine,
Magic-built to last a season;
Masterpiece of love benign,
Fairer that expansive reason
Whose omen 'tis, and sign.
Wilt thou not ope thy heart to know
What rainbows teach, and sunsets show?
Verdict which accumulates
From lengthening scroll of human fates,
Voice of earth to earth returned,
Prayers of saints that inly burned,
Saying, *What is excellent,*
As God lives, is permanent;
Hearts are dust, hearts' loves remain;
Heart's love will meet thee again.
Revere the Maker; fetch thine eye
Up to his style, and manners of the sky.
Not of adamant and gold
Built he heaven stark and cold;
No, but a nest of bending reeds,

Flowering grass and scented weeds;
Or like a traveler's fleeing tent,
Or bow above the tempest bent;
Built of tears and sacred flames,
And virtue reaching to its aims;
Built of furtherance and pursuing,
Not of spent deeds, but of doing.
Silent rushes the swift Lord
Through ruined systems still restored,
Broadsowing, bleak and void to bless,
Plants with worlds the wilderness;
Waters with tears of ancient sorrow
Apples of Eden ripe tomorrow.
House and tenant go to ground,
Lost in God, in Godhead found."

CONCORD HYMN

SUNG AT THE COMPLETION OF
THE BATTLE MONUMENT, APRIL 19, 1836.

By the rude bridge that arched the flood,
   Their flag to April's breeze unfurled,
Here once the embattled farmers stood,
   And fired the shot heard round the world.

The foe long since in silence slept;
   Alike the conqueror silent sleeps;
And Time the ruined bridge has swept
   Down the dark stream which seaward creeps.

On this green bank, by this soft stream,
   We set today a votive stone;
That memory may their deed redeem,
   When, like our sires, our sons are gone.

Spirit, that made those heroes dare
   To die, and leave their children free,
Bid Time and Nature gently spare
   The shaft we raise to them and thee.

BRAHMA

If the red slayer think he slays,
   Or if the slain think he is slain,
They know not well the subtle ways
   I keep, and pass, and turn again.

Far or forgot to me is near;
   Shadow and sunlight are the same;
The vanished gods to me appear;
   And one to me are shame and fame.

They reckon ill who leave me out;
   When me they fly, I am the wings;
I am the doubter and the doubt,
   And I the hymn the Brahmin sings.

The strong gods pine for my abode,
   And pine in vain the sacred Seven;
But thou, meek lover of the good!
   Find me, and turn thy back on heaven.

DAYS

Daughters of Time, the hypocritic Days,
Muffled and dumb like barefoot dervishes,
And marching single in an endless file,
Bring diadems and fagots in their hands.
To each they offer gifts after his will,
Bread, kingdoms, stars, and sky that holds them all.
I, in my pleached garden, watched the pomp,
Forgot my morning wishes, hastily
Took a few herbs and apples, and the Day
Turned and departed silent. I, too late,
Under her solemn fillet saw the scorn.

TWO RIVERS

Thy summer voice, Musketaquit,
Repeats the music of the rain;
But sweeter rivers pulsing flit
Through thee, as thou through Concord Plain.

Thou in thy narrow banks art pent:
The stream I love unbounded goes
Through flood and sea and firmament;
Through light, through life, it forward flows.

I see the inundation sweet,
I hear the spending of the stream
Through years, through men, through nature fleet,
Through love and thought, through power and dream.

Musketaquit, a goblin strong,
Of shard and flint makes jewels gay;
They lose their grief who hear his song,
And where he winds is the day of day.

So forth and brighter fares my stream,
Who drink it shall not thirst again;
No darkness stains its equal gleam,
And ages drop in it like rain.

MUSIC

Let me go where'er I will
I hear a sky-born music still:
It sounds from all things old,
It sounds from all things young,
From all that's fair, from all that's foul,
Peals out a cheerful song.
It is not only in the rose,
It is not only in the bird,
Not only where the rainbow glows,
Nor in the song of woman heard,
But in the darkest, meanest things
There alway, alway something sings.

'Tis not in the high stars alone,
Nor in the cups of budding flowers,
Nor in the redbreast's mellow tone,
Nor in the bow that smiles in showers,
But in the mud and scum of things
There alway, alway something sings.

TERMINUS

It is time to be old,
To take in sail:
The god of bounds,
Who sets to seas a shore,
Came to me in his fatal rounds,
And said: "No more!
No farther shoot
Thy broad ambitious branches, and thy root.
Fancy departs: no more invent;
Contract thy firmament
To compass of a tent.
There's not enough for this and that,
Make thy option which of two;
Economize the failing river,
Not the less revere the Giver,
Leave the many and hold the few.
Timely wise accept the terms,
Soften the fall with wary foot;
A little while
Still plan and smile,
And—fault of novel germs—
Mature the unfallen fruit.

Curse, if thou wilt, thy sires,
Bad husbands of their fires,
Who, when they gave thee breath,
Failed to bequeath
The needful sinew stark as once,
The Baresark marrow to thy bones,
But left a legacy of ebbing veins,
Inconstant heat and nerveless reins,
Amid the Muses, left thee deaf and dumb,
Amid the gladiators, halt and numb."

As the bird trims her to the gale,
I trim myself to the storm of time,
I man the rudder, reef the sail,
Obey the voice at eve obeyed at prime:
"Lowly faithful, banish fear,
Right onward drive unharmed;
The port, well worth the cruise, is near,
And every wave is charmed."

FRAGMENTS

Of all wit's uses the main one
Is to live well with who has none.

That each should in his house abide,
Therefore was the world so wide.

People

People

EDITOR'S NOTE

EMERSON'S theory of the individual is basic to his thought, but his writing is nowhere better than when it concerns itself with particular persons. His finest portrait, in *English Traits,* is of a people, and of that people in terms of its "personal force." Carlyle called *English Traits* a "book by a real *man,* with eyes in his head; nobleness, wisdom, humor, and many other things, in the heart of him." The bulk of the book, reprinted here, reveals Emerson's powers in their happiest state. The chapter called "Literature" is omitted because much of what it discusses is no longer of the first interest; yet its opening sentence must be salvaged. "A strong common sense, which it is not easy to unseat or disturb, marks the English mind for a thousand years: a rude strength newly applied to thought, as of sailors and soldiers who had lately learned to read." The rest of the work is worthy of that sentence. It is all brilliant, all witty, all serious, and all particular. Here are the fabulous Victorians in their essence, presented feature by feature, praised in the curious language of comedy, complimented even while they are shown to be grotesque. The book has no equal in its kind.

The essay on Montaigne, from *Representative Men,* and the speech on Burns (1859), are both different in method from the paper on Carlyle (1881), or from the classic memorial to Thoreau (1862). All four pay tribute to literary figures, but in fashions appropriate to their subjects. The essay on Montaigne spreads over the universe of chance and change which the great skeptic reviewed. The eulogy of Burns is passionate and lyrical, rising like a skylark to its most moving, most generous conclusion. The portrait of Carlyle is borrowed from letters Emerson had written back from England, and from the *Journals*. The inimitable sketch of Thoreau comes mostly from the *Journals*, where Emerson had described many walks with his younger friend, the naturalist who was also a philosopher; but it comes also from memory, and from his feeling, at Thoreau's grave, that a unique spirit had been lost to the earth.

Emerson's aunt, Mary Moody Emerson, lives now in the account he read of her at Boston in 1869. And she truly lives, for among other things Emerson knew how to present her in her own words, as he had known how to present Thoreau in his. The art of quotation was never more clearly an art than Emerson here showed it to be. The famous *Historic Notes of Life and Letters in New England*, written probably in 1867, was published as a posthumous article in the *Atlantic Monthly* for October, 1883. The remark Emerson "recalls" in the opening paragraph is recalled in fact from the *Journals* where it had been safely put away. And so with much of what follows; though it is true that Emerson did write much of the piece from memory. He wrote it all with a remarkable mixture of humorous relish and profound respect. It is the history of a culture, and as such is a model for other efforts in the field.

ENGLISH TRAITS

LAND

ALFIERI thought Italy and England the only countries worth living in; the former because there Nature vindicates her rights and triumphs over the evils inflicted by the governments; the latter because art conquers nature and transforms a rude, ungenial land into a paradise of comfort and plenty. England is a garden. Under an ash-colored sky, the fields have been combed and rolled till they appear to have been finished with a pencil instead of a plough. The solidity of the structures that compose the towns speaks the industry of ages. Nothing is left as it was made. Rivers, hills, valleys, the sea itself, feel the hand of a master. The long habitation of a powerful and ingenious race has turned every rood of land to its best use, has found all the capabilities, the arable soil, the quarriable rock, the highways, the by-ways, the fords, the navigable waters; and the new arts of intercourse meet you everywhere; so that England is a huge phalanstery, where all that man wants is provided within the precinct. Cushioned and comforted in every manner, the traveler rides as on a cannon-ball, high and low, over rivers and towns, through mountains in tunnels of three or four miles, at near twice the speed of our trains; and reads quietly the *Times* newspaper, which, by its immense correspondence and reporting seems to have machinized the rest of the world for his occasion.

The problem of the traveler landing at Liverpool is,

Why England is England? What are the elements of that power which the English hold over other nations? If there be one test of national genius universally accepted, it is success; and if there be one successful country in the universe for the last millennium, that country is England.

A wise traveler will naturally choose to visit the best of actual nations; and an American has more reasons than another to draw him to Britain. In all that is done or begun by the Americans towards right thinking or practice, we are met by a civilization already settled and overpowering. The culture of the day, the thoughts and aims of men, are English thoughts and aims. A nation considerable for a thousand years since Egbert, it has, in the last centuries, obtained the ascendant, and stamped the knowledge, activity and power of mankind with its impress. Those who resist it do not feel it or obey it less. The Russian in his snows is aiming to be English. The Turk and Chinese also are making awkward efforts to be English. The practical common-sense of modern society, the utilitarian direction which labor, laws, opinion, religion take, is the natural genius of the British mind. The influence of France is a constituent of modern civility, but not enough opposed to the English for the most wholesome effect. The American is only the continuation of the English genius into new conditions, more or less propitious.

See what books fill our libraries. Every book we read, every biography, play, romance, in whatever form, is still English history and manners. So that a sensible Englishman once said to me, "As long as you do not grant us copyright, we shall have the teaching of you."

But we have the same difficulty in making a social or moral estimate of England, that the sheriff finds in drawing a jury to try some cause which has agitated the whole community and on which everybody finds himself an interested party. Officers, jurors, judges have all taken sides. England has inoculated all nations with her civilization, intelligence and tastes; and to resist the tyranny and prepossession of the British element, a serious man must aid himself by comparing with it the civilizations of the farthest east and west, the old Greek, the Oriental, and, much more, the ideal standard; if only by means of the very impatience which English forms are sure to awaken in independent minds.

Besides, if we will visit London, the present time is the best time, as some signs portend that it has reached its highest point. It is observed that the English interest us a little less within a few years; and hence the impression that the British power has culminated, is in solstice, or already declining.

As soon as you enter England, which, with Wales, is no larger than the State of Georgia,[1] this little land stretches by an illusion to the dimensions of an empire. The innumerable details, the crowded succession of towns, cities, cathedrals, castles and great and decorated estates, the number and power of the trades and guilds, the military strength and splendor, the multitudes of rich and of remarkable people, the servants and equipages—all these catching the eye and never allowing it to pause, hide all boundaries by the impression of magnificence and endless wealth.

I reply to all the urgencies that refer me to this and that object indispensably to be seen—Yes, to see England well needs a hundred years; for what they told me was the merit of Sir John Soane's Museum, in London —that it was well packed and well saved—is the merit of England; it is stuffed full, in all corners and crevices,

---

[1] Add South Carolina, and you have more than an equivalent for the area of Scotland.

with towns, towers, churches, villas, palaces, hospitals and charity-houses. In the history of art it is a long way from a cromlech to York minster; yet all the intermediate steps may still be traced in this all-preserving island.

The territory has a singular perfection. The climate is warmer by many degrees than it is entitled to by latitude. Neither hot nor cold, there is no hour in the whole year when one cannot work. Here is no winter, but such days as we have in Massachusetts in November, a temperature which makes no exhausting demand on human strength, but allows the attainment of the largest stature. Charles the Second said "It invited men abroad more days in the year and more hours in the day than another country." Then England has all the materials of a working country except wood. The constant rain—a rain with every tide, in some parts of the island—keeps its multitude of rivers full and brings agricultural production up to the highest point. It has plenty of water, of stone, of potter's clay, of coal, of salt and of iron. The land naturally abounds with game; immense heaths and downs are paved with quails, grouse and woodcock, and the shores are animated by water-birds. The rivers and the surrounding sea spawn with fish; there are salmon for the rich and sprats and herrings for the poor. In the northern lochs, the herring are in innumerable shoals; at one season, the country people say, the lakes contain one part water and two parts fish.

The only drawback on this industrial conveniency is the darkness of its sky. The night and day are too nearly of a color. It strains the eyes to read and to write. Add the coal smoke. In the manufacturing towns, the fine soot or *blacks* darken the day, give white sheep the color of black sheep, discolor the human saliva, contaminate the air, poison many plants and corrode the monuments and buildings.

The London fog aggravates the distempers of the sky, and sometimes justifies the epigram on the climate by an English wit, "in a fine day, looking up a chimney; in a foul day, looking down one." A gentleman in Liverpool told me that he found he could do without a fire in his parlor about one day in the year. It is however pretended that the enormous consumption of coal in the island is also felt in modifying the general climate.

Factitious climate, factitious position. England resembles a ship in its shape, and if it were one, its best admiral could not have worked it or anchored it in a more judicious or effective position. Sir John Herschel said, "London is the center of the terrene globe." The shopkeeping nation, to use a shop word, has a *good stand*. The old Venetians pleased themselves with the flattery that Venice was in 45°, midway between the poles and the line; as if that were an imperial centrality. Long of old, the Greeks fancied Delphi the navel of the earth, in their favorite mode of fabling the earth to be an animal. The Jews believed Jerusalem to be the center. I have seen a kratometric chart designed to show that the city of Philadelphia was in the same thermic belt, and by inference in the same belt of empire, as the cities of Athens, Rome and London. It was drawn by a patriotic Philadelphian, and was examined with pleasure, under his showing, by the inhabitants of Chestnut Street. But when carried to Charleston, to New Orleans and to Boston, it somehow failed to convince the ingenious scholars of all those capitals.

But England is anchored at the side of Europe, and right in the heart of the modern world. The sea, which, according to Virgil's famous line, divided the poor Britons utterly from the world, proved to be the ring of marriage with all nations. It is not down in the books— it is written only in the geologic strata—that fortunate day when a wave of the German Ocean burst the old isthmus which joined Kent and Cornwall to France, and gave to this fragment of Europe its impregnable sea-wall, cutting off an island of eight hundred miles in length, with an irregular breadth reaching to three hundred miles; a territory large enough for independence, enriched with every seed of national power, so near that it can see the harvests of the continent, and so far that who would cross the strait must be an expert mariner, ready for tempests. As America, Europe and Asia lie, these Britons have precisely the best commercial position in the whole planet, and are sure of a market for all the goods they can manufacture. And to make these advantages avail, the river Thames must dig its spacious outlet to the sea from the heart of the kingdom, giving road and landing to innumerable ships, and all the conveniency to trade that a people so skilful and sufficient in economizing waterfront by docks, warehouses and lighters required. When James the First declared his purpose of punishing London by removing his Court, the Lord Mayor replied that "in removing his royal presence from his lieges, they hoped he would leave them the Thames."

In the variety of surface, Britain is a miniature of Europe, having plain, forest, marsh, river, seashore; mines in Cornwall; caves in Matlock and Derbyshire; delicious landscape in Dovedale, delicious sea-view at Tor Bay, Highlands in Scotland, Snowdon in Wales, and in Westmoreland and Cumberland a pocket Switzerland, in which the lakes and mountains are on a sufficient scale to fill the eye and touch the imagination. It is a nation conveniently small. Fontenelle thought that nature had sometimes a little affectation; and there is such an artificial completeness in this nation of artificers as if there were a design from the beginning to elaborate a bigger Birmingham. Nature held counsel with herself and said, "My Romans are gone. To build my new empire, I will choose a rude race, all masculine, with brutish strength. I will not grudge a competition of the roughest males. Let buffalo gore buffalo, and the pasture to the strongest! For I have work that requires the best will and sinew. Sharp and temperate northern breezes shall blow, to keep that will alive and alert. The sea shall disjoin the people from others, and knit them to a fierce nationality. It shall give them markets on every side. Long time I will keep them on their feet, by poverty, border-wars, seafaring, sea-risks and the stimulus of gain. An island—but not so large, the people not so many as to glut the great markets and depress one another, but proportioned to the size of Europe and the continents."

With its fruits, and wares, and money, must its civil influence radiate. It is a singular coincidence to this geographic centrality, the spiritual centrality which Emanuel Swedenborg ascribes to the people. "For the English nation, the best of them are in the center of all Christians, because they have interior intellectual light. This appears conspicuously in the spiritual world. This light they derive from the liberty of speaking and writing, and thereby of thinking."

RACE

An ingenious anatomist has written a book[1] to prove that races are imperishable, but nations are pliant political constructions, easily changed or destroyed. But this writer did not found his assumed races on any necessary law, disclosing their ideal or metaphysical necessity; nor

---

[1] *The Races, a Fragment.* By Robert Knox. London: 1850.

did he on the other hand count with precision the existing races and settle the true bounds; a point of nicety, and the popular test of the theory. The individuals at the extremes of divergence in one race of men are as unlike as the wolf to the lapdog. Yet each variety shades down imperceptibly into the next, and you cannot draw the line where a race begins or ends. Hence every writer makes a different count. Blumenbach reckons five races; Humboldt, three; and Mr. Pickering, who lately in our Exploring Expedition thinks he saw all the kinds of men that can be on the planet, makes eleven.

The British Empire is reckoned to contain (in 1848) 222,000,000 souls—perhaps a fifth of the population of the globe; and to comprise a territory of 5,000,000 square miles. So far have British people predominated. Perhaps forty of these millions are of British stock. Add the United States of America, which reckon (in the same year), exclusive of slaves, 20,000,000 of people, on a territory of 3,000,000 square miles, and in which the foreign element, however considerable, is rapidly assimilated, and you have a population of English descent and language of 60,000,000, and governing a population of 245,000,000 souls.

The British census proper reckons twenty-seven and a half millions in the home countries. What makes this census important is the quality of the units that compose it. They are free forcible men, in a country where life is safe and has reached the greatest value. They give the bias to the current age; and that, not by chance or by mass, but by their character and by the number of individuals among them of personal ability. It has been denied that the English have genius. Be it as it may, men of vast intellect have been born on their soil, and they have made or applied the principal inventions. They have sound bodies and supreme endurance in war and in labor. The spawning force of the race has sufficed to the colonization of great parts of the world; yet it remains to be seen whether they can make good the exodus of millions from Great Britain, amounting in 1852 to more than a thousand a day. They have assimilating force, since they are imitated by their foreign subjects; and they are still aggressive and propagandist, enlarging the dominion of their arts and liberty. Their laws are hospitable, and slavery does not exist under them. What oppression exists is incidental and temporary; their success is not sudden or fortunate, but they have maintained constancy and self-equality for many ages.

Is this power due to their race, or to some other cause? Men hear gladly of the power of blood or race. Everybody likes to know that his advantages cannot be attributed to air, soil, sea, or to local wealth, as mines and quarries, nor to laws and traditions, nor to fortune; but to superior brain, as it makes the praise more personal to him.

We anticipate in the doctrine of race something like that law of physiology that whatever bone, muscle, or essential organ is found in one healthy individual, the same part or organ may be found in or near the same place in its congener; and we look to find in the son every mental and moral property that existed in the ancestor. In race, it is not the broad shoulders, or litheness, or stature that give advantage, but a symmetry that reaches as far as to the wit. Then the miracle and renown begin. Then first we care to examine the pedigree, and copy heedfully the training—what food they ate, what nursing, school, and exercises they had, which resulted in this mother-wit, delicacy of thought and robust wisdom. How came such men as King Alfred, and Roger Bacon, William of Wykeham, Walter Raleigh, Philip Sidney, Isaac Newton, William Shakespeare, George

Chapman, Francis Bacon, George Herbert, Henry Vane, to exist here? What made these delicate natures? was it the air? was it the sea? was it the parentage? For it is certain that these men are samples of their contemporaries. The hearing ear is always found close to the speaking tongue, and no genius can long or often utter anything which is not invited and gladly entertained by men around him.

It is race, is it not? that puts the hundred millions of India under the dominion of a remote island in the north of Europe. Race avails much, if that be true which is alleged, that all Celts are Catholics and all Saxons are Protestants; that Celts love unity of power, and Saxons the representative principle. Race is a controlling influence in the Jew, who, for two millenniums, under every climate, has preserved the same character and employments. Race in the Negro is of appalling importance. The French in Canada, cut off from all intercourse with the parent people, have held their national traits. I chanced to read Tacitus *On the Manners of the Germans,* not long since, in Missouri and the heart of Illinois, and I found abundant points of resemblance between the Germans of the Hercynian forest, and our "Hoosiers," "Suckers" and "Badgers" of the American woods.

But whilst race works immortally to keep its own, it is resisted by other forces. Civilization is a re-agent, and eats away the old traits. The Arabs of today are the Arabs of Pharaoh; but the Briton of today is a very different person from Cassibelaunus or Ossian. Each religious sect has its physiognomy. The Methodists have acquired a face; the Quakers, a face; the nuns, a face. An Englishman will pick out a dissenter by his manners. Trades and professions carve their own lines on face and form. Certain circumstances of English life are not less effective; as personal liberty; plenty of food; good ale and mutton; open market, or good wages for every kind of labor; high bribes to talent and skill; the island life, or the million opportunities and outlets for expanding and misplaced talent; readiness of combination among themselves for politics or for business; strikes; and sense of superiority founded on habit of victory in labor and in war: and the appetite for superiority grows by feeding.

It is easy to add to the counteracting forces to race. Credence is a main element. 'Tis said that the views of nature held by any people determine all their institutions. Whatever influences add to mental or moral faculty, take men out of nationality as out of other conditions, and make the national life a culpable compromise.

These limitations of the formidable doctrine of race suggest others which threaten to undermine it, as not sufficiently based. The fixity or inconvertibleness of races as we see them is a weak argument for the eternity of these frail boundaries, since all our historical period is a point to the duration in which nature has wrought. Any the least and solitariest fact in our natural history, such as the melioration of fruits and of animal stocks, has the worth of a *power* in the opportunity of geologic periods. Moreover, though we flatter the self-love of men and nations by the legend of pure races, all our experience is of the gradation and resolution of races, and strange resemblances meet us everywhere. It need not puzzle us that Malay and Papuan, Celt and Roman, Saxon and Tartar should mix, when we see the rudiments of tiger and baboon in our human form, and know that the barriers of races are not so firm but that some spray sprinkles us from the antediluvian seas.

The low organizations are simplest; a mere mouth, a jelly, or a straight worm. As the scale mounts, the organtzations become complex. We are piqued with pure de-scent, but nature loves inoculation. A child blends in his face the faces of both parents and some feature from every ancestor whose face hangs on the wall. The best nations are those most widely related; and navigation, as effecting a world-wide mixture, is the most potent ad-vancer of nations.

The English composite character betrays a mixed ori-gin. Everything English is a fusion of distant and antag-onistic elements. The language is mixed; the names of men are of different nations—three languages, three or four nations—the currents of thought are counter: con-templation and practical skill; active intellect and dead conservatism; world-wide enterprise and devoted use and wont; aggressive freedom and hospitable law with bitter class-legislation; a people scattered by their wars and affairs over the face of the whole earth, and home-sick to a man; a country of extremes—dukes and chart-ists, Bishops of Durham and naked heathen colliers—nothing can be praised in it without damning exceptions, and nothing denounced without salvos of cordial praise.

Neither do this people appear to be of one stem, but collectively a better race than any from which they are derived. Nor is it easy to trace it home to its original seats. Who can call by right names what races are in Britain? Who can trace them historically? Who can dis-criminate them anatomically, or metaphysically?

In the impossibility of arriving at satisfaction on the historical question of race, and—come of whatever dis-putable ancestry—the indisputable Englishman before me, himself very well marked, and nowhere else to be found—I fancied I could leave quite aside the choice of a tribe as his lineal progenitors. Defoe said in his wrath, "the Englishman was the mud of all races." I incline to the belief that, as water, lime, and sand make mortar, so certain temperaments marry well, and, by well-managed contrarieties, develop as drastic a character as the English. On the whole it is not so much a history of one or of certain tribes of Saxons, Jutes, or Frisians, coming from one place and genetically identical, as it is an anthology of temperaments out of them all. Certain temperaments suit the sky and soil of England, say eight or ten or twenty varieties, as, out of a hundred pear trees, eight or ten suit the soil of an orchard and thrive— whilst all the unadapted temperaments die out.

The English derive their pedigree from such a range of nationalities that there needs sea-room and land-room to unfold the varieties of talent and character. Perhaps the ocean serves as a galvanic battery, to distribute acids at one pole and alkalies at the other. So England tends to accumulate her liberals in America, and her conservatives at London. The Scandinavians in her race still hear in every age the murmurs of their mother, the ocean; the Briton in the blood hugs the homestead still.

Again, as if to intensate the influences that are not of race, what we think of when we talk of English traits really narrows itself to a small district. It excludes Ireland and Scotland and Wales, and reduces itself at last to London, that is, to those who come and go thither. The portraits that hang on the walls in the Academy Exhibition at London, the figures in *Punch's* drawings of the public men or of the club-houses, the prints in the shop-windows, are distinctive English, and not American, no, nor Scotch, nor Irish: but 'tis a very restricted nationality. As you go north into the manufacturing and agricultural districts, and to the population that never travels; as you go into Yorkshire, as you enter Scotland, the world's Englishman is no longer found. In Scotland there is a rapid loss of all grandeur of mien and manners; a provincial eagerness and acuteness appear;

the poverty of the country makes itself remarked, and a coarseness of manners; and, among the intellectual, is the insanity of dialectics. In Ireland are the same climate and soil as in England, but less food, no right relation to the land, political dependence, small tenantry and an inferior or misplaced race.

These queries concerning ancestry and blood may be well allowed, for there is no prosperity that seems more to depend on the kind of man than British prosperity. Only a hardy and wise people could have made this small territory great. We say, in a regatta or yacht-race, that if the boats are anywhere nearly matched, it is the man that wins. Put the best sailing-master into either boat, and he will win.

Yet it is fine for us to speculate in face of unbroken traditions, though vague and losing themselves in fable. The traditions have got footing, and refuse to be disturbed. The kitchen-clock is more convenient than sidereal time. We must use the popular category, as we do the Linnaean classification, for convenience, and not as exact and final. Otherwise we are presently confounded when the best-settled traits of one race are claimed by some new ethnologist as precisely characteristic of the rival tribe.

I found plenty of well-marked English types, the ruddy complexion fair and plump, robust men, with faces cut like a die, and a strong island speech and accent; a Norman type, with the complacency that belongs to that constitution. Others who might be Americans, for anything that appeared in their complexion or form; and their speech was much less marked and their thought much less bound. We will call them Saxons. Then the Roman has implanted his dark complexion in the trinity or quaternity of bloods.

1. The sources from which tradition derives their stock are mainly three. And first they are of the oldest blood of the world—the Celtic. Some peoples are deciduous or transitory. Where are the Greeks? Where the Etrurians? Where the Romans? But the Celts or Sidonides are an old family, of whose beginning there is no memory, and their end is likely to be still more remote in the future; for they have endurance and productiveness. They planted Britain, and gave to the seas and mountains names which are poems and imitate the pure voices of nature. They are favorably remembered in the oldest records of Europe. They had no violent feudal tenure, but the husbandman owned the land. They had an alphabet, astronomy, priestly culture and a sublime creed. They have a hidden and precarious genius. They made the best popular literature of the Middle Ages in the songs of Merlin and the tender and delicious mythology of Arthur.

2. The English come mainly from the Germans, whom the Romans found hard to conquer in two hundred and ten years—say impossible to conquer, when one remembers the long sequel—a people about whom in the old empire the rumor ran there was never any that meddled with them that repented it not.

3. Charlemagne, halting one day in a town of Narbonnese Gaul, looked out of a window and saw a fleet of Northmen cruising in the Mediterranean. They even entered the port of the town where he was, causing no small alarm and sudden manning and arming of his galleys. As they put out to sea again, the emperor gazed long after them, his eyes bathed in tears. "I am tormented with sorrow," he said, "when I foresee the evils they will bring on my posterity." There was reason for these Xerxes' tears. The men who have built a ship and invented the rig, cordage, sail, compass and pump; the working in and out of port, have acquired much more than a ship. Now arm them and every shore is at their mercy. For if they have not numerical superiority where they anchor, they have only to sail a mile or two to find it. Bonaparte's art of war, namely of concentrating force on the point of attack, must always be theirs who have the choice of the battle-ground. Of course they come into the fight from a higher ground of power than the landnations; and can engage them on shore with a victorious advantage in the retreat. As soon as the shores are sufficiently peopled to make piracy a losing business, the same skill and courage are ready for the service of trade.

The *Heimskringla*,[1] or *Sagas of the Kings of Norway*, collected by Snorro Sturleson, is the Iliad and Odyssey of English history. Its portraits, like Homer's, are strongly individualized. The *Sagas* describe a monarchical republic like Sparta. The government disappears before the importance of citizens. In Norway, no Persian masses fight and perish to aggrandize a king, but the actors are bonders or landholders, every one of whom is named and personally and patronymically described, as the king's friend and companion. A sparse population gives this high worth to every man. Individuals are often noticed as very handsome persons, which trait only brings the story nearer to the English race. Then the solid material interest predominates, so dear to English understanding, wherein the association is logical, between merit and land. The heroes of the *Sagas* are not the knights of South Europe. No vaporing of France and Spain has corrupted them. They are substantial farmers whom the rough times have forced to defend their properties. They have weapons which they use in a deter-

---

[1] *Heimskringla.* Translated by Samuel Laing, Esq. London: 1844.

mined manner, by no means for chivalry, but for their acres. They are people considerably advanced in rural arts, living amphibiously on a rough coast, and drawing half their food from the sea and half from the land. They have herds of cows, and malt, wheat, bacon, butter, and cheese. They fish in the fiord and hunt the deer. A king among these farmers has a varying power, sometimes not exceeding the authority of a sheriff. A king was maintained, much as in some of our country districts a winter-schoolmaster is quartered, a week here, a week there, and a fortnight on the next farm—on all the farms in rotation. This the king calls going into guest-quarters; and it was the only way in which, in a poor country, a poor king with many retainers could be kept alive when he leaves his own farm to collect his dues through the kingdom.

These Norsemen are excellent persons in the main, with good sense, steadiness, wise speech and prompt action. But they have a singular turn for homicide; their chief end of man is to murder or to be murdered; oars, scythes, harpoons, crowbars, peatknives and hayforks are tools valued by them all the more for their charming aptitude for assassinations. A pair of kings, after dinner, will divert themselves by thrusting each his sword through the other's body, as did Yngve and Alf. Another pair ride out on a morning for a frolic, and finding no weapon near, will take the bits out of their horses' mouths and crush each other's heads with them, as did Alric and Eric. The sight of a tent-cord or a cloak-string puts them on hanging somebody, a wife, or a husband, or, best of all, a king. If a farmer has so much as a hayfork, he sticks it into a King Dag. King Ingiald finds it vastly amusing to burn up half a dozen kings in a hall, after getting them drunk. Never was poor gentleman so surfeited with life, so furious to be rid of it, as the Northman. If he cannot pick any other quarrel, he will get himself comfortably gored by a bull's horns, like Egil, or slain by a landslide, like the agricultural King Onund. Odin died in his bed, in Sweden; but it was a proverb of ill condition to die the death of old age. King Hake of Sweden cuts and slashes in battle, as long as he can stand, then orders his warship, loaded with his dead men and their weapons, to be taken out to sea, the tiller shipped and the sails spread; being left alone he sets fire to some tar-wood and lies down contented on deck. The wind blew off the land, the ship flew, burning in clear flame, out between the islets into the ocean, and there was the right end of King Hake.

The early *Sagas* are sanguinary and piratical; the later are of a noble strain. History rarely yields us better passages than the conversation between King Sigurd the Crusader and King Eystein his brother, on their respective merits—one the soldier, and the other a lover of the arts of peace.

But the reader of the Norman history must steel himself by holding fast the remote compensations which result from animal vigor. As the old fossil world shows that the first steps of reducing the chaos were confided to saurians and other huge and horrible animals, so the foundations of the new civility were to be laid by the most savage men.

The Normans came out of France into England worse men than they went into it one hundred and sixty years before. They had lost their own language and learned the Romance or barbarous Latin of the Gauls, and had acquired, with the language, all the vices it had names for. The conquest has obtained in the chronicles the name of the "memory of sorrow." Twenty thousand thieves landed at Hastings. These founders of the House of Lords were greedy and ferocious dragoons, sons of greedy and ferocious pirates. They were all alike, they took everything they could carry, they burned, harried, violated, tortured and killed, until everything English was brought to the verge of ruin. Such however is the illusion of antiquity and wealth, that decent and dignified men now existing boast their descent from these filthy thieves, who showed a far juster conviction of their own merits, by assuming for their types the swine, goat, jackal, leopard, wolf and snake, which they severally resembled.

England yielded to the Danes and Northmen in the tenth and eleventh centuries, and was the receptacle into which all the mettle of that strenuous population was poured. The continued draught of the best men in Norway, Sweden and Denmark to these piratical expeditions exhausted those countries, like a tree which bears much fruit when young, and these have been second-rate powers ever since. The power of the race migrated and left Norway void. King Olaf said, "When King Harold, my father, went westward to England, the chosen men in Norway followed him; but Norway was so emptied then, that such men have not since been to find in the country, nor especially such a leader as King Harold was for wisdom and bravery."

It was a tardy recoil of these invasions, when, in 1801, the British government sent Nelson to bombard the Danish forts in the Sound, and, in 1807, Lord Cathcart, at Copenhagen, took the entire Danish fleet, as it lay in the basins, and all the equipments from the Arsenal, and carried them to England. Konghelle, the town where the kings of Norway, Sweden and Denmark were wont to meet, is now rented to a private English gentleman for a hunting ground.

It took many generations to trim and comb and perfume the first boat-load of Norse pirates into royal highnesses and most noble Knights of the Garter; but every sparkle of ornament dates back to the Norse boat. There will be time enough to mellow this strength into civility and religion. It is a medical fact that the children of the blind see; the children of felons have a healthy conscience. Many a mean, dastardly boy is, at the age of puberty, transformed into a serious and generous youth.

The mildness of the following ages has not quite effaced these traits of Odin; as the rudiment of a structure matured in the tiger is said to be still found unabsorbed in the Caucasian man. The nation has a tough, acrid, animal nature, which centuries of churching and civilizing have not been able to sweeten. Alfieri said "the crimes of Italy were the proof of the superiority of the stock"; and one may say of England that this watch moves on a splinter of adamant. The English uncultured are a brutal nation. The crimes recorded in their calendars leave nothing to be desired in the way of cold malignity. Dear to the English heart is a fair stand-up fight. The brutality of the manners in the lower class appears in the boxing, bear-baiting, cock-fighting, love of executions, and in the readiness for a set-to in the streets, delightful to the English of all classes. The costermongers of London streets hold cowardice in loathing—"we must work our fists well; we are all handy with our fists." The public schools are charged with being bear-gardens of brutal strength, and are liked by the people for that cause. The fagging is a trait of the same quality. Medwin, in the *Life of Shelley*, relates that at a military school they rolled up a young man in a snowball, and left him so in his room while the other cadets went to church—and crippled him for life. They have retained impressment, deck-flogging, army-flogging and school-flogging. Such is the ferocity of the army discipline that a soldier, sentenced to flogging, sometimes prays that his sentence may be commuted to death. Flogging, banished from the armies of Western Europe, remains here by the sanction of the Duke of Wellington. The right of the husband to sell the wife has been retained down to our times. The Jews have been the favorite victims of royal and popular persecution. Henry III mortgaged all the Jews in the kingdom to his brother the Earl of Cornwall, as security for money which he borrowed. The torture of criminals, and the rack for extorting evidence, were slowly disused. Of the criminal statutes, Sir Samuel Romilly said: "I have examined the codes of all nations, and ours is the worst, and worthy of the Anthropophagi." In the last session (1848), the House of Commons was listening to the details of flogging and torture practised in the jails.

As soon as this land, thus geographically posted, got a hardy people into it, they could not help becoming the sailors and factors of the globe. From childhood, they dabbled in water, they swam like fishes, their playthings were boats. In the case of the ship-money, the judges delivered it for law, that "England being an island, the very midland shires therein are all to be accounted maritime"; and Fuller adds, "the genius even of landlocked counties driving the natives with a maritime dexterity." As early as the conquest it is remarked, in explanation of the wealth of England, that its merchants trade to all countries.

The English at the present day have great vigor of body and endurance. Other countrymen look slight and undersized beside them, and invalids. They are bigger men than the Americans. I suppose a hundred English taken at random out of the street would weigh a fourth more than so many Americans. Yet, I am told, the skeleton is not larger. They are round, ruddy, and handsome; at least the whole bust is well formed, and there is a tendency to stout and powerful frames. I remarked the stoutness on my first landing at Liverpool; porter, dray-man, coachman, guard—what substantial, respectable, grandfatherly figures, with costume and manners to suit. The American has arrived at the old mansion-house and finds himself among uncles, aunts and grandsires. The pictures on the chimney-tiles of his nursery were pic-tures of these people. Here they are in the identical cos-tumes and air which so took him.

It is the fault of their forms that they grow stocky, and the women have that disadvantage—few tall, slen-der figures of flowing shape, but stunted and thickset persons. The French say that the Englishwomen have two left hands. But in all ages they are a handsome race. The bronze monuments of crusaders lying cross-legged in the Temple Church at London, and those in Worces-ter and in Salisbury Cathedrals, which are seven hun-dred years old, are of the same type as the best youthful heads of men now in England—please by beauty of the same character, an expression blending good nature, valor and refinement, and mainly by that uncorrupt youth in the face of manhood, which is daily seen in the streets of London.

Both branches of the Scandinavian race are distin-quished for beauty. The anecdote of the handsome cap-tives which Saint Gregory found at Rome, A.D. 600, is matched by the testimony of the Norman chroniclers, five centuries later, who wondered at the beauty and long flowing hair of the young English captives. Mean-time the *Heimskringla* has frequent occasion to speak of the personal beauty of its heroes. When it is considered what humanity, what resources of mental and moral power the traits of the blond race betoken, its accession to empire marks a new and finer epoch, wherein the old mineral force shall be subjugated at last by humanity

and shall plough in its furrow henceforward. It is not a
final race, once a crab always crab—but a race with a
future.

On the English face are combined decision and nerve
with the fair complexion, blue eyes and open and florid
aspect. Hence the love of truth, hence the sensibility,
the fine perception and poetic construction. The fair
Saxon man, with open front and honest meaning, domestic, affectionate, is not the wood out of which cannibal,
or inquisitor, or assassin is made, but he is molded for
law, lawful trade, civility, marriage, the nurture of children, for colleges, churches, charities and colonies.

They are rather manly than warlike. When the war is
over, the mask falls from the affectionate and domestic
tastes, which make them women in kindness. This union
of qualities is fabled in their national legend of *Beauty
and the Beast*, or, long before, in the Greek legend of
Hermaphrodite. The two sexes are co-present in the
English mind. I apply to Britannia, queen of seas and
colonies, the words in which her latest novelist portrays
his heroine; "She is as mild as she is game, and as game
as she is mild." The English delight in the antagonism
which combines in one person the extremes of courage
and tenderness. Nelson, dying at Trafalgar, sends his
love to Lord Collingwood, and like an innocent school-
boy that goes to bed, says "Kiss me, Hardy," and turns
to sleep. Lord Collingwood, his comrade, was of a nature
the most affectionate and domestic. Admiral Rodney's
figure approached to delicacy and effeminacy, and he
declared himself very sensible to fear, which he surmounted only by considerations of honor and public
duty. Clarendon says the Duke of Buckingham was so
modest and gentle, that some courtiers attempted to put
affronts on him, until they found that this modesty and
effeminacy was only a mask for the most terrible deter-

mination. And Sir Edward Parry said of Sir John Franklin, that "if he found Wellington Sound open, he
explored it; for he was a man who never turned his back
on a danger, yet of that tenderness that he would not
brush away a mosquito." Even for their highwaymen the
same virtue is claimed, and Robin Hood comes described
to us as *mitissimus proedonum;* the gentlest thief. But
they know where their war-dogs lie. Cromwell, Blake,
Marlborough, Chatham, Nelson and Wellington are not
to be trifled with, and the brutal strength which lies at
the bottom of society, the animal ferocity of the quays
and cockpits, the bullies of the costermongers of Shore-
ditch, Seven Dials and Spitalfields, they know how to
wake up.

They have a vigorous health and last well into middle
and old age. The old men are as red as roses, and still
handsome. A clear skin, a peach-bloom complexion and
good teeth are found all over the island. They use a
plentiful and nutritious diet. The operative cannot sub-
sist on water cresses. Beef, mutton, wheat-bread and
malt-liquors are universal among the first-class laborers.
Good feeding is a chief point of national pride among
the vulgar, and in their caricatures they represent the
Frenchman as a poor, starved body. It is curious that
Tacitus found the English beer already in use among
the Germans: "They make from barley or wheat a drink
corrupted into some resemblance to wine." Lord Chief
Justice Fortescue, in Henry VI's time, says "The inhabitants of England drink no water, unless at certain times
on a religious score and by way of penance." The extremes of poverty and ascetic penance, it would seem,
never reach cold water in England. Wood the antiquary,
in describing the poverty and maceration of Father
Lacey, an English Jesuit, does not deny him beer. He
says: "His bed was under a thatching, and the way to

it up a ladder; his fare was coarse; his drink, of a penny a gawn, or gallon."

They have more constitutional energy than any other people. They think, with Henri Quatre, that manly exercises are the foundation of that elevation of mind which gives one nature ascendant over another; or with the Arabs, that the days spent in the chase are not counted in the length of life. They box, run, shoot, ride, row, and sail from pole to pole. They eat and drink, and live jolly in the open air, putting a bar of solid sleep between day and day. They walk and ride as fast as they can, their head bent forward, as if urged on some pressing affair. The French say that Englishmen in the street always walk straight before them like mad dogs. Men and women walk with infatuation. As soon as he can handle a gun, hunting is the fine art of every Englishman of condition. They are the most voracious people of prey that ever existed. Every season turns out the aristocracy into the country to shoot and fish. The more vigorous run out of the island to America, to Asia, to Africa and Australia, to hunt with fury by gun, by trap, by harpoon, by lasso, with dog, with horse, with elephant or with dromedary, all the game that is in nature. These men have written the game-books of all countries, as Hawker, Scrope, Murray, Herbert, Maxwell, Cumming, and a host of travelers. The people at home are addicted to boxing, running, leaping and rowing matches.

I suppose the dogs and horses must be thanked for the fact that the men have muscles almost as tough and supple as their own. If in every efficient man there is first a fine animal, in the English race it is of the best breed, a wealthy, juicy, broad-chested creature, steeped in ale and good cheer and a little overloaded by his flesh. Men of animal nature rely, like animals, on their instincts. The Englishman associates well with dogs and horses. His attachment to the horse arises from the courage and address required to manage it. The horse finds out who is afraid of it, and does not disguise its opinion. Their young boiling clerks and lusty collegians like the company of horses better than the company of professors. I suppose the horses are better company for them. The horse has more uses than Buffon noted. If you go into the streets, every driver in bus or dray is a bully, and if I wanted a good troop of soldiers, I should recruit among the stables. Add a certain degree of refinement to the vivacity of these riders, and you obtain the precise quality which makes the men and women of polite society formidable.

They come honestly by their horsemanship, with Hengst and Horsa for their Saxon founders. The other branch of their race had been Tartar nomads. The horse was all their wealth. The children were fed on mares' milk. The pastures of Tartary were still remembered by the tenacious practice of the Norsemen to eat horseflesh at religious feasts. In the Danish invasions the marauders seized upon horses where they landed, and were at once converted into a body of expert cavalry.

At one time this skill seems to have declined. Two centuries ago the English horse never performed any eminent service beyond the seas; and the reason assigned was that the genius of the English hath always more inclined them to foot-service, as pure and proper manhood, without any mixture; whilst in a victory on horseback, the credit ought to be divided betwixt the man and his horse. But in two hundred years a change has taken place. Now, they boast that they understand horses better than any other people in the world, and that their horses are become their second selves.

"William the Conqueror being," says Camden, "better affected to beasts than to men, imposed heavy fines and punishments on those that should meddle with his game." The *Saxon Chronicle* says "he loved the tall deer as if he were their father." And rich Englishmen have followed his example, according to their ability, ever since, in encroaching on the tillage and commons with their game-preserves. It is a proverb in England that it is safer to shoot a man than a hare. The severity of the game-laws certainly indicates an extravagant sympathy of the nation with horses and hunters. The gentlemen are always on horseback, and have brought horses to an ideal perfection; the English racer is a factitious breed. A score or two of mounted gentlemen may frequently be seen running like centaurs down a hill nearly as steep as the roof of a house. Every inn-room is lined with pictures of races; telegraphs communicate, every hour, tidings of the heats from Newmarket and Ascot; and the House of Commons adjourns over the Derby Day.

ABILITY

The Saxon and the Northman are both Scandinavians. History does not allow us to fix the limits of the application of these names with any accuracy, but from the residence of a portion of these people in France, and from some effect of that powerful soil on their blood and manners, the Norman has come popularly to represent in England the aristocratic, and the Saxon the democratic principle. And though, I doubt not, the nobles are of both tribes, and the workers of both, yet we are forced to use the names a little mythically, one to represent the worker and the other the enjoyer.

The island was a prize for the best race. Each of the dominant races tried its fortune in turn. The Phoenician, the Celt and the Goth had already got in. The Roman came, but in the very day when his fortune culminated. He looked in the eyes of a new people that was to supplant his own. He disembarked his legions, erected his camps and towers—presently he heard bad news from Italy, and worse and worse, every year; at last, he made a handsome compliment of roads and walls, and departed. But the Saxon seriously settled in the land, builded, tilled, fished and traded, with German truth and adhesiveness. The Dane came and divided with him. Last of all the Norman or French-Dane arrived, and formally conquered, harried and ruled the kingdom. A century later it came out that the Saxon had the most bottom and longevity, had managed to make the victor speak the language and accept the law and usage of the victim; forced the baron to dictate Saxon terms to Norman kings; and, step by step, got all the essential securities of civil liberty invented and confirmed. The genius of the race and the genius of the place conspired to this effect. The island is lucrative to free labor, but not worth possession on other terms. The race was so intellectual that a feudal or military tenure could not last longer than the war. The power of the Saxon-Danes, so thoroughly beaten in the war that the name of English and villein were synonymous, yet so vivacious as to extort charters from the kings, stood on the strong personality of these people. Sense and economy must rule in a world which is made of sense and economy, and the banker, with his seven per cent, drives the earl out of his castle. A nobility of soldiers cannot keep down a commonalty of shrewd scientific persons. What signifies a pedigree of a hundred links, against a cotton-spinner with steam in his mill; or against a company of broad-shouldered Liverpool merchants, for whom Stephenson and Brunel are contriving locomotives and a tubular bridge?

These Saxons are the hands of mankind. They have

the taste for toil, a distaste for pleasure or repose, and the telescopic appreciation of distant gain. They are the wealth-makers—and by dint of mental faculty which has its own conditions. The Saxon works after liking, or only for himself; and to set him at work and to begin to draw his monstrous values out of barren Britain, all dishonor, fret and barrier must be removed, and then his energies begin to play.

The Scandinavian fancied himself surrounded by Trolls—a kind of goblin men with vast power of work and skilful production—divine stevedores, carpenters, reapers, smiths and masons, swift to reward every kindness done them, with gifts of gold and silver. In all English history this dream comes to pass. Certain Trolls or working brains, under the names of Alfred, Bede, Caxton, Bracton, Camden, Drake, Selden, Dugdale, Newton, Gibbon, Brindley, Watt, Wedgwood, dwell in the troll-mounts of Britain and turn the sweat of their face to power and renown.

If the race is good, so is the place. Nobody landed on this spellbound island with impunity. The enchantments of barren shingle and rough weather transformed every adventurer into a laborer. Each vagabond that arrived bent his neck to the yoke of gain, or found the air too tense for him. The strong survived, the weaker went to the ground. Even the pleasure-hunters and sots of England are of a tougher texture. A hard temperament had been formed by Saxon and Saxon-Dane, and such of these French or Normans as could reach it were naturalized in every sense.

All the admirable expedients or means hit upon in England must be looked at as growths or irresistible offshoots of the expanding mind of the race. A man of that brain thinks and acts thus; and his neighbor, being afflicted with the same kind of brain, though he is rich and called a baron or a duke, thinks the same thing, and is ready to allow the justice of the thought and act in his retainer or tenant, though sorely against his baronial or ducal will.

The island was renowned in antiquity for its breed of mastiffs, so fierce that when their teeth were set you must cut their heads off to part them. The man was like his dog. The people have that nervous bilious temperament which is known by medical men to resist every means employed to make its possessor subservient to the will of others. The English game is main force to main force, the planting of foot to foot, fair play and open field, a rough tug without trick or dodging, till one or both come to pieces. King Ethelwald spoke the language of his race when he planted himself at Wimborne and said he "would do one of two things, or there live, or there lie." They hate craft and subtlety. They neither poison, nor waylay, nor assassinate; and when they have pounded each other to a poultice, they will shake hands and be friends for the remainder of their lives.

You shall trace these Gothic touches at school, at country fairs, at the hustings and in parliament. No artifice, no breach of truth and plain dealing—not so much as secret ballot, is suffered in the island. In parliament, the tactics of the opposition is to resist every step of the government by a pitiless attack: and in a bargain, no prospect of advantage is so dear to the merchant as the thought of being tricked is mortifying.

Sir Kenelm Digby, a courtier of Charles and James, who won the sea-fight of Scanderoon, was a model Englishman in his day. "His person was handsome and gigantic, he had so graceful elocution and noble address, that, had he been dropt out of the clouds in any part of the world, he would have made himself respected: he

was skilled in six tongues, and master of arts and arms." [1]
Sir Kenelm wrote a book, *Of Bodies and of Souls,* in
which he propounds, that "syllogisms do breed or rather
are all the variety of man's life. They are the steps by
which we walk in all our businesses. Man, as he is man,
doth nothing else but weave such chains. Whatsoever
he doth, swerving from this work, he doth as deficient
from the nature of man: and, if he do aught beyond this,
by breaking out into divers sorts of exterior actions, he
findeth, nevertheless, in this linked sequel of simple discourses, the art, the cause, the rule, the bounds and the
model of it." [2]

There spoke the genius of the English people. There
is a necessity on them to be logical. They would hardly
greet the good that did not logically fall—as if it excluded their own merit, or shook their understandings.
They are jealous of minds that have much facility of
association, from an instinctive fear that the seeing many
relations to their thought might impair this serial continuity and lucrative concentration. They are impatient
of genius, or of minds addicted to contemplation, and
cannot conceal their contempt for sallies of thought,
however lawful, whose steps they cannot count by their
wonted rule. Neither do they reckon better a syllogism
that ends in syllogism. For they have a supreme eye to
facts, and theirs is a logic that brings salt to soup, hammer to nail, oar to boat; the logic of cooks, carpenters
and chemists, following the sequence of nature, and one
on which words make no impression. Their mind is not
dazzled by its own means, but locked and bolted to
results. They love men who, like Samuel Johnson, a
doctor in the schools, would jump out of his syllogism

---

[1] Antony Wood.
[2] *Man's Soule,* p. 29.

the instant his major proposition was in danger, to save that at all hazards. Their practical vision is spacious, and they can hold many threads without entangling them. All the steps they orderly take; but with the high logic of never confounding the minor and major proposition; keeping their eye on their aim, in all the complicity and delay incident to the several series of means they employ. There is room in their minds for this and that—a science of degrees. In the courts the independence of the judges and the loyalty of the suitors are equally excellent. In Parliament they have hit on that capital invention of freedom, a constitutional opposition. And when courts and parliament are both deaf, the plaintiff is not silenced. Calm, patient, his weapon of defence from year to year is the obstinate reproduction of the grievance, with calculations and estimates. But, meantime, he is drawing numbers and money to his opinion, resolved that if all remedy fails, right of revolution is at the bottom of his charter-box. They are bound to see their measure carried, and stick to it through ages of defeat.

Into this English logic, however, an infusion of justice enters, not so apparent in other races—a belief in the existence of two sides, and the resolution to see fair play. There is on every question an appeal from the assertion of the parties to the proof of what is asserted. They kiss the dust before a fact. Is it a machine, is it a charter, is it a boxer in the ring, is it a candidate on the hustings—the universe of Englishmen will suspend their judgment until the trial can be had. They are not to be led by a phrase, they want a working plan, a working machine, a working constitution, and will sit out the trial and abide by the issue and reject all preconceived theories. In politics they put blunt questions, which must be answered; Who is to pay the taxes? What will you do for trade? What for corn? What for the spinner?

This singular fairness and its results strike the French with surprise. Philip de Commines says, "Now, in my opinion, among all the sovereignties I know in the world, that in which the public good is best attended to, and the least violence exercised on the people, is that of England." Life is safe, and personal rights; and what is freedom without security? whilst, in France, "fraternity," "equality," and "indivisible unity" are names for assassination. Montesquieu said, "England is the freest country in the world. If a man in England had as many enemies as hairs on his head, no harm would happen to him."

Their self-respect, their faith in causation, and their realistic logic or coupling of means to ends, have given them the leadership of the modern world. Montesquieu said, "No people have true common sense but those who are born in England." This common sense is a preception of all the conditions of our earthly existence; of laws that can be stated, and of laws that cannot be stated, or that are learned only by practice, in which allowance for friction is made. They are impious in their skepticism of theory, and in high departments they are cramped and sterile. But the unconditional surrender to facts, and the choice of means to reach their ends, are as admirable as with ants and bees.

The bias of the nation is a passion for utility. They love the lever, the screw and pulley, the Flanders draught-horse, the waterfall, windmills, tidemills; the sea and the wind to bear their freight ships. More than the diamond Koh-i-noor, which glitters among their crown jewels, they prize that dull pebble which is wiser than a man, whose poles turn themselves to the poles of the world and whose axis is parallel to the axis of the world. Now, their toys are steam and galvanism. They are heavy at the fine arts, but adroit at the coarse; not good in jewelry or mosaics, but the best iron-masters, colliers, woolcombers and tanners in Europe. They apply themselves to agriculture, to draining, to resisting encroachments of sea, wind, traveling sands, cold and wet subsoil; to fishery, to manufacture of indispensable staples—salt, plumbago, leather, wool, glass, pottery and brick—to bees and silkworms—and by their steady combinations they succeed. A manufacturer sits down to dinner in a suit of clothes which was wool on a sheep's back at sunrise. You dine with a gentleman on venison, pheasant, quail, pigeons, poultry, mushrooms and pineapples, all the growth of his estate. They are neat husbands for ordering all their tools pertaining to house and field.

All are well kept. There is no want and no waste. They study use and fitness in their building, in the order of their dwellings and in their dress. The Frenchman invented the ruffle; the Englishman added the shirt. The Englishman wears a sensible coat buttoned to the chin, of rough but solid and lasting texture. If he is a lord, he dresses a little worse than a commoner. They have diffused the taste for plain substantial hats, shoes and coats through Europe. They think him the best-dressed man whose dress is so fit for his use that you cannot notice or remember to describe it.

They secure the essentials in their diet, in their arts and manufactures. Every article of cutlery shows, in its shape, thought and long experience of workmen. They put the expense in the right place, as, in their sea-steamers, in the solidity of the machinery and the strength of the boat. The admirable equipment of their arctic ships carries London to the pole. They build roads aqueducts; warm and ventilate houses. And they have impressed their directness and practical habit on modern civilization.

In trade, the Englishman believes that nobody breaks who ought not to break; and that if he do not make trade everything, it will make him nothing; and acts on this belief. The spirit of system, attention to details, and the subordination of details, or the not driving things too finely, (which is charged on the Germans,) constitute that despatch of business which makes the mercantile power of England.

In war, the Englishman looks to his means. He is the opinion of Civilis, his German ancestor, whom Tacitus reports as holding that "the gods are on the side of the strongest"—a sentence which Bonaparte unconsciously translated, when he said that "he had noticed that Providence always favored the heaviest battalion." Their military science propounds that if the weight of the advancing column is greater than that of the resisting, the latter is destroyed. Therefore Wellington, when he came to the army in Spain, had every man weighed, first with accoutrements, and then without; believing that the force of an army depended on the weight and power of the individual soldiers, in spite of cannon. Lord Palmerston told the House of Commons that more care is taken of the health and comfort of English troops than of any other troops in the world; and that hence the English can put more men into the rank, on the day of action, on the field of battle, than any other army. Before the bombardment of the Danish forts in the Baltic, Nelson spent day after day, himself, in the boats, on the exhausting service of sounding the channel. Clerk of Eldin's celebrated maneuver of breaking the line of sea-battle, and Nelson's feat of *doubling*, or stationing his ships one on the outer bow, and another on the outer quarter of each of the enemy's, were only translations into naval tactics of Bonaparte's rule of concentration. Lord Collingwood was accustomed to tell his men that if they could fire three well-directed broadsides in five minutes, no vessel could resist them; and from constant practice they came to do it in three minutes and a half.

But conscious that no race of better men exists, they rely most on the simplest means, and do not like ponderous and difficult tactics, but delight to bring the affair hand to hand; where the victory lies with the strength, courage and endurance of the individual combatants. They adopt every improvement in rig, in motor, in weapons, but they fundamentally believe that the best stratagem in naval war is to lay your ship close alongside of the enemy's ship and bring all your guns to bear on him, until you or he go to the bottom. This is the old fashion, which never goes out of fashion, neither in nor out of England.

It is not usually a point of honor, nor a religious sentiment, and never any whim, that they will shed their blood for; but usually property, and right measured by property, that breeds revolution. They have no Indian taste for a tomahawk-dance, no French taste for a badge or a proclamation. The Englishman is peaceably minding his business and earning his day's wages. But if you offer to lay hand on his day's wages, on his cow, or his right in common, or his shop, he will fight to the Judgment. Magna Charta, jury trial, *habeas corpus*, star-chamber, ship money, Popery, Plymouth colony, American Revolution, are all questions involving a yeoman's right to his dinner, and except as touching that, would not have lashed the British nation to rage and revolt.

Whilst they are thus instinct with a spirit of order and of calculation, it must be owned they are capable of larger views; but the indulgence is expensive to them, costs great crises, or accumulations of mental power. In common, the horse works best with blinders. Nothing is more in the line of English thought than our unvarnished Connecticut question "Pray, sir, how do you get your living when you are at home?" The questions of freedom, of taxation, of privilege, are money questions. Heavy fellows, steeped in beer and fleshpots, they are hard of hearing and dim of sight. Their drowsy minds need to be flagellated by war and trade and politics and persecution. They cannot well read a principle, except by the light of fagots and of burning towns.

Tacitus says of the Germans, "Powerful only in sudden efforts, they are impatient of toil and labor." This highly destined race, if it had not somewhere added the chamber of patience to its brain, would not have built London. I know not from which of the tribes and temperaments that went to the composition of the people this tenacity was supplied, but they clinch every nail they drive. They have no running for luck, and no immoderate speed. They spend largely on their fabric, and await the slow return. Their leather lies tanning seven years in the vat. At Rogers's mills, in Sheffield, where I was shown the process of making a razor and a penknife, I was told there is no luck in making good steel; that they make no mistakes, every blade in the hundred and in the thousand is good. And that is characteristic of all their work—no more is attempted than is done.

When Thor and his companions arrive at Utgard, he is told that "nobody is permitted to remain here, unless he understand some art, and excel in it all other men." The same question is still put to the posterity of Thor. A nation of laborers, every man is trained to some one art or detail and aims at perfection in that; not content unless he has something in which he thinks he surpasses all other men. He would rather not do anything at all than not do it well. I suppose no people have such thoroughness—from the highest to the lowest, every man meaning to be master of his art.

"To show capacity," a Frenchman described as the end of a speech in debate: "No," said an Englishman, "but to set your shoulder at the wheel—to advance the business." Sir Samuel Romilly refused to speak in popular assemblies, confining himself to the House of Commons, where a measure can be carried by a speech. The business of the House of Commons is conducted by a few persons, but these are hard-worked. Sir Robert Peel "knew the Blue Books by heart." His colleagues and rivals carry Hansard in their heads. The high civil and legal offices are not beds of ease, but posts which exact frightful amounts of mental labor. Many of the great leaders, like Pitt, Canning, Castlereagh, Romilly, are soon worked to death. They are excellent judges in England of a good worker, and when they find one, like Clarendon, Sir Philip Warwick, Sir William Coventry, Ashley, Burke, Thurlow, Mansfield, Pitt, Eldon, Peel, or Russell, there is nothing too good or too high for him.

They have a wonderful heat in the pursuit of a public aim. Private persons exhibit, in scientific and antiquarian researches, the same pertinacity as the nation showed in the coalitions in which it yoked Europe against the empire of Bonaparte, one after the other defeated, and still renewed, until the sixth hurled him from his seat.

Sir John Herschel, in completion of the work of his father, who had made the catalogue of the stars of the northern hemisphere, expatriated himself for years at the Cape of Good Hope, finished his inventory of the southern heaven, came home, and redacted it in eight years more—a work whose value does not begin until thirty years have elapsed, and thenceforward a record to

all ages of the highest import. The Admiralty sent out
the Arctic expeditions year after year, in search of Sir
John Franklin, until at last they have threaded their way
through polar pack and Behring's Straits and solved the
geographical problem. Lord Elgin, at Athens, saw the
imminent ruin of the Greek remains, set up his scaffold-
ings, in spite of epigrams, and, after five years' labor to
collect them, got his marbles on shipboard. The ship
struck a rock and went to the bottom. He had them all
fished up by divers, at a vast expense, and brought to
London; not knowing that Haydon, Fuseli and Canova,
and all good heads in all the world, were to be his ap-
plauders. In the same spirit, were the excavation and
research by Sir Charles Fellowes for the Xanthian monument, and of Layard for his Nineveh sculptures.

The nation sits in the immense city they have builded,
a London extended into every man's mind, though he
live in Van Dieman's Land or Capetown. Faithful performance of what is undertaken to be performed, they
honor in themselves, and exact in others, as certificate of
equality with themselves. The modern world is theirs.
They have made and make it day by day. The commercial relations of the world are so intimately drawn to
London, that every dollar on earth contributes to the
strength of the English government. And if all the
wealth in the planet should perish by war or deluge, they
know themselves competent to replace it.

They have approved their Saxon blood, by their sea-
going qualities; their descent from Odin's smiths, by
their hereditary skill in working in iron; their British
birth, by husbandry and immense wheat harvests; and
justified their occupancy of the center of habitable land,
by their supreme ability and cosmopolitan spirit. They
have tilled, builded, forged, spun and woven. They have
made the island a thoroughfare, and London a shop, a

law-court, a record-office and scientific bureau, inviting to strangers; a sanctuary to refugees of every political and religious opinion; and such a city that almost every active man, in any nation, finds himself at one time or other forced to visit it.

In every path of practical activity they have gone even with the best. There is no secret of war in which they have not shown mastery. The steam-chamber of Watt, the locomotive of Stephenson, the cotton-mule of Roberts, perform the labor of the world. There is no department of literature, of science, or of useful art, in which they have not produced a first-rate book. It is England whose opinion is waited for on the merit of a new invention, an improved science. And in the complications of the trade and politics of their vast empire, they have been equal to every exigency, with counsel and with conduct. Is it their luck, or is it in the chambers of their brain—it is their commercial advantage that whatever light appears in better method or happy invention, breaks out *in their race.* They are a family to which a destiny attaches, and the Banshee has sworn that a male heir shall never be wanting. They have a wealth of men to fill important posts, and the vigilance of party criticism insures the selection of a competent person.

A proof of the energy of the British people is the highly artificial construction of the whole fabric. The climate and geography, I said, were factitious, as if the hands of man had arranged the conditions. The same character pervades the whole kingdom. Bacon said, "Rome was a state not subject to paradoxes"; but England subsists by antagonisms and contradictions. The foundations of its greatness are the rolling waves; and from first to last it is a museum of anomalies This foggy and rainy country furnishes the world with astronomical observations. Its short rivers do not afford water-power, but the land shakes under the thunder of the mills. There is no gold-mine of any importance, but there is more gold in England than in all other countries. It is too far north for the culture of the vine, but the wines of all countries are in its docks. The French Comte de Lauraguais said, "No fruit ripens in England but a baked apple"; but oranges and pineapples are as cheap in London as in the Mediterranean. The Mark-Lane Express, or the Custom House Returns, bear out to the letter the vaunt of Pope—

> Let India boast her palms, nor envy we
> The weeping amber, nor the spicy tree,
> While, by our oaks, those precious loads are borne,
> And realms commanded which those trees adorn.

The native cattle are extinct, but the island is full of artificial breeds. The agriculturist Bakewell created sheep and cows and horses to order, and breeds in which everything was omitted but what is economical. The cow is sacrificed to her bag, the ox to his sirloin. Stall-feeding makes sperm-mills of the cattle, and converts the stable to a chemical factory. The rivers, lakes and ponds, too much fished, or obstructed by factories, are artificially filled with the eggs of salmon, turbot, and herring.

Chat Moss and the fens of Lincolnshire and Cambridgeshire are unhealthy and too barren to pay rent. By cylindrical tiles and guttapercha tubes, five millions of acres of bad land have been drained and put on equality with the best, for rape-culture and grass. The climate too, which was already believed to have become milder and drier by the enormous consumption of coal, is so far reached by this new action, that fogs and storms are said to disappear. In due course, all England will be drained and rise a second time out of the waters. The latest step was to call in the aid of steam to agriculture. Steam is almost an Englishman. I do not know but they will send him to Parliament next, to make laws. He weaves, forges, saws, pounds, fans, and now he must pump, grind, dig and plough for the farmer. The markets created by the manufacturing population have erected agriculture into a great thriving and spending industry. The value of the houses in Britain is equal to the value of the soil. Artificial aids of all kinds are cheaper than the natural resources. No man can afford to walk, when the parliamentary-train carries him for a penny a mile. Gas-burners are cheaper than daylight in numberless floors in the cities. All the houses in London buy their water. The English trade does not exist for the exportation of native products, but on its manufactures, or the making well everything which is ill-made elsewhere. They make ponchos for the Mexican, bandannas for the Hindu, ginseng for the Chinese, beads for the Indian, laces for the Flemings, telescopes for astronomers, cannons for kings.

The Board of Trade caused the best models of Greece and Italy to be placed within the reach of every manufacturing population. They caused to be translated from foreign languages and illustrated by elaborate drawings, the most approved works of Munich, Berlin and Paris. They have ransacked Italy to find new forms, to add a grace to the products of their looms, their potteries and their foundries.[1]

The nearer we look, the more artificial is their social system. Their law is a network of fictions. Their property, a scrip or certificate of right to interest on money that no man ever saw. Their social classes are made by statute. Their ratios of power and representation are his-

---

[1] See *Memorial of H. Greenough*, p. 66, New York, 1853.

torical and legal. The last Reform bill took away political power from a mound, a ruin and a stone-wall, whilst Birmingham and Manchester, whose mills paid for the wars of Europe, had no representative. Purity in the elective Parliament is secured by the Purchase of seats.[2] Foreign power is kept by armed colonies; power at home, by a standing army of police. The pauper lives better than the free laborer, the thief better than the pauper, and the transported felon better than the one under imprisonment. The crimes are factitious; as smuggling, poaching, non-conformity, heresy and treason. The sovereignty of the seas is maintained by the impressment of seamen. "The impressment of seamen," said Lord Eldon, "is the life of our navy." Solvency is maintained by means of a national debt, on the principle, "If you will not lend me the money, how can I pay you?" For the administration of justice, Sir Samuel Romilly's expedient for clearing the arrears of business in Chancery was, the Chancellor's staying away entirely from his court. Their system of education is factitious. The Universities galvanize dead languages into a semblance of life. Their church is artificial. The manners and customs of society are artificial—made-up men with made-up manners—and thus the whole is Birminghamized, and we have a nation whose existence is a work of art—a cold, barren, almost arctic isle being made the most fruitful, luxurious and imperial land in the whole earth.

Man in England submits to be a product of political economy. On a bleak moor a mill is built, a banking-house is opened, and men come in as water in a sluice-way, and towns and cities rise. Man is made as a Bir-

---

[2] Sir S. Romilly, purest of English patriots, decided that the only independent mode of entering Parliament was to buy a seat, and he bought Horsham.

mingham button. The rapid doubling of the population dates from Watt's steam-engine. A landlord who owns a province, says "The tenantry are unprofitable; let me have sheep." He unroofs the houses and ships the population to America. The nation is accustomed to the instantaneous creation of wealth. It is the maxim of their economists, "that the greater part in value of the wealth now existing in England has been produced by human hands within the last twelve months." Meantime, three or four days' rain will reduce hundreds to starving in London.

One secret of their power is their mutual good understanding. Not only good minds are born among them, but all the people have good minds. Every nation has yielded some good wit, if, as has chanced to many tribes, only one. But the intellectual organization of the English admits a communicableness of knowledge and ideas among them all. An electric touch by any of their national ideas, melts them into one family and brings the hoards of power which their individuality is always hiving, into use and play for all. Is it the smallness of the country, or is it the pride and affection of race—they have solidarity, or responsibleness, and trust in each other.

Their minds, like wool, admit of a dye which is more lasting than the cloth. They embrace their cause with more tenacity than their life. Though not military, yet every common subject by the poll is fit to make a soldier of. These private, reserved, mute family-men can adopt a public end with all their heat, and this strength of affection makes the romance of their heroes. The difference of rank does not divide the national heart. The Danish poet Oehlenschläger complains that who writes in Danish writes to two hundred readers. In Germany there is one speech for the learned, and another for the masses, to that extent that, it is said, no sentiment or phrase from the works of any great German writer is ever heard among the lower classes. But in England, the language of the noble is the language of the poor. In Parliament, in pulpits, in theaters, when the speakers rise to thought and passion, the language becomes idiomatic; the people in the street best understand the best words. And their language seems drawn from the Bible, the Common Law and the works of Shakespeare, Bacon, Milton, Pope, Young, Cowper, Burns and Scott. The island has produced two or three of the greatest men that ever existed, but they were not solitary in their own time. Men quickly embodied what Newton found out, in Greenwich observatories and practical navigation. The boys know all that Hutton knew of strata, or Dalton of atoms, or Harvey of blood vessels; and these studies, once dangerous, are in fashion. So what is invented or known in agriculture, or in trade, or in war, or in art, or in literature and antiquities. A great ability, not amassed on a few giants, but poured into the general mind, so that each of them could at a pinch stand in the shoes of the other; and they are more bound in character than differenced in ability or in rank. The laborer is a possible lord. The lord is a possible basket-maker. Every man carries the English system in his brain, knows what is confided to him and does therein the best he can. The chancellor carries England on his mace, the midshipman at the point of his dirk, the smith on his hammer, the cook in the bowl of his spoon; the postilion cracks his whip for England, and the sailor times his oars to "God save the King!" The very felons have their pride in each other's English stanchness. In politics and in war they hold together as by hooks of steel. The charm in Nelson's history is the unselfish greatness, the assurance of being supported to the uttermost by those whom he supports to the uttermost. Whilst they are some ages ahead of the rest of the world in the art of living; whilst in some directions they do not represent the modern spirit but constitute it—this vanguard of civility and power they coldly hold, marching in phalanx, lockstep, foot after foot, file after file of heroes, ten thousand deep.

MANNERS

I find the Englishman to be him of all men who stands firmest in his shoes. They have in themselves what they value in their horses—mettle and bottom. On the day of my arrival at Liverpool, a gentleman, in describing to me the Lord Lieutenant of Ireland, happened to say, "Lord Clarendon has pluck like a cock and will fight till he dies"; and what I heard first I heard last, and the one thing the English value is *pluck*. The word is not beautiful, but on the quality they signify by it the nation is unanimous. The cabmen have it; the merchants have it; the bishops have it; the women have it; the journals have it—the *Times* newspaper they say is the pluckiest thing in England, and Sydney Smith had made it a proverb that little Lord John Russell, the minister, would take the command of the Channel fleet tomorrow.

They require you to dare to be of your own opinion, and they hate the practical cowards who cannot in affairs answer directly yes or no. They dare to displease, nay, they will let you break all the commandments, if you do it natively and with spirit. You must be somebody; then you may do this or that, as you will.

Machinery has been applied to all work, and carried to such perfection that little is left for the men but to

mind the engines and feed the furnaces. But the machines require punctual service, and as they never tire,
they prove too much for their tenders. Mines, forges,
mills, breweries, railroads, steam-pump, steam-plough,
drill of regiments, drill of police, rule of court and shop-
rule have operated to give a mechanical regularity to all
the habit and action of men. A terrible machine has
possessed itself of the ground, the air, the men and
women, and hardly even thought is free.

The mechanical might and organization requires in
the people constitution and answering spirits; and he
who goes among them must have some weight of metal.
At last, you take your hint from the fury of life you find,
and say, one thing is plain, this is no country for faint-
hearted people: don't creep about diffidently; make up
your mind; take your own course, and you shall find
respect and furtherance.

It requires, men say, a good constitution to travel in
Spain. I say as much of England, for other cause, simply
on account of the vigor and brawn of the people. Nothing but the most serious business could give one any
counterweight to these Baresarks, though they were
only to order eggs and muffins for their breakfast. The
Englishman speaks with all his body. His elocution is
stomachic—as the American's is labial. The Englishman is very petulant and precise about his accommodation at inns and on the roads; a quiddle about his toast
and his chop and every species of convenience, and loud
and pungent in his expressions of impatience at any
neglect. His vivacity betrays itself at all points, in his
manners, in his respiration, and the inarticulate noises
he makes in clearing the throat—all significant of burly
strength. He has stamina; he can take the initiative in
emergencies. He has that *aplomb* which results from a
good adjustment of the moral and physical nature and

the obedience of all the powers to the will; as if the axes of his eyes were united to his backbone, and only moved with the trunk.

This vigor appears in the incuriosity and stony neglect, each of every other. Each man walks, eats, drinks, shaves, dresses, gesticulates, and, in every manner, acts and suffers without reference to the by-standers, in his own fashion, only careful not to interfere with them or annoy them; not that he is trained to neglect the eyes of his neighbors—he is really occupied with his own affair and does not think of them. Every man in this polished country consults only his convenience, as much as a solitary pioneer in Wisconsin. I know not where any personal eccentricity is so freely allowed, and no man gives himself any concern with it. An Englishman walks in a pouring rain, swinging his closed umbrella like a walking-stick; wears a wig, or a shawl, or a saddle, or stands on his head, and no remark is made. And as he has been doing this for several generations, it is now in the blood.

In short, every one of these islanders is an island himself, safe, tranquil, incommunicable. In a company of strangers you would think him deaf; his eyes never wander from his table and newspaper. He is never betrayed into any curiosity or unbecoming emotion. They have all been trained in one severe school of manners, and never put off the harness. He does not give his hand. He does not let you meet his eye. It is almost an affront to look a man in the face without being introduced. In mixed or in select companies they do not introduce persons; so that a presentation is a circumstance as valid as a contract. Introductions are sacraments. He withholds his name. At the hotel, he is hardly willing to whisper it to the clerk at the book-office. If he give you his private address on a card, it is like an avowal of friendship; and his bearing, on being introduced, is cold, even though he is seeking your acquaintance and is studying how he shall serve you.

It was an odd proof of this impressive energy, that in my lectures I hesitated to read and threw out for its impertinence many a disparaging phrase which I had been accustomed to spin, about poor, thin, unable mortals—so much had the fine physique and the personal vigor of this robust race worked on my imagination.

I happened to arrive in England at the moment of a commercial crisis. But it was evident that let who will fail, England will not. These people have sat here a thousand years, and here will continue to sit. They will not break up, or arrive at any desperate revolution, like their neighbors; for they have as much energy, as much continence of character as they ever had. The power and possession which surround them are their own creation, and they exert the same commanding industry at this moment.

They are positive, methodical, cleanly and formal, loving routine and conventional ways; loving truth and religion, to be sure, but inexorable on points of form. All the world praises the comfort and private appointments of an English inn, and of English households. You are sure of neatness and of personal decorum. A Frenchman may possibly be clean; an Englishman is conscientiously clean. A certain order and complete propriety is found in his dress and in his belongings.

Born in a harsh and wet climate, which keeps him indoors whenever he is at rest, and being of an affectionate and loyal temper, he dearly loves his house. If he is rich, he buys a demesne and builds a hall; if he is in middle condition, he spares no expense on his house. Without, it is all planted; within, it is wainscoted, carved, curtained, hung with pictures and filled with good furniture. 'Tis a passion which survives all others, to deck and improve it. Hither he brings all that is rare and costly, and with the national tendency to sit fast in the same spot for many generations, it comes to be, in the course of time, a museum of heirlooms, gifts and trophies of the adventures and exploits of the family. He is very fond of silver plate, and though he have no gallery of portraits of his ancestors, he has of their punch-bowls and porringers. Incredible amounts of plate are found in good houses, and the poorest have some spoon or saucepan, gift of a godmother, saved out of better times.

An English family consists of a few persons, who, from youth to age, are found revolving within a few feet of each other, as if tied by some invisible ligature, tense as that cartilage which we have seen attaching the two Siamese. England produces under favorable conditions of ease and culture the finest women in the world. And as the men are affectionate and true-hearted, the women inspire and refine them. Nothing can be more delicate without being fantastical, nothing more firm and based in nature and sentiment, than the courtship and mutual carriage of the sexes. The song of 1596 says, "the wife of every Englishman is counted blest." The sentiment of Imogen in *Cymbeline* is copied from English nature; and not less the Portia of Brutus, the Kate Percy and the Desdemona. The romance does not exceed the height of noble passion in Mrs. Lucy Hutchinson, or in Lady Russell, or even as one discerns through the plain prose of *Pepys's Diary*, the sacred habit of an English wife. Sir Samuel Romilly could not bear the death of his wife. Every class has its noble and tender examples.

Domesticity is the taproot which enables the nation to branch wide and high. The motive and end of their trade and empire is to guard the independence and privacy of their homes. Nothing so much marks their manners as the concentration on their household ties. This domesticity is carried into court and camp. Wellington governed India and Spain and his own troops, and fought battles, like a good family-man, paid his debts, and though general of an army in Spain, could not stir abroad for fear of public creditors. This taste for house and parish merits has of course its doting and foolish side. Mr. Cobbett attributes the huge popularity of Perceval, prime minister in 1810, to the fact that he was wont to go to church every Sunday, with a large quarto gilt prayer-book under one arm, his wife hanging on the other, and followed by a long brood of children.

They keep their old customs, costumes, and pomps, their wig and mace, sceptre and crown. The Middle Ages still lurk in the streets of London. The Knights of the Bath take oath to defend injured ladies; the gold-stick-in-waiting survives. They repeated the ceremonies of the eleventh century in the coronation of the present Queen. A hereditary tenure is natural to them. Offices, farms, trades and traditions descend so. Their leases run for a hundred and a thousand years. Terms of service and partnership are lifelong, or are inherited. "Holdship has been with me," said Lord Eldon, "eight-and-twenty years, knows all my business and books." Antiquity of usage is sanction enough. Wordsworth says of the small freeholders of Westmoreland, "Many of these humble sons of the hills had a consciousness that the land which they tilled had for more than five hundred years been possessed by men of the same name and blood." The ship-carpenter in the public yards, my lord's gardener and porter, have been there for more than a hundred years, grandfather, father, and son.

The English power resides also in their dislike of change. They have difficulty in bringing their reason to act, and on all occasions use their memory first. As soon as they have rid themselves of some grievance and settled the better practice, they make haste to fix it as a finality, and never wish to hear of alteration more.

Every Englishman is an embryonic chancellor: his instinct is to search for a precedent. The favorite phrase of their law is, "a custom whereof the memory of man runneth not back to the contrary." The barons say, "*Nolumus mutari*"; and the cockneys stifle the curiosity of the foreigner on the reason of any practice with "Lord, sir, it was always so." They hate innovation. Bacon told them, Time was the right reformer; Chatham, that "confidence was a plant of slow growth"; Canning, to "advance with the times"; and Wellington, that "habit was ten times nature." All their statesmen learn the irresistibility of the tide of custom, and have invented many fine phrases to cover this slowness of perception and prehensility of tail.

A sea-shell should be the crest of England, not only because it represents a power built on the waves, but also the hard finish of the men. The Englishman is finished like a cowry or a murex. After the spire and the spines are formed, or with the formation, a juice exudes and a hard enamel varnishes every part. The keeping of the proprieties is as indispensable as clean linen. No merit quite countervails the want of this, whilst this sometimes stands in lieu of all. " 'Tis in bad taste," is the most formidable word an Englishman can pronounce. But this japan costs them dear. There is a prose in certain Englishmen which exceeds in wooden deadness all rivalry with other countrymen. There is a knell in the conceit and externality of their voice, which seems to say, *Leave all hope behind.* In this Gibraltar of propriety, mediocrity gets intrenched and consolidated and founded in adamant. An Englishman of fashion is like one of those souvenirs, bound in gold vellum, enriched with delicate engravings on thick hot-pressed paper, fit for the hands of ladies and princes, but with nothing in it worth reading or remembering.

A severe decorum rules the court and the cottage. When Thalberg the pianist was one evening performing before the Queen at Windsor, in a private party, the Queen accompanied him with her voice. The circumstance took air, and all England shuddered from sea to sea. The indecorum was never repeated. Cold, repressive manners prevail. No enthusiasm is permitted except at the opera. They avoid everything marked. They require a tone of voice that excites no attention in the room. Sir Philip Sidney is one of the patron saints of England, of whom Wotton said, "His wit was the measure of congruity."

Pretension and vaporing are once for all distasteful. They keep to the other extreme of low tone in dress and manners. They avoid pretension and go right to the heart of the thing. They hate nonsense, sentimentalism and highflown expression; they use a studied plainness. Even Brummell, their fop, was marked by the severest simplicity in dress. They value themselves on the absence of everything theatrical in the public business, and on conciseness and going to the point, in private affairs.

In an aristocratical country like England, not the Trial by Jury, but the dinner, is the capital institution. It is the mode of doing honor to a stranger, to invite him to eat—and has been for many hundred years. "And they think," says the Venetian traveler of 1500, "no greater honor can be conferred or received, than to invite others to eat with them, or to be invited themselves, and they would sooner give five or six ducats to provide an entertainment for a person, than a groat to assist him in any distress." [1] It is reserved to the end of the day, the family-hour being generally six, in London, and if any company is expected, one or two hours later. Everyone dresses for dinner, in his own house, or in another man's. The guests are expected to arrive within half an hour of the time fixed by card of invitation, and nothing but death or mutilation is permitted to detain them. The English dinner is precisely the model on which our own are constructed in the Atlantic cities. The company sit one or two hours before the ladies leave the table. The gentlemen remain over their wine an hour longer, and rejoin the ladies in the drawing-room and take coffee. The dress-dinner generates a talent of table-talk which reaches great perfection: the stories are so good that one is sure they must have been often told before, to have got such happy turns. Hither come all manner of clever projects, bits of popular science, of practical invention, of miscellaneous humor; political, literary and personal news; railroads, horses, diamonds, agriculture, horticulture, pisciculture and wine.

English stories *bon-mots* and the recorded table-talk of their wits, are as good as the best of the French. In America, we are apt scholars, but have not yet attained the same perfection: for the range of nations from which London draws, and the steep contrasts of condition, create the picturesque in society, as broken country makes picturesque landscape: whilst our prevailing equality makes a prairie tameness: and secondly, because the usage of a dress-dinner every day at dark has a tendency to hive and produce to advantage everything good. Much attrition has worn every sentence into a bullet. Also one meets now and then with polished men

---

[1] *Relation of England.* Printed by the Camden Society.

who know everything, have tried everything, and can
do everything, and are quite superior to letters and
science. What could they not, if only they would?

TRUTH

The Teutonic tribes have a national singleness of
heart, which contrasts with the Latin races. The German
name has a proverbial significance of sincerity and
honest meaning. The arts bear testimony to it. The faces
of clergy and laity in old sculptures and illuminated
missals are charged with earnest belief. Add to this hereditary rectitude the punctuality and precise dealing
which commerce creates, and you have the English truth
and credit. The government strictly performs its engagements. The subjects do not understand trifling on its
part. When any breach of promise occurred, in the old
days of prerogative, it was resented by the people as an
intolerable grievance. And in modern times, any slipperi-
ness in the government of political faith, or any repudia-
tion or crookedness in matters of finance, would bring
the whole nation to a committee of inquiry and reform.
Private men keep their promises, never so trivial. Down
goes the flying word on the tablets, and is indelible as
Domesday Book.

Their practical power rests on their national sincerity.
Veracity derives from instinct, and marks superiority in
organization. Nature has endowed some animals with
cunning, as a compensation for strength withheld; but
it has provoked the malice of all others, as if avengers of
public wrong. In the nobler kinds, where strength could
be afforded, her races are loyal to truth, as truth is the
foundation of the social state. Beasts that make no truce

with man, do not break with each other. 'Tis said that the wolf, who makes a *cache* of his prey and brings his fellows with him to the spot, if, on digging, it is not found, is instantly and unresistingly torn in pieces. English veracity seems to result on a sounder animal structure, as if they could afford it. They are blunt in saying what they think, sparing of promises, and they require plain dealing of others. We will not have to do with a man in a mask. Let us know the truth. Draw a straight line, hit whom and where it will. Alfred, whom the affection of the nation makes the type of their race, is called by a writer at the Norman Conquest, the *truth-speaker; Alueredus veridicus.* Geoffrey of Monmouth says of King Aurelius, uncle of Arthur, that "above all things he hated a lie." The Northman Guttorm said to King Olaf, "It is royal work to fulfil royal words." The mottoes of their families are monitory proverbs, as, *Fare fac*—Say, do—of the Fairfaxes; *Say and seal,* of the House of Fiennes; *Vero nil verius,* of the DeVeres. To be king of their word is their pride. When they unmask cant, they say, "The English of this is," etc.; and to give the lie is the extreme insult. The phrase of the lowest of the people is "honor-bright," and their vulgar praise, "His word is as good as his bond." They hate shuffling and equivocation, and the cause is damaged in the public opinion, on which any paltering can be fixed. Even Lord Chesterfield, with his French breeding, when he came to define a gentleman, declared that truth made his distinction; and nothing ever spoken by him would find so hearty a suffrage from his nation. The Duke of Wellington, who had the best right to say so, advises the French General Kellermann that he may rely on the parole of an English officer. The English, of all classes, value themselves on this trait, as distinguishing them from the French, who, in the popular belief, are more polite than true. An Englishman understates, avoids the superlative, checks himself in compliments, alleging that in the French language one cannot speak without lying.

They love reality in wealth, power, hospitality, and do not easily learn to make a show, and take the world as it goes. They are not fond of ornaments, and if they wear them, they must be gems. They read gladly in old Fuller that a lady, in the reign of Elizabeth, "would have as patiently digested a lie, as the wearing of false stones or pendants of counterfeit pearl." They have the earth-hunger, or preference for property in land, which is said to mark the Teutonic nations. They build of stone: public and private buildings are massive and durable. In comparing their ships' houses and public offices with the American, it is commonly said that they spend a pound where we spend a dollar. Plain rich clothes, plain rich equipage, plain rich finish throughout their house and belongings mark the English truth.

They confide in each other—English believes in English. The French feel the superiority of this probity. The Englishman is not springing a trap for his admiration, but is honestly minding his business. The Frenchman is vain. Madame de Staël says that the English irritated Napoleon, mainly because they have found out how to unite success with honesty. She was not aware how wide an application her foreign readers would give to the remark. Wellington discovered the ruin of Bonaparte's affairs, by his own probity. He augured ill of the empire, as soon as he saw that it was mendacious and lived by war. If war do not bring in its sequel new trade, better agriculture and manufactures, but only games, fireworks and spectacles—no prosperity could support it; much less a nation decimated for conscripts and out of pocket, like France. So he drudged for years on his military works at Lisbon, and from this base at last extended his gigantic lines to Waterloo, believing in his countrymen and their syllogisms above all the *rhodo-montade* of Europe.

At a St. George's festival, in Montreal, where I happened to be a guest since my return home, I observed that the chairman complimented his compatriots, by saying, "they confided that wherever they met an Englishman, they found a man who would speak the truth." And one cannot think this festival fruitless, if, all over the world, on the 23rd of April, wherever two or three English are found, they meet to encourage each other in the nationality of veracity.

In the power of saying rude truth, sometimes in the lion's mouth, no men surpass them. On the king's birthday, when each bishop was expected to offer the king a purse of gold, Latimer gave Henry VIII a copy of the *Vulgate*, with a mark at the passage, "Whoremongers and adulterers God will judge"; and they so honor stoutness in each other that the king passed it over. They are tenacious of their belief and cannot easily change their opinions to suit the hour. They are like ships with too much head on to come quickly about, nor will prosperity or even adversity be allowed to shake their habitual view of conduct. Whilst I was in London, M. Guizot arrived there on his escape from Paris, in February, 1848. Many private friends called on him. His name was immediately proposed as an honorary member of the Athenaeum. M. Guizot was blackballed. Certainly they knew the distinction of his name. But the Englishman is not fickle. He had really made up his mind now for years as he read his newspaper, to hate and despise M. Guizot; and the altered position of the man as an illustrious exile and a guest in the country, makes no difference to him, as it would instantly to an American.

They require the same adherence, thorough conviction and reality, in public men. It is the want of character which makes the low reputation of the Irish members. "See them," they said, "one hundred and twenty-seven all voting like sheep, never proposing anything, and all but four voting the income tax," which was an ill-judged concession of the government, relieving Irish property from the burdens charged on English.

They have a horror of adventurers in or out of Parliament. The ruling passion of Englishmen in these days is a terror of humbug. In the same proportion they value honesty, stoutness, and adherence to your own. They like a man committed to his objects. They hate the French, as frivolous; they hate the Irish, as aimless; they hate the Germans, as professors. In February 1848, they said, Look, the French king and his party fell for want of a shot; they had not conscience to shoot, so entirely was the pith and heart of monarchy eaten out.

They attack their own politicians every day, on the same grounds, as adventurers. They love stoutness in standing for your right, in declining money or promotion that costs any concession. The barrister refuses the silk gown of Queen's Counsel, if his junior have it one day earlier. Lord Collingwood would not accept his medal for victory on 14th February, 1797, if he did not receive one for victory on 1st June, 1794; and the long withholden medal was accorded. When Castlereagh dissuaded Lord Wellington from going to the king's levee until the unpopular Cintra business had been explained, he replied, "You furnish me a reason for going. I will go to this, or I will never go to a king's levee." The radical mob at Oxford cried after the Tory Lord Eldon, "There's old Eldon; cheer him; he never ratted." They have given the parliamentary nickname of *Trimmers* to the time-servers, whom English character does not love.[1]

They are very liable in their politics to extraordinary delusions; thus to believe what stands recorded in the gravest books, that the movement of 10th April, 1848, was urged or assisted by foreigners: which, to be sure, is paralleled by the democratic whimsy in this country which I have noticed to be shared by men sane on other points, that the English are at the bottom of the agitation of slavery, in American politics: and then again by the French popular legends on the subject of *perfidious Albion*. But suspicion will make fools of nations as of citizens.

A slow temperament makes them less rapid and ready than other countrymen, and has given occasion to the observation that English wit comes afterwards—which the French denote as *esprit d'escalier*. This dulness makes their attachment to home and their adherence in all foreign countries to home habits. The Englishman who visits Mount Etna will carry his teakettle to the top. The old Italian author of the *Relation of England* (in 1500), says, "I have it on the best information, that, when the war is actually raging most furiously, they will seek for good eating and all their other comforts, without thinking what harm might befall them." Then their eyes seem to be set at the bottom of a tunnel, and they affirm the one small fact they know, with the best faith

---

[1] It is an unlucky moment to remember these sparkles of solitary virtue in the face of the honors lately paid in England to the Emperor Louis Napoleon. I am sure that no Englishman whom I had the happiness to know, consented, when the aristocracy and the commons of London cringed like a Neapolitan rabble, before a successful thief. But—how to resist one step, though odious, in a linked series of state necessities? Governments must always learn too late, that the use of dishonest agents is as ruinous for nations as for single men.

in the world that nothing else exists. And as their own belief in guineas is perfect, they readily, on all occasions, apply the pecuniary argument as final. Thus when the Rochester rappings began to be heard of in England, a man deposited £100 in a sealed box in the Dublin Bank, and then advertised in the newspapers to all somnambulists, mesmerizers and others, that whoever could tell him the number of his note should have the money. He let it lie there six months, the newspapers now and then, at his instance, stimulating the attention of the adepts; but none could ever tell him; and he said, "Now let me never be bothered more with this proven lie." It is told of a good Sir John that he heard a case stated by counsel, and made up his mind; then the counsel for the other side taking their turn to speak, he found himself so unsettled and perplexed that he exclaimed, "So help me God! I will never listen to evidence again." Any number of delightful examples of this English stolidity are the anecdotes of Europe. I knew a very worthy man—a magistrate, I believe he was, in the town of Derby—who went to the opera to see Malibran. In one scene, the heroine was to rush across a ruined bridge. Mr. B. arose and mildly yet firmly called the attention of the audience and the performers to the fact that, in his judgment, the bridge was unsafe! This English stolidity contrasts with French wit and tact. The French, it is commonly said, have greatly more influence in Europe than the English. What influence the English have is by brute force of wealth and power; that of the French by affinity and talent. The Italian is subtle, the Spaniard treacherous: tortures, it is said, could never wrest from an Egyptian the confession of a secret. None of these traits belong to the Englishman. His choler and conceit force everything out. Defoe, who knew his countrymen well, says of them—

In close intrigue, their faculty's but weak,
For generally whate'er they know, they speak,
And often their own counsels undermine
By mere infirmity without design;
From whence, the learned say, it doth proceed,
That English treasons never can succeed;
For they're so open-hearted, you may know
Their own most secret thoughts, and others' too.

CHARACTER

The English race are reputed morose. I do not know
that they have sadder brows than their neighbors of
northern climates. They are sad by comparison with the
singing and dancing nations: not sadder, but slow and
staid, as finding their joys at home. They, too, believe
that where there is no enjoyment of life there can be no
vigor and art in speech or thought; that your merry heart
goes all the way, your sad one tires in a mile. This trait
of gloom has been fixed on them by French travelers,
who, from Froissart, Voltaire, Le Sage, Mirabeau, down
to the lively journalists of the *feuilletons,* have spent
their wit on the solemnity of their neighbors. The French
say, gay conversation is unknown in their island. The
Englishman finds no relief from reflection, except in reflection. When he wishes for amusement, he goes to
work. His hilarity is like an attack of fever. Religion, the
theater and the reading the books of his country all feed
and increase his natural melancholy. The police does
not interfere with public diversions. It thinks itself bound
in duty to respect the pleasures and rare gayety of this
inconsolable nation; and their well-known courage is
entirely attributable to their disgust of life.

I suppose their gravity of demeanor and their few

words have obtained this reputation. As compared with the Americans, I think them cheerful and contented. Young people in this country are much more prone to melancholy. The English have a mild aspect and a ringing cheerful voice. They are large-natured and not so easily amused as the southerners, and are among them as grown people among children, requiring war, or trade, or engineering, or science, instead of frivolous games. They are proud and private, and even if disposed to recreation, will avoid an open garden. They sported sadly; *ils s'amusaient tristement, selon la coutume de leur pays,* said Froissart; and I suppose never nation built their party-walls so thick, or their garden-fences so high. Meat and wine produce no effect on them. They are just as cold, quiet and composed, at the end, as at the beginning of dinner.

The reputation of taciturnity they have enjoyed for six or seven hundred years; and a kind of pride in bad public speaking is noted in the House of Commons, as if they were willing to show that they did not live by their tongues, or thought they spoke well enough if they had the tone of gentlemen. In mixed company they shut their mouths. A Yorkshire mill-owner told me he had ridden more than once all the way from London to Leeds, in the first-class carriage, with the same persons, and no word exchanged. The club-houses were established to cultivate social habits, and it is rare that more than two eat together, and oftenest one eats alone. Was it then a stroke of humor in the serious Swedenborg, or was it only his pitiless logic, that made him shut up the English souls in a heaven by themselves?

They are contradictorily described as sour, splenetic and stubborn—and as mild, sweet and sensible. The truth is they have great range and variety of character.

Commerce sends abroad multitudes of different classes. The choleric Welshman, the fervid Scot, the bilious resident in the East or West Indies, are wide of the perfect behavior of the educated and dignified man of family. So is the burly farmer; so is the country squire, with his narrow and violent life. In every inn is the Commercial-Room, in which "travelers," or bagmen who carry patterns and solicit orders for the manufacturers, are wont to be entertained. It easily happens that this class should characterize England to the foreigner, who meets them on the road and at every public house, whilst the gentry avoid the taverns, or seclude themselves whilst in them.

But these classes are the right English stock, and may fairly show the national qualities, before yet art and education have dealt with them. They are good lovers, good haters, slow but obstinate admirers, and in all things very much steeped in their temperament, like men hardly awaked from deep sleep, which they enjoy. Their habits and instincts cleave to nature. They are of the earth, earthy; and of the sea, as the sea-kinds, attached to it for what it yields them, and not from any sentiment. They are full of coarse strength, rude exercise, butcher's meat and sound sleep; and suspect any poetic insinuation or any hint for the conduct of life which reflects on this animal existence, as if somebody were fumbling at the umbilical cord and might stop their supplies. They doubt a man's sound judgment if he does not eat with appetite, and shake their heads if he is particularly chaste. Take them as they come, you shall find in the common people a surly indifference, sometimes gruffness and ill temper; and in minds of more power, magazines of inexhaustible war, challenging

The ruggedest hour that time and spite dare bring
To frown upon the enraged Northumberland.

They are headstrong believers and defenders of their opinion, and not less resolute in maintaining their whim and perversity. Hezekiah Woodward wrote a book against the Lord's Prayer. And one can believe that Burton, the Anatomist of Melancholy, having predicted from the stars the hour of his death, slipped the knot himself round his own neck, not to falsify his horoscope.

Their looks bespeak an invincible stoutness: they have extreme difficulty to run away, and will die game. Wellington said of the young coxcombs of the Life-Guards, delicately brought up, "But the puppies fight well"; and Nelson said of his sailors, "They really mind shot no more than peas." Of absolute stoutness no nation has more or better examples. They are good at storming redoubts, at boarding frigates, at dying in the last ditch, or any desperate service which has daylight and honor in it; but not, I think, at enduring the rack, or any passive obedience, like jumping off a castle-roof at the word of a czar, being both vascular and highly organized, so as to be very sensible of pain; and intellectual, so as to see reason and glory in a matter.

Of that constitutional force which yields the supplies of the day, they have the more than enough; the excess which creates courage on fortitude, genius in poetry, invention in mechanics, enterprise in trade, magnificence in wealth, splendor in ceremonies, petulance and projects in youth. The young men have a rude health which runs into peccant humors. They drink brandy like water, cannot expend their quantities of waste strength on riding, hunting, swimming and fencing, and run into absurd frolics with the gravity of the Eumenides. They stoutly carry into every nook and corner of the earth their turbulent sense; leaving no lie uncontradicted; no pretension unexamined. They chew hasheesh; cut themselves with poisoned creases; swing their hammock in the boughs of the Bohon Upas; taste every poison; buy every secret; at Naples they put St. Januarius's blood in an alembic; they saw a hole into the head of the "winking Virgin," to know why she winks; measure with an English footrule every cell of the Inquisition, every Turkish caaba, every Holy of holies; translate and send to Bentley the arcanum bribed and bullied away from shuddering Brahmins; and measure their own strength by the terror they cause. These travelers are of every class, the best and the worst; and it may easily happen that those of rudest behavior are taken notice of and remembered. The Saxon melancholy in the vulgar rich and poor appears as gushes of ill-humor, which every check exasperates into sarcasm and vituperation. There are multitudes of rude young English who have the self-sufficiency and bluntness of their nation, and who, with their disdain of the rest of mankind and with this indigestion and choler, have made the English traveler a proverb for uncomfortable and offensive manners. It was no bad description of the Briton generically, what was said two hundred years ago of one particular Oxford scholar: "He was a very bold man, uttered anything that came into his mind, not only among his companions, but in public coffee-houses, and would often speak his mind of particular persons then accidentally present, without examining the company he was in; for which he was often reprimanded and several times threatened to be kicked and beaten."

The common Englishman is prone to forget a cardinal article in the bill of social rights, that every man has a right to his own ears. No man can claim to usurp more than a few cubic feet of the audibilities of a public room, or to put upon the company with the loud statement of his crotchets or personalities.

But it is in the deep traits of race that the fortunes of

nations are written, and however derived—whether a happier tribe or mixture of tribes, the air, or what circumstance that mixed for them the golden mean of temperament—here exists the best stock in the world, broad-fronted, broad-bottomed, best for depth, range and equability; men of aplomb and reserves, great range and many moods, strong instincts, yet apt for culture; war-class as well as clerks; earls and tradesmen; wise minority, as well as foolish majority; abysmal temperament, hiding wells of wrath, and glooms on which no sunshine settles, alternated with a common-sense and humanity which hold them fast to every piece of cheerful duty; making this temperament a sea to which all storms are superficial; a race to which their fortunes flow, as if they alone had the elastic organization at once fine and robust enough for dominion; as if the burly inexpressive, now mute and contumacious, now fierce and sharp-tongued dragon, which once made the island light with his fiery breath, had bequeathed his ferocity to his conqueror. They hide virtues under vices, or the semblance of them. It is the misshapen hairy Scandinavian troll again, who lifts the cart out of the mire, or "threshes the corn that ten day-laborers could not end," but it is done in the dark and with muttered maledictions. He is a churl with a soft place in his heart, whose speech is a brash of bitter waters, but who loves to help you at a pinch. He says no, and serves you, and your thanks disgust him. Here was lately a cross-grained miser, odd and ugly, resembling in countenance the portrait of Punch with the laugh left out; rich by his own industry; sulking in a lonely house; who never gave a dinner to any man and disdained all courtesies; yet as true a worshipper of beauty in form and color as ever existed, and profusely pouring over the cold mind of his countrymen creations of grace and truth, removing the reproach of sterility from English art, catching from their savage climate every fine hint, and importing into their galleries every tint and trait of sunnier cities and skies; making an era in painting; and when he saw that the splendor of one of his pictures in the Exhibition dimmed his rival's that hung next it, secretly took a brush and blackened his own.

They do not wear their heart in their sleeve for daws to peck at. They have that phlegm or staidness which it is a compliment to disturb. "Great men," said Aristotle, "are always of a nature originally melancholy." 'Tis the habit of a mind which attaches to abstractions with a passion which gives vast results. They dare to displease, they do not speak to expectation. They like the sayers of No, better than the sayers of Yes. Each of them has an opinion which he feels it becomes him to express all the more that it differs from yours. They are meditating opposition. This gravity is inseparable from minds of great resources.

There is an English hero superior to the French, the German, the Italian, or the Greek. When he is brought to the strife with fate, he sacrifices a richer material possession, and on more purely metaphysical grounds. He is there with his own consent, face to face with fortune, which he defies. On deliberate choice and from grounds of character, he has elected his part to live and die for, and dies with grandeur. This race has added new elements to humanity and has a deeper root in the world.

They have great range of scale, from ferocity to exquisite refinement. With larger scale, they have great retrieving power. After running each tendency to an extreme, they try another tack with equal heat. More intellectual than other races, when they live with other races they do not take their language, but bestow their own. They subsidize other nations, and are not subsidized. They proselyte, and are not proselyted. They assimilate other races to themselves, and are not assimilated. The English did not calculate the conquest of the Indies. It fell to their character. So they administer, in different parts of the world, the codes of every empire and race; in Canada, old French law; in the Mauritius, the Code Napoleon; in the West Indies, the edicts of the Spanish Cortes; in the East Indies, the Laws of Menu; in the Isle of Man, of the Scandinavian Thing; at the Cape of Good Hope, of the old Netherlands; and in the Ionian Islands, the Pandects of Justinian.

They are very conscious of their advantageous position in history. England is the lawgiver, the patron, the instructor, the ally. Compare the tone of the French and of the English press: the first querulous, captious, sensitive about English opinion; the English press never timorous about French opinion, but arrogant and contemptuous.

They are testy and headstrong through an excess of will and bias; churlish as men sometimes please to be who do not forget a debt, who ask no favors and who will do what they like with their own. With education and intercourse, these asperities wear off and leave the good-will pure. If anatomy is reformed according to national tendencies, I suppose the spleen will hereafter be found in the Englishman, not found in the American, and differencing the one from the other. I anticipate another anatomical discovery, that this organ will be found to be cortical and caducous; that they are superficially morose, but at last tender-hearted, herein differing from Rome and the Latin nations. Nothing savage, nothing mean resides in the English heart. They are subject to panics of credulity and of rage, but the temper of the nation, however disturbed, settles itself soon and easily, as, in this temperate zone, the sky after whatever storms clears again, and serenity is its normal condition.

A saving stupidity masks and protects their perception, as the curtain of the eagle's eye. Our swifter Americans, when they first deal with English, pronounce them stupid; but, later, do them justice as people who wear well, or hide their strength. To understand the power of performance that is in their finest wits, in the patient Newton, or in the versatile transcendent poets, or in the Dugdales, Gibbons, Hallams, Eldons and Peels, one should see how English day-laborers hold out. High and low, they are of an unctuous texture. There is an adipocere in their constitution, as if they had oil also for their mental wheels and could perform vast amounts of work without damaging themselves.

Even the scale of expense on which people live, and to which scholars and professional men conform, proves the tension of their muscle, when vast numbers are found who can each lift this enormous load. I might even add, their daily feasts argue a savage vigor of body.

No nation was ever so rich in able men; "Gentlemen," as Charles I said of Strafford, "whose abilities might make a prince rather afraid than ashamed in the greatest affairs of state"; men of such temper, that, like Baron Vere, "had one seen him returning from a victory, he would by his silence have suspected that he had lost the day; and, had he beheld him in a retreat, he would have collected him a conqueror by the cheerfulness of his spirit."[1]

The following passage from the *Heimskringla* might almost stand as a portrait of the modern Englishman —"Haldor was very stout and strong and remarkably handsome in appearances. King Harold gave him this testimony, that he, among all his men, cared least about

---

[1] Fuller, *Worthies of England*.

doubtful circumstances, whether they betokened danger or pleasure; for, whatever turned up, he was never in higher nor in lower spirits, never slept less nor more on account of them, nor ate nor drank but according to his custom. Haldor was not a man of many words, but short in conversation, told his opinion bluntly and was obstinate and hard: and this could not please the king, who had many clever people about him, zealous in his service. Haldor remained a short time with the king, and then came to Iceland, where he took up his abode in Hiardaholt and dwelt in that farm to a very advanced age."[2]

The national temper, in the civil history, is not flashy or whiffling. The slow, deep English mass smolders with fire, which at last sets all its borders in flame. The wrath of London is not French wrath, but has a long memory, and, in its hottest heat, a register and rule.

Half their strength they put not forth. They are capable of a sublime resolution, and if hereafter the war of races, often predicted, and making itself a war of opinions also (a question of despotism and liberty coming from Eastern Europe), should menace the English civilization, these sea-kings may take once again to their floating castles and find a new home and a second millennium of power in their colonies.

The stability of England is the security of the modern world. If the English race were as mutable as the French, what reliance? But the English stand for liberty. The conservative, money-loving, lord-loving English are yet liberty-loving; and so freedom is safe: for they have more personal force than any other people. The nation always resist the immoral action of their government.

---

[2] *Heimskringla*, Laing's translation, vol. iii. p. 37.

They think humanely on the affairs of France, of Turkey, of Poland, of Hungary, of Schleswig Holstein, though overborne by the statecraft of the rulers at last.

Does the early history of each tribe show the permanent bias, which, though not less potent, is masked as the tribe spreads its activity into colonies, commerce, codes, arts, letters? The early history shows it, as the musician plays the air which he proceeds to conceal in a tempest of variations. In Alfred, in the Northmen, one may read the genius of the English society, namely that private life is the place of honor. Glory, a career, and ambition, words familiar to the longitude of Paris, are seldom heard in English speech. Nelson wrote from their hearts his homely telegraph, "England expects every man to do his duty."

For actual service, for the dignity of a profession, or to appease diseased or inflamed talent, the army and navy may be entered (the worst boys doing well in the navy); and the civil service in departments where serious official work is done; and they hold in esteem the barrister engaged in the severer studies of the law. But the calm, sound and most British Briton shrinks from public life as charlatanism, and respects an economy founded on agriculture, coal-mines, manufactures or trade, which secures an independence through the creation of real values.

They wish neither to command nor obey, but to be kings in their own houses. They are intellectual and deeply enjoy literature; they like well to have the world served up to them in books, maps, models, and every mode of exact information, and, though not creators in art, they value its refinement. They are ready for leisure, can direct and fill their own day, nor need so much as others the constraint of a necessity. But the history of the nation discloses, at every turn, this original predilection for private independence, and however this inclination may have been disturbed by the bribes with which their vast colonial power has warped men out of orbit, the inclination endures, and forms and reforms the laws, letters, manners and occupations. They choose that welfare which is compatible with the commonwealth, knowing that such alone is stable; as wise merchants prefer investments in the three per cents.

COCKAYNE

The English are a nation of humorists. Individual right is pushed to the uttermost bound compatible with public order. Property is so perfect that it seems the craft of that race, and not to exist elsewhere. The king cannot step on an acre which the peasant refuses to sell. A testator endows a dog or a rookery, and Europe cannot interfere with his absurdity. Every individual has his particular way of living, which he pushes to folly, and the decided sympathy of his compatriots is engaged to back up Mr. Crump's whim by statutes and chancellors and horse-guards. There is no freak so ridiculous but some Englishman has attempted to immortalize by money and law. British citizenship is as omnipotent as Roman was. Mr. Cockayne is very sensible of this. The pursy man means by freedom the right to do as he pleases, and does wrong in order to feel his freedom, and makes a conscience of persisting in it.

He is intensely patriotic, for his country is so small. His confidence in the power and performance of his nation makes him provokingly incurious about other nations. He dislikes foreigners. Swedenborg, who lived much in England, notes "the similitude of minds among the English, in consequence of which they contract fa-

miliarity with friends who are of that nation, and seldom
with others; and they regard foreigners as one looking
through a telescope from the top of a palace regards
those who dwell or wander about out of the city." A
much older traveler, the Venetian who wrote the *Relation of England*,[1] in 1500, says—"The English are great
lovers of themselves and of everything belonging to
them. They think that there are no other men than
themselves and no other world but England; and whenever they see a handsome foreigner, they say that he
looks like an Englishman and it is a great pity he should
not be an Englishman; and whenever they partake of
any delicacy with a foreigner, they ask him whether such
a thing is made in his country." When he adds epithets
of praise, his climax is, "So English"; and when he
wishes to pay you the highest compliment, he says, I
should not know you from an Englishman. France is, by
its natural contrast, a kind of blackboard on which English character draws its own traits in chalk. This arrogance habitually exhibits itself in allusions to the French.
I suppose that all men of English blood in America,
Europe, or Asia, have a secret feeling of joy that they
are not French natives. Mr. Coleridge is said to have
given public thanks to God, at the close of a lecture, that
he had defended him from being able to utter a single
sentence in the French language. I have found that Englishmen have such a good opinion of England, that the
ordinary phrases in all good society, of postponing or
disparaging one's own things in talking with a stranger,
are seriously mistaken by them for an insuppressible
homage to the merits of their nation; and the New
Yorker or Pennsylvanian who modestly laments the dis-

---

[1] Printed by the Camden Society.

advantage of a new country, log-huts and savages, is surprised by the instant and unfeigned commiseration of the whole company, who plainly account all the world out of England a heap of rubbish.

The same insular limitation pinches his foreign politics. He sticks to his traditions and usages, and, so help him God! he will force his island by-laws down the throat of great countries, like India, China, Canada, Australia, and not only so, but impose Wapping on the Congress of Vienna and trample down all nationalities with his taxed boots. Lord Chatham goes for liberty and no taxation without representation—for that is British law; but not a hobnail shall they dare make in America, but buy their nails in England—for that also is British law; and the fact that British commerce was to be re-created by the independence of America, took them all by surprise.

In short, I am afraid that English nature is so rank and aggressive as to be a little incompatible with every other. The world is not wide enough for two.

But beyond this nationality, it must be admitted, the island offers a daily worship to the old Norse god Brage, celebrated among our Scandinavian forefathers for his eloquence and majestic air. The English have a steady courage that fits them for great attempts and endurance: they have also a petty courage, through which every man delights in showing himself for what he is and in doing what he can; so that in all companies, each of them has too good an opinion of himself to imitate anybody. He hides no defect of his form, features, dress, connection, or birthplace, for he thinks every circumstance belonging to him comes recommended to you. If one of them have a bald, or a red, or a green head, or bow legs, or a scar, or mark, or a paunch, or a squeaking or a raven voice, he has persuaded himself that there is something modish and becoming in it, and that it sits well on him.

But nature makes nothing in vain, and this little super-fluity of self-regard in the English brain is one of the secrets of their power and history. It sets every man on being and doing what he really is and can. It takes away a dodging, skulking, secondary air, and encourages a frank and manly bearing, so that each man makes the most of himself and loses no opportunity for want of pushing. A man's personal defects will commonly have, with the rest of the world, precisely that importance which they have to himself. If he makes light of them, so will other men. We all find in these a convenient meter of character, since a little man would be ruined by the vexation. I remember a shrewd politician, in one of our western cities, told me that "he had known several successful statesmen made by their foible." And another, an ex-governor of Illinois, said to me, "If the man knew anything, he would sit in a corner and be modest; but he is such an ignorant peacock that he goes bustling up and down and hits on extraordinary discoveries."

There is also this benefit in brag, that the speaker is unconsciously expressing his own ideal. Humor him by all means, draw it all out and hold him to it. Their culture generally enables the traveled English to avoid any ridiculous extremes of this self-pleasing, and to give it an agreeable air. Then the natural disposition is fostered by the respect which they find entertained in the world for English ability. It was said of Louis XIV, that his gait and air were becoming enough in so great a monarch, yet would have been ridiculous in another man; so the prestige of the English name warrants a certain confident bearing, which a Frenchman or Belgian could not carry. At all events, they feel themselves at liberty to assume the most extraordinary tone on the subject of English merits.

An English lady on the Rhine hearing a German speaking of her party as foreigners, exclaimed, "No, we are not foreigners; we are English; it is you that are foreigners." They tell you daily in London the story of the Frenchman and Englishman who quarreled. Both were unwilling to fight, but their companions put them up to it; at last it was agreed that they should fight alone, in the dark, and with pistols: the candles were put out, and the Englishman, to make sure not to hit anybody, fired up the chimney—and brought down the Frenchman. They have no curiosity about foreigners, and answer any information you may volunteer with "Oh, Oh!" until the informant makes up his mind that they shall die in their ignorance, for any help he will offer. There are really no limits to this conceit, though brighter men among them make painful efforts to be candid.

The habit of brag runs through all classes, from the *Times* newspaper through politicians and poets, through Wordsworth, Carlyle, Mill and Sydney Smith, down to the boys of Eton. In the gravest treatise on political economy, in a philosophical essay, in books of science, one is surprised by the most innocent exhibition of unflinching nationality. In a tract on Corn, a most amiable and accomplished gentleman writes thus—"Though Britain, according to Bishop Berkeley's idea, were surrounded by a wall of brass ten thousand cubits in height, still she would as far excel the rest of the globe in riches, as she now does both in this secondary quality and in the more important ones of freedom, virtue and science."[1]

The English dislike the American structure of society,

[1] William Spence.

whilst yet trade, mills, public education and Chartism are doing what they can to create in England the same social condition. America is the paradise of the economists; is the favorable exception invariably quoted to the rules of ruin; but when he speaks directly of the Americans the islander forgets his philosophy and remembers his disparaging anecdotes.

But this childish patriotism costs something, like all narrowness. The English sway of their colonies has no root of kindness. They govern by their arts and ability; they are more just than kind; and whenever an abatement of their power is felt, they have not conciliated the affection on which to rely.

Coarse local distinctions, as those of nation, province, or town, are useful in the absence of real ones; but we must not insist on these accidental lines. Individual traits are always triumphing over national ones. There is no fence in metaphysics discriminating Greek, or English, or Spanish science. Æsop and Montaigne, Cervantes and Saadi are men of the world; and to wave our own flag at the dinner table or in the University is to carry the boisterous dulness of a fire-club into a polite circle. Nature and destiny are always on the watch for our follies. Nature trips us up when we strut; and there are curious examples in history on this very point of national pride.

George of Cappadocia, born at Epiphania in Cilicia, was a low parasite who got a lucrative contract to supply the army with bacon. A rogue and informer, he got rich and was forced to run from justice. He saved his money, embraced Arianism, collected a library, and got promoted by a faction to the episcopal throne of Alexandria. When Julian came, A.D. 361, George was dragged to prison; the prison was burst open by the mob and George was lynched, as he deserved. And this precious knave became, in good time, Saint George of England, patron of chivalry, emblem of victory and civility and the pride of the best blood of the modern world.

Strange, that the solid truth-speaking Briton should derive from an impostor. Strange, that the New World should have no better luck—that broad America must wear the name of a thief. Amerigo Vespucci, the pickle-dealer at Seville, who went out, in 1499, a subaltern with Hojeda, and whose highest naval rank was boat-swain's mate in an expedition that never sailed, managed in this lying world to supplant Columbus and baptize half the earth with his own dishonest name. Thus no-body can throw stones. We are equally badly off in our founders; and the false pickledealer is an offset to the false bacon-seller.

WEALTH

There is no country in which so absolute a homage is paid to wealth. In America there is a touch of shame when a man exhibits the evidences of large property, as if after all it needed apology. But the Englishman has pure pride in his wealth, and esteems it a final certificate. A coarse logic rules throughout all English souls—if you have merit, can you not show it by your good clothes and coach and horses? How can a man be a gentleman without a pipe of wine? Haydon says, "There is a fierce resolution to make every man live according to the means he possesses." There is a mixture of religion in it. They are under the Jewish law, and read with sonorous emphasis that their days shall be long in the land, they shall have sons and daughters, flocks and herds, wine and oil. In exact proportion is the reproach of poverty. They do not wish to be represented except by opulent

men. An Englishman who has lost his fortune is said to
have died of a broken heart. The last term of insult is,
"a beggar." Nelson said, "The want of fortune is a crime
which I can never get over." Sydney Smith said, "Poverty is infamous in England." And one of their recent
writers speaks, in reference to a private and scholastic
life, of "the grave moral deterioration which follows an
empty exchequer." You shall find this sentiment, if not
so frankly put, yet deeply implied in the novels and
romances of the present century, and not only in these,
but in biography and in the votes of public assemblies,
in the tone of the preaching and in the table-talk.

I was lately turning over Wood's *Athenæ Oxonienses*,
and looking naturally for another standard in a chronicle
of the scholars of Oxford for two hundred years. But I
found the two disgraces in that, as in most English
books, are, first, disloyalty to Church and State, and second, to be born poor, or to come to poverty. A natural
fruit of England is the brutal political economy. Malthus
finds no cover laid at nature's table for the laborer's son.
In 1809, the majority in Parliament expressed itself by
the language of Mr. Fuller in the House of Commons,
"If you do not like the country, damn you, you can leave
it." When Sir S. Romilly proposed his bill forbidding
parish officers to bind children apprentices at a greater
distance than forty miles from their home, Peel opposed,
and Mr. Wortley said, "though, in the higher ranks, to
cultivate family affections was a good thing, it was not
so among the lower orders. Better take them away from
those who might deprave them. And it was highly injurious to trade to stop binding to manufacturers, as it
must raise the price of labor and of manufactured
goods."

The respect for truth of facts in England is equaled
only by the respect for wealth. It is at once the pride of

art of the Saxon, as he is a wealth-maker, and his passion for independence. The Englishman believes that every man must take care of himself, and has himself to thank if he do not mend his condition. To pay their debts is their national point of honor. From the Exchequer and the East India House to the huckster's shop, everything prospers because it is solvent. The British armies are solvent and pay for what they take. The British empire is solvent; for in spite of the huge national debt, the valuation mounts. During the war from 1789 to 1815, whilst they complained that they were taxed within an inch of their lives, and by dint of enormous taxes were subsidizing all the continent against France, the English were growing rich every year faster than any people ever grew before. It is their maxim that the weight of taxes must be calculated, not by what is taken, but by what is left. Solvency is in the ideas and mechanism of an Englishman. The Crystal Palace is not considered honest until it pays; no matter how much convenience, beauty, or *éclat*, it must be self-supporting. They are contented with slower steamers, as long as they know that swifter boats lose money. They proceed logically by the double method of labor and thrift. Every household exhibits an exact economy, and nothing of that uncalculated headlong expenditure which families use in America. If they cannot pay, they do not buy; for they have no presumption of better fortunes next year, as our people have; and they say without shame, I cannot afford it. Gentlemen do not hesitate to ride in the second-class cars, or in the second cabin. An economist, or a man who can proportion his means and his ambition, or bring the year round with expenditure which expresses his character without embarrassing one day of his future, is already a master of life, and a freeman. Lord Burleigh writes to his son that "one ought never to devote more than two-thirds of his income to the ordinary expenses of life, since the extraordinary will be certain to absorb the other third."

The ambition to create value evokes every kind of ability; government becomes a manufacturing corporation, and every house a mill. The headlong bias to utility will let no talent lie in a napkin—if possible will teach spiders to weave silk stockings. An Englishman, while he eats and drinks no more or not much more than another man, labors three times as many hours in the course of a year as another European; or, his life as a workman is three lives. He works fast. Everything in England is at a quick pace. They have reinforced their own productivity by the creation of that marvelous machinery which differences this age from any other age.

It is a curious chapter in modern history, the growth of the machine-shop. Six hundred years ago, Roger Bacon explained the precession of the equinoxes, the consequent necessity of the reform of the calendar; measured the length of the year; invented gunpowder; and announced (as if looking from his lofty cell, over five centuries, into ours), that "machines can be constructed to drive ships more rapidly than a whole galley of rowers could do; nor would they need anything but a pilot to steer them. Carriages also might be constructed to move with an incredible speed, without the aid of any animal. Finally, it would not be impossible to make machines which by means of a suit of wings should fly in the air in the manner of birds." But the secret slept with Bacon. The six hundred years have not yet fulfilled his words. Two centuries ago the sawing of timber was done by hand; the carriage wheels ran on wooden axles; the land was tilled by wooden ploughs. And it was to little purpose that they had pit-coal, or that looms were improved, unless Watt and Stephenson had taught them to work force-pumps and power-looms by steam. The great strides were all taken within the last hundred years. *The Life of Sir Robert Peel,* in his day the model Englishman, very properly has, for a frontispiece, a drawing of the spinning-jenny, which wove the web of his fortunes. Hargreaves invented the spinning-jenny, and died in a workhouse. Arkwright improved the invention, and the machine dispensed with the work of ninety-nine men; that is, one spinner could do as much work as one hundred had done before. The loom was improved further. But the men would sometimes strike for wages and combine against the masters, and, about 1829-30, much fear was felt lest the trade would be drawn away by these interruptions and the emigration of the spinners to Belgium and the United States. Iron and steel are very obedient. Whether it were not possible to make a spinner that would not rebel, nor mutter, nor scowl, nor strike for wages, nor emigrate? At the solicitation of the masters, after a mob and riot at Staley Bridge, Mr. Roberts of Manchester undertook to create this peaceful fellow, instead of the quarrelsome fellow God had made. After a few trials, he succeeded, and in 1830 procured a patent for his self-acting mule; a creation, the delight of mill-owners, and "destined," they said, "to restore order among the industrious classes"; a machine requiring only a child's hand to piece the broken yarns. As Arkwright had destroyed domestic spinning, so Roberts destroyed the factory spinner. The power of machinery in Great Britain, in mills, has been computed to be equal to 600,000,000 men, one man being able by the aid of steam to do the work which required two hundred and fifty men to accomplish fifty years ago. The production has been commensurate. England already had this laborious race, rich soil, water, wood, coal, iron and favorable climate. Eight hundred years ago commerce had made it rich, and it was recorded, "England is the richest of all the northern nations." The Norman historians recite that "in 1067, William carried with him into Normandy, from England, more gold and silver than had ever before been seen in Gaul." But when, to this labor and trade and these native resources was added this goblin of steam, with his myriad arms, never tired, working night and day everlastingly, the amassing of property has run out of all figures. It makes the motor of the last ninety years. The steampipe has added to her population and wealth the equivalent of four or five Englands. Forty thousand ships are entered in Lloyd's lists. The yield of wheat has gone on from 2,000,000 quarters in the time of the Stuarts, to 13,000,000 in 1854. A thousand million of pounds sterling are said to compose the floating money of commerce. In 1848, Lord John Russell stated that the people of this country had laid out £300,000,000 of capital in railways, in the last four years. But a better measure than these sounding figures is the estimate that there is wealth enough in England to support the entire population in idleness for one year.

The wise, versatile, all-giving machinery makes chisels, roads, locomotives, telegraphs. Whitworth divides a bar to a millionth of an inch. Steam twines huge cannon into wreaths, as easily as it braids straw, and vies with the volcanic forces which twisted the strata. It can clothe shingle mountains with ship-oaks, make swordblades that will cut gun-barrels in two. In Egypt, it can plant forests, and bring rain after three thousand years. Already it is ruddering the balloon, and the next war will be fought in the air. But another machine more potent in England than steam is the Bank. It votes an issue of bills, population is stimulated and cities rise; it refuses loans, and emigration empties the country;

trade sinks; revolutions break out; kings are dethroned. By these new agents our social system is molded. By dint of steam and of money, war and commerce are changed. Nations have lost their old omnipotence; the patriotic tie does not hold. Nations are getting obsolete, we go and live where we will. Steam has enabled men to choose what law they will live under. Money makes place for them. The telegraph is a limp band that will hold the Fenris-wolf of war. For now that a telegraph line runs through France and Europe from London, every message it transmits makes stronger by one thread the band which war will have to cut.

The introduction of these elements gives new resources to existing proprietors. A sporting duke may fancy that the state depends on the House of Lords, but the engineer sees that every stroke of the steam-piston gives value to the duke's land, fills it with tenants; doubles, quadruples, centuples the duke's capital, and creates new measures and new necessities for the culture of his children. Of course it draws the nobility into the competition, as stock-holders in the mine, the canal, the railway, in the application of steam to agriculture, and sometimes into trade. But it also introduces large classes into the same competition; the old energy of the Norse race arms itself with these magnificent powers; new men prove an overmatch for the land-owner, and the mill buys out the castle. Scandinavian Thor, who once forged his bolts in icy Hecla and built galleys by lonely fiords, in England has advanced with the times, has shorn his beard, enters Parliament, sits down at a desk in the India House and lends Miollnir to Birmingham for a steam-hammer.

The creation of wealth in England in the last ninety years is a main fact in modern history. The wealth of London determines prices all over the globe. All things precious, or useful, or amusing, or intoxicating, are sucked into this commerce and floated to London. Some English private fortunes reach, and some exceed a million of dollars a year. A hundred thousand palaces adorn the island. All that can feed the senses and passions, all that can succor the talent or arm the hands of the intelligent middle class, who never spare in what they buy for their own consumption; all that can aid science, gratify taste, or soothe comfort, is in open market. Whatever is excellent and beautiful in civil, rural, or ecclesiastic architecture, in fountain, garden, or grounds—the English noble crosses sea and land to see and to copy at home. The taste and science of thirty peaceful generations; the gardens which Evelyn planted; the temples and pleasure-houses which Inigo Jones and Christopher Wren built; the wood that Gibbons carved; the taste of foreign and domestic artists, Shenstone, Pope, Brown, Loudon, Paxton—are in the vast auction, and the hereditary principle heaps on the owner of today the benefit of ages of owners. The present possessors are to the full as absolute as any of their fathers in choosing and procuring what they like. This comfort and splendor, the breadth of lake and mountain, tillage, pasture and park, sumptuous castle and modern villa—all consist with perfect order. They have no revolutions; no horse-guards dictating to the crown; no Parisian *poissardes* and barricades; no mob: but drowsy habitude, daily dress-dinners, wine and ale and beer and gin and sleep.

With this power of creation and this passion for independence, property has reached an ideal perfection. It is felt and treated as the national life-blood. The laws are framed to give property the securest possible basis, and the provisions to lock and transmit it have exercised the cunningest heads in a profession which never admits a fool. The rights of property nothing but felony and treason can override. The house is a castle which the king cannot enter. The Bank is a strongbox to which the king has no key. Whatever surly sweetness possession can give, is tasted in England to the dregs. Vested rights are awful things, and absolute possession gives the smallest freeholder identity of interest with the duke. High stone fences and padlocked garden-gates announce the absolute will of the owner to be alone. Every whim of exaggerated egotism is put into stone and iron, into silver and gold, with costly deliberation and detail.

An Englishman hears that the Queen Dowager wishes to establish some claim to put her park paling a rod forward into his grounds, so as to get a coachway and save her a mile to the avenue. Instantly he transforms his paling into stone-masonry, solid as the walls of Cuma, and all Europe cannot prevail on him to sell or compound for an inch of the land. They delight in a freak as the proof of their sovereign freedom. Sir Edward Boynton, at Spic Park at Cadenham, on a precipice of incomparable prospect, built a house like a long barn, which had not a window on the prospect side. Strawberry Hill of Horace Walpole, Fonthill Abbey of Mr. Beckford, were freaks; and Newstead Abbey became one in the hands of Lord Byron.

But the proudest result of this creation has been the great and refined forces it has put at the disposal of the private citizen. In the social world an Englishman today has the best lot. He is a king in a plain coat. He goes with the most powerful protection, keeps the best company, is armed by the best education, is seconded by wealth; and his English name and accidents are like a flourish of trumpets announcing him. This, with his quiet style of manners, gives him the power of a sovereign without the inconveniences which belong to that rank. I much prefer the condition of an English gentleman of the better class to that of any potentate in Europe —whether for travel, or for opportunity of society, or for access to means of science or study, or for mere comfort and easy healthy relation to people at home.

Such as we have seen is the wealth of England; a mighty mass, and made good in whatever details we care to explore. The cause and spring of it is the wealth of temperament in the people. The wonder of Britain is this plenteous nature. Her worthies are ever surrounded by as good men as themselves; each is a captain a hundred strong, and that wealth of men is represented again in the faculty of each individual—that he has waste strength, power to spare. The English are so rich and seem to have established a tap-root in the bowels of the planet, because they are constitutionally fertile and creative.

But a man must keep an eye on his servants, if he would not have them rule him. Man is a shrewd inventor and is ever taking the hint of a new machine from his own structure, adapting some secret of his own anatomy in iron, wood and leather to some required function in the work of the world. But it is found that the machine unmans the user. What he gains in making cloth, he loses in general power. There should be temperance in making cloth, as well as in eating. A man should not be a silk-worm, nor a nation a tent of caterpillars. The robust rural Saxon degenerates in the mills to the Leicester stockinger, to the imbecile Manchester spinner—far on the way to be spiders and needles. The incessant repetition of the same handwork dwarfs the man, robs him of his strength, wit and versatility, to make a pin-polisher, a buckle-maker, or any other specialty; and presently, in a change of industry, whole towns are sacrificed like ant-hills, when the fashion of shoe-strings supersedes buckles, when cotton takes the place of linen, or rail-

ways of turnpikes, or when commons are inclosed by
landlords. Then society is admonished of the mischief
of the division of labor, and that the best political economy is care and culture of men; for in these crises all
are ruined except such as are proper individuals, capable
of thought and of new choice and the application of
their talent to new labor. Then again come in new calamities. England is aghast at the disclosure of her fraud
in the adulteration of food, of drugs and of almost every
fabric in her mills and shops; finding that milk will not
nourish, nor sugar sweeten, nor bread satisfy, nor pepper bite the tongue, nor glue stick. In true England all is
false and forged. This too is the reaction of machinery,
but of the larger machinery of commerce. 'Tis not, I suppose, want of probity, so much as the tyranny of trade,
which necessitates a perpetual competition of under-
selling, and that again a perpetual deterioration of the
fabric.

The machinery has proved, like the balloon, unman-
ageable, and flies away with the aeronaut. Steam from
the first hissed and screamed to warn him; it was dreadful with its explosion, and crushed the engineer. The
machinist has wrought and watched, engineers and fire-
men without number have been sacrificed in learning to
tame and guide the monster. But harder still it has
proved to resist and rule the dragon Money, with his
paper wings. Chancellors and Boards of Trade, Pitt,
Peel and Robinson and their Parliaments and their whole
generation adopted false principles, and went to their
graves in the belief that they were enriching the country
which they were impoverishing. They congratulated each
other on ruinous expedients. It is rare to find a merchant
who knows why a crisis occurs in trade, why prices rise or
fall, or who knows the mischief of paper-money. In the
culmination of national prosperity, in the annexation of

countries; building of ships, depots, towns; in the influx of tons of gold and silver; amid the chuckle of chancellors and financiers, it was found that bread rose to famine prices, that the yeoman was forced to sell his cow and pig, his tools and his acre of land; and the dreadful barometer of the poor-rates was touching the point of ruin. The poor-rate was sucking in the solvent classes and forcing an exodus of farmers and mechanics. What befalls from the violence of financial crises, befalls daily in the violence of artificial legislation.

Such a wealth has England earned, ever new, bounteous and augmenting. But the question recurs, does she take the step beyond, namely to the wise use, in view of the supreme wealth of nations? We estimate the wisdom of nations by seeing what they did with their surplus capital. And, in view of these injuries, some compensation has been attempted in England. A part of the money earned returns to the brain to buy schools, libraries, bishops, astronomers, chemists and artists with; and a part to repair the wrongs of this intemperate weaving, by hospitals, savings banks, Mechanics' Institutes, public grounds and other charities and amenities. But the antidotes are frightfully inadequate, and the evil requires a deeper cure, which time and a simpler social organization must supply. At present she does not rule her wealth. She is simply a good England, but no divinity, or wise and instructed soul. She too is in the stream of fate, one victim more in a common catastrophe.

But being in the fault, she has the misfortune of greatness to be held as the chief offender. England must be held responsible for the despotism of expense. Her prosperity, the splendor which so much manhood and talent and perseverance has thrown upon vulgar aims, is the very argument of materialism. Her success strengthens the hands of base wealth. Who can propose to youth poverty and wisdom, when mean gain has arrived at the conquest of letters and arts; when English success has grown out of the very renunciation of principles, and the dedication to outsides? A civility of trifles, of money and expense, an erudition of sensation takes place, and the putting as many impediments as we can between the man and his objects. Hardly the bravest among them have the manliness to resist it successfully. Hence it has come that not the aims of a manly life, but the means of meeting a certain ponderous expense, is that which is to be considered by a youth in England emerging from his minority. A large family is reckoned a misfortune. And it is a consolation in the death of the young, that a source of expense is closed.

ARISTOCRACY

The feudal character of the English state, now that it is getting obsolete, glares a little, in contrast with the democratic tendencies. The inequality of power and property shocks republican nerves. Palaces, halls, villas, walled parks, all over England, rival the splendor of royal seats. Many of the halls, like Haddon or Kedleston, are beautiful desolations. The proprietor never saw them, or never lived in them. Primogeniture built these sumptuous piles, and I suppose it is the sentiment of every traveler, as it was mine, It was well to come ere these were gone. Primogeniture is a cardinal rule of English property and institutions. Laws, customs, manners, the very persons and faces, affirm it.

The frame of society is aristocratic, the taste of the people is loyal. The estates, names and manners of the nobles flatter the fancy of the people and conciliate the necessary support. In spite of broken faith, stolen charters and the devastation of society by the profligacy of the court, we take sides as we read for the loyal England and King Charles's "return to his right" with his Cavaliers—knowing what a heartless trifler he is, and what a crew of God-forsaken robbers they are. The people of England knew as much. But the fair idea of a settled government connecting itself with heraldic names, with the written and oral history of Europe, and, at last, with the Hebrew religion and the oldest traditions of the world, was too pleasing a vision to be shattered by a few offensive realities and the politics of shoe-makers and costermongers. The hopes of the commoners take the same direction with the interest of the patricians. Every man who becomes rich buys land and does what he can to fortify the nobility, into which he hopes to rise. The Anglican clergy are identified with the aristocracy. Time and law have made the joining and molding perfect in every part. The Cathedrals, the Universities, the national music, the popular romances, conspire to uphold the heraldry which the current politics of the day are sapping. The taste of the people is conservative. They are proud of the castles, and of the language and symbol of chivalry. Even the word *lord* is the luckiest style that is used in any language to designate a patrician. The superior education and manners of the nobles recommend them to the country.

The Norwegian pirate got what he could and held it for his eldest son. The Norman noble, who was the Norwegian pirate baptized, did likewise. There was this advantage of Western over Oriental nobility, that this was recruited from below. English history is aristocracy with the doors open. Who has courage and faculty, let him come in. Of course the terms of admission to this club are hard and high. The selfishness of the nobles comes in aid of the interest of the nation to require signal merit. Piracy and war gave place to trade, politics and letters; the war-lord to the law-lord; the law-lord to the merchant and the mill-owner; but the privilege was kept, whilst the means of obtaining it were changed.

The foundations of these families lie deep in Norwegian exploits by sea and Saxon sturdiness on land. All nobility in its beginnings was somebody's natural superiority. The things these English have done were not done without peril of life, nor without wisdom and conduct; and the first hands, it may be presumed, were often challenged to show their right to their honors, or yield them to better men. "He that will be a head, let him be a bridge," said the Welsh chief Benegridran, when he carried all his men over the river on his back. "He shall have the book," said the mother of Alfred, "who can read it"; and Alfred won it by that title: and I make no doubt that feudal tenure was no sinecure, but baron, knight and tenant often had their memories refreshed, in regard to the service by which they held their lands. The De Veres, Bohuns, Mowbrays and Plantagenets were not addicted to contemplation. The Middle Age adorned itself with proofs of manhood and devotion. Of Richard Beauchamp, Earl of Warwick, the Emperor told Henry V that no Christian king had such another knight for wisdom, nurture and manhood, and caused him to be named, "Father of curtesie." "Our success in France," says the historian, "lived and died with him."[1]

The war-lord earned his honors, and no donation of land was large, as long as it brought the duty of protecting it, hour by hour, against a terrible enemy. In France and in England, the nobles were, down to a late day, born and bred to war: and the duel, which in peace still

---

[1] Fuller's *Worthies*, II. p. 472.

held them to the risks of war, diminished the envy that in trading and studious nations would else have pried into their title. They were looked on as men who played high for a great stake.

Great estates are not sinecures, if they are to be kept great. A creative economy is the fuel of magnificence. In the same line of Warwick, the successor next but one to Beauchamp was the stout earl of Henry VI and Edward IV. Few esteemed themselves in the mode, whose heads were not adorned with the black ragged staff, his badge. At his house in London, six oxen were daily eaten at a breakfast, and every tavern was full of his meat, and who had any acquaintance in his family should have as much boiled and roast as he could carry on a long dagger.

The new age brings new qualities into request; the virtues of pirates gave way to those of planters, merchants, senators and scholars. Comity, social talent and fine manners, no doubt, have had their part also. I have met somewhere with a historiette, which, whether more or less true in its particulars, carries a general truth. "How came the Duke of Bedford by his great landed estates? His ancestor having traveled on the continent, a lively, pleasant man, became the companion of a foreign prince wrecked on the Dorsetshire coast, where Mr. Russell lived. The prince recommended him to Henry VIII, who, liking his company, gave him a large share of the plundered church lands."

The pretence is that the noble is of unbroken descent from the Norman, and has never worked for eight hundred years. But the fact is otherwise. Where is Bohun? where is De Vere? The lawyer, the farmer, the silkmercer lies *perdu* under the coronet, and winks to the antiquary to say nothing; especially skilful lawyers, nobody's sons, who did some piece of work at a nice moment for government and were rewarded with ermine.

The national tastes of the English do not lead them to the life of the courtier, but to secure the comfort and independence of their homes. The aristocracy are marked by their predilection for country-life. They are called the county-families. They have often no residence in London and only go thither a short time, during the season, to see the opera; but they concentrate the love and labor of many generations on the building, planting and decoration of their homesteads. Some of them are too old and too proud to wear titles, or, as Sheridan said of Coke, "disdain to hide their head in a coronet"; and some curious examples are cited to show the stability of English families. Their proverb is, that fifty miles from London, a family will last a hundred years; at a hundred miles, two hundred years; and so on; but I doubt that steam, the enemy of time as well as of space, will disturb these ancient rules. Sir Henry Wotton says of the first Duke of Buckingham, "He was born at Brookeby in Leicestershire, where his ancestors had chiefly continued about the space of four hundred years, rather without obscurity, than with any great lustre."[1] Wraxall says that in 1781, Lord Surrey, afterwards Duke of Norfolk, told him that when the year 1783 should arrive, he meant to give a grand festival to all the descendants of the body of Jockey of Norfolk, to mark the day when the dukedom should have remained three hundred years in their house, since its creation by Richard III. Pepys tells us, in writing of an Earl Oxford, in 1666, that the honor had now remained in that name and blood six hundred years.

This long descent of families and this cleaving

---

[1] Reliquiæ Wottonianæ, p. 208.

through ages to the same spot of ground, captivates the imagination. It has too a connection with the names of the towns and districts of the country.

The names are excellent—an atmosphere of legendary melody spread over the land. Older than all epics and histories which clothe a nation, this undershirt sits close to the body. What history too, and what stores of primitive and savage observation it infolds! Cambridge is the bridge of the Cam; Sheffield the field of the river Sheaf; Leicester the *castra,* or camp, of the Lear, or Leir (now Soar); Rochdale, of the Roch; Exeter or Excester, the *castra* of the Ex; Exmouth, Dartmouth, Sidmouth, Teignmouth, the mouths of the Ex, Dart, Sid and Teign rivers. Waltham is strong town; Radcliffe is red cliff; and so on —a sincerity and use in naming very striking to an American, whose country is whitewashed all over by unmeaning names, the cast-off clothes of the country from which its emigrants came; or named at a pinch from a psalm-tune. But the English are those "barbarians" of Jamblichus, who "are stable in their manners, and firmly continue to employ the same words, which also are dear to the gods."

'Tis an old sneer that the Irish peerage drew their names from playbooks. The English lords do not call their lands after their own names, but call themselves after their lands, as if the man represented the country that bred him; and they rightly wear the token of the glebe that gave them birth, suggesting that the tie is not cut, but that there in London—the crags of Argyle, the kail of Cornwall, the downs of Devon, the iron of Wales, the clays of Stafford are neither forgetting nor forgotten, but know the man who was born by them and who, like the long line of his fathers, has carried that crag, that shore, dale, fen, or woodland, in his blood and manners. It has, too, the advantage of suggesting responsibleness. A susceptible man could not wear a name which represented in a strict sense a city or a county of England, without hearing in it a challenge to duty and honor.

The predilection of the patricians for residence in the country, combined with the degree of liberty possessed by the peasant, makes the safety of the English hall. Mirabeau wrote prophetically from England, in 1784, "If revolution break out in France, I tremble for the aristocracy: their chateaux will be reduced to ashes and their blood spilt in torrents. The English tenant would defend his lord to the last extremity." The English go to their estates for grandeur. The French live at court, and exile themselves to their estates for economy. As they do not mean to live with their tenants, they do not conciliate them, but wring from them the last *sous*. Evelyn writes from Blois, in 1644: "The wolves are here in such numbers, that they often come and take children out of the streets; yet will not the Duke, who is sovereign here, permit them to be destroyed."

In evidence of the wealth amassed by ancient families, the traveler is shown the palaces in Piccadilly, Burlington House, Devonshire House, Lansdowne House in Berkshire Square, and lower down in the city, a few noble houses which still withstand in all their amplitude the encroachment of streets. The Duke of Bedford includes or included a mile square in the heart of London, where the British Museum, once Montague House, now stands, and the land occupied by Woburn Square, Bedford Square, Russell Square. The Marquis of Westminster built within a few years the series of squares called Belgravia. Stafford House is the noblest palace in London. Northumberland House holds its place by Charing Cross. Chesterfield House remains in Audley Street. Sion House and Holland House are in the suburbs. But most of the historical houses are masked or lost in the modern uses to which trade or charity has converted them. A multitude of town palaces contain inestimable galleries of art.

In the country, the size of private estates is more impressive. From Barnard Castle I rode on the highway twenty-three miles from High Force, a fall of the Tees, towards Darlington, past Raby Castle, through the estate of the Duke of Cleveland. The Marquis of Breadalbane rides out of his house a hundred miles in a straight line to the sea, on his own property. The Duke of Sutherland owns the county of Sutherland, stretching across Scotland from sea to sea. The Duke of Devonshire, besides his other estates, own 96,000 acres in the County of Derby. The Duke of Richmond has 40,000 acres at Goodwood and 300,000 at Gordon Castle. The Duke of Norfolk's park in Sussex is fifteen miles in circuit. An agriculturist bought lately the island of Lewes, in Hebrides, containing 500,000 acres. The possessions of the Earl of Lonsdale gave him eight seats in Parliament. This is the Heptarchy again; and before the Reform of 1832, one hundred and fifty-four persons sent three hundred and seven members to Parliament. The borough-mongers governed England.

These large domains are growing larger. The great estates are absorbing the small freeholds. In 1786 the soil of England was owned by 250,000 corporations and proprietors; and in 1822, by 32,000. These broad estates find room in this narrow island. All over England, scattered at short intervals among ship-yards, mills, mines and forges, are the paradises of the nobles, where the livelong repose and refinement are heightened by the contrast with the roar of industry and necessity, out of which you have stepped aside.

I was surprised to observe the very small attendance usually in the House of Lords. Out of 573 peers, on ordinary days only twenty or thirty. Where are they? I asked. "At home on their estates, devoured by *ennui,* or in the Alps, or up the Rhine, in the Harz Mountains, or in Egypt, or in India, on the Ghauts." But, with such interests at stake, how can these men afford to neglect them? "O," replied my friend, "why should they work for themselves, when every man in England works for them and will suffer before they come to harm?" The hardest radical instantly uncovers and changes his tone to a lord. It was remarked, on the 10th April, 1848 (the day of the Chartist demonstration), that the upper classes were for the first time actively interesting themselves in their own defence, and men of rank were sworn special constables with the rest. "Besides, why need they sit out the debate? Has not the Duke of Wellington, at this moment, their proxies—the proxies of fifty peers— in his pocket, to vote for them if there be an emergency?"

It is however true that the existence of the House of Peers as a branch of the government entitles them to fill half the Cabinet; and their weight of property and station gives them a virtual nomination of the other half; whilst they have their share in the subordinate offices, as a school of training. This monopoly of political power has given them their intellectual and social eminence in Europe. A few law lords and a few political lords take the brunt of public business. In the army, the nobility fill a large part of the high commissions, and give to these a tone of expense and splendor and also of exclusiveness. They have borne their full share of duty and danger in this service, and there are few noble families which have not paid, in some of their members, the debt of life or limb in the sacrifices of the Russian war. For the rest, the nobility have the lead in matters of state and of expense; in questions of taste, in social usages, in convivial and domestic hospitalities. In general, all that is required of them is to sit securely, to preside at public meetings, to countenance charities and to give the example of that decorum so dear to the British heart.

If one asks, in the critical spirit of the day, what service this class have rendered?—uses appear, or they would have perished long ago. Some of these are easily enumerated, others more subtle make a part of unconscious history. Their institution is one step in the progress of society. For a race yields a nobility in some form, however we name the lords, as surely as it yields women.

The English nobles are high-spirited, active, educated men, born to wealth and power, who have run through every country and kept in every country the best company, have seen every secret of art and nature, and, when men of any ability or ambition, have been consulted in the conduct of every important action. You cannot wield great agencies without lending yourself to them, and when it happens that the spirit of the earl meets his rank and duties, we have the best examples of behavior. Power of any kind readily appears in the manners; and beneficent power, *le talent de bien faire,* gives a majesty which cannot be concealed or resisted.

These people seem to gain as much as they lose by their position. They survey society as from the top of St. Paul's, and if they never hear plain truth from men, they see the best of everything, in every kind, and they see things so grouped and amassed as to infer easily the sum and genius, instead of tedious particularities. Their good behavior deserves all its fame, and they have that simplicity and that air of repose which are the finest ornament of greatness.

The upper classes have only birth, say the people here, and not thoughts. Yes, but they have manners, and it is wonderful how much talent runs into manners —nowhere and never so much as in England. They have the sense of superiority, the absence of all the ambitious effort which disgusts in the aspiring classes, a pure tone of thought and feeling, and the power to command, among their other luxuries, the presence of the most accomplished men in their festive meetings.

Loyalty is in the English a sub-religion. They wear the laws as ornaments, and walk by their faith in their painted May-Fair as if among the forms of gods. The economist of 1855 who asks, Of what use are the lords? may learn of Franklin to ask, Of what use is a baby? They have been a social church proper to inspire sentiments mutually honoring the lover and the loved. Politeness is the ritual of society, as prayers are of the church, a school of manners, and a gentle blessing to the age in which it grew. 'Tis a romance adorning English life with a larger horizon; a midway heaven, fulfilling to their sense their fairy tales and poetry. This, just as far as the breeding of the nobleman really made him brave, handsome, accomplished and great-hearted.

On general grounds, whatever tends to form manners or to finish men, has a great value. Every one who has tasted the delight of friendship will respect every social guard which our manners can establish, tending to secure from the intrusion of frivolous and distasteful people. The jealousy of every class to guard itself is a testimony to the reality they have found in life. When a man once knows that he has done justice to himself, let him dismiss all terrors of aristocracy as superstitions, so far as he is concerned. He who keeps the door of a mine, whether of cobalt, or mercury, or nickel, or plumbago, securely knows that the world cannot do without him. Everybody who is real is open and ready for that which is also real.

Besides, these are they who make England that strongbox and museum it is; who gather and protect works of art, dragged from amidst burning cities and revolutionary countries, and brought hither out of all the world. I look with respect at houses six, seven, eight hundred, or, like Warwick Castle, nine hundred years old. I pardoned high park-fences, when I saw that besides does and pheasants, these have preserved Arundel marbles, Townley galleries, Howard and Spenserian libraries, Warwick and Portland vases, Saxon manuscripts, monastic architectures, millennial trees and breeds of cattle elsewhere extinct. In these manors, after the frenzy of war and destruction subsides a little, the antiquary finds the frailest Roman jar or crumbling Egyptian mummy-case, without so much as a new layer of dust, keeping the series of history unbroken and waiting for its interpreter, who is sure to arrive. These lords are the treasurers and librarians of mankind, engaged by their pride and wealth to this function.

Yet there were other works for British dukes to do. George Loudon, Quintinye, Evelyn, had taught them to make gardens. Arthur Young, Bakewell and Mechi have made them argricultural. Scotland was a camp until the day of Culloden. The Dukes of Athol, Sutherland, Buccleugh and the Marquis of Breadalbane have introduced the rape-culture, the sheep-farm, wheat, drainage, the plantation of forests, the artificial replenishment of lakes and ponds with fish, the renting of game-preserves. Against the cry of the old tenantry and the sympathetic cry of the English press, they have rooted out and planted anew, and now six millions of people live, and live better, on the same land that fed three millions.

The English barons, in every period, have been brave and great, after the estimate and opinion of their times. The grand old halls scattered up and down in England, are dumb vouchers to the state and broad hospitality of their ancient lords. Shakespeare's portraits of good Duke Humphrey, of Warwick, of Northumberland, of Talbot, were drawn in strict consonance with the traditions. A sketch of the Earl of Shrewsbury, from the pen of Queen Elizabeth's archbishop Parker;[1] Lord Herbert of Cherbury's autobiography; the letters and essays of Sir Philip Sidney; the anecdotes preserved by the antiquaries Fuller and Collins; some glimpses at the interiors of noble houses, which we owe to Pepys and Evelyn; the details which Ben Jonson's masques (performed at Kenilworth, Althorpe, Belvoir and other noble houses), record or suggest; down to Aubrey's passages of the life of Hobbes in the house of the Earl of Devon, are favorable pictures of a romantic style of manners. Penshurst still shines for us, and its Christmas revels, "where logs not burn, but men." At Wilton House the "Arcadia" was written, amidst conversations with Fulke Greville, Lord Brooke, a man of no vulgar mind, as his own poems declare him. I must hold Ludlow Castle an honest house, for which Milton's "Comus" was written, and the company nobly bred which performed it with knowledge and sympathy. In the roll of nobles are found poets, philosophers, chemists, astronomers, also men of solid virtues and of lofty sentiments; often they have been the friends and patrons of genius and learning, and especially of the fine arts; and at this moment, almost every great house has its sumptuous picture-gallery.

Of course there is another side to this gorgeous show. Every victory was the defeat of a party only less worthy.

---

[1] Dibdin's *Literary Reminiscences,* vol. 1, xii.

Castles are proud things, but 'tis safest to be outside of them. War is a foul game, and yet war is not the worst part of aristocratic history. In later times, when the baron, educated only for war, with his brains paralyzed by his stomach, found himself idle at home, he grew fat and wanton and a sorry brute. Grammont, Pepys and Evelyn show the kennels to which the king and court went in quest of pleasure. Prostitutes taken from the theaters were made duchesses, their bastards dukes and earls. "The young men sat uppermost, the old serious lords were out of favor." The discourse that the king's companions had with him was "poor and frothy." No man who valued his head might do what these pot-companions familiarly did with the king. In logical sequence of these dignified revels, Pepys can tell the beggarly shifts to which the king was reduced, who could not find paper at his council table, and "no hand-kerchers" in his wardrobe, "and but three bands to his neck," and the linen-draper and the stationer were out of pocket and refusing to trust him, and the baker will not bring bread any longer. Meantime the English Channel was swept and London threatened by the Dutch fleet, manned too by English sailors, who, having been cheated of their pay for years by the king, enlisted with the enemy.

The Selwyn correspondence, in the reign of George III, discloses a rottenness in the aristocracy which threatened to decompose the state. The sycophancy and sale of votes and honor, for place and title; lewdness, gaming, smuggling, bribery and cheating; the sneer at the childish indiscretion of quarreling with ten thousand a year; the want of ideas; the splendor of the titles, and the apathy of the nation, are instructive, and make the reader pause and explore the firm bounds which confined these vices to a handful of rich men. In the reign of the Fourth George, things do not seem to have mended, and the rotten debauchee let down from a window by an inclined plane into his coach to take the air, was a scandal to Europe which the ill fame of his queen and of his family did nothing to retrieve.

Under the present reign the perfect decorum of the Court is thought to have put a check on the gross vices of the aristocracy; yet gaming, racing, drinking and mistresses bring them down, and the democrat can still gather scandals, if he will. Dismal anecdotes abound, verifying the gossip of the last generation, of dukes served by bailiffs, with all their plate in pawn; of great lords living by the showing of their houses, and of an old man wheeled in his chair from room to room, whilst his chambers are exhibited to the visitor for money; of ruined dukes and earls living in exile for debt. The historic names of the Buckinghams, Beauforts, Marlboroughs and Hertfords have gained no new lustre, and now and then darker scandals break out, ominous as the new chapters added under the Orleans dynasty to the *causes célèbres* in France. Even peers who are men of worth and public spirit are overtaken and embarrassed by their vast expense. The respectable Duke of Devonshire, willing to be the Mecænas and Lucullus of his island, is reported to have said that he cannot live at Chatsworth but one month in the year. Their many houses eat them up. They cannot sell them, because they are entailed. They will not let them, for pride's sake, but keep them empty, aired, and the grounds mown and dressed, at a cost of four or five thousand pounds a year. The spending is for a great part in servants, in many houses exceeding a hundred.

Most of them are only chargeable with idleness, which, because it squanders such vast power of benefit, has the mischief of crime. "They might be little Providences on earth," said my friend, "and they are, for the most part, jockeys and fops." Campbell says, "Acquaintance with the nobility, I could never keep up. It requires a life of idleness, dressing and attendance on their parties." I suppose too that a feeling of self-respect is driving cultivated men out of this society, as if the noble were slow to receive the lessons of the times and had not learned to disguise his pride of place. A man of wit, who is also one of the celebrities of wealth and fashion, confessed to his friend that he could not enter their houses without being made to feel that they were great lords, and he a low plebeian. With the tribe of *artistes,* including the musical tribe, the patrician morgue keeps no terms, but excludes them. When Julia Grisi and Mario sang at the houses of the Duke of Wellington and other grandees, a cord was stretched between the singer and the company.

When every noble was a soldier, they were carefully bred to great personal prowess. The education of a soldier is a simpler affair than that of an earl in the nineteenth century. And this was very seriously pursued; they were expert in every species of equitation, to the most dangerous practices, and this down to the accession of William of Orange. But graver men appear to have trained their sons for civil affairs. Elizabeth extended her thought to the future; and Sir Philip Sidney in his letter to his brother, and Milton and Evelyn, gave plain and hearty counsel. Already too the English noble and squire were preparing for the career of the country-gentleman and his peaceable expense. They went from city to city, learning receipts to make perfumes, sweet powders, pomanders, antidotes, gathering seeds, gems, coins and divers curiosities, preparing for a private life thereafter, in which they should take pleasure in these recreations.

All advantages given to absolve the young patrician

from intellectual labor are of course mistaken. "In the university, noblemen are exempted from the public exercises for the degree, etc., by which they attain a degree called *honorary*. At the same time, the fees they have to pay for matriculation, and on all other occasions, are much higher."[1] Fuller records "the observation of foreigners, that Englishmen, by making their children gentlemen before they are men, cause they are so seldom wise men." This cockering justifies Dr. Johnson's bitter apology for primogeniture, that "it makes but one fool in a family."

The revolution in society has reached this class. The great powers of industrial art have no exclusion of name or blood. The tools of our time, namely steam, ships, printing, money and popular education, belong to those who can handle them; and their effect has been that advantages once confined to men of family are now open to the whole middle class. The road that grandeur levels for his coach, toil can travel in his cart.

This is more manifest every day, but I think it is true throughout English history. English history, wisely read, is the vindication of the brain of that people. Here at last were climate and condition friendly to the working faculty. Who now will work and dare, shall rule. This is the charter, or the chartism, which fogs and seas and rains proclaimed—that intellect and personal force should make the law; that industry and administrative talent should administer; that work should wear the crown. I know that not this, but something else is pretended. The fiction with which the noble and the bystander equally please themselves is that the former is of unbroken descent from the Norman, and so has never worked for eight hundred years. All the families are

---

[1] Huber, *History of English Universities.*

new, but the name is old, and they have made a covenant with their memories not to disturb it. But the analysis of the peerage and gentry shows the rapid decay and
extinction of old families, the continual recruiting of
these from new blood. The doors, though ostentatiously
guarded, are really open, and hence the power of the
bribe. All the barriers to rank only whet the thirst and
enhance the prize. "Now," said Nelson, when clearing
for battle, "a peerage, or Westminster Abbey!" "I have
no illusion left," said Sydney Smith, "but the Archbishop
of Canterbury." "The lawyers," said Burke, "are only
birds of passage in this House of Commons," and then
added, with a new figure, "they have their best bower
anchor in the House of Lords."

Another stride that has been taken appears in the
perishing of heraldry. Whilst the privileges of nobility
are passing to the middle class, the badge is discredited
and the titles of lordship are getting musty and cumber-
some. I wonder that sensible men have not been already
impatient of them. They belong, with wigs, powder and
scarlet coats, to an earlier age and may be advanta-
geously consigned, with paint and tattoo, to the digni-
taries of Australia and Polynesia.

A multitude of English, educated at the universities,
bred into their society with manners, ability and the
gifts of fortune, are every day confronting the peers on
a footing of equality, and outstripping them, as often, in
the race of honor and influence. That cultivated class is
large and ever enlarging. It is computed that, with titles
and without, there are seventy thousand of these people
coming and going in London, who make up what is
called high society. They cannot shut their eyes to the
fact that an untitled nobility possess all the power without the inconveniences that belong to rank, and the rich
Englishman goes over the world at the present day,

drawing more than all the advantages which the strongest of his kings could command.

UNIVERSITIES

Of British universities, Cambridge has the most illustrious names on its list. At the present day too, it has the advantage of Oxford, counting in its *alumni* a greater number of distinguished scholars. I regret that I had but a single day wherein to see King's College Chapel, the beautiful lawns and gardens of the colleges, and a few of its gownsmen.

But I availed myself of some repeated invitations to Oxford, where I had introductions to Dr. Daubeny, Professor of Botany, and to the Regius Professor of Divinity, as well as to a valued friend, a Fellow of Oriel, and went thither on the last day of March, 1848. I was the guest of my friend in Oriel, was housed close upon that college, and I lived on college hospitalities.

My new friends showed me their cloisters, the Bodleian Library, the Randolph Gallery, Merton Hall and the rest. I saw several faithful, high-minded young men, some of them in the mood of making sacrifices for peace of mind—a topic, of course, on which I had no counsel to offer. Their affectionate and gregarious ways reminded me at once of the habits of *our* Cambridge men, though I imputed to these English an advantage in their secure and polished manners. The halls are rich with oaken wainscoting and ceiling. The pictures of the founders hang from the walls; the tables glitter with plate. A youth came forward to the upper table and pronounced the ancient form of grace before meals, which, I suppose, has been in use here for ages, *Benedictus benedicat; benedictur, benedicatur.*

It is a curious proof of the English use and wont, or of their good nature, that these young men are locked up every night at nine o'clock, and the porter at each hall is required to give the name of any belated student who is admitted after that hour. Still more descriptive is the fact that out of twelve hundred young men, comprising the most spirited of the aristocracy, a duel has never occurred.

Oxford is old, even in England, and conservative. Its foundations date from Alfred and even from Arthur, if, as is alleged, the Pheryllt of the Druids had a seminary here. In the reign of Edward I, it is pretended, here were thirty thousand students; and nineteen most noble foundations were then established. Chaucer found it as firm as if it had always stood; and it is, in British story, rich with great names, the school of the island and the link of England to the learned of Europe. Hither came Erasmus, with delight, in 1497. Albericus Gentilis, in 1580, was relieved and maintained by the university. Albert Alaskie, a noble Polonian, Prince of Sirad, who visited England to admire the wisdom of Queen Elizabeth, was entertained with stage plays in the Refectory of Christ-Church in 1583. Isaac Casaubon, coming from Henri Quatre of France by invitation of James I, was admitted to Christ-Church, in July, 1613. I saw the Ashmolean Museum, whither Elias Ashmole in 1682 sent twelve cart-loads of rarities. Here indeed was the Olympia of all Antony Wood's and Aubrey's games and heroes, and every inch of ground has its lustre. For Wood's *Athenæ Oxonienses,* or calendar of the writers of Oxford for two hundred years, is a lively record of English manners and merits, and as much a national monument as Purchas's Pilgrims or Hansard's Register. On every side, Oxford is redolent of age and authority. Its gates shut of themselves against modern innovation. It is still gov-

erned by the statutes of Archbishop Laud. The books in
Merton Library are still chained to the wall. Here, on
August 27, 1660, John Milton's *Pro Populo Anglicano
Defensio* and *Iconoclastes* were committed to the flames.
I saw the school-court or quadrangle where, in 1683, the
Convocation caused the *Leviathan* of Thomas Hobbes
to be publicly burnt. I do not know whether this learned
body have yet heard of the Declaration of American
Independence, or whether the Ptolemaic astronomy does
not still hold its ground against the novelties of Coperni-
cus.

As many sons, almost so many benefactors. It is usual
for a nobleman, or indeed for almost every wealthy
student, on quitting college to leave behind him some
article of plate; and gifts of all values, from a hall or a
fellowship or a library, down to a picture or a spoon,
are continually accruing, in the course of a century. My
friend Doctor J. gave me the following anecdote. In Sir
Thomas Lawrence's collection at London were the
cartoons of Raphael and Michael Angelo. This inestimable prize was offered to Oxford University for seven
thousand pounds. The offer was accepted, and the committee charged with the affair had collected three thousand pounds, when, among other friends, they called on
Lord Eldon. Instead of a hundred pounds, he surprised
them by putting down his name for three thousand
pounds. They told him they should now very easily raise
the remainder. "No," he said, "your men have probably
already contributed all they can spare; I can as well give
the rest": and he withdrew his cheque for three thousand, and wrote four thousand pounds. I saw the whole
collection in April, 1848.

In the Bodleian Library, Dr. Bandinel showed me the
manuscript Plato, of the date of A.D. 896, brought by Dr.
Clarke from Egypt; a manuscript Virgil of the same

century; the first Bible printed at Mentz (I believe in
1450); and a duplicate of the same, which had been
deficient in about twenty leaves at the end. But one day,
being in Venice, he bought a room full of books and
manuscripts—every scrap and fragment—for four thousand louis d'ors, and had the doors locked and sealed by
the consul. On proceeding afterwards to examine his
purchase, he found the twenty deficient pages of his
Mentz Bible, in perfect order; brought them to Oxford
with the rest of his purchase, and placed them in the
volume; but has too much awe for the Providence that
appears in bibliography also, to suffer the reunited parts
to be re-bound. The oldest building here is two hundred
years younger than the frail manuscript brought by Dr.
Clarke from Egypt. No candle or fire is ever lighted in
the Bodleian. Its catalogue is the standard catalogue on
the desk of every library in Oxford. In each several
college they underscore in red ink on this catalogue the
titles of books contained in the library of that college—
the theory being that the Bodleian has all books. This
rich library spent during the last year (1847), for the
purchase of books, £1,668.

The logical English train a scholar as they train an
engineer. Oxford is a Greek factory, as Wilton mills
weave carpet and Sheffield grinds steel. They know the
use of a tutor, as they know the use of a horse; and they
draw the greatest amount of benefit out of both. The
reading men are kept, by hard walking, hard riding and
measured eating and drinking, at the top of their condition, and two days before the examination, do no work,
but lounge, ride, or run, to be fresh on the college
doomsday. Seven years' residence is the theoretic period
for a master's degree. In point of fact, it has long been
three years' residence, and four years more of standing.

This "three years" is about twenty-one months in all.[1]

"The whole expense," says Professor Sewel, "of ordinary college tuition at Oxford, is about sixteen guineas a year." But this plausible statement may deceive a reader unacquainted with the fact that the principal teaching relied on is private tuition. And the expenses of private tuition are reckoned at from £50 to £70 a year, or $1,000 for the whole course of three years and a half. At Cambridge, $750 a year is economical, and $1,500 not extravagant.[2]

The number of students and of residents, the dignity of the authorities, the value of the foundations, the history and the architecture, the known sympathy of entire Britain in what is done there, justify a dedication to study in the undergraduate such as cannot easily be in America, where his college is half suspected by the Freshman to be insignificant in the scale beside trade and politics. Oxford is a little aristocracy in itself, numerous and dignified enough to rank with other estates in the realm; and where fame and secular promotion are to be had for study, and in a direction which has the unanimous respect of all cultivated nations.

This aristocracy, of course, repairs its own losses; fills places, as they fall vacant, from the body of students. The number of fellowships at Oxford is 540, averaging £200 a year, with lodging and diet at the college. If a young American, loving learning and hindered by poverty, were offered a home, a table, the walks and the library in one of these academical palaces, and a thousand dollars a year, as long as he chose to remain a bachelor, he would dance for joy. Yet these young men thus happily placed, and paid to read, are impatient of

[1] Huber, ii. p. 304.
[2] Bristed, *Five Years at an English University.*

their few checks, and many of them preparing to resign their fellowships. They shuddered at the prospect of dying a Fellow, and they pointed out to me a paralytic old man, who was assisted into the hall. As the number of undergraduates at Oxford is only about 1,200 or 1,300, and many of these are never competitors, the chance of a fellowship is very great. The income of the nineteen colleges is conjectured at £150,000 a year.

The effect of this drill is the radical knowledge of Greek and Latin and of mathematics, and the solidity and taste of English criticism. Whatever luck there may be in this or that award, an Eton captain can write Latin longs and shorts, can turn the Court-Guide into hexameters, and it is certain that a Senior Classic can quote correctly from the *Corpus Poetarum* and is critically learned in all the humanities. Greek erudition exists on the Isis and Cam, whether the Maud man or the Brasenose man be properly ranked or not; the atmosphere is loaded with Greek learning; the whole river has reached a certain height, and kills all that growth of weeds which this Castalian water kills. The English nature takes culture kindly. So Milton thought. It refines the Norseman. Access to the Greek mind lifts his standard of taste. He has enough to think of, and, unless of an impulsive nature, is indisposed from writing or speaking, by the fulness of his mind and the new severity of his taste. The great silent crowd of thoroughbred Grecians always known to be around him, the English writer cannot ignore. They prune his orations and point his pen. Hence the style and tone of English journalism. The men have learned accuracy and comprehension, logic, and pace, or speed of working. They have bottom, endurance, wind. When born with good constitutions, they make those eupeptic studying-mills, the cast-iron men, the *dura ilia,* whose powers of performance compare with ours as the steam-hammer with the music-box—Cokes, Mansfields, Seldens and Bentleys, and when it happens that a superior brain puts a rider on this admirable horse, we obtain those masters of the world who combine the highest energy in affairs with a supreme culture.

It is contended by those who have been bred at Eton, Harrow, Rugby and Westminster, that the public sentiment within each of those schools is high-toned and manly; that, in their playgrounds, courage is universally admired, meanness despised, manly feelings and generous conduct are encouraged: that an unwritten code of honor deals to the spoiled child of rank and to the child of upstart wealth, an even-handed justice, purges their nonsense out of both and does all that can be done to make them gentlemen.

Again, at the universities, it is urged that all goes to form what England values as the flower of its national life—a well-educated gentleman. The German Huber, in describing to his countrymen the attributes of an English gentleman, frankly admits that "in Germany, we have nothing of the kind. A gentleman must possess a political character, an independent and public position, or at least the right of assuming it. He must have average opulence, either of his own, or in his family. He should also have bodily activity and strength, unattainable by our sedentary life in public offices. The race of English gentlemen presents an appearance of manly vigor and form not elsewhere to be found among an equal number of persons. No other nation produces the stock. And in England, it has deteriorated. The university is a decided presumption in any man's favor. And so eminent are the members that a glance at the calendars will show that in all the world one cannot be in better company than on the books of one of the larger Oxford or Cambridge colleges." [1]

These seminaries are finishing schools for the upper classes, and not for the poor. The useful is exploded. The definition of a public school is "a school which excludes all that could fit a man for standing behind a counter." [2]

No doubt, the foundations have been perverted. Oxford, which equals in wealth several of the smaller European states, shuts up the lectureships which were made "public for all men thereunto to have concourse"; misspends the revenues bestowed for such youths "as should be most meet for towardness, poverty and painfulness"; there is gross favoritism; many chairs and many fellowships are made beds of ease; and it is likely that the university will know how to resist and make inoperative the terrors of parliamentary inquiry; no doubt their learning is grown obsolete—but Oxford also has its merits, and I found here also proof of the national fidelity and thoroughness. Such knowledge as they prize they possess and impart. Whether in course or by indirection, whether by a cramming tutor or by examiners with prizes and foundation scholarships, education, according to the English notion of it, is arrived at. I looked over the Examination Papers of the year 1848, for the various scholarships and fellowships, the Lusby, the Hertford, the Dean-Ireland and the University (copies of which were kindly given me by a Greek professor), containing the tasks which many competitors had victoriously performed, and I believed they would prove too severe tests for the candidates for a Bachelor's degree in Yale or

---

[1] Huber, *History of the English Universities*, Newman's Translation.

[2] See Bristed, *Five Years in an English University*. New York, 1852.

Harvard. And in general, here was proof of a more searching study in the appointed directions, and the knowledge pretended to be conveyed was conveyed. Oxford sends out yearly twenty or thirty very able men and three or four hundred well-educated men.

The diet and rough exercise secure a certain amount of old Norse power. A fop will fight, and in exigent circumstances will play the manly part. In seeing these youths I believed I saw aleady an advantage in vigor and color and general habit, over their contemporaries in the American colleges. No doubt much of the power and brilliancy of the reading-men is merely constitutional or hygienic. With a hardier habit and resolute gymnastics, with five miles more walking, or five ounces less eating, or with a saddle and gallop of twenty miles a day, with skating and rowing-matches, the American would arrive at as robust exegesis and cheery and hilarious tone. I should readily concede these advantages, which it would be easy to acquire, if I did not find also that they read better than we, and write better.

English wealth falling on their school and university training, makes a systematic reading of the best authors, and to the end of a knowledge how the things whereof they treat really stand: whilst pamphleteer or journalist, reading for an argument for a party, or reading to write, or at all events for some by-end imposed on them, must read meanly and fragmentarily. Charles I said that he understood English law as well as a gentleman ought to understand it.

Then they have access to books; the rich libraries collected at every one of many thousands of houses, give an advantage not to be attained by a youth in this country, when one thinks how much more and better may be learned by a scholar who, immediately on hearing of a book, can consult it, than by one who is on the quest, for years, and reads inferior books because he cannot find the best.

Again, the great number of cultivated men keep each other up to a high standard. The habit of meeting well-read and knowing men teaches the art of omission and selection.

Universities are of course hostile to geniuses, which seeing and using ways of their own, discredit the routine: as churches and monasteries persecute youthful saints. Yet we all send our sons to college, and though he be a genius, the youth must take his chance. The university must be retrospective. The gale that gives direction to the vanes on all its towers blows out of antiquity. Oxford is a library, and the professors must be librarians. And I should as soon think of quarreling with the janitor for not magnifying his office by hostile sallies into the street, like the Governor of Kertch or Kinburn, as of quarreling with the professors for not admiring the young neologists who pluck the beards of Euclid and Aristotle, or for not attempting themselves to fill their vacant shelves as original writers.

It is easy to carp at colleges, and the college, if we will wait for it, will have its own turn. Genius exists there also, but will not answer a call of a committee of the House of Commons. It is rare, precarious, eccentric and darkling. England is the land of mixture and surprise, and when you have settled it that the universities are moribund, out comes a poetic influence from the heart of Oxford, to mold the opinions of cities, to build their houses as simply as birds their nests, to give veracity to art and charm mankind, as an appeal to moral order always must. But besides this restorative genius, the best poetry of England of this age, in the old forms, comes from two graduates of Cambridge.

RELIGION

No people at the present day can be explained by their national religion. They do not feel responsible for it; it lies far outside of them. Their loyalty to truth and their labor and expenditure rest on real foundations, and not on a national church. And English life, it is evident, does not grow out of the Athanasian creed, or the Articles, or the Eucharist. It is with religion as with marriage. A youth marries in haste; afterwards, when his mind is opened to the reason of the conduct of life, he is asked what he thinks of the institution of marriage and of the right relations of the sexes? "I should have much to say," he might reply, "if the question were open, but I have a wife and children, and all question is closed for me." In the barbarous days of a nation, some *cultus* is formed or imported; altars are built, tithes are paid, priests ordained. The education and expenditure of the country take that direction, and when wealth, refinement, great men, and ties to the world supervene, its prudent men say, Why fight against Fate, or lift these absurdities which are now mountainous? Better find some niche or crevice in this mountain of stone which religious ages have quarried and carved, wherein to bestow yourself, than attempt anything ridiculously and dangerously above your strength, like removing it.

In seeing old castles and cathedrals, I sometimes say, as today in front of Dundee Church tower, which is eight hundred years old, "This was built by another and a better race than any that now look on it." And plainly there has been great power of sentiment at work in this island, of which these buildings are the proofs; as volcanic basalts show the work of fire which has been extinguished for ages. England felt the full heat of the

Christianity which fermented Europe, and drew, like the chemistry of fire, a firm line between barbarism and culture. The power of the religious sentiment put an end to human sacrifices, checked appetite, inspired the crusades, inspired resistance to tyrants, inspired self-respect, set bounds to serfdom and slavery, founded liberty, created the religious architecture—York, Newstead, Westminster, Fountains Abbey, Ripon, Beverley and Dundee —works to which the key is lost, with the sentiment which created them; inspired the English Bible, the liturgy, the monkish histories, the chronicle of Richard of Devizes. The priest translated the *Vulgate*, and translated the sanctities of old hagiology into English virtues on English ground. It was a certain affirmative or aggressive state of the Caucasian races. Man awoke refreshed by the sleep of ages. The violence of the northern savages exasperated Christianity into power. It lived by the love of the people. Bishop Wilfrid manumitted two hundred and fifty serfs, whom he found attached to the soil. The clergy obtained respite from labor for the boor on the Sabbath and on church festivals. "The lord who compelled his boor to labor between sunset on Saturday and sunset on Sunday, foreited him altogether." The priest came out of the people and sympathized with his class. The church was the mediator, check and democratic principle, in Europe. Latimer, Wicliffe, Arundel, Cobham, Antony Parsons, Sir Harry Vane, George Fox, Penn, Bunyan are the democrats, as well as the saints of their times. The Catholic Church, thrown on this toiling, serious people, has made in fourteen centuries a massive system, close-fitted to the manners and genius of the country, at once domestical and stately. In the long time, it has blended with everything in heaven above and the earth beneath. It moves through a zodiac of feasts and fasts, names every day of the year, every town and market and headland and monument, and has coupled itself with the almanac, that no court can be held, no field ploughed, no horse shod, without some leave from the church. All maxims of prudence or shop or farm are fixed and dated by the church. Hence its strength in the agricultural districts. The distribution of land into parishes enforces a church sanction to every civil privilege; and the gradation of the clergy—prelates for the rich and curates for the poor—with the fact that a classical education has been secured to the clergyman, makes them "the link which unites the sequestered peasantry with the intellectual advancement of the age."[1]

The English Church has many certificates to show of humble effective service in humanizing the people, in cheering and refining men, feeding, healing and educating. It has the zeal of martyrs and confessors; the noblest books; a sublime architecture; a ritual marked by the same secular merits, nothing cheap or purchasable.

From this slow-grown church important reactions proceed; much for culture, much for giving a direction to the nation's affection and will today. The carved and pictured chapel—its entire surface animated with image and emblem—made the parish-church a sort of book and Bible to the people's eye.

Then, when the Saxon instinct had secured a service in the vernacular tongue, it was the tutor and university of the people. In York minster, on the day of the enthronization of the new archbishop, I heard the service of evening prayer read and chanted in the choir. It was strange to hear the pretty pastoral of the betrothal of Rebecca and Isaac, in the morning of the world, read with circumstantiality in York minster, on the 13th January, 1848, to the decorous English audience, just fresh

---

[1] Wordsworth.

from the *Times* newspaper and their wine, and listening with all the devotion of national pride. That was binding old and new to some purpose. The reverence for the Scriptures is an element of civilization, for thus has the history of the world been preserved and is preserved. Here in England every day a chapter of Genesis, and a leader in the *Times*.

Another part of the same service on this occasion was not insignificant. Handel's coronation anthem "God save the King," was played by Dr. Camidge on the organ, with sublime effect. The minster and the music were made for each other. It was a hint of the part the church plays as a political engine. From his infancy, every Englishman is accustomed to hear daily prayers for the queen, for the royal family and the Parliament, by name; and this lifelong consecration cannot be without influence on his opinions.

The universities also are parcel of the ecclesiastical system, and their first design is to form the clergy. Thus the clergy for a thousand years have been the scholars of the nation.

The national temperament deeply enjoys the unbroken order and tradition of its church; the liturgy, ceremony, architecture; the sober grace, the good company, the connection with the throne and with history, which adorn it. And whilst it endears itself thus to men of more taste than activity, the stability of the English nation is passionately enlisted to its support, from its inextricable connection with the cause of public order, with politics and with funds.

Good churches are not built by bad men; at least there must be probity and enthusiasm somewhere in the society. These minsters were neither built nor filled by atheists. No church has had more learned, industrious or devoted men; plenty of "clerks and bishops, who, out of their gowns, would turn their backs on no man." [1] Their architecture still glows with faith in immortality. Heats and genial periods arrive in history, or, shall we say, plenitudes of Divine Presence, by which high tides are caused in the human spirit, and great virtues and talents appear, as in the eleventh, twelfth, thirteenth, and again in the sixteenth and seventeenth centuries, when the nation was full of genius and piety.

But the age of the Wicliffes, Cobhams, Arundels, Beckets; of the Latimers, Mores, Cranmers; of the Taylors, Leightons, Herberts; of the Sherlocks and Butlers, is gone. Silent revolutions in opinion have made it impossible that men like these should return, or find a place in their once sacred stalls. The spirit that dwelt in this church has glided away to animate other activities, and they who come to the old shrines find apes and players rustling the old garments.

The religion of England is part of good breeding. When you see on the continent the well-dressed Englishman come into his ambassador's chapel and put his face for silent prayer into his smooth-brushed hat, you cannot help feeling how much national pride prays with him, and the religion of a gentleman. So far is he from attaching any meaning to the words, that he believes himself to have done almost the generous thing, and that it is very condescending in him to pray to God. A great duke said on the occasion of a victory, in the House of Lords, that he thought the Almighty God had not been well used by them, and that it would become their magnanimity, after so great successes, to take order that a proper acknowledgment be made. It is the church of the gentry, but it is not the church of the poor. The

---

[1] Fuller.

operatives do not own it, and gentlemen lately testified in the House of Commons that in their lives they never saw a poor man in a ragged coat inside a church.

The torpidity on the side of religion of the vigorous English understanding shows how much wit and folly can agree in one brain. Their religion is a quotation; their church is a doll; and any examination is interdicted with screams of terror. In good company you expect them to laugh at the fanaticism of the vulgar; but they do not; they are the vulgar.

The English, in common perhaps with Christendom in the nineteenth century, do not respect power, but only performance; value ideas only for an economic result. Wellington esteems a saint only as far as he can be an army chaplain: "Mr. Briscoll, by his admirable conduct and good sense, got the better of Methodism, which had appeared among the soldiers and once among the officers." They value a philosopher as they value an apothecary who brings bark or a drench; and inspiration is only some blowpipe, or a finer mechanical aid.

I suspect that there is in an Englishman's brain a valve that can be closed at pleasure, as an engineer shuts off steam. The most sensible and well-informed men possess the power of thinking just so far as the bishop in religious matters, and as the chancellor of the exchequer in politics. They talk with courage and logic, and show you magnificent results, but the same men who have brought free trade or geology to their present standing, look grave and lofty and shut down their valve as soon as the conversation approaches the English Church. After that, you talk with a box-turtle.

The action of the university, both in what is taught and in the spirit of the place, is directed more on producing an English gentleman, than a saint or a psychologist. It ripens a bishop, and extrudes a philosopher. I do not know that there is more cabalism in the Anglican than in other churches, but the Anglican clergy are identified with the aristocracy. They say here, that if you talk with a clergyman, you are sure to find him well-bred, informed and candid: he entertains your thought or your project with sympathy and praise. But if a second clergyman come in, the sympathy is at an end: two together are inaccessible to your thought, and whenever it comes to action, the clergyman invariably sides with his church.

The Anglican Church is marked by the grace and good sense of its forms, by the manly grace of its clergy. The gospel it preaches is "By taste are ye saved." It keeps the old structures in repair, spends a world of money in music and building, and in buying Pugin and architectural literature. It has a general good name for amenity and mildness. It is not in ordinary a persecuting church; it is not inquisitorial, not even inquisitive; is perfectly well-bred, and can shut its eyes on all proper occasions. If you let it alone, it will let you alone. But its instinct is hostile to all change in politics, literature, or social arts. The church has not been the founder of the London University, of the Mechanics' Institutes, of the Free School, of whatever aims at diffusion of knowledge. The Platonists of Oxford are as bitter against this heresy, as Thomas Taylor.

The doctrine of the Old Testament is the religion of England. The first leaf of the New Testament it does not open. It believes in a Providence which does not treat with levity a pound sterling. They are neither transcendentalists nor Christians. They put up no Socratic prayer, much less any saintly prayer for the queen's mind; ask neither for light nor right, but say bluntly, "Grant her in health and wealth long to live." And one traces this Jewish prayer in all English private history, from the prayers of King Richard, in Richard of Devizes' *Chronicle,* to those in the diaries of Sir Samuel Romilly and of Haydon the painter. "Abroad with my wife," writes Pepys piously, "the first time that ever I rode in my own coach; which do make my heart rejoice and praise God, and pray him to bless it to me, and continue it." The bill for the naturalization of the Jews (in 1753) was resisted by petitions from all parts of the kingdom, and by petition from the city of London, reprobating this bill, as "tending extremely to the dishonor of the Christian religion, and extremely injurious to the interests and commerce of the kingdom in general, and of the city of London in particular."

But they have not been able to congeal humanity by act of Parliament. "The heavens journey still and sojourn not," and arts, wars, discoveries and opinion go onward at their own pace. The new age has new desires, new enemies, new trades, new charities, and reads the Scriptures with new eyes. The chatter of French politics, the steam-whistle, the hum of the mill and the noise of embarking emigrants had quite put most of the old legends out of mind; so that when you came to read the liturgy to a modern congregation, it was almost absurd in its unfitness, and suggested a masquerade of old costumes.

No chemist has prospered in the attempt to crystallize a religion. It is endogenous, like the skin and other vital organs. A new statement every day. The prophet and apostle knew this, and the nonconformist confutes the conformists, by quoting the texts they must allow. It is the condition of a religion to require religion for its expositor. Prophet and apostle can only be rightly understood by prophet and apostle. The statesman knows that the religious element will not fail, any more than the supply of fibrine and chyle; but it is in its nature constructive, and will organize such a church as its wants.

The wise legislator will spend on temples, schools, libraries, colleges, but will shun the enriching of priests. If in any manner he can leave the election and paying of the priest to the people, he will do well. Like the Quakers, he may resist the separation of a class of priests, and create opportunity and expectation in the society to run to meet natural endowment in this kind. But when wealth accrues to a chaplaincy, a bishopric, or rectorship, it requires moneyed men for its stewards, who will give it another direction than to the mystics of their day. Of course, money will do after its kind, and will steadily work to unspiritualize and unchurch the people to whom it was bequeathed. The class certain to be excluded from all preferment are the religious—and driven to other churches; which is nature's *vis medicatrix*.

The curates are ill-paid, and the prelates are overpaid. This abuse draws into the church the children of the nobility and other unfit persons who have a taste for expense. Thus a bishop is only a surpliced merchant. Through his lawn I can see the bright buttons of the shopman's coat glitter. A wealth like that of Durham makes almost a premium on felony. Brougham, in a speech in the House of Commons on the Irish elective franchise, said, "How will the reverend bishops of the other house be able to express their due abhorrence of the crime of perjury, who solemnly declare in the presence of God that when they are called upon to accept a living, perhaps of £4,000 a year, at that very instant they are moved by the Holy Ghost to accept the office and administration thereof, and for no other reason whatever?" The modes of initiation are more damaging than custom-house oaths. The bishop is elected by the dean and prebends of the cathedral. The queen sends these gentlemen a *congé d'élire*, or leave to elect: but also sends them the name of the person whom they are to elect. They go into the cathedral, chant and pray and beseech the Holy Ghost to assist them in their choice; and, after these invocations, invariably find that the dictates of the Holy Ghost agree with the recommendations of the Queen.

But you must pay for conformity. All goes well as long as you run with conformists. But you, who are an honest man in other particulars, know that there is alive somewhere a man whose honesty reaches to this point also that he shall not kneel to false gods, and on the day when you meet him, you sink into the class of counterfeits. Besides, this succumbing has grave penalties. If you take in a lie, you must take in all that belongs to it. England accepts this ornamented national church, and it glazes the eyes, bloats the flesh, gives the voice a stertorous clang, and clouds the understanding of the receivers.

The English Church, undermined by German criticism, had nothing left but tradition; and was led logically back to Romanism. But that was an element which only hot heads could breathe: in view of the educated class, generally, it was not a fact to front the sun; and the alienation of such men from the church became complete.

Nature, to be sure, had her remedy. Religious persons are driven out of the Established Church into sects, which instantly rise to credit and hold the Establishment in check. Nature has sharper remedies, also. The English, abhorring change in all things, abhorring it most in matters of religion, cling to the last rag of form, and are dreadfully given to cant. The English (and I wish it were confined to them, but 'tis a taint in the Anglo-Saxon blood in both hemispheres)—the English and the Americans cant beyond all other nations. The French relin-

quish all that industry to them. What is so odious as the
polite bows to God, in our books and newspapers? The
popular press is flagitious in the exact measure of its
sanctimony, and the religion of the day is a theatrical
Sinai, where the thunders are supplied by the property-
man. The fanaticism and hypocrisy create satire. *Punch*
finds an inexhaustible material. Dickens writes novels on
Exeter-Hall humanity. Thackeray exposes the heartless
high life. Nature revenges herself more summarily by the
heathenism of the lower classes. Lord Shaftesbury calls
the poor thieves together and reads sermons to them,
and they call it "gas." George Borrow summons the
Gypsies to hear his discourse on the Hebrews in Egypt,
and reads to them the Apostles' Creed in Romany.
"When I had concluded," he says, "I looked around me.
The features of the assembly were twisted, and the eyes
of all turned upon me with a frightful squint: not an
individual present but squinted; the genteel Pepa, the
good-humored Chicharona, the Cosdami, all squinted;
the Gypsy jockey squinted worst of all."

The Church at this moment is much to be pitied. She
has nothing left but possession. If a bishop meets an
intelligent gentleman and reads fatal interrogations in
his eyes, he has no resource but to take wine with him.
False position introduces cant, perjury, simony and ever
a lower class of mind and character into the clergy: and,
when the hierarchy is afraid of science and education,
afraid of piety, afraid of tradition and afraid of theology,
there is nothing left but to quit a church which is no
longer one.

But the religion of England—is it the Established
Church? no; is it the sects? no; they are only perpetua-
tions of some private man's dissent, and are to the Established Church as cabs are to a coach, cheaper and more
convenient, but really the same thing. Where dwells the

religion? Tell me first where dwells electricity, or motion, or thought, or gesture. They do not dwell or stay at all. Electricity cannot be made fast, mortared up and ended, like London Monument or the Tower, so that you shall know where to find it, and keep it fixed, as the English do with their things, forevermore; it is passing, glancing, gesticular; it is a traveler, a newness, a surprise, a secret, which perplexes them and puts them out. Yet, if religion be the doing of all good, and for its sake the suffering of all evil, *souffrir de tout le monde, et ne faire souffrir personne,* that divine secret has existed in England from the days of Alfred to those of Romilly, of Clarkson and of Florence Nightingale, and in thousands who have no fame.

RESULT

England is the best of actual nations. It is no ideal framework, it is an old pile built in different ages, with repairs, additions and makeshifts; but you see the poor best you have got. London is the epitome of our times, and the Rome of today. Broad-fronted, broad-bottomed Teutons, they stand in solid phalanx four-square to the points of compass; they constitute the modern world, they have earned their vantage ground and held it through ages of adverse possession. They are well marked and differing from other leading races. England is tender-hearted. Rome was not. England is not so public in its bias; private life is its place of honor. Truth in private life, untruth in public, marks these home-loving men. Their political conduct is not decided by general views, but by internal intrigues and personal and family interest. They cannot readily see beyond

England. The history of Rome and Greece, when written by their scholars, degenerates into English party pamphlets. They cannot see beyond England, nor in England can they transcend the interests of the governing classes. "English principles" mean a primary regard to the interests of property. England, Scotland and Ireland combine to check the colonies. England and Scotland combine to check Irish manufactures and trade. England rallies at home to check Scotland. In England, the strong classes check the weaker. In the home population of near thirty millions, there are but one million voters. The Church punishes dissent, punishes education. Down to a late day, marriages performed by dissenters were illegal. A bitter class-legislation gives power to those who are rich enough to buy a law. The game-laws are a proverb of oppression. Pauperism incrusts and clogs the state, and in hard times becomes hideous. In bad seasons, the porridge was diluted. Multitudes lived miserably by shell-fish and sea-ware. In cities, the children are trained to beg, until they shall be old enough to rob. Men and women were convicted of poisoning scores of children for burial fees. In Irish districts, men deteriorated in size and shape, the nose sunk, the gums were exposed, with diminished brain and brutal form. During the Australian emigration, multitudes were rejected by the commissioners as being too emaciated for useful colonists. During the Russian war, few of those that offered as recruits were found up to the medical standard, though it had been reduced.

The foreign policy of England, though ambitious and lavish of money, has not often been generous or just. It has a principal regard to the interest of trade, checked however by the aristocratic bias of the ambassador, which usually puts him in sympathy with the continental

Courts. It sanctioned the partition of Poland, it betrayed Genoa, Sicily, Parga, Greece, Turkey, Rome and Hungary.

Some public regards they have. They have abolished slavery in the West Indies and put an end to human sacrifices in the East. At home they have a certain statute hospitality. England keeps open doors, as a trading country must, to all nations. It is one of their fixed ideas, and wrathfully supported by their laws in unbroken sequence for a thousand years. In *Magna Charta* it was ordained that all "merchants shall have safe and secure conduct to go out and come into England, and to stay there, and to pass as well by land as by water, to buy and sell by the ancient allowed customs, without any evil toll, except in time of war, or when they shall be of any nation at war with us." It is a statute and obliged hospitality and peremptorily maintained. But this shop-rule had one magnificent effect. It extends its cold unalterable courtesy to political exiles of every opinion, and is a fact which might give additional light to that portion of the planet seen from the farthest star. But this perfunctory hospitality puts no sweetness into their unaccommodating manners, no check on that puissant nationality which makes their existence incompatible with all that is not English.

What we must say about a nation is a superficial dealing with symptoms. We cannot go deep enough into the biography of the spirit who never throws himself entire into one hero, but delegates his energy in parts or spasms to vicious and defective individuals. But the wealth of the source is seen in the plenitude of English nature. What variety of power and talent; what facility and plenteousness of knighthood, lordship, ladyship, royalty, loyalty; what a proud chivalry is indicated in *Collins's Peerage*, through eight hundred years! What dignity resting on what reality and stoutness! What courage in war, what sinew in labor, what cunning workmen, what inventors and engineers, what seamen and pilots, what clerks and scholars! No one man and no few men can represent them. It is a people of myriad personalities. Their many-headedness is owing to the advantageous position of the middle class, who are always the source of letters and science. Hence the vast plenty of their esthetic production. As they are many-headed, so they are many-nationed: their colonization annexes archipelagoes and continents, and their speech seems destined to be the universal language of men. I have noted the reserve of power in the English temperament. In the island, they never let out all the length of all the reins, there is no Berserker rage, no abandonment or ecstasy of will or intellect, like that of the Arabs in the time of Mahomet, or like that which intoxicated France in 1789. But who would see the uncoiling of that tremendous spring, the explosion of their well-husbanded forces, must follow the swarms which pouring now for two hundred years from the British islands, have sailed and rode and traded and planted through all climates, mainly following the belt of empire, the temperate zones, carrying the Saxon seed, with its instinct for liberty and law, for arts and for thought—acquiring under some skies a more electric energy than the native air allows—to the conquest of the globe. Their colonial policy, obeying the necessities of a vast empire, has become liberal. Canada and Australia have been contented with substantial independence. They are expiating the wrongs of India by benefits; first, in works for the irrigation of the peninsula, and roads, and telegraphs; and secondly, in the instruction of the people, to qualify them for self-government, when the British power shall be finally called home.

Their mind is in a state of arrested development—a divine cripple like Vulcan; a blind *savant* like Huber and Sanderson. They do not occupy themselves on matters of general and lasting import, but on a corporeal civilization, on goods that perish in the using. But they read with good intent, and what they learn they incarnate. The English mind turns every abstraction it can receive into a portable utensil, or a working institution. Such is their tenacity and such their practical turn, that they hold all they gain. Hence we say that only the English race can be trusted with freedom—freedom which is double-edged and dangerous to any but the wise and robust. The English designate the kingdoms emulous of free institutions, as the sentimental nations. Their culture is not an outside varnish, but is thorough and secular in families and the race. They are oppressive with their temperament, and all the more that they are refined. I have sometimes seen them walk with my countrymen when I was forced to allow them every advantage, and their companions seemed bags of bones.

There is cramp limitation in their habit of thought, sleepy routine, and a tortoise's instinct to hold hard to the ground with his claws, lest he should be thrown on his back. There is a drag of inertia which resists reform in every shape—law-reform, army-reform, extension of suffrage, Jewish franchise, Catholic emancipation—the abolition of slavery, of impressment, penal code and entails. They praise this drag, under the formula that it is the excellence of the British constitution that no law can anticipate the public opinion. These poor tortoises must hold hard, for they feel no wings sprouting at their shoulders. Yet somewhat divine warms at their heart and waits a happier hour. It hides in their sturdy will. "Will," said the old philosophy, "is the measure of power," and personality is the token of this race. *Quid vult valde vult.*

What they do they do with a will. You cannot account for their success by their Christianity, commerce, charter, common law, Parliament, or letters, but by the contumacious sharp-tongued energy of English *naturel,* with a poise impossible to disturb, which makes all these its instruments. They are slow and reticent, and are like a dull good horse which lets every nag pass him, but with whip and spur will run down every racer in the field. They are right in their feeling, though wrong in their speculation.

The feudal system survives in the steep inequality of property and privilege, in the limited franchise, in the social barriers which confine patronage and promotion to a caste, and still more in the submissive ideas pervading these people. The fagging of the schools is repeated in the social classes. An Englishman shows no mercy to those below him in the social scale, as he looks for none from those above him; any forbearance from his superiors surprises him, and they suffer in his good opinion. But the feudal system can be seen with less pain on large historical grounds. It was pleaded in mitigation of the rotten borough, that it worked well, that substantial justice was done. Fox, Burke, Pitt, Erskine, Wilberforce, Sheridan, Romilly, or whatever national man, were by this means sent to Parliament, when their return by large constituencies would have been doubtful. So now we say that the right measures of England are the men it bred; that it has yielded more able men in five hundred years than any other nation; and, though we must not play Providence and balance the chances of producing ten great men against the comfort of ten thousand mean men, yet retrospectively, we may strike the balance and prefer one Alfred, one Shakespeare, one Milton, one Sidney, one Raleigh, one Wellington, to a million foolish democrats.

The American system is more democratic, more humane; yet the American people do not yield better or more able men, or more inventions or books or benefits than the English. Congress is not wiser or better than Parliament. France has abolished its suffocating old *régime*, but is not recently marked by any more wisdom or virtue.

The power of performance has not been exceeded—the creation of value. The English have given importance to individuals, a principal end and fruit of every society. Every man is allowed and encouraged to be what he is, and is guarded in the indulgence of his whim. "Magna Charta," said Rushworth, "is such a fellow that he will have no sovereign." By this general activity and by this sacredness of individuals, they have in seven hundred years evolved the principles of freedom. It is the land of patriots, martyrs, sages and bards, and if the ocean out of which it emerged should wash it away, it will be remembered as an island famous for immortal laws, for the announcements of original right which make the stone tables of liberty.

MONTAIGNE: OR, THE SKEPTIC

EVERY fact is related on one side to sensation, and on the other to morals. The game of thought is, on the appearance of one of these two sides, to find the other: given the upper, to find the under side. Nothing so thin but has these two faces, and when the observer has seen the obverse, he turns it over to see the reverse. Life is a pitching of this penny—heads or tails. We never tire of this game, because there is still a slight shudder of astonishment at the exhibition of the other face, at the contrast of the two faces. A man is flushed with success, and bethinks himself what this good luck signifies. He drives his bargain in the street; but it occurs that he also is bought and sold. He sees the beauty of a human face, and searches the cause of that beauty, which must be more beautiful. He builds his fortunes, maintains the laws, cherishes his children; but he asks himself, Why? and whereto? This head and this tail are called, in the language of philosophy, Infinite and Finite; Relative and Absolute; Apparent and Real; and many fine names beside.

Each man is born with a predisposition to one or the other of these sides of nature; and it will easily happen that men will be found devoted to one or the other. One class has the perception of difference, and is conversant with facts and surfaces, cities and persons, and the bringing certain things to pass—the men of talent and action. Another class have the perception of identity, and are men of faith and philosophy, men of genius.

Each of these riders drives too fast. Plotinus believes only in philosophers; Fenelon, in saints; Pindar and Byron, in poets. Read the haughty language in which Plato and the Platonists speak of all men who are not devoted to their own shining abstractions: other men are rats and mice. The literary class is usually proud and exclusive. The correspondence of Pope and Swift describes mankind around them as monsters; and that of Goethe and Schiller, in our own time, is scarcely more kind.

It is easy to see how this arrogance comes. The genius is a genius by the first look he casts on any object. Is his eye creative? Does he not rest in angles and colors, but beholds the design?—he will presently undervalue the actual object. In powerful moments, his thought has dissolved the works of art and nature into their causes, so that the works appear heavy and faulty. He has a conception of beauty which the sculptor cannot embody. Picture, statue, temple, railroad, steam-engine, existed first in an artist's mind, without flaw, mistake, or friction, which impair the executed models. So did the Church, the State, college, court, social circle, and all the institutions. It is not strange that these men, remembering what they have seen and hoped of ideas, should affirm disdainfully the superiority of ideas. Having at some time seen that the happy soul will carry all the arts in power, they say, Why cumber ourselves with superfluous realizations? and like dreaming beggars they assume to speak and act as if these values were already substantiated.

On the other part, the men of toil and trade and luxury—the animal world, including the animal in the philosopher and poet also, and the practical world, including the painful drudgeries which are never excused to philosopher or poet any more than to the rest—weigh heavily on the other side. The trade in our streets believes in no metaphysical causes, thinks nothing of the force which necessitated traders and a trading planet to exist: no, but sticks to cotton, sugar, wool and salt. The ward meetings, on election days, are not softened by any misgiving of the value of these ballotings. Hot life is streaming in a single direction. To the men of this world, to the animal strength and spirits, to the men of practical power, whilst immersed in it, the man of ideas appears out of his reason. They alone have reason.

Things always bring their own philosophy with them, that is, prudence. No man acquires property without acquiring with it a little arithmetic also. In England, the richest country that ever existed, property stands for more, compared with personal ability, than in any other. After dinner, a man believes less, denies more: verities have lost some charm. After dinner, arithmetic is the only science: ideas are disturbing, incendiary, follies of young men, repudiated by the solid portion of society: and a man comes to be valued by his athletic and animal qualities. Spence relates that Mr. Pope was with Sir Godfrey Kneller one day, when his nephew, a Guinea trader, came in. "Nephew," said Sir Godfrey, "you have the honor of seeing the two greatest men in the world." "I don't know how great men you may be," said the Guinea man, "but I don't like your looks. I have often bought a man much better than both of you, all muscles and bones, for ten guineas." Thus the men of the senses revenge themselves on the professors and repay scorn for scorn. The first had leaped to conclusions not yet ripe, and say more than is true; the others make themselves merry with the philosopher, and weigh man by the pound. They believe that mustard bites the tongue, that pepper is hot, friction-matches incendiary, revolvers are to be avoided, and suspenders hold up pantaloons; that there is much sentiment in a chest of tea; and a man will be eloquent, if you give him good wine. Are you tender and scrupulous—you must eat more mince pie. They hold that Luther had milk in him when he said—

> *Wer nicht liebt Wein, Weiber, Gesang,*
> *Der bleibt ein Narr sein Leben lang;—*

and when he advised a young scholar, perplexed with fore-ordination and free-will, to get well drunk. "The nerves," says Cabanis, "they are the man." My neighbor, a jolly farmer, in the tavern bar-room, thinks that the use of money is sure and speedy spending. For his part, he says, he puts his down his neck and gets the good of it.

The inconvenience of this way of thinking is that it runs into indifferentism and then into disgust. Life is eating us up. We shall be fables presently. Keep cool: it will be all one a hundred years hence. Life's well enough, but we shall be glad to get out of it, and they will all be glad to have us. Why should we fret and drudge? Our meat will taste tomorrow as it did yesterday, and we may at last have had enough of it. "Ah," said my languid gentleman at Oxford, "there's nothing new or true—and no matter."

With a little more bitterness, the cynic moans; our life is like an ass led to market by a bundle of hay being carried before him; he sees nothing but the bundle of hay. "There is so much trouble in coming into the world," said Lord Bolingbroke, "and so much more, as well as meanness, in going out of it, that 'tis hardly worth while to be here at all." I knew a philosopher of this kidney who was accustomed briefly to sum up his experience of human nature in saying, "Mankind is a damned rascal": and the natural corollary is pretty sure to follow—"The world lives by humbug, and so will I."

The abstractionist and the materialist thus mutually exasperating each other, and the scoffer expressing the worst of materialism, there arises a third party to occupy the middle ground between these two, the skeptic, namely. He finds both wrong by being in extremes. He labors to plant his feet, to be the beam of the balance. He will not go beyond his card. He sees the one-sidedness of these men of the street; he will not be a Gibeonite; he stands for the intellectual faculties, a cool head and whatever serves to keep it cool; no unadvised industry, no unrewarded self-devotion, no loss of the brains in toil. Am I an ox, or a dray? You are both in extremes, he says. You that will have all solid, and a world of pig-lead, deceive yourselves grossly. You believe yourselves rooted and grounded on adamant; and yet, if we uncover the last facts of our knowledge, you are spinning like bubbles in a river, you know not whither or whence, and you are bottomed and capped and wrapped in delusions. Neither will he be betrayed to a book and wrapped in a gown. The studious class are their own victims; they are thin and pale, their feet are cold, their heads are hot, the night is without sleep, the day a fear of interruption—pallor, squalor, hunger and egotism. If you come near them and see what conceits they entertain—they are abstractionists, and spend their days and nights in dreaming some dream; in expecting the homage of society to some precious scheme, built on a truth, but destitute of proportion in its presentment, of justness in its application, and of all energy of will in the schemer to embody and vitalize it.

But I see plainly, he says, that I cannot see. I know that human strength is not in extremes, but in avoiding extremes. I, at least, will shun the weakness of philosophizing beyond my depth. What is the use of pretending to powers we have not? What is the use of pretending to assurances we have not, respecting the other life? Why exaggerate the power of virtue? Why be an angel before your time? These strings, wound up too high, will snap. If there is a wish for immortality, and no evidence, why not say just that? If there are conflicting evidences, why not state them? If there is not ground for a candid thinker to make up his mind, yea or nay—why not suspend the judgment? I weary of these dogmatizers. I tire of these hacks of routine, who deny the dogmas. I neither affirm nor deny. I stand here to try the case. I am here to consider, σκοπεῖν, to consider how it is. I will try to keep the balance true. Of what use to take the chair and glibly rattle off theories of society, religion and nature, when I know that practical objections lie in the way, insurmountable by me and by my mates? Why so talkative in public, when each of my neighbors can pin me to my seat by arguments I cannot refute? Why pretend that life is so simple a game, when we know how subtle and elusive the Proteus is? Why think to shut up all things in your narrow coop, when we know there are not one or two only, but ten, twenty, a thousand things, and unlike? Why fancy that you have all the truth in your keeping? There is much to say on all sides.

Who shall forbid a wise skepticism, seeing that there is no practical question on which anything more than an approximate solution can be had? Is not marriage an open question, when it is alleged, from the beginning of the world, that such as are in the institution wish to get out, and such as are out wish to get in? And the reply of Socrates, to him who asked whether he should choose a wife, still remains reasonable, that "whether he should choose one or not, he would repent it." Is not the State a question? All society is divided in opinion on the subject of the State. Nobody loves it; great numbers dislike it and suffer conscientious scruples to allegiance; and the only defence set up, is the fear of doing worse in disorganizing. Is it otherwise with the Church? Or, to put any of the questions which touch mankind nearest— shall the young man aim at a leading part in law, in politics, in trade? It will not be pretended that a success in either of these kinds is quite coincident with what is best and inmost in his mind. Shall he then, cutting the stays that hold him fast to the social state, put out to sea with no guidance but his genius? There is much to say on both sides. Remember the open question between the present order of "competition" and the friends of "attractive and associated labor." The generous minds embrace the proposition of labor shared by all; it is the only honesty; nothing else is safe. It is from the poor man's hut alone that strength and virtue come: and yet, on the other side, it is alleged that labor impairs the form and breaks the spirit of man, and the laborers cry unanimously, "We have no thoughts." Culture, how indispensable! I cannot forgive you the want of accomplishments; and yet culture will instantly impair that chiefest beauty of spontaneousness. Excellent is culture for a savage; but once let him read in the book, and he is no longer able not to think of Plutarch's heroes. In short, since true fortitude of understanding consists "in not letting what we know be embarrassed by what we do not know," we ought to secure those advantages which we can command, and not risk them by clutching after the airy and unattainable. Come, no chimeras! Let us go abroad; let us mix in affairs; let us learn and get and have and climb. "Men are a sort of moving plants, and, like trees, receive a great part of their nourishment from the air. If they keep too much at home, they pine." Let us have a robust, manly life; let us know what we know, for certain; what we have, let it be solid and seasonable and our own. A world in the hand is worth two in the bush. Let us have to do with real men and women, and not with skipping ghosts.

This then is the right ground of the skeptic—this of consideration, of self-containing; not at all of unbelief; not at all of universal denying, nor of universal doubting —doubting even that he doubts; least of all of scoffing and profligate jeering at all that is stable and good. These are no more his moods than are those of religion and philosophy. He is the considerer, the prudent, taking in sail, counting stock, husbanding his means, believing that a man has too many enemies than that he can afford to be his own foe; that we cannot give ourselves too many advantages in this unequal conflict, with powers so vast and unweariable ranged on one side, and this little conceited vulnerable popinjay that a man is, bobbing up and down into every danger, on the other. It is a position taken up for better defence, as of more safety, and one that can be maintained; and it is one of more opportunity and range: as, when we build a house, the rule is to set it not too high nor too low, under the wind, but out of the dirt.

The philosophy we want is one of fluxions and mobility. The Spartan and Stoic schemes are too stark and stiff for our occasion. A theory of Saint John, and of nonresistance, seems, on the other hand, too thin and aerial. We want some coat woven of elastic steel, stout as the first and limber as the second. We want a ship in these billows we inhabit. An angular, dogmatic house would be rent to chips and splinters in this storm of many elements. No, it must be tight, and fit to the form of man, to live at all; as a shell must dictate the architecture of a house founded on the sea. The soul of man must be the type of our scheme, just as the body of man is the type after which a dwelling-house is built. Adaptiveness is the peculiarity of human nature. We are golden averages, volitant stabilities, compensated or periodic errors, houses founded on the sea. The wise skeptic wishes to have a near view of the best game and the chief players; what is best in the planet; art and nature, places and events; but mainly men. Everything that is excellent in mankind—a form of grace, an arm of iron, lips of persuasion, a brain of resources, every one skilful to play and win—he will see and judge.

The terms of admission to this spectacle are, that he have a certain solid and intelligible way of living of his own; some method of answering the inevitable needs of human life; proof that he has played with skill and success; that he has evinced the temper, stoutness and the range of qualities which, among his contemporaries and countrymen, entitle him to fellowship and trust. For the secrets of life are not shown except to sympathy and likeness. Men do not confide themselves to boys, or coxcombs, or pedants, but to their peers. Some wise limitation, as the modern phrase is; some condition between the extremes, and having, itself, a positive quality; some stark and sufficient man, who is not salt or sugar, but sufficiently related to the world to do justice to Paris or London, and, at the same time, a vigorous and original thinker, whom cities can not overawe, but who uses them—is the fit person to occupy this ground of speculation.

These qualities meet in the character of Montaigne. And yet, since the personal regard which I entertain for Montaigne may be unduly great, I will, under the shield of this prince of egotists, offer, as an apology for electing him as the representative of skepticism, a word or two to explain how my love began and grew for this admirable gossip.

A single odd volume of Cotton's translation of the *Essays* remained to me from my father's library, when a boy. It lay long neglected, until, after many years, when I was newly escaped from college, I read the book, and procured the remaining volumes. I remember the delight and wonder in which I lived with it. It seemed to me as if I had myself written the book, in some former life, so sincerely it spoke to my thought and experience. It happened, when in Paris, in 1833, that, in the cemetery of Père Lachaise, I came to a tomb of Auguste Collignon, who died in 1830, aged sixty-eight years, and who, said the monument, "lived to do right, and had formed himself to virtue on the *Essays of Montaigne.*" Some years later, I became acquainted with an accomplished English poet, John Sterling; and, in prosecuting my correspondence, I found that, from a love of

Montaigne, he had made a pilgrimage to his chateau, still standing near Castellan, in Perigord, and, after two hundred and fifty years, had copied from the walls of his library the inscriptions which Montaigne had written there. That *Journal* of Mr. Sterling's, published in the *Westminster Review,* Mr. Hazlitt has reprinted in the *Prolegomena* to his edition of the *Essays.* I heard with pleasure that one of the newly discovered autographs of William Shakespeare was in a copy of Florio's translation of Montaigne. It is the only book which we certainly know to have been in the poet's library. And, oddly enough, the duplicate copy of Florio, which the British Museum purchased with a view of protecting the Shakespeare autograph (as I was informed in the Museum), turned out to have the autograph of Ben Jonson in the fly-leaf. Leigh Hunt relates of Lord Byron, that Montaigne was the only great writer of past times whom he read with avowed satisfaction. Other coincidences, not needful to be mentioned here, concurred to make this old Gascon still new and immortal for me.

In 1571, on the death of his father, Montaigne, then thirty-eight years old, retired from the practice of law at Bordeaux, and settled himself on his estate. Though he had been a man of pleasure and sometimes a courtier, his studious habits now grew on him, and he loved the compass, staidness and independence of the country-gentleman's life. He took up his economy in good earnest, and made his farms yield the most. Downright and plain-dealing, and abhorring to be deceived or to deceive, he was esteemed in the country for his sense and probity. In the civil wars of the League, which converted every house into a fort, Montaigne kept his gates open and his house without defence. All parties freely came and went, his courage and honor being universally esteemed. The neighboring lords and gentry brought jewels and papers to him for safe-keeping. Gibbon reckons, in these bigoted times, but two men of liberality in France—Henry IV and Montaigne.

Montaigne is the frankest and honestest of all writers. His French freedom runs into grossness; but he has anticipated all censure by the bounty of his own confessions. In his times, books were written to one sex only, and almost all were written in Latin; so that in a humorist a certain nakedness of statement was permitted, which our manners, of a literature addressed equally to both sexes, do not allow. But though a biblical plainness coupled with a most uncanonical levity may shut his pages to many sensitive readers, yet the offence is superficial. He parades it: he makes the most of it: nobody can think or say worse of him than he does. He pretends to most of the vices; and, if there be any virtue in him, he says, it got in by stealth. There is no man, in his opinion, who has not deserved hanging five or six times; and he pretends no exception in his own behalf. "Five or six as ridiculous stories," too, he says, "can be told of me, as of any man living." But, with all this really superfluous frankness, the opinion of an invincible probity grows into every reader's mind. "When I the most strictly and religiously confess myself, I find that the best virtue I have has in it some tincture of vice; and I, who am as sincere and perfect a lover of virtue of that stamp as any other whatever, am afraid that Plato, in his purest virtue, if he had listened and laid his ear close to himself, would have heard some jarring sound of human mixture; but faint and remote and only to be perceived by himself."

Here is an impatience and fastidiousness at color or pretence of any kind. He has been in courts so long as to have conceived a furious disgust at appearances; he will indulge himself with a little cursing and swearing; he will talk with sailors and gipsies, use flash and street ballads; he has stayed indoors till he is deadly sick; he will to the open air, though it rain bullets. He has seen too much of gentlemen of the long robe, until he wishes for cannibals; and is so nervous, by factitious life, that he thinks the more barbarous man is, the better he is. He likes his saddle. You may read theology, and grammar, and metaphysics elsewhere. Whatever you get here shall smack of the earth and of real life, sweet, or smart, or stinging. He makes no hesitation to entertain you with the records of his disease, and his journey to Italy is quite full of that matter. He took and kept this position of equilibrium. Over his name he drew an emblematic pair of scales, and wrote *Que sçais je?* under it. As I look at his effigy opposite the title page, I seem to hear him say, "You may play old Poz, if you will; you may rail and exaggerate—I stand here for truth, and will not, for all the states and churches and revenues and personal reputations of Europe, overstate the dry fact, as I see it; I will rather mumble and prose about what I certainly know—my house and barns; my father, my wife and my tenants; my old lean bald pate; my knives and forks; what meats I eat and what drinks I prefer, and a hundred straws just as ridiculous—than I will write, with a fine crow-quill, a fine romance. I like gray days, and autumn and winter weather. I am gray and autumnal myself, and think an undress and old shoes that do not pinch my feet, and old friends who do not constrain me, and plain topics where I do not need to strain myself and pump my brains, the most suitable. Our condition as men is risky and ticklish enough. One cannot be sure of himself and his fortune an hour, but he may be whisked off into some pitiable or ridiculous plight. Why should I vapor and play the philosopher, instead of ballasting, the best I can, this dancing balloon? So, at least, I live within compass, keep myself ready for action, and can shoot the gulf at last with decency. If there be anything farcical in such a life, the blame is not mine: let it lie at fate's and nature's door."

The *Essays*, therefore, are an entertaining soliloquy on every random topic that comes into his head; treating everything without ceremony, yet with masculine sense. There have been men with deeper insight; but, one would say, never a man with such abundance of thoughts: he is never dull, never insincere, and has the genius to make the reader care for all that he cares for.

The sincerity and marrow of the man reaches to his sentences. I know not anywhere the book that seems less written. It is the language of conversation transferred to a book. Cut these words, and they would bleed; they are vascular and alive. One has the same pleasure in it that he feels in listening to the necessary speech of men about their work, when any unusual circumstance gives momentary importance to the dialogue. For blacksmiths and teamsters do not trip in their speech; it is a shower of bullets. It is Cambridge men who correct themselves and begin again at every half sentence, and, moreover, will pun, and refine too much, and swerve from the matter to the expression. Montaigne talks with shrewdness, knows the world and books and himself, and uses the positive degree; never shrieks, or protests, or prays: no weakness, no convulsion, no superlative: does not wish to jump out of his skin, or play any antics, or annihilate space or time, but is stout and solid; tastes every moment of the day; likes pain because it makes him feel himself and realize things; as we pinch ourselves to know that we are awake. He keeps the plain; he rarely mounts or sinks; likes to feel solid ground and the stones underneath. His writing has no enthusiasms, no aspiration; contented, self-respecting and keeping the middle of the road. There is but one exception—in his love for Socrates. In speaking of him, for once his cheek flushes and his style rises to passion.

Montaigne died of a quinsy, at the age of sixty, in 1592. When he came to die he caused the mass to be celebrated in his chamber. At the age of thirty-three, he had been married. "But," he says, "might I have had my own will, I would not have married Wisdom herself, if she would have had me: but 'tis to much purpose to evade it, the common custom and use of life will have it so. Most of my actions are guided by example, not choice." In the hour of death, he gave the same weight to custom. *Que sçais je?* What do I know?

This book of Montaigne the world has endorsed by translating it into all tongues and printing seventy-five editions of it in Europe; and that, too, a circulation somewhat chosen, namely among courtiers, soldiers, princes, men of the world and men of wit and generosity.

Shall we say that Montaigne has spoken wisely, and given the right and permanent expression of the human mind, on the conduct of life?

We are natural believers. Truth, or the connection between cause and effect, alone interests us. We are persuaded that a thread runs through all things: all worlds are strung on it, as beads; and men, and events, and life, come to us only because of that thread: they pass and repass only that we may know the direction and continuity of that line. A book or statement which goes to show that there is no line, but random and chaos, a calamity out of nothing, a prosperity and no account of it, a hero born from a fool, a fool from a hero—dispirits us. Seen or unseen, we believe the tie exists. Talent makes counterfeit ties; genius finds the real ones.

We hearken to the man of science, because we anticipate the sequence in natural phenomena which he uncovers. We love whatever affirms, connects, preserves; and dislike what scatters or pulls down. One man appears whose nature is to all men's eyes conserving and constructive; his presence supposes a well-ordered society, agriculture, trade, large institutions and empire. If these did not exist, they would begin to exist through his endeavors. Therefore he cheers and comforts men, who feel all this in him very readily. The nonconformist and the rebel say all manner of unanswerable things against the existing republic, but discover to our sense no plan of house or state of their own. Therefore, though the town and state and way of living, which our counsellor contemplated, might be a very modest or musty prosperity, yet men rightly go for him, and reject the reformer so long as he comes only with ax and crowbar.

But though we are natural conservers and causationists, and reject a sour, dumpish unbelief, the skeptical class, which Montaigne represents, have reason, and every man, at some time, belongs to it. Every superior mind will pass through this domain of equilibration—I should rather say, will know how to avail himself of the checks and balances in nature, as a natural weapon against the exaggeration and formalism of bigots and blockheads.

Skepticism is the attitude assumed by the student in relation to the particulars which society adores, but which he sees to be reverend only in their tendency and spirit. The ground occupied by the skeptic is the vestibule of the temple. Society does not like to have any breath of question blown on the existing order. But the interrogation of custom at all points is an inevitable stage in the growth of every superior mind, and is the evidence of its perception of the flowing power which remains itself in all changes.

The superior mind will find itself equally at odds with the evils of society and with the projects that are offered to relieve them. The wise skeptic is a bad citizen; no conservative, he sees the selfishness of property and the drowsiness of institutions. But neither is he fit to work with any democratic party that ever was constituted; for parties wish every one committed, and he penetrates the popular patriotism. His politics are those of the *Soul's Errand* of Sir Walter Raleigh; or of Krishna, in the *Bhagavat*, "There is none who is worthy of my love or hatred"; whilst he sentences law, physic, divinity, commerce and custom. He is a reformer; yet he is no better member of the philanthropic association. It turns out that he is not the champion of the operative, the pauper, the prisoner, the slave. It stands in his mind that our life in this world is not of quite so easy interpretation as churches and school-books say. He does not wish to take ground against these benevolences, to play the part of devil's attorney, and blazon every doubt and sneer that darkens the sun for him. But he says, There are doubts.

I mean to use the occasion, and celebrate the calendar-day of our Saint Michel de Montaigne, by counting and describing these doubts or negations. I wish to ferret them out of their holes and sun them a little. We must do with them as the police do with old rogues, who are shown up to the public at the marshal's office. They will never be so formidable when once they have been identified and registered. But I mean honestly by them—that justice shall be done to their terrors. I shall not take Sunday objections, made up on purpose to be put down. I shall take the worst I can find, whether I can dispose of them or they of me.

I do not press the skepticism of the materialist. I know the quadruped opinion will not prevail. 'Tis of no importance what bats and oxen think. The first danger-ous symptom I report is, the levity of intellect; as if it were fatal to earnestness to know much. Knowledge is the knowing that we can not know. The dull pray; the geniuses are light mockers. How respectable is earnest-ness on every platform! but intellect kills it. Nay, San Carlo, my subtle and admirable friend, one of the most penetrating of men, finds that all direct ascension, even of lofty piety, leads to this ghastly insight and sends back the votary orphaned. My astonishing San Carlo thought the lawgivers and saints infected. They found the ark empty; saw, and would not tell; and tried to choke off their approaching followers, by saying, "Ac-tion, action, my dear fellows, is for you!" Bad as was to me this detection by San Carlo, this frost in July, this blow from a bride, there was still a worse, namely the cloy or satiety of the saints. In the mount of vision, ere they have yet risen from their knees, they say, "We dis-cover that this our homage and beatitude is partial and deformed: we must fly for relief to the suspected and reviled Intellect, to the Understanding, the Mephistoph-eles, to the gymnastics of talent."

This is hobgoblin the first; and, though it has been the subject of much elegy in our nineteenth century, from Byron, Goethe and other poets of less fame, not to mention many distinguished private observers—I con-fess it is not very affecting to my imagination; for it seems to concern the shattering of baby-houses and crockery-shops. What flutters the Church of Rome, or of England, or of Geneva, or of Boston, may yet be very

far from touching any principle of faith. I think that
the intellect and moral sentiment are unanimous; and
that though philosophy extirpates bugbears, yet it supplies the natural checks of vice, and polarity to the soul.
I think that the wiser a man is, the more stupendous he
finds the natural and moral economy, and lifts himself
to a more absolute reliance.

There is the power of moods, each setting at nought
all but its own tissue of facts and beliefs. There is the
power of complexions, obviously modifying the dispositions and sentiments. The beliefs and unbeliefs appear to be structural; and as soon as each man attains the
poise and vivacity which allow the whole machinery
to play, he will not need extreme examples, but will
rapidly alternate all opinions in his own life. Our life is
March weather, savage and serene in one hour. We go
forth austere, dedicated, believing in the iron links of
Destiny, and will not turn on our heel to save our life:
but a book, or a bust, or only the sound of a name,
shoots a spark through the nerves, and we suddenly believe in will: my finger-ring shall be the seal of Solomon;
fate is for imbeciles; all is possible to the resolved mind.
Presently a new experience gives a new turn to our
thoughts: common sense resumes its tyranny; we say,
"Well, the army, after all, is the gate to fame, manners
and poetry: and, look you—on the whole, selfishness
plants best, prunes best, makes the best commerce and
the best citizen." Are the opinions of a man on right and
wrong, on fate and causation, at the mercy of a broken
sleep or an indigestion? Is his belief in God and Duty
no deeper than a stomach evidence? And what guaranty
for the permanence of his opinions? I like not the French
celerity—a new Church and State once a week. This is
the second negation; and I shall let it pass for what it
will. As far as it asserts rotation of states of mind, I sup-

pose it suggests its own remedy, namely in the record of
larger periods. What is the mean of many states; of all
the states? Does the general voice of ages affirm any
principle, or is no community of sentiment discoverable
in distant times and places? And when it shows the
power of self-interest, I accept that as part of the divine
law and must reconcile it with aspiration the best I can.

The word Fate, or Destiny, expresses the sense of
mankind, in all ages, that the laws of the world do not
always befriend, but often hurt and crush us. Fate, in
the shape of *Kinde* or nature, grows over us like grass.
We paint Time with a scythe; Love and Fortune, blind;
and Destiny, deaf. We have too little power of resistance
against this ferocity which champs us up. What front
can we make against these unavoidable, victorious,
maleficent forces? What can I do against the influence
of Race, in my history? What can I do against hereditary and constitutional habits; against scrofula, lymph,
impotence? against climate, against barbarism, in my
country? I can reason down or deny everything, except
this perpetual Belly: feed he must and will, and I cannot make him respectable.

But the main resistance which the affirmative impulse
finds, and one including all others, is in the doctrine of
the Illusionists. There is a painful rumor in circulation
that we have been practised upon in all the principal
performances of life, and free agency is the emptiest
name. We have been sopped and drugged with the air,
with food, with woman, with children, with sciences,
with events, which leave us exactly where they found
us. The mathematics, 'tis complained, leave the mind
where they find it: so do all sciences; and so do all
events and actions. I find a man who has passed through
all the sciences, the churl he was; and, through all the

offices, learned, civil and social, can detect the child.
We are not the less necessitated to dedicate life to them.
In fact we may come to accept it as the fixed rule and
theory of our state of education, that God is a substance,
and his method is illusion. The eastern sages owned the
goddess Yoganidra, the great illusory energy of Vishnu,
by whom, as utter ignorance, the whole world is beguiled.

Or shall I state it thus?—The astonishment of life
is the absence of any appearance of reconciliation between the theory and practice of life. Reason, the prized
reality, the Law, is apprehended, now and then, for a
serene and profound moment amidst the hubbub of
cares and works which have no direct bearing on it—
is then lost for months or years, and again found for an
interval, to be lost again. If we compute it in time, we
may, in fifty years, have half a dozen reasonable hours.
But what are these cares and works the better? A method
in the world we do not see, but this parallelism of great
and little, which never react on each other, nor discover
the smallest tendency to converge. Experiences, fortunes, governings, readings, writings, are nothing to the
purpose; as when a man comes into the room it does
not appear whether he has been fed on yams or buffalo
—he has contrived to get so much bone and fibre as he
wants, out of rice or out of snow. So vast is the disproportion between the sky of law and the pismire of performance under it, that whether he is a man of worth
or a sot is not so great a matter as we say. Shall I add,
as one juggle of this enchantment, the stunning non-
intercourse law which makes cooperation impossible?
The young spirit pants to enter society. But all the ways
of culture and greatness lead to solitary imprisonment.
He has been often balked. He did not expect a sympathy with his thought from the village, but he went

with it to the chosen and intelligent, and found no entertainment for it, but mere misapprehension, distaste and scoffing. Men are strangely mistimed and misapplied; and the excellence of each is an inflamed individualism which separates him more.

There are these, and more than these diseases of thought, which our ordinary teachers do not attempt to remove. Now shall we, because a good nature inclines us to virtue's side, say, There are no doubts—and lie for the right? Is life to be led in a brave or in a cowardly manner? and is not the satisfaction of the doubts essential to all manliness? Is the name of virtue to be a barrier to that which is virtue? Can you not believe that a man of earnest and burly habit may find small good in tea, essays and catechism, and want a rougher instruction, want men, labor, trade, farming, war, hunger, plenty, love, hatred, doubt and terror to make things plain to him; and has he not a right to insist on being convinced in his own way? When he is convinced, he will be worth the pains.

Belief consists in accepting the affirmations of the soul; unbelief, in denying them. Some minds are incapable of skepticism. The doubts they profess to entertain are rather a civility or accommodation to the common discourse of their company. They may well give themselves leave to speculate, for they are secure of a return. Once admitted to the heaven of thought, they see no relapse into night, but infinite invitation on the other side. Heaven is within heaven, and sky over sky, and they are encompassed with divinities. Others there are to whom the heaven is brass, and it shuts down to the surface of the earth. It is a question of temperament, or of more or less immersion in nature. The last class must needs have a reflex or parasite faith; not a sight of realities, but an instinctive reliance on the seers and believers of realities. The manners and thoughts of believers astonish them and convince them that these have seen something which is hid from themselves. But their sensual habit would fix the believer to his last position, whilst he as inevitably advances; and presently the unbeliever, for love of belief, burns the believer.

Great believers are always reckoned infidels, impracticable, fantastic, atheistic, and really men of no account. The spiritualist finds himself driven to express his faith by a series of skepticisms. Charitable souls come with their projects and ask his cooperation. How can he hesitate? It is the rule of mere comity and courtesy to agree where you can, and to turn your sentence with something auspicious, and not freezing and sinister. But he is forced to say, "O, these things will be as they must be: what can you do? These particular griefs and crimes are the foliage and fruit of such trees as we see growing. It is vain to complain of the leaf or the berry; cut it off, it will bear another just as bad. You must begin your cure lower down." The generosities of the day prove an intractable element for him. The people's questions are not his; their methods are not his; and against all the dictates of good nature he is driven to say he has no pleasure in them.

Even the doctrines dear to the hope of man, of the divine Providence and of the immortality of the soul, his neighbors can not put the statement so that he shall affirm it. But he denies out of more faith, and not less. He denies out of honesty. He had rather stand charged with the imbecility of skepticism, than with untruth. I believe, he says, in the moral design of the universe; it exists hospitably for the weal of souls; but your dogmas seem to me caricatures: why should I make believe them? Will any say, This is cold and infidel? The wise and magnanimous will not say so. They will exult in his far-sighted good will that can abandon to the adversary all the ground of tradition and common belief, without losing a jot of strength. It sees to the end of all transgression. George Fox saw that there was "an ocean of darkness and death; but withal an infinite ocean of light and love which flowed over that of darkness."

The final solution in which skepticism is lost, is in the moral sentiment, which never forfeits its supremacy. All moods may be safely tried, and their weight allowed to all objections: the moral sentiment as easily outweighs them all, as any one. This is the drop which balances the sea. I play with the miscellany of facts, and take those superficial views which we call skepticism; but I know that they will presently appear to me in that order which makes skepticism impossible. A man of thought must feel the thought that is parent of the universe; that the masses of nature do undulate and flow.

This faith avails to the whole emergency of life and objects. The world is saturated with deity and with law. He is content with just and unjust, with sots and fools, with the triumph of folly and fraud. He can behold with serenity the yawning gulf between the ambition of man and his power of performance, between the demand and supply of power, which makes the tragedy of all souls.

Charles Fourier announced that "the attractions of man are proportioned to his destinies"; in other words, that every desire predicts its own satisfaction. Yet all experience exhibits the reverse of this; the incompetency of power is the universal grief of young and ardent minds. They accuse the divine providence of a certain parsimony. It has shown the heaven and earth to every child and filled him with a desire for the whole; a desire raging, infinite; a hunger, as of space to be filled with planets; a cry of famine, as of devils for souls.

Then for the satisfaction—to each man is administered a single drop, a bead of dew of vital power, *per day*— a cup as large as space, and one drop of the water of life in it. Each man woke in the morning with an appetite that could eat the solar system like a cake; a spirit for action and passion without bounds; he could lay his hand on the morning star; he could try conclusions with gravitation or chemistry; but, on the first motion to prove his strength—hands, feet, senses, gave way and would not serve him. He was an emperor deserted by his states, and left to whistle by himself, or thrust into a mob of emperors, all whistling: and still the sirens sang, "The attractions are proportioned to the destinies." In every house, in the heart of each maiden and of each boy, in the soul of the soaring saint, this chasm is found —between the largest promise of ideal power, and the shabby experience.

The expansive nature of truth comes to our succor, elastic, not to be surrounded. Man helps himself by larger generalizations. The lesson of life is practically to generalize; to believe what the years and the centuries say, against the hours; to resist the usurpation of particulars; to penetrate to their catholic sense. Things seem to say one thing, and say the reverse. The appearance is immoral; the result is moral. Things seem to tend downward, to justify despondency, to promote rogues, to defeat the just; and by knaves as by martyrs the just cause is carried forward. Although knaves win in every political struggle, although society seems to be delivered over from the hands of one set of criminals into the hands of another set of criminals, as fast as the government is changed, and the march of civilization is a train of felonies—yet, general ends are somehow answered. We see, now, events forced on which seem to retard or retrograde the civility of ages. But the world-spirit is a good swimmer, and storms and waves cannot drown him. He snaps his finger at laws: and so, throughout history, heaven seems to affect low and poor means. Through the years and the centuries, through evil agents, through toys and atoms, a great and beneficent tendency irresistibly streams.

Let a man learn to look for the permanent in the mutable and fleeting; let him learn to bear the disappearance of things he was wont to reverence without losing his reverence; let him learn that he is here, not to work but to be worked upon; and that, though abyss open under abyss, and opinion displace opinion, all are at last contained in the Eternal Cause—

> If my bark sink, 'tis to another sea.

HISTORIC NOTES
OF LIFE AND LETTERS
IN NEW ENGLAND

> For Joy and Beauty planted it
> With faerie gardens cheered,
> And boding Fancy haunted it
> With men and women weird.

THE ancient manners were giving way. There grew a certain tenderness on the people, not before remarked. Children had been repressed and kept in the background; now they were considered, cosseted and pampered. I recall the remark of a witty physician who remembered the hardships of his own youth; he said,

"It was a misfortune to have been born when children were nothing, and to live till men were nothing."

There are always two parties, the party of the Past and the party of the Future; the Establishment and the Movement. At times the resistance is reanimated, the schism runs under the world and appears in Literature, Philosophy, Church, State, and social customs. It is not easy to date these eras of activity with any precision, but in this region one made itself remarked, say in 1820 and the twenty years following.

It seemed a war between intellect and affection; a crack in nature, which split every church in Christendom into Papal and Protestant; Calvinism into Old and New schools; Quakerism into Old and New; brought new divisions in politics; as the new conscience touching temperance and slavery. The key to the period appeared to be that the mind had become aware of itself. Men grew reflective and intellectual. There was a new consciousness. The former generations acted under the belief that a shining social prosperity was the beatitude of man, and sacrificed uniformly the citizen to the State. The modern mind believed that the nation existed for the individual, for the guardianship and education of every man. This idea, roughly written in revolutions and national movements, in the mind of the philosopher had far more precision; the individual is the world.

This perception is a sword such as was never drawn before. It divides and detaches bone and marrow, soul and body, yea, almost the man from himself. It is the age of severance, of dissociation, of freedom, of analysis, of detachment. Every man for himself. The public speaker disclaims speaking for any other; he answers only for himself. The social sentiments are weak; the sentiment of patriotism is weak; veneration is low; the natural affections feebler than they were. People grow

philosophical about native land and parents and relations. There is an universal resistance to ties and liga-
ments once supposed essential to civil society. The new
race is stiff, heady and rebellious; they are fanatics in
freedom; they hate tolls, taxes, turnpikes, banks, hierarchies, governors, yea, almost laws. They have a neck of
unspeakable tenderness; it winces at a hair. They rebel
against theological as against political dogmas; against
mediation, or saints, or any nobility in the unseen.

The age tends to solitude. The association of the time
is accidental and momentary and hypocritical, the detachment intrinsic and progressive. The association is
for power, merely—for means; the end being the enlargement and independency of the individual. An-
ciently, society was in the course of things. There was a
Sacred Band, a Theban Phalanx. There can be none
now. College classes, military corps, or trades-unions
may fancy themselves indissoluble for a moment, over
their wine; but it is a painted hoop, and has no girth.
The age of arithmetic and of criticism has set in. The
structures of old faith in every department of society a
few centuries have sufficed to destroy. Astrology, magic,
palmistry, are long gone. The very last ghost is laid.
Demonology is on its last legs. Prerogative, government,
goes to pieces day by day. Europe is strewn with
wrecks; a constitution once a week. In social manners
and morals the revolution is just as evident. In the law
courts, crimes of fraud have taken the place of crimes
of force. The stockholder has stepped into the place of
the warlike baron. The nobles shall not any longer, as
feudal lords, have power of life and death over the
churls, but now, in another shape, as capitalists, shall in
all love and peace eat them up as before. Nay, government itself becomes the resort of those whom government was invented to restrain. "Are there any brigands

on the road?" inquired the traveler in France. "Oh, no, set your heart at rest on that point," said the landlord; "what should these fellows keep the highway for, when they can rob just as effectually, and much more at their ease, in the bureaus of office?"

In literature the effect appeared in the decided tendency of criticism. The most remarkable literary work of the age has for its hero and subject precisely this introversion: I mean the poem of Faust. In philosophy, Immanuel Kant has made the best catalogue of the human faculties and the best analysis of the mind. Hegel also, especially. In science the French *savant,* exact, pitiless, with barometer, crucible, chemic test and calculus in hand, travels into all nooks and islands, to weigh, to analyze and report. And chemistry, which is the analysis of matter, has taught us that we eat gas, drink gas, tread on gas, and are gas. The same decomposition has changed the whole face of physics; the like in all arts, modes. Authority falls, in Church, College, Courts of Law, Faculties, Medicine. Experiment is credible; antiquity is grown ridiculous.

It marked itself by a certain predominance of the intellect in the balance of powers. The warm swart Earth-spirit which made the strength of past ages, mightier than it knew, with instincts instead of science, like a mother yielding food from her own breast instead of preparing it through chemic and culinary skill—warm Negro ages of sentiment and vegetation—all gone; another hour had struck and other forms arose. Instead of the social existence which all shared, was now separation. Every one for himself; driven to find all his resources, hopes, rewards, society and deity within himself.

The young men were born with knives in their brain, a tendency to introversion, self-dissection, anatomizing

of motives. The popular religion of our fathers had received many severe shocks from the new times; from the
Arminians, which was the current name of the back-
sliders from Calvinism, sixty years ago; then from the
English philosophic theologians, Hartley and Priestley
and Belsham, the followers of Locke; and then I should
say much later from the slow but extraordinary influence
of Swedenborg; a man of prodigious mind, though as I
think tainted with a certain suspicion of insanity, and
therefore generally disowned, but exerting a singular
power over an important intellectual class; then the
powerful influence of the genius and character of Dr.
Channing.

Germany had created criticism in vain for us until
1820, when Edward Everett returned from his five years
in Europe, and brought to Cambridge his rich results,
which no one was so fitted by natural grace and the
splendor of his rhetoric to introduce and recommend.
He made us for the first time acquainted with Wolff's
theory of the Homeric writings, with the criticism of
Heyne. The novelty of the learning lost nothing in the
skill and genius of his relation, and the rudest undergraduate found a new morning opened to him in the
lecture room of Harvard Hall.

There was an influence on the young people from the
genius of Everett which was almost comparable to that
of Pericles in Athens. He had an inspiration which did
not go beyond his head, but which made him the master
of elegance. If any of my readers were at that period in
Boston or Cambridge, they will easily remember his
radiant beauty of person, of a classic style, his heavy
large eye, marble lids, which gave the impression of
mass which the slightness of his form needed; sculptured lips; a voice of such rich tones, such precise and
perfect utterance, that, although slightly nasal, it was

the most mellow and beautiful and correct of all the instruments of the time. The word that he spoke, in the manner in which he spoke it, became current and classical in New England. He had a great talent for collecting facts, and for bringing those he had to bear with ingenious felicity on the topic of the moment. Let him rise to speak on what occasion soever, a fact had always just transpired which composed, with some other fact well known to the audience, the most pregnant and happy coincidence. It was remarked that for a man who threw out so many facts he was seldom convicted of a blunder. He had a good deal of special learning, and all his learning was available for purposes of the hour. It was all new learning, that wonderfully took and stimulated the young men. It was so coldly and weightily communicated from so commanding a platform, as if in the consciousness and consideration of all history and all learning—adorned with so many simple and austere beauties of expression, and enriched with so many excellent digressions and significant quotations, that, though nothing could be conceived beforehand less attractive or indeed less fit for green boys from Connecticut, New Hampshire and Massachusetts, with their unripe Latin and Greek reading, than exegetical discourses in the style of Voss and Wolff and Ruhnken, on the Orphic and Ante-Homeric remains—yet this learning instantly took the highest place to our imagination in our unoccupied American Parnassus. All his auditors felt the extreme beauty and dignity of the manner, and even the coarsest were contented to go punctually to listen, for the manner, when they had found out that the subject-matter was not for them. In the lecture room, he abstained from all ornament, and pleased himself with the play of detailing erudition in a style of perfect simplicity. In the pulpit (for he was then a clergyman) he made amends to himself and his auditor for the self-denial of the professor's chair, and, with an infantine simplicity still, of manner, he gave the reins to his florid, quaint and affluent fancy.

Then was exhibited all the richness of a rhetoric which we have never seen rivaled in this country. Wonderful how memorable were words made which were only pleasing pictures, and covered no new or valid thoughts. He abounded in sentences, in wit, in satire, in splendid allusion, in quotation impossible to forget, in daring imagery, in parable and even in a sort of defying experiment of his own wit and skill in giving an oracular weight to Hebrew or Rabbinical words—feats which no man could better accomplish, such was his self-command and the security of his manner. All his speech was music, and with such variety and invention that the ear was never tired. Especially beautiful were his poetic quotations. He delighted in quoting Milton, and with such sweet modulation that he seemed to give as much beauty as he borrowed; and whatever he has quoted will be remembered by any who heard him, with inseparable association with his voice and genius. He had nothing in common with vulgarity and infirmity, but, speaking, walking, sitting, was as much aloof and uncommon as a star. The smallest anecdote of his behavior or conversation was eagerly caught and repeated, and every young scholar could recite brilliant sentences from his sermons, with mimicry, good or bad, of his voice. This influence went much farther, for he who was heard with such throbbing hearts and sparkling eyes in the lighted and crowded churches, did not let go his hearers when the church was dismissed, but the bright image of that eloquent form followed the boy home to his bed-chamber; and not a sentence was written in academic exercises, not a declamation attempted in the college chapel, but showed the omnipresence of his genius to youthful heads. This made every youth his defender, and boys filled their mouths with arguments to prove that the orator had a heart. This was a triumph of Rhetoric. It was not the intellectual or the moral principles which he had to teach. It was not thoughts. When Massachusetts was full of his fame it was not contended that he had thrown any truths into circulation. But his power lay in the magic of form; it was in the graces of manner; in a new perception of Grecian beauty, to which he had opened our eyes. There was that finish about this person which is about women, and which distinguishes every piece of genius from the works of talent—that these last are more or less matured in every degree of completeness according to the time bestowed on them, but works of genius in their first and slightest form are still wholes. In every public discourse there was nothing left for the indulgence of his hearer, no marks of late hours and anxious, unfinished study, but the goddess of grace had breathed on the work a last fragrancy and glitter.

By a series of lectures largely and fashionably attended for two winters in Boston he made a beginning of popular literary and miscellaneous lecturing, which in that region at least had important results. It is acquiring greater importance every day, and becoming a national institution. I am quite certain that this purely literary influence was of the first importance to the American mind.

In the pulpit Dr. Frothingham, an excellent classical and German scholar, had already made us acquainted, if prudently, with the genius of Eichhorn's theologic criticism. And Professor Norton a little later gave form and method to the like studies in the then infant Divinity School. But I think the paramount source of the religious revolution was Modern Science; beginning with Copernicus, who destroyed the pagan fictions of the Church, by showing mankind that the earth on which we live was not the center of the Universe, around which the sun and stars revolved every day, and thus fitted to be the platform on which the Drama of the Divine Judgment was played before the assembled Angels of Heaven—"the scaffold of the divine vengeance" Saurin called it—but a little scrap of a planet, rushing round the sun in our system, which in turn was too minute to be seen at the distance of many stars which we behold. Astronomy taught us our insignificance in Nature; showed that our sacred as our profane history had been written in gross ignorance of the laws, which were far grander than we knew; and compelled a certain extension and uplifting of our views of the Deity and his Providence. This correction of our superstitions was confirmed by the new science of geology, and the whole train of discoveries in every department. But we presently saw also that the religious nature in man was not affected by these errors in his understanding. The religious sentiment made nothing of bulk or size, or far or near; triumphed over time as well as space; and every lesson of humility, or justice, or charity, which the old ignorant saints had taught him, was still forever true.

Whether from these influences, or whether by a reaction of the general mind against the too formal science, religion and social life of the earlier period—there was, in the first quarter of our nineteenth century, a certain sharpness of criticism, an eagerness for reform, which showed itself in every quarter. It appeared in the popularity of Lavater's *Physiognomy*, now almost forgotten. Gall and Spurzheim's *Phrenology* laid a rough hand on the mysteries of animal and spiritual nature, dragging down every sacred secret to a street show. The attempt was coarse and odious to scientific men, but had a certain truth in it; it felt connection where the professors denied it, and was a leading to a truth which had not yet been announced. On the heels of this intruder came Mesmerism, which broke into the inmost shrines, attempted the explanation of miracle and prophecy, as well as of creation. What could be more revolting to the contemplative philosopher! But a certain success attended it, against all expectation. It was human, it was genial, it affirmed unity and connection between remote points, and as such was excellent criticism on the narrow and dead classification of what passed for science; and the joy with which it was greeted was an instinct of the people which no true philosopher would fail to profit by. But while society remained in doubt between the indignation of the old school and the audacity of the new, a higher note sounded. Unexpected aid from high quarters came to iconoclasts. The German poet Goethe revolted against the science of the day, against French and English science, declared war against the great name of Newton, proposed his own new and simple optics: in botany, his simple theory of metamorphosis—the eye of a leaf is all; every part of the plant from root to fruit is only a modified leaf, the branch of a tree is nothing but a leaf whose serratures have become twigs. He extended this into anatomy and animal life, and his views were accepted. The revolt became a revolution. Schelling and Oken introduced their ideal natural philosophy, Hegel his metaphysics, and extended it to civil history.

The result in literature and the general mind was a return to law; in science, in politics, in social life; as distinguished from the profligate manners and politics of earlier times. The age was moral. Every immorality is a departure from nature, and is punished by natural loss and deformity. The popularity of Combe's *Constitution of Man;* the humanity which was the aim of all the multitudinous works of Dickens; the tendency even of *Punch's* caricature, was all on the side of the people. There was a breath of new air, much vague expectation, a consciousness of power not yet finding its determinate aim.

I attribute much importance to two papers of Dr. Channing, one on Milton and one on Napoleon, which were the first specimens in this country of that large criticism which in England had given power and fame to the *Edinburgh Review.* They were widely read, and of course immediately fruitful in provoking emulation which lifted the style of journalism. Dr. Channing, whilst he lived, was the star of the American Church, and we then thought, if we do not still think, that he left no successor in the pulpit. He could never be reported, for his eye and voice could not be printed, and his discourses lose their best in losing them. He was made for the public; his cold temperament made him the most unprofitable private companion; but all America would have been impoverished in wanting him. We could not then spare a single word he uttered in public, not so much as the reading a lesson in Scripture, or a hymn, and it is curious that his printed writings are almost a history of the times; as there was no great public interest, political, literary, or even economical (for he wrote on the Tariff), on which he did not leave some printed record of his brave and thoughtful opinion. A poor little invalid all his life, he is yet one of those men who vindicate the power of the American race to produce greatness.

Dr. Channing took counsel in 1840 with George Ripley, to the point whether it were possible to bring cultivated, thoughtful people together, and make society that deserved the name. He had earlier talked with Dr. John Collins Warren on the like purpose, who admitted the wisdom of the design and undertook to aid him in making the experiment. Dr. Channing repaired to Dr. Warren's house on the appointed evening, with large thoughts which he wished to open. He found a well-chosen assembly of gentlemen variously distinguished; there was mutual greeting and introduction, and they were chatting agreeably on indifferent matters and drawing gently towards their great expectation, when a side-door opened, the whole company streamed in to an oyster supper, crowned by excellent wines; and so ended the first attempt to establish aesthetic society in Boston.

Some time afterwards Dr. Channing opened his mind to Mr. and Mrs. Ripley, and with some care they invited a limited party of ladies and gentlemen. I had the honor to be present. Though I recall the fact, I do not retain any instant consequence of this attempt, or any connection between it and the new zeal of the friends who at that time began to be drawn together by sympathy of studies and of aspiration. Margaret Fuller, George Ripley, Dr. Convers Francis, Theodore Parker, Dr. Hedge, Mr. Brownson, James Freeman Clarke, William H. Channing, and many others, gradually drew together and from time to time spent an afternoon at each other's houses in a serious conversation. With them was always one well-known form, a pure idealist, not at all a man of letters, nor of any practical talent, nor a writer of books; a man quite too cold and contemplative for the alliances of friendship, with rare simplicity and grandeur of perception, who read Plato as an equal, and inspired his companions only in proportion as they were intellectual—whilst the men of talent complained of the want of point and precision in this abstract and religious thinker.

These fine conversations, of course, were incomprehensible to some in the company, and they had their revenge in their little joke. One declared that "It seemed to him like going to heaven in a swing"; another reported that, at a knotty point in the discourse, a sympathizing Englishman with a squeaking voice interrupted with the question, "Mr. Alcott, a lady near me desires to inquire whether omnipotence abnegates attribute?"

I think there prevailed at that time a general belief in Boston that there was some concert of *doctrinaires* to establish certain opinions and inaugurate some movement in literature, philosophy, and religion, of which design the supposed conspirators were quite innocent; for there was no concert, and only here and there two or three men or women who read and wrote, each alone, with unusual vivacity. Perhaps they only agreed in having fallen upon Coleridge and Wordsworth and Goethe, then on Carlyle, with pleasure and sympathy. Otherwise, their education and reading were not marked, but had the American superficialness, and their studies were solitary. I suppose all of them were surprised at this rumor of a school or sect, and certainly at the name of Transcendentalism, given nobody knows by whom, or when it was first applied. As these persons became in the common chances of society acquainted with each other, there resulted certainly strong friendships, which of course were exclusive in proportion to their heat: and perhaps those persons who were mutually the best friends were the most private and had no ambition of publishing their letters, diaries, or conversation.

From that time meetings were held for conversation, with very little form, from house to house, of people engaged in studies, fond of books, and watchful of all the intellectual light from whatever quarter it flowed. Nothing could be less formal, yet the intelligence and character and varied ability of the company gave it some notoriety and perhaps waked curiosity as to its aims and results.

Nothing more serious came of it than the modest quarterly journal called *The Dial* which, under the editorship of Margaret Fuller, and later of some other, enjoyed its obscurity for four years. All its papers were unpaid contributions, and it was rather a work of friendship among the narrow circle of students than the organ of any party. Perhaps its writers were its chief readers: yet it contained some noble papers by Margaret Fuller, and some numbers had an instant exhausting sale, because of papers by Theodore Parker.

Theodore Parker was our Savonarola, an excellent scholar, in frank and affectionate communication with the best minds of his day, yet the tribune of the people, and the stout Reformer to urge and defend every cause of humanity with and for the humblest of mankind. He was no artist. Highly refined persons might easily miss in him the element of beauty. What he said was mere fact, almost offended you, so bald and detached; little cared he. He stood altogether for practical truth; and so to the last. He used every day and hour of his short life, and his character appeared in the last moments with the same firm control as in the mid-day of strength. I habitually apply to him the words of a French philosopher who speaks of "the man of Nature who abominates the steam-engine and the factory. His vast lungs breathe independence with the air of the mountains and the woods."

The vulgar politician disposed of this circle cheaply as "the sentimental class." State Street had an instinct that they invalidated contracts and threatened the

stability of stocks; and it did not fancy brusque manners.
Society always values, even in its teachers, inoffensive
people, susceptible of conventional polish. The clergyman who would live in the city *may* have piety, but
must have taste, whilst there was often coming, among
these, some John the Baptist, wild from the woods, rude,
hairy, careless of dress and quite scornful of the etiquette of cities. There was a pilgrim in those days walking in the country who stopped at every door where he
hoped to find hearing for his doctrine, which was, Never
to give or receive money. He was a poor printer, and
explained with simple warmth the belief of himself and
five or six young men with whom he agreed in opinion,
of the vast mischief of our insidious coin. He thought
everyone should labor at some necessary product, and
as soon as he had made more than enough for himself,
were it corn, or paper, or cloth, or boot-jacks, he should
give of the commodity to any applicant, and in turn
go to his neighbor for any article which he had to spare.
Of course we were curious to know how he sped in his
experiments on the neighbor, and his anecdotes were
interesting, and often highly creditable. But he had the
courage which so stern a return to Arcadian manners required, and had learned to sleep, in cold nights, when
the farmer at whose door he knocked declined to give
him a bed, on a wagon covered with the buffalo-robe
under the shed—or under the stars, when the farmer
denied the shed and the buffalo-robe. I think he per-
sisted for two years in his brave practice, but did not enlarge his church of believers.

These reformers were a new class. Instead of the fiery
souls of the Puritans, bent on hanging the Quaker, burning the witch and banishing the Romanist, these were
gentle souls, with peaceful and even with genial dispositions, casting sheep's-eyes even on Fourier and his

houris. It was a time when the air was full of reform.
Robert Owen of Lanark came hither from England in
1845, and read lectures or held conversations wherever
he found listeners; the most amiable, sanguine and candid of men. He had not the least doubt that he had hit
on a right and perfect socialism, or that all mankind
would adopt it. He was then seventy years old, and
being asked, "Well, Mr. Owen, who is your disciple?
How many men are there possessed of your views who
will remain after you are gone, to put them in practice?"
"Not one," was his reply. Robert Owen knew Fourier in
his old age. He said that Fourier learned of him all the
truth he had; the rest of his system was imagination, and
the imagination of a banker. Owen made the best impression by his rare benevolence. His love of men made
us forget his "Three Errors." His charitable construction of men and their actions was invariable. He was
the better Christian in his controversy with Christians,
and he interpreted with great generosity the acts of the
Holy Alliance, and Prince Metternich, with whom the
persevering *doctrinaire* had obtained interviews; "Ah,"
he said, "you may depend on it there are as tender
hearts and as much good-will to serve men, in palaces,
as in colleges."

And truly I honor the generous ideas of the Socialists,
the magnificence of their theories, and the enthusiasm
with which they have been urged. They appeared the
inspired men of their time. Mr. Owen preached his
doctrine of labor and reward, with the fidelity and devotion of a saint, to the slow ears of his generation.
Fourier, almost as wonderful an example of the mathematical mind of France as La Place or Napoleon, turned
a truly vast arithmetic to the question of social misery,
and has put men under the obligation which a generous
mind always confers, of conceiving magnificent hopes

and making great demands as the right of man. He took his measure of that which all should and might enjoy, from no soup-society or charity-concert, but from the refinements of palaces, the wealth of universities, and the triumphs of artists. He thought nobly. A man is entitled to pure air, and to the air of good conversation in his bringing up, and not, as we or so many of us, to the poor smell and musty chambers, cats and fools. Fourier carried a whole French Revolution in his head, and much more. Here was arithmetic on a huge scale. His ciphering goes where ciphering never went before, namely, into stars, atmospheres, and animals, and men and women, and classes of every character. It was the most entertaining of French romances, and could not but suggest vast possibilities of reform to the coldest and least sanguine.

We had an opportunity of learning something of these Socialists and their theory, from the indefatigable apostle of the sect in New York, Albert Brisbane. Mr. Brisbane pushed his doctrine with all the force of memory, talent, honest faith and importunacy. As we listened to his exposition it appeared to us the sublime of mechanical philosophy; for the system was the perfection of arrangement and contrivance. The force of arrangement could no farther go. The merit of the plan was that it was a system; that it had not the partiality and hint-and-fragment character of most popular schemes, but was coherent and comprehensive of facts to a wonderful degree. It was not daunted by distance, or magnitude, or remoteness of any sort, but strode about nature with a giant's step, and skipped no fact, but wove its large Ptolemaic web of cycle and epicycle, of phalanx and phalanstery, with laudable assiduity. Mechanics were pushed so far as fairly to meet spiritualism. One could not but be struck with strange coin-

cidences betwixt Fourier and Swedenborg. Genius
hitherto has been shamefully misapplied, a mere trifler.
It must now set itself to raise the social condition of
man and to redress the disorders of the planet he in-
habits. The Desert of Sahara, the Campagna di Roma,
the frozen Polar circles, which by their pestilential or
hot or cold airs poison the temperate regions, accuse
man. Society, concert, cooperation, is the secret of the
coming Paradise. By reason of the isolation of men at
the present day, all work is drudgery. By concert and
the allowing each laborer to choose his own work, it becomes pleasure. "Attractive Industry" would speedily
subdue, by adventurous scientific and persistent tillage,
the pestilential tracts; would equalize temperature, give
health to the globe and cause the earth to yield "healthy
imponderable fluids" to the solar system, as now it yields
noxious fluids. The hyena, the jackal, the gnat, the bug,
the flea, were all beneficent parts of the system; the
good Fourier knew what those creatures should have
been, had not the mold slipped, through the bad state
of the atmosphere; caused no doubt by the same vicious
imponderable fluids. All these shall be redressed by
human culture, and the useful goat and dog and innocent poetical moth, or the wood-tick to consume decom-
posing wood, shall take their place. It takes sixteen hundred and eighty men to make one Man, complete in all
the faculties; that is, to be sure that you have got a good
joiner, a good cook, a barber, a poet, a judge, an um-
brella-maker, a mayor and alderman, and so on. Your
community should consist of two thousand persons, to
prevent accidents of omission; and each community
should take up six thousand acres of land. Now fancy
the earth planted with fifties and hundreds of these
phalanxes side by side—what tillage, what architecture,
what refectories, what dormitories, what reading-rooms,

what concerts, what lectures, what gardens, what baths! What is not in one will be in another, and many will be within easy distance. Then know you one and all, that Constantinople is the natural capital of the globe. There, in the Golden Horn, will the Arch-Phalanx be established; there will the Omniarch reside. Aladdin and his magician, or the beautiful Scheherezade can alone, in these prosaic times before the sight, describe the material splendors collected there. Poverty shall be abolished; deformity, stupidity and crime shall be no more. Genius, grace, art, shall abound, and it is not to be doubted but that in the reign of "Attractive Industry" all men will speak in blank verse.

Certainly we listened with great pleasure to such gay and magnificent pictures. The ability and earnestness of the advocate and his friends, the comprehensiveness of their theory, its apparent directness of proceeding to the end they would secure, the indignation they felt and uttered in the presence of so much social misery, commanded our attention and respect. It contained so much truth, and promised in the attempts that shall be made to realize it so much valuable instruction, that we are engaged to observe every step of its progress. Yet in spite of the assurances of its friends that it was new and widely discriminated from all other plans for the regeneration of society, we could not exempt it from the criticism which we apply to so many projects for reform with which the brain of the age teems. Our feeling was that Fourier had skipped no fact but one, namely Life. He treats man as a plastic thing, something that may be put up or down, ripened or retarded, molded, polished, made into solid or fluid or gas, at the will of the leader; or perhaps as a vegetable, from which, though now a poor crab, a very good peach can by manure and exposure be in time produced—but skips the faculty of life, which spawns and scorns system and system-makers; which eludes all conditions; which makes or supplants a thousand phalanxes and New Harmonies with each pulsation. There is an order in which in a sound mind the faculties always appear, and which, according to the strength of the individual, they seek to realize in the surrounding world. The value of Fourier's system is that it is a statement of such an order externized, or carried outward into its correspondence in facts. The mistake is that this particular order and series is to be imposed, by force or preaching and votes, on all men, and carried into rigid execution. But what is true and good must not only be begun by life, but must be conducted to its issues by life. Could not the conceiver of this design have also believed that a similar model lay in every mind, and that the method of each associate might be trusted, as well as that of his particular Committee and General Office, No. 200 Broadway? Nay, that it would be better to say, Let us be lovers and servants of that which is just, and straightway every man becomes a center of a holy and beneficent republic, which he sees to include all men in its law, like that of Plato, and of Christ. Before such a man the whole world becomes Fourierized or Christized or humanized, and in obedience to his most private being he finds himself, according to his presentiment, though against all sensuous probability, acting in strict concert with all others who followed their private light.

Yet, in a day of small, sour and fierce schemes, one is admonished and cheered by a project of such friendly aims and of such bold and generous proportion; there is an intellectual courage and strength in it which is superior and commanding; it certifies the presence of so much truth in the theory, and in so far is destined to be fact.

It argued singular courage, the adoption of Fourier's system, to even a limited extent, with his books lying before the world only defended by the thin veil of the French language. The Stoic said, Forbear; Fourier said, Indulge. Fourier was of the opinion of St. Evremond; abstinence from pleasure appeared to him a great sin. Fourier was very French indeed. He labored under a misapprehension of the nature of women. The Fourier marriage was a calculation how to secure the greatest amount of kissing that the infirmity of human constitution admitted. It was false and prurient, full of absurd French superstitions about women; ignorant how serious and how moral their nature always is; how chaste is their organization; how lawful a class.

It is the worst of community that it must inevitably transform into charlatans the leaders, by the endeavor continually to meet the expectation and admiration of this eager crowd of men and women seeking they know not what. Unless he have a Cossack roughness of clearing himself of what belongs not, charlatan he must be.

It was easy to see what must be the fate of this fine system in any serious and comprehensive attempt to set it on foot in this country. As soon as our people got wind of the doctrine of Marriage held by this master, it would fall at once into the hands of a lawless crew who would flock in troops to so fair a game, and, like the dreams of poetic people on the first outbreak of the old French Revolution, so theirs would disappear in a slime of mire and blood.

There is of course to every theory a tendency to run to an extreme, and to forget the limitations. In our free institutions, where every man is at liberty to choose his home and his trade, and all possible modes of working and gaining are open to him, fortunes are easily made by thousands, as in no other country. Then property proves too much for the man, and the men of science, art, intellect, are pretty sure to degenerate into selfish housekeepers, dependent on wine, coffee, furnace-heat, gas-light and fine furniture. Then instantly things swing the other way, and we suddenly find that civilization crowed too soon; that what we bragged as triumphs were treacheries: that we have opened the wrong door and let the enemy into the castle; that civilization was a mistake; that nothing is so vulgar as a great warehouse of rooms full of furniture and trumpery; that, in the circumstances, the best wisdom were an auction or a fire. Since the foxes and the birds have the right of it, with a warm hole to keep out the weather, and no more—a penthouse to fend the sun and rain is the house which lays no tax on the owner's time and thoughts, and which he can leave, when the sun is warm, and defy the robber. This was Thoreau's doctrine, who said that the Fourierists had a sense of duty which led them to devote themselves to their second-best. And Thoreau gave in flesh and blood and pertinacious Saxon belief the purest ethics. He was more real and practically believing in them than any of his company, and fortified you at all times with an affirmative experience which refused to be set aside. Thoreau was in his own person a practical answer, almost a refutation, to the theories of the socialists. He required no Phalanx, no Government, no society, almost no memory. He lived extempore from hour to hour, like the birds and the angels; brought every day a new proposition, as revolutionary as that of yesterday, but different: the only man of leisure in his town; and his independence made all others look like slaves. He was a good Abbot Sampson, and carried a counsel in his breast. "Again and again I congratulate myself on my so-called poverty, I could not overstate this advantage." "What you call bareness and poverty, is to me simplicity. God could not be unkind to me if he should try. I love best to have each thing in its season only, and enjoy doing without it at all other times. It is the greatest of all advantages to enjoy no advantage at all. I have never got over my surprise that I should have been born into the most estimable place in all the world, and in the very nick of time too." There's an optimist for you.

I regard these philanthropists as themselves the effects of the age in which we live, and, in common with so many other good facts, the efflorescence of the period, and predicting a good fruit that ripens. They were not the creators they believed themselves, but they were unconscious prophets of a true state of society; one which the tendencies of nature lead unto, one which always establishes itself for the sane soul, though not in that manner in which they paint it; but they were describers of that which is really being done. The large cities are phalansteries; and the theorists drew all their argument from facts already taking place in our experience. The cheap way is to make every man do what he was born for. One merchant to whom I described the Fourier project, thought it must not only succeed, but that argricultural association must presently fix the price of bread, and drive single farmers into association in self-defence, as the great commercial and manufacturing companies had done. Society in England and in America is trying the experiment again in small pieces, in cooperative associations, in cheap eating-houses, as well as in the economies of clubhouses and in cheap reading-rooms.

It chanced that here in one family were two brothers, one a brilliant and fertile inventor, and close by him his own brother, a man of business, who knew how to direct his faculty and make it instantly and permanently lucrative. Why could not the like partnership be formed between the inventor and the man of executive talent everywhere? Each man of thought is surrounded by wiser men than he, if they cannot write as well. Cannot he and they combine? Talents supplement each other. Beaumont and Fletcher and many French novelists have known how to utilize such partnerships. Why not have a larger one, and with more various members?

Housekeepers say, "There are a thousand things to everything," and if one must study all the strokes to be laid, all the faults to be shunned in a building or work of art, of its keeping, its composition, its site, its color, there would be no end. But the architect, acting under a necessity to build the house for its purpose, finds himself helped, he knows not how, into all these merits of detail, and steering clear, though in the dark, of those dangers which might have shipwrecked him.

BROOK FARM

The West Roxbury association was formed in 1841, by a society of members, men and women, who bought a farm in West Roxbury, of about two hundred acres, and took possession of the place in April. Mr. George Ripley was the President, and I think Mr. Charles Dana (afterwards well known as one of the editors of the *New York Tribune*), was the secretary. Many members took shares by paying money, others held shares by their labor. An old house on the place was enlarged, and three new houses built. William Allen was at first and for some time the head farmer, and the work was distributed in orderly committees to the men and women. There were many employments more or less lucrative found for, or brought hither by these members—shoemakers, joiners, sempstresses. They had good scholars among them, and so received pupils for their education. The parents of the children in some instances wished to live there, and were received as boarders. Many persons attracted by the beauty of the place and the culture and ambition of the community, joined them as boarders, and lived there for years. I think the numbers of this mixed community soon reached eighty or ninety souls.

It was a noble and generous movement in the projectors, to try an experiment of better living. They had the feeling that our ways of living were too conventional and expensive, not allowing each to do what he had a talent for, and not permitting men to combine cultivation of mind and heart with a reasonable amount of daily labor. At the same time, it was an attempt to lift others with themselves, and to share the advantages they should attain, with others now deprived of them.

There was no doubt great variety of character and purpose in the members of the community. It consisted in the main of young people—few of middle age, and none old. Those who inspired and organized it were of course persons impatient of the routine, the uniformity, perhaps they would say the squalid contentment of society around them, which was so timid and skeptical of any progress. One would say then that impulse was the rule in the society, without centripetal balance; perhaps it would not be severe to say, intellectual *sansculottism,* an impatience of the formal, routinary character of our educational, religious, social and economical life in Massachusetts. Yet there was immense hope in these young people. There was nobleness; there were self-sacrificing victims who compensated for the levity and rashness of their companions. The young people lived a great deal in a short time, and came forth some of them perhaps with shattered constitutions. And a few grave sanitary influences of character were happily there, which, I was assured, were always felt.

George W. Curtis of New York, and his brother, of English Oxford, were members of the family from the first. Theodore Parker, the near neighbor of the farm and the most intimate friend of Mr. Ripley, was a frequent visitor. Mr. Ichabod Morton of Plymouth, a plain man formerly engaged through many years in the fisheries with success—eccentric, with a persevering interest in education, and of a very democratic religion, came and built a house on the farm, and he, or members of his family, continued there to the end. Margaret Fuller, with her joyful conversation and large sympathy, was often a guest, and always in correspondence with her friends. Many ladies, whom to name were to praise, gave character and varied attraction to the place.

In and around Brook Farm, whether as members, boarders, or visitors, were many remarkable persons, for character, intellect, or accomplishments. I recall one youth of the subtlest mind, I believe I must say the subtlest observer and diviner of character I ever met, living, reading, writing, talking there, perhaps as long as the colony held together; his mind fed and overfed by whatever is exalted in genius, whether in Poetry or Art, in Drama or Music, or in social accomplishment and elegancy; a man of no employment or practical aims, a student and philosopher, who found his daily enjoyment not with the elders or his exact contemporaries so much as with the fine boys who were skating and playing ball or bird-hunting; forming the closest friendships with such, and finding his delight in the petulant heroisms of boys; yet was he the chosen counsellor to whom the guardians would repair on any hitch or difficulty that occurred, and draw from him a wise counsel. A fine, subtle, inward genius, puny in body and habit as a girl, yet with an *aplomb* like a general, never disconcerted. He lived and thought, in 1842, such worlds of life; all hinging on the thought of Being or Reality as opposed to consciousness; hating intellect with the ferocity of a Swedenborg. He was the Abbé or spiritual father, from his religious bias. His reading lay in Æschylus, Plato, Dante, Calderon, Shakespeare, and in modern novels and romances of merit. There too was Hawthorne, with his cold yet gentle genius, if he failed to do justice to this temporary home. There was the accomplished Doctor of Music, who has presided over its literature ever since in our metropolis. Rev. William Henry Channing, now of London, was from the first a student of Socialism in France and England, and in perfect sympathy with this experiment. An English baronet, Sir John Caldwell, was a frequent visitor, and more or less directly interested in the leaders and the success.

Hawthorne drew some sketches, not happily, as I think; I should rather say, quite unworthy of his genius. No friend who knew Margaret Fuller could recognize her rich and brilliant genius under the dismal mask which the public fancied was meant for her in that disagreeable story.

The founders of Brook Farm should have this praise, that they made what all people try to make, an agreeable place to live in. All comers, even the most fastidious, found it the pleasantest of residences. It is certain that freedom from household routine, variety of character and talent, variety of work, variety of means of thought and instruction, art, music, poetry, reading, masquerade, did not permit sluggishness or despondency; broke up routine. There is agreement in the testimony that it was, to most of the associates, education; to many, the most important period of their life, the birth of valued friendships, their first acquaintance with

the riches of conversation, their training in behavior.
The art of letter-writing, it is said, was immensely cultivated. Letters were always flying not only from house
to house, but from room to room. It was a perpetual
picnic, a French Revolution in small, an Age of Reason
in a patty-pan.

In the American social communities, the gossip found
such vent and sway as to become despotic. The institutions were whispering-galleries, in which the adored
Saxon privacy was lost. Married women I believe uniformly decided against the community. It was to them
like the brassy and lacquered life in hotels. The common
school was well enough, but to the common nursery
they had grave objections. Eggs might be hatched in
ovens, but the hen on her own account much preferred
the old way. A hen without her chickens was but half
a hen.

It was a curious experience of the patrons and leaders
of this noted community, in which the agreement with
many parties was that they should give so many hours
of instruction in mathematics, in music, in moral and
intellectual philosophy, and so forth—that in every instance the newcomers showed themselves keenly alive
to the advantages of the society, and were sure to avail
themselves of every means of instruction; their knowledge was increased, their manners refined—but they
became in that proportion averse to labor, and were
charged by the heads of the departments with a certain
indolence and selfishness.

In practice it is always found that virtue is occasional,
spotty, and not linear or cubic. Good people are as bad
as rogues if steady performance is claimed; the conscience of the conscientious runs in veins, and the most
punctilious in some particulars are latitudinarian in

others. It was very gently said that people on whom beforehand all persons would put the utmost reliance were not responsible. They saw the necessity that the work must be done, and did it not, and it of course fell to be done by the few religious workers. No doubt there was in many a certain strength drawn from the fury of dissent. Thus Mr. Ripley told Theodore Parker, "There is your accomplished friend——: he would hoe corn all Sunday if I would let him, but all Massachusetts could not make him do it on Monday."

Of course every visitor found that there was a comic side to this Paradise of shepherds and shepherdesses. There was a stove in every chamber, and every one might burn as much wood as he or she would saw. The ladies took cold on washingday; so it was ordained that the gentlemen-shepherds should wring and hang out clothes; which they punctually did. And it would sometimes occur that when they danced in the evening, clothes-pins dropped plentifully from their pockets. The country members naturally were surprised to observe that one man ploughed all day and one looked out of the window all day, and perhaps drew his picture, and both received at night the same wages. One would meet also some modest pride in their advanced condition, signified by a frequent phrase, "Before we came out of civilization."

The question which occurs to you had occurred much earlier to Fourier: "How in this charming Elysium is the dirty work to be done?" And long ago Fourier had exclaimed, "Ah! I have it," and jumped with joy. "Don't you see," he cried, "that nothing so delights the young Caucasian child as dirt? See the mud-pies that all children will make if you will let them. See how much more joy they find in pouring their pudding on the table-cloth

than into their beautiful mouths. The children from six
to eight, organized into companies with flags and uni-
forms, shall do this last function of civilization."

In Brook Farm was this peculiarity, that there was no
head. In every family is the father; in every factory, a
foreman; in a shop, a master; in a boat, the skipper;
but in this Farm, no authority; each was master or mis-
tress of his or her actions; happy, hapless anarchists.
They expressed, after much perilous experience, the
conviction that plain-dealing was the best defence of
manners and moral between the sexes. People cannot
live together in any but necessary ways. The only candidates who will present themselves will be those who
have tried the experiment of independence and ambition, and have failed; and none others will barter for
the most comfortable equality the chance of superiority.
Then all communities have quarreled. Few people can
live together on their merits. There must be kindred, or
mutual economy, or a common interest in their business,
or other external tie.

The society at Brook Farm existed, I think, about
six or seven years, and then broke up, the Farm was
sold, and I believe all the partners came out with
pecuniary loss. Some of them had spent on it the accumulations of years. I suppose they all, at the moment,
regarded it as a failure. I do not think they can so
regard it now, but probably as an important chapter in
their experience which has been of lifelong value. What
knowledge of themselves and of each other, what various practical wisdom, what personal power, what
studies of character, what accumulated culture many of
the members owed to it! What mutual measure they
took of each other! It was a close union, like that in a
ship's cabin, of clergymen, young collegians, merchants,
mechanics, farmers' sons and daughters, with men and

women of rare opportunities and delicate culture, yet assembled there by a sentiment which all shared, some of them hotly shared, of the honesty of a life of labor and of the beauty of a life of humanity. The yeoman saw refined manners in persons who were his friends; and the lady or the romantic scholar saw the continuous strength and faculty in people who would have disgusted them but that these powers were now spent in the direction of their own theory of life.

I recall these few selected facts, none of them of much independent interest, but symptomatic of the times and country. I please myself with the thought that our American mind is not now eccentric or rude in its strength, but is beginning to show a quiet power, drawn from wide and abundant sources, proper to a Continent and to an educated people. If I have owed much to the special influences I have indicated, I am not less aware of that excellent and increasing circle of masters in arts and in song and in science, who cheer the intellect of our cities and this country today—whose genius is not a lucky accident, but normal, and with broad foundation of culture, and so inspires the hope of steady strength advancing on itself, and a day without night.

MARY MOODY EMERSON

I WISH to meet the invitation with which the ladies have honored me by offering them a portrait of real life. It is a representative life, such as could hardly have appeared out of New England; of an age now past, and of which I think no types survive. Perhaps I deceive myself and overestimate its interest. It has to me a value like that which many readers find in Madame Guyon, in Rahel, in Eugénie de Guérin, but it is purely original and hardly admits of a duplicate. Then it is a fruit of Calvinism and New England, and marks the precise time when the power of the old creed yielded to the influence of modern science and humanity.

I have found that I could only bring you this portrait by selections from the diary of my heroine, premising a sketch of her time and place. I report some of the thoughts and soliloquies of a country girl, poor, solitary —"a goody" as she called herself—growing from youth to age amid slender opportunities and usually very humble company.

Mary Moody Emerson was born just before the outbreak of the Revolution. When introduced to Lafayette at Portland, she told him that she was "in arms" at the Concord Fight. Her father, the minister of Concord, a warm patriot in 1775, went as a chaplain to the American army at Ticonderoga: he carried his infant daughter, before he went, to his mother in Malden and told her to keep the child until he returned. He died at Rutland, Vermont, of army fever, the next year, and Mary remained at Malden with her grandmother, and, after her death, with her father's sister, in whose house she grew up, rarely seeing her brothers and sisters in Concord. This aunt and her husband lived on a farm, were getting old, and the husband a shiftless, easy man. There was plenty of work for the little niece to do day by day, and not always bread enough in the house.

One of her tasks, it appears, was to watch for the approach of the deputy-sheriff, who might come to confiscate the spoons or arrest the uncle for debt. Later, another aunt, who had become insane, was brought hither to end her days. More and sadder work for this young girl. She had no companions, lived in entire solitude with these old people, very rarely cheered by short visits from her brothers and sisters. Her mother had married again—married the minister who succeeded her husband in the parish at Concord, [Dr. Ezra Ripley,] and had now a young family growing up around her.

Her aunt became strongly attached to Mary, and persuaded the family to give the child up to her as a daughter, on some terms embracing a care of her future interests. She would leave the farm to her by will. This promise was kept; she came into possession of the property many years after, and her dealings with it gave her no small trouble, though they give much piquancy to her letters in after years. Finally it was sold, and its price invested in a share of a farm in Maine, where she lived as a boarder with her sister, for many years. It was in a picturesque country, within sight of the White Mountains, with a little lake in front at the foot of a high hill called Bear Mountain. Not far from the house was a brook running over a granite floor like the Franconia Flume, and noble forests around. Every word she writes about this farm ("Elm Vale," Waterford), her dealings and vexations about it, her joys and raptures of religion and Nature, interest like a romance, and to those who may hereafter read her letters, will make its obscure acres amiable.

In Malden she lived through all her youth and early womanhood, with the habit of visiting the families of her brothers and sisters on any necessity of theirs. Her good-will to serve in time of sickness or of pressure was known to them, and promptly claimed, and her attachment to the youths and maidens growing up in those families was secure for any trait of talent or of character.

Her sympathy for young people who pleased her was almost passionate, and was sure to make her arrival in each house a holiday.

Her early reading was Milton, Young, Akenside, Samuel Clarke, Jonathan Edwards, and always the Bible. Later, Plato, Plotinus, Marcus Antoninus, Stewart, Coleridge, Cousin, Herder, Locke, Madame De Staël, Channing, Mackintosh, Byron. Nobody can read in her manuscript, or recall the conversation of old-school people, without seeing that Milton and Young had a religious authority in their mind, and nowise the slight, merely entertaining quality of modern bards. And Plato, Aristotle, Plotinus—how venerable and organic as Nature they are in her mind! What a subject is her mind and life for the finest novel! When I read Dante, the other day, and his paraphrases to signify with more adequateness Christ or Jehovah, whom do you think I was reminded of? Whom but Mary Emerson and her eloquent theology? She had a deep sympathy with genius. When it was unhallowed, as in Byron, she had none the less, whilst she deplored and affected to denounce him. But she adored it when ennobled by character. She liked to notice that the greatest geniuses have died ignorant of their power and influence. She wished you to scorn to shine. "My opinion," she writes, [is] "that a mind like Byron's would never be satisfied with modern Unitarianism—that the fiery depths of Calvinism, its high and mysterious elections to eternal bliss, beyond angels, and all its attendant wonders would have alone been fitted to fix his imagination."

Her wit was so fertile, and only used to strike, that she never used it for display, any more than a wasp would parade his sting. It was ever the will and not the phrase that concerned her. Yet certain expressions, when they marked a memorable state of mind in her experience, recurred to her afterwards, and she would vindicate herself as having said to Dr. R—— or Uncle L—— so and so, at such a period of her life. But they were intensely true when first spoken. All her language was happy, but inimitable, unattainable by talent, as if caught from some dream. She calls herself "the puny pilgrim, whose sole talent is sympathy." "I like that kind of apathy that is a triumph to overset."

She writes to her nephew Charles Emerson, in 1833 —"I could never have adorned the garden. If I had been in aught but dreary deserts, I should have idolized my friends, despised the world and been haughty. I never expected connections and matrimony. My taste was formed in romance, and I knew I was not destined to please. I love God and his creation as I never else could. I scarcely feel the sympathies of this life enough to agitate the pool. This in general, one case or so excepted, and even this is a relation to God through you. 'Twas so in my happiest early days, when you were at my side."

Destitution is the Muse of her genius—Destitution and Death. I used to propose that her epitaph should be: "Here lies the angel of Death." And wonderfully as she varies and poetically repeats that image in every page and day, yet not less fondly and sublimely she returns to the other—the grandeur of humility and privation, as thus; "The chief witness which I have had of a Godlike principle of action and feeling is in the disinterested joy felt in others' superiority. For the love of superior virtue is mine own gift from God." "Where were thine own intellect if others had not lived?"

She had many acquaintances among the notables of the time; and now and then in her migrations from town to town in Maine and Massachusetts, in search of a new boarding-place, discovered some preacher with sense or piety, or both. For on her arrival at any new home she was likely to steer first to the minister's house and pray his wife to take a boarder; and as the minister found quickly that she knew all his books and many more, and made shrewd guesses at his character and possibilities, she would easily rouse his curiosity, as a person who could read his secret and tell him his fortune.

She delighted in success, in youth, in beauty, in genius, in manners. When she met a young person who interested her, she made herself acquainted and intimate with him or her at once, by sympathy, by flattery, by raillery, by anecdotes, by wit, by rebuke, and stormed the castle. None but was attracted or piqued by her interest and wit and wide acquaintance with books and with eminent names. She said she gave herself full swing in these sudden intimacies, for she knew she should disgust them soon, and resolved to have their best hours. "Society is shrewd to detect those who do not belong to her train, and seldom wastes her attentions." She surprised, attracted, chided and denounced her companion by turns, and pretty rapid turns. But no intelligent youth or maiden could have once met her without remembering her with interest, and learning something of value. Scorn trifles, lift your aims: do what you are afraid to do: sublimity of character must come from sublimity of motive: these were the lessons which were urged with vivacity, in ever new language. But if her companion was dull, her impatience knew no bounds. She tired presently of dull conversations, and asked to be read to, and so disposed of the visitor. If the voice or the reading tired her, she would ask the friend if he or she would do an errand for her, and so dismiss them. If her companion were a little ambitious, and asked her opinions on books or matters on which she did not wish rude hands laid, she did not hesitate to stop the intruder with "How's your cat, Mrs. Tenner?"

"I was disappointed," she writes, "in finding my little Calvinist no companion, a cold little thing who lives in society alone, and is looked up to as a specimen of genius. I performed a mission in secretly undermining his vanity, or trying to. Alas! never done but by mortifying affliction." From the country she writes to her sister in town, "You cannot help saying that my epistle is a striking specimen of egotism. To which I can only answer that, in the country, we converse so much more with ourselves, that we are almost led to forget everybody else. The very sound of your bells and the rattling of the carriages have a tendency to divert selfishness." "This seems a world rather of trying each others' dispositions than of enjoying each others' virtues."

She had the misfortune of spinning with a greater velocity than any of the other tops. She would tear into the chaise or out of it, into the house or out of it, into the conversation, into the thought, into the character of the stranger—disdaining all the graduation by which her fellows time their steps: and though she might do very happily in a planet where others moved with the like velocity, she was offended here by the phlegm of all her fellow creatures, and disgusted them by her impatience. She could keep step with no human being. Her nephew [R.W.E.] wrote of her: "I am glad the friendship with Aunt Mary is ripening. As by seeing a high tragedy, reading a true poem, or a novel like *Corinne,* so, by society with her, one's mind is electrified and purged. She is no statute book of practical commandments, nor orderly digest of any system of Philosophy, divine or human, but a Bible, miscellaneous in its parts but one in its spirit, wherein are sentences of condemnation, promises and covenants of love that make foolish the wisdom of the world with the power of God."

Our Delphian was fantastic enough, Heaven knows, yet could always be tamed by large and sincere conversation. Was there thought and eloquence, she would listen like a child. Her aspiration and prayer would begin, and the whim and petulance in which by diseased habit she had grown to indulge without suspecting it, was burned up in the glow of her pure and poetic spirit, which dearly loved the Infinite.

She writes: "August, 1847: *Vale*—My oddities were never designed—effect of an uncalculating constitution, at first, then through isolation; and as to dress, from duty. To be singular of choice, without singular talents and virtues, is as ridiculous as ungrateful." "It is so universal with all classes to avoid contact with me that I blame none. The fact has generally increased piety and self-love." "As a traveler enters some fine palace and finds all the doors closed, and he only allowed the use of some avenues and passages, so have I wandered from the cradle over the apartments of social affections, or the cabinets of natural or moral philosophy, the recesses of ancient and modern lore. All say—Forbear to enter the pales of the initiated by birth, wealth, talents and patronage. I submit with delight, for it is the echo of a decree from above; and from the highway hedges where I get lodging, and from the rays which burst forth when the crowd are entering these noble salons, whilst I stand in the doors, I get a pleasing vision which is an earnest of the interminable skies where the mansions are prepared for the poor."

"To live to give pain rather than pleasure (the latter so delicious) seems the spider-like necessity of my being on earth, and I have gone on my queer way with joy, saying, 'Shall the clay interrogate?' But in every actual case, 'tis hard, and we lose sight of the first necessity—here too amid works red with default in all great and grand and infinite aims. Yet with intentions disinterested, though uncontrolled by proper reverence for others."

When Mrs. Thoreau called on her one day, wearing pink ribbons, she shut her eyes, and so conversed with her for a time. By and by she said, "Mrs. Theoreau, I don't know whether you have observed that my eyes are shut." "Yes, Madam, I have observed it." "Perhaps you would like to know the reasons?" "Yes, I should." "I don't like to see a person of your age guilty of such levity in her dress."

When her cherished favorite, E. H., was at the Vale, and had gone out to walk in the forest with Hannah, her niece, Aunt Mary feared they were lost, and found a man in the next house and begged him to go and look for them. The man went and returned saying that he could not find them. "Go and cry, 'Elizabeth!'" The man rather declined this service, as he did not know Miss H. She was highly offended, and exclaimed, "God has given you a voice that you might use it in the service of your fellow creatures. Go instantly and call 'Elizabeth' till you find them." The man went immediately, and did as he was bid, and having found them apologized for calling thus, by telling what Miss Emerson had said to him.

When some ladies of my acquaintance by an unusual chance found themselves in her neighborhood and visited her, I told them that she was no whistle that every mouth could play on, but a quite clannish instrument, a pibroch, for example, from which none but a native Highlander could draw music.

In her solitude of twenty years, with fewest books

and those only sermons, and a copy of *Paradise Lost*, without covers or title page, so that later, when she heard much of Milton and sought his work, she found it was her very book which she knew so well—she was driven to find Nature her companion and solace. She speaks of "her attempts in Malden, to wake up the soul amid the dreary scenes of monotonous Sabbaths, when Nature looked like a pulpit."

"Malden, November 15th, 1805—What a rich day, so fully occupied in pursuing truth that I scorned to touch a novel which for so many years I have wanted. How insipid is fiction to a mind touched with immortal views! November 16th—I am so small in my expectations, that a week of industry delights. Rose before light every morn; visited from necessity once, and again for books; read Butler's *Analogy*; commented on the Scriptures; read in a little book—Cicero's *Letters*—a few: touched Shakespeare—washed, carded, cleaned house, and baked. Today cannot recall an error, nor scarcely a sacrifice, but more fulness of content in the labors of a day never was felt. There is a sweet pleasure in bending to circumstances while superior to them."

"Malden, September, 1807—The rapture of feeling I would part from, for days more devoted to higher discipline. But when Nature beams with such excess of beauty, when the heart thrills with hope in its Author—feels that it is related to him more than by any ties of Creation—it exults, too fondly perhaps for a state of trial. But in dead of night, nearer morning, when the eastern stars glow or appear to glow with more indescribable lustre, a lustre which penetrates the spirit with wonder and curiosity—then, however awed, who can fear? Since Sabbath, Aunt B—— [the insane aunt] was brought here. Ah! mortifying sight! instinct perhaps triumphs over reason, and every dignified respect to herself, in her anxiety about recovery, and the smallest means connected. Not one wish of others detains her, not one care. But it alarms me not, I shall delight to return to God. His name my fullest confidence. His sole presence ineffable pleasure.

"I walked yesterday five or more miles, lost to mental or heart existence, through fatigue—just fit for the society I went into, all mildness and the most commonplace virtue. The lady is celebrated for her cleverness, and she was never so good to me. Met a lady in the morning walk, a foreigner—conversed on the accomplishments of Miss T. My mind expanded with novel and innocent pleasure. Ah! were virtue, and that of dear heavenly meekness attached by any necessity to a lower rank of genteel people, who would sympathize with the exalted with satisfaction? But that is not the case, I believe. A mediocrity does seem to me more distant from eminent virtue than the extremes of station; though after all it must depend on the nature of the heart. A mediocre mind will be deranged in either extreme of wealth or poverty, praise or censure, society or solitude. The feverish lust of notice perhaps in all these cases would injure the heart of common refinement and virtue."

Later she writes of her early days in Malden: "When I get a glimpse of the revolutions of nations—that retribution which seems forever going on in this part of creation—I remember with great satisfaction that from all the ills suffered, in childhood and since, from others, I felt that it was rather the order of things than their individual fault. It was from being early impressed by my poor unpractical aunt, that Providence and Prayer were all in all. Poor woman! Could her own temper in childhood or age have been subdued, how happy for herself, who had a warm heart; but for me would have prevented those early lessons of fortitude, which her caprices taught me to practise. Had I prospered in life, what a proud, excited being, even to feverishness, I might have been. Loving to shine, flattered and flattering, anxious, and wrapped in others, frail and feverish as myself."

She alludes to the early days of her solitude, sixty years afterward, on her own farm in Maine, speaking sadly the thoughts suggested by the rich autumn landscape around her: "Ah! as I walked out this afternoon, so sad was wearied Nature that I felt her whisper to me, 'Even these leaves you use to think my better emblems have lost their charm on me too, and I weary of my pilgrimage—tired that I must again be clothed in the grandeurs of winter, and anon be bedizened in flowers and cascades. Oh, if there be a power superior to me—and that there is, my own dread fetters proclaim —when will He let my lights go out, my tides cease to an eternal ebb? Oh for transformation! I am not infinite, nor have I power or will, but bound and imprisoned, the tool of mind, even of the beings I feed and adorn. Vital, I feel not: not active, but passive, and cannot aid the creatures which seem my progeny—myself. But you are ingrate to tire of me, now you want to look beyond. 'Twas I who soothed your thorny childhood, though you knew me not, and you were placed in my most leafless waste. Yet I comforted thee when going on the daily errand, fed thee with my mallows, on the first young day of bread failing. More, I led thee when thou knewest not a syllable of my active Cause, (any more than if it had been dead eternal matter), to that Cause; and from the solitary heart taught thee to say, at first womanhood, Alive with God is enough—'tis rapture.'"

"This morning rich in existence; the remembrance of

past destitution in the deep poverty of my aunt, and her most unhappy temper; of bitterer days of youth and age, when my senses and understanding seemed but means of labor, or to learn my own unpopular destiny, and that—but no more—joy, hope and resignation unite me to Him whose mysterious Will adjusts everything, and the darkest and lightest are alike welcome. Oh! could this state of mind continue, death would not be longed for." "I felt, till above twenty years old, as though Christianity were as necessary to the world as existence—was ignorant that it was lately promulged, or partially received." Later: "Could I have those hours in which in fresh youth I said, To obey God is joy, though there were no hereafter, I should rejoice, though returning to dust.

"Folly follows me as the shadow does the form. Yet my whole life devoted to find some new truth which will link me closer to God. And the simple principle which made me say, in youth and laborious poverty, that, should He make me a blot on the fair face of his Creation, I should rejoice in His will, has never been equaled, though it returns in the long life of destitution like an Angel. I end days of fine health and cheerfulness without getting upward now. How did I use to think them lost! If more liberal views of the divine government make me think nothing lost which carries me to His now-hidden presence, there may be danger of losing and causing others the loss of that awe and sobriety so indispensable."

She was addressed and offered marriage by a man of talents, education and good social position, whom she respected. The proposal gave her pause and much to think, but after consideration she refused it, I know not on what grounds: but a few allusions to it in her diary suggest that it was a religious act, and it is easy to see that she could hardly promise herself sympathy in her religious abandonment with any but a rarely found partner.

"1807. Jan. 19, Malden [alluding to the sale of her farm]. Last night I spoke two sentences about that foolish place, which I most bitterly lament—not because they were improper, but they arose from anger. It is difficult, when we have no kind of barrier, to command our feelings. But this shall teach me. It humbles me beyond anything I have met, to find myself for a moment affected with hope, fear, or especially anger, about interest. But I did overcome and return kindness for the repeated provocations. What is it? My uncle has been the means of lessening my property. Ridiculous to wound him for that. He was honestly seeking his own. But at last, this very night, the bargain is closed, and I am delighted with myself—my dear self has done well. Never did I so exult in a trifle. Happy beginning of my bargain, though the sale of the place appears to me one of the worst things for me at this time."

"Jan. 21. Weary at times of objects so tedious to hear and see. O the power of vision, then the delicate power of the nerve which receives impressions from sounds! If ever I am blest with a social life, let the accent be grateful. Could I at times be regaled with music, it would remind me that there are *sounds*. Shut up in this severe weather with careful, infirm, afflicted age, it is wonderful, my spirits: hopes I can have none. Not a prospect but is dark on earth, as to knowledge and joy from externals: but the prospect of a dying bed reflects lustre on all the rest.

"The evening is fine, but I dare not enjoy it. The moon and stars reproach me, because I had to do with mean fools. Should I take so much care to save a few dollars? Never was I so much ashamed. Did I say with what rapture I might dispose of them to the poor? Pho! self-preservation, dignity, confidence in the future, contempt of trifles! Alas, I am disgraced. Took a momentary revenge on —— for worrying me."

"Jan. 30. I walked to Captain Dexter's. Sick. Promised never to put that ring on. Ended miserably the month which began so worldly.

"It was the choice of the Eternal that gave the glowing seraph his joys, and to me my vile imprisonment. I adore Him. It was His will that gives my superiors to shine in wisdom, friendship, and ardent pursuits, while I pass my youth, its last traces, in the veriest shades of ignorance and complete destitution of society. I praise Him, though when my strength of body falters, it is a trial not easily described.

"True, I must finger the very farthing candle-ends— the duty assigned to my pride; and indeed so poor are some of those allotted to join me on the weary needy path, that 'tis benevolence enjoins self-denial. Could I but dare it in the bread-and-water diet! Could I but live free from calculation, as in the first half of life, when my poor aunt lived. I had ten dollars a year for clothes and charity, and I never remember to have been needy, though I never had but two or three aids in those six years of earning my home. That ten dollars my dear father earned, and one hundred dollars remain, and I can't bear to take it, and don't know what to do. Yet I would not breathe to —— or —— my want. 'Tis only now that I would not let —— pay my hotel bill. They have enough to do. Besides, it would send me packing to depend for anything. Better anything than dishonest dependence, which robs the poorer, and despoils friendship of equal connection."

In 1830, in one of her distant homes, she reproaches herself with some sudden passion she has for visiting her old home and friends in the city, where she had lived for a while with her brother [Mr. Emerson's father] and afterwards with his widow. "Do I yearn to be in Boston? 'Twould fatigue, disappoint; I, who have so long despised means, who have always found it a sort of rebellion to seek them? Yet the old desire for the worm is not so greedy as [mine] to find myself in my old haunts."

1833. "The difficulty of getting places of low board for a lady, is obvious. And, at moments, I am tired out. Yet how independent, how better than to hang on friends! And sometimes I fancy that I am emptied and peeled to carry some seed to the ignorant, which no idler wind can so well dispense." "Hard to contend for a health which is daily used in petition for a final close." "Am I, poor victim, swept on through the sternest ordinations of nature's laws which slay? yet I'll trust." "There was great truth in what a pious enthusiast said, that, if God should cast him into hell, he would yet clasp his hands around Him."

"Newburyport, Sept. 1822. High, solemn, entrancing noon, prophetic of the approach of the Presiding Spirit of Autumn. God preserve my reason! Alone, feeling strongly, fully, that I have deserved nothing; according to Adam Smith's idea of society, 'done nothing'; doing nothing, never expect to; yet joying in existence, perhaps striving to beautify one individual of God's creation.

"Our civilization is not always mending our poetry. It is sauced and spiced with our complexity of arts and inventions, but lacks somewhat of the grandeur that belongs to a Doric and unphilosophical age. In a religious contemplative public it would have less outward variety, but simpler and grander means; a few pulsations of created beings, a few successions of acts, a few

lamps held out in the firmament enable us to talk of
Time, make epochs, write histories—to do more—to
date the revelations of God to man. But these lamps
are held to measure out some of the moments of
eternity, to divide the history of God's operations in the
birth and death of nations, of worlds. It is a goodly
name for our notions of breathing, suffering, enjoying,
acting. We personify it. We call it by every name of
fleeting, dreaming, vaporing imagery. Yet it is nothing.
We exist in eternity. Dissolve the body and the night
is gone, the stars are extinguished, and we measure
duration by the number of our thoughts, by the activity
of reason, the discovery of truths, the acquirement of
virtue, the approach to God. And the gray-headed god
throws his shadows all around, and his slaves catch,
now at this, now at that, one at the halo he throws
around poetry, or pebbles, bugs, or bubbles. Sometimes
they climb, sometimes creep into the meanest holes—
but they are all alike in vanishing, like the shadow of a
cloud."

To her nephew Charles: "War; what do I think of it?
Why in your ear I think it so much better than oppression that if it were ravaging the whole geography of
despotism it would be an omen of high and glorious
import. Channing paints its miseries, but does he know
those of a worse war—private animosities, pinching,
bitter warfare of the human heart, the cruel oppression
of the poor by the rich, which corrupts old worlds?
How much better, more honest, are storming and conflagration of towns! They are but letting blood which
corrupts into worms and dragons. A war-trump would
be harmony to the jars of theologians and statesmen
such as the papers bring. It was the glory of the Chosen
People, nay, it is said there was war in Heaven. War
is among the means of discipline, the rough meliorators,

and no worse than the strife with poverty, malice and ignorance. War devastates the conscience of men, yet corrupt peace does not less. And if you tell me of the miseries of the battlefield, with the sensitive Channing (of whose love of life I am ashamed), what of a few days of agony, what of a vulture being the bier, tomb and parson of a hero, compared to the long years of sticking on a bed and wished away? For the widows and orphans—Oh, I could give facts of the long-drawn years of imprisoned minds and hearts, which uneducated orphans endure!"

"O Time! Thou loiterer. Thou, whose might has laid low the vastest and crushed the worm, restest on thy hoary throne, with like potency over thy agitations and thy graves. When will thy routines give way to higher and lasting institutions? When thy trophies and thy name and all its wizard forms be lost in the Genius of Eternity? In Eternity, no deceitful promises, no fantastic illusions, no riddles concealed by thy shrouds, none of thy Arachnean webs, which decoy and destroy. Hasten to finish thy motley work, on which frightful Gorgons are at play, spite of holy ghosts. 'Tis already moth-eaten and its shuttles quaver, as the beams of the loom are shaken."

"Sat. 25. Hail requiem of departed Time! Never was incumbent's funeral followed by expectant heir with more satisfaction. Yet not his hope is mine. For in the weary womb are prolific numbers of the same sad hour, colored by the memory of defeats in virtue, by the prophecy of others, more dreary, blind and sickly. Yet He who formed thy web, who stretched thy warp from long ages, has graciously given man to throw his shuttle, or feel he does, and irradiate the filling woof with many a flowery rainbow—labors, rather—evanescent efforts, which will wear like flowerets in brighter soils—has attuned his mind in such unison with the harp of the universe, that he is never without some chord of hope's music. 'Tis not in the nature of existence, while there is a God, to be without the pale of excitement. When the dreamy pages of life seem all turned and folded down to very weariness, even this idea of those who fill the hour with crowded virtues, lifts the spectator to other worlds, and he adores the eternal purposes of Him who lifteth up and casteth down, bringeth to dust, and raiseth to the skies. 'Tis a strange deficiency in Brougham's title of a *System of Natural Theology,* when the moral constitution of the being for whom these contrivances were made is not recognized. The wonderful inhabitant of the building to which unknown ages were the mechanics, is left out as to that part where the Creator had put his own lighted candle, placed a vicegerent. Not to complain of the poor old earth's chaotic state, brought so near in its long and gloomy transmutings by the geologist. Yet its youthful charms as decked by the hand of Moses' Cosmogony, will linger about the heart, while Poetry succumbs to Science. Yet there is a sombre music in the whirl of times so long gone by. And the bare bones of this poor embryo earth may give the idea of the Infinite far, far better than when dignified with arts and industry—its oceans, when beating the symbols of ceaseless ages, than when covered with cargoes of war and oppression. How grand its preparation for souls—souls who were to feel the Divinity, before Science had dissected the emotions, and applied its steely analysis to that state of being which recognizes neither psychology nor element."

"September, 1836. *Vale.* The mystic dream which is shed over the season. O, to dream more deeply; to lose external objects a little more! Yet the hold on them is so slight, that duty is lost sight of perhaps, at times.

Sadness is better than walking, talking, acting, somnambulism. Yes, this entire solitude with the Being who makes the powers of life! Even Fame, which lives in other states of Virtue, palls. Usefulness, if it requires action, seems less like existence than the desire of being absorbed in God, retaining consciousness. Number the waste-places of the journey—the secret martydom of youth, heavier than the stake, I thought, the narrow limits which know no outlet, the bitter dregs of the cup —and all are sweetened by the purpose of Him I love. The idea of being no mate for those intellectualists I've loved to admire, is no pain. Hereafter the same solitary joy will go with me, were I not to live, as I expect, in the vision of the Infinite. Never do the feelings of the Infinite, and the consciousness of finite frailty and ignorance, harmonize so well as at this mystic season in the deserts of life. Contradictions, the modern German says, of the Infinite and finite."

I sometimes fancy I detect in her writings, a certain —shall I say—polite and courtly homage to the name and dignity of Jesus, not at all spontaneous, but growing out of her respect to the Revelation, and really veiling and betraying her organic dislike to any interference, any mediation between her and the Author of her being, assurance of whose direct dealing with her she incessantly invokes: for example, the parenthesis "Saving thy presence, Priest and Medium of all this approach for a sinful creature!" "Were it possible that the Creator was not virtually present with the spirits and bodies which He has made—if it were in the nature of things possible He could withdraw himself—I would hold on to the faith, that, at some moment of His existence, I was present: that, though cast from Him, my sorrows, my ignorance and meanness were a part of His plan: my death, too, however long and tediously delayed to prayer—was decreed, was fixed. Oh how weary in youth—more so scarcely now, not whenever I can breathe, as it seems, the atmosphere of the Omnipresence: then I ask not faith nor knowledge; honors, pleasures, labors, I always refuse, compared to this divine partaking of existence—but how rare, how dependent on the organs through which the soul operates!

"The sickness of the last week was fine medicine; pain disintegrated the spirit, or became spiritual. I rose —I felt that I had given to God more perhaps than an angel could—had promised Him in youth that to be a blot on this fair world, at His command, would be acceptable. Constantly offer myself to continue the obscurist and loneliest thing ever heard of, with one proviso—His agency. Yes, love Thee, and all Thou dost, while Thou sheddest frost and darkness on every path of mine."

For years she had her bed made in the form of a coffin; and delighted herself with the discovery of the figure of a coffin made every evening on their sidewalk, by the shadow of a church tower which adjoined the house.

Saladin caused his shroud to be made, and carried it to battle as his standard. She made up her shroud, and death still refusing to come, and she thinking it a pity to let it lie idle, wore it as a night-gown, or a day-gown, nay, went out to ride in it, on horseback, in her mountain roads, until it was worn out. Then she had another made up, and as she never traveled without being provided for this dear and indispensable contingency, I believe she wore out a great many.

"1833. I have given up, the last year or two, the hope of dying. In the lowest ebb of health nothing is ominous; diet and exercise restore. So it seems best to get that very humbling business of insurance. I

enter my dear sixty the last of this month." "1835,
June 16. Tedious indisposition—hoped, as it took a
new form, it would open the cool, sweet grave. Now
existence itself in any form is sweet. Away with
knowledge—God alone. He communicates this our condition and humble waiting, or I should never perceive Him. Science, Nature—O, I've yearned to open
some page—not now, too late. Ill health and nerves. O
dear worms—how they will at some sure time take
down this tedious tabernacle, most valuable companions, instructors in the science of mind, by gnawing
away the meshes which have chained it. A very Beatrice
in showing the Paradise. Yes, I irk under contact with
forms of depravity, while I am resigned to being nothing, never expect a palm, a laurel, hereafter."

"1826, July. If one could choose, and without crime
be gibbeted—were it not altogether better than the
long drooping away by age without mentality or devotion? The vulture and crow would *caw caw,* and, unconscious of any deformity in the mutilated body, would
relish their meal, make no grimace of affected sympathy,
nor suffer any real compassion. I pray to die, though
happier myriads and mine own companions press nearer
to the throne. His coldest beam will purify and render
me forever holy. Had I the highest place of acquisition
and diffusing virtue here, the principle of human
sympathy would be too strong for that rapt emotion,
that severe delight which I crave; nay for that kind of
obscure virtue which is so rich to lay at the feet of the
Author of morality. Those economists (Adam Smith)
who say nothing is added to the wealth of a nation but
what is dug out of the earth, and that, whatever disposition of virtue may exist, unless something is done
for society, deserves no fame—why I am content with

such paradoxical kind of facts; but one secret sentiment of virtue, disinterested (or perhaps not), is worthy, and will tell, in the world of spirits, of God's immediate presence, more than the blood of many a martyr who has it not." "I have heard that the greatest geniuses have died ignorant of their power and influence on the arts and sciences. I believe thus much, that their large perception consumed their egotism, or made it impossible for them to make small calculations.

"That greatest of all gifts, however small my power of receiving—the capacity, the element to love the All-perfect, without regard to personal happiness—happiness?—'tis itself." She checks herself amid her passionate prayers for immediate communion with God, "I who never made a sacrifice to record—I cowering in the nest of quiet for so many years—I indulge the delight of sympathizing with great virtues—blessing their Original: Have I this right?" "While I am sympathizing in the government of God over the world, perhaps I lose nearer views. Well, I learned his existence *a priori*. No object of science or observation ever was pointed out to me by my poor aunt, but His Being and commands; and oh how much I trusted Him with every event till I learned the order of human events from the pressure of wants.

"What a timid, ungrateful creature! Fear the deepest pitfalls of age, when pressing on, in imagination at least, to Him with whom a day is a thousand years—with whom all miseries and irregularities are conforming to universal good! Shame on me who have learned within three years to sit whole days in peace and enjoyment without the least apparent benefit to any, or knowledge to myself—resigned, too, to the memory of long years of slavery passed in labor and ignorance, to the loss of that character which I once thought and felt so sure of, without ever being conscious of acting from calculation."

Her friends used to say to her, "I wish you joy of the worm." And when at last her release arrived, the event of her death had really such a comic tinge in the eyes of every one who knew her, that her friends feared they might, at her funeral, not dare to look at each other, lest they should forget the serious proprieties of the hour.

She gave high counsels. It was the privilege of certain boys to have this immeasurably high standard indicated to their childhood; a blessing which nothing else in education could supply. It is frivolous to ask—"And was she ever a Christian in practice?" Cassandra uttered, to a frivolous, skeptical time, the arcana of the Gods: but it is easy to believe that Cassandra domesticated in a lady's house would have proved a troublesome boarder. Is it the less desirable to have the lofty abstractions because the abstractionist is nervous and irritable? Shall we not keep Flamsteed and Herschel in the observatory, though it should even be proved that they neglected to rectify their own kitchen clock? It is essential to the safety of every mackerel fisher that latitudes and longitudes should be astronomically ascertained; and so every banker, shopkeeper and wood-sawyer has a stake in the elevation of the moral code by saint and prophet. Very rightly, then, the Christian ages, proceeding on a grand instinct, have said: Faith alone, Faith alone.

THOREAU

HENRY DAVID THOREAU was the last male descendant of a French ancestor who came to this country from the Isle of Guernsey. His character exhibited occasional traits drawn from this blood, in singular combination with a very strong Saxon genius.

He was born in Concord, Massachusetts, on the 12th of July, 1817. He was graduated at Harvard College in 1837, but without any literary distinction. An iconoclast in literature, he seldom thanked colleges for their service to him, holding them in small esteem, whilst yet his debt to them was important. After leaving the University, he joined his brother in teaching a private school, which he soon renounced. His father was a manufacturer of lead pencils, and Henry applied himself for a time to this craft, believing he could make a better pencil than was then in use. After completing his experiments, he exhibited his work to chemists and artists in Boston, and having obtained their certificates to its excellence and to its equality with the best London manufacture, he returned home contented. His friends congratulated him that he had now opened his way to fortune. But he replied, that he should never make another pencil. "Why should I? I would not do again what I have done once." He resumed his endless walks and miscellaneous studies, making every day some new acquaintance with Nature, though as yet never speaking of zoology or botany, since, though very studious of natural facts, he was incurious of technical and textual science.

At this time, a strong, healthy youth, fresh from college, whilst all his companions were choosing their profession, or eager to begin some lucrative employment, it was inevitable that his thoughts should be exercised on the same question, and it required rare decision to refuse all the accustomed paths and keep his solitary freedom at the cost of disappointing the natural expectations of his family and friends: all the more difficult that he had a perfect probity, was exact in securing his own independence, and in holding every man to the like duty. But Thoreau never faltered. He was a born protestant. He declined to give up his large ambition of knowledge and action for any narrow craft or profession, aiming at a much more comprehensive calling, the art of living well. If he slighted and defied the opinions of others, it was only that he was more intent to reconcile his practice with his own belief. Never idle or self-indulgent, he preferred, when he wanted money, earning it by some piece of manual labor agreeable to him, as building a boat or a fence, planting, grafting, surveying, or other short work, to any long engagements. With his hardy habits and few wants, his skill in woodcraft, and his powerful arithmetic, he was very competent to live in any part of the world. It would cost him less time to supply his wants than another. He was therefore secure of his leisure.

A natural skill for mensuration, growing out of his mathematical knowledge and his habit of ascertaining the measures and distances of objects which interested him, the size of trees, the depth and extent of ponds and rivers, the height of mountains, and the air-line distance of his favorite summits—this, and his intimate knowledge of the territory about Concord, made him drift into the profession of land-surveyor. It had the advantage for him that it led him continually into new and secluded grounds, and helped his studies of Nature. His accuracy and skill in this work were readily appreciated, and he found all the employment he wanted.

He could easily solve the problems of the surveyor, but he was daily beset with graver questions, which he manfully confronted. He interrogated every custom, and wished to settle all his practice on an ideal foundation. He was a protestant *à outrance*, and few lives contain so many renunciations. He was bred to no profession; he never married; he lived alone; he never went to church; he never voted; he refused to pay a tax to the State; he ate no flesh, he drank no wine, he never knew the use of tobacco; and, though a naturalist, he used neither trap nor gun. He chose, wisely no doubt for himself, to be the bachelor of thought and Nature. He had no talent for wealth, and knew how to be poor without the least hint of squalor or inelegance. Perhaps he fell into his way of living without forecasting it much, but approved it with later wisdom. "I am often reminded," he wrote in his journal, "that if I had bestowed on me the wealth of Crœsus, my aims must be still the same, and my means essentially the same." He had no temptations to fight against—no appetites, no passions, no taste for elegant trifles. A fine house, dress, the manners and talk of highly cultivated people were all thrown away on him. He much preferred a good Indian, and considered these refinements as impediments to conversation, wishing to meet his companion on the simplest terms. He declined invitations to dinner-parties, because there each was in every one's way, and he could not meet the individuals to any purpose. "They make their pride," he said, "in making their dinner cost much; I make my pride in making my dinner cost little." When asked at table what dish he preferred, he answered, "The nearest." He did not like the taste of wine, and never had a vice in his life. He said, "I have a faint recollection of pleasure derived from smoking dried lily-stems, before I was a man. I had commonly a supply of these. I have never smoked anything more noxious."

He chose to be rich by making his wants few, and supplying them himself. In his travels, he used the railroad only to get over so much country as was unimportant to the present purpose, walking hundreds of miles, avoiding taverns, buying a lodging in farmers' and fishermen's houses, as cheaper, and more agreeable to him, and because there he could better find the men and the information he wanted.

There was somewhat military in his nature, not to be subdued, always manly and able, but rarely tender, as if he did not feel himself except in opposition. He wanted a fallacy to expose, a blunder to pillory, I may say required a little sense of victory, a roll of the drum, to call his powers into full exercise. It cost him nothing to say No; indeed he found it much easier than to say Yes. It seemed as if his first instinct on hearing a proposition was to controvert it, so impatient was he of the limitations of our daily thought. This habit, of course, is a little chilling to the social affections; and though the companion would in the end acquit him of any malice or untruth, yet it mars conversation. Hence, no equal companion stood in affectionate relations with one so pure and guileless. "I love Henry," said one of his friends, "but I cannot like him; and as for taking his arm, I should as soon think of taking the arm of an elm tree."

Yet, hermit and stoic as he was, he was really fond of sympathy, and threw himself heartily and childlike into the company of young people whom he loved, and whom he delighted to entertain, as he only could, with the varied and endless anecdotes of his experiences by field and river: and he was always ready to lead a huckleberry-party or a search for chestnuts or grapes. Talking, one day, of a public discourse, Henry remarked, that whatever succeeded with the audience was bad. I said, "Who would not like to write something which all can read, like Robinson Crusoe? and who does not see with regret that his page is not solid with a right materialistic treatment, which delights everybody?" Henry objected, of course, and vaunted the better lectures which reached only a few persons. But, at supper, a young girl, understanding that he was to lecture at the Lyceum, sharply asked him, whether his lecture would be a nice, interesting story, such as she wished to hear, or whether it was one of those old philosophical things that she did not care about. Henry turned to her, and bethought himself, and, I saw, was trying to believe that he had matter that might fit her and her brother, who were to sit up and go to the lecture, if it was a good one for them.

He was a speaker and actor of the truth, born such, and was ever running into dramatic situations from this cause. In any circumstance it interested all by-standers to know what part Henry would take, and what he would say; and he did not disappoint expectation, but used an original judgment on each emergency. In 1845 he built himself a small framed house on the shores of Walden Pond, and lived there two years alone, a life of labor and study. This action was quite native and fit for him. No one who knew him would tax him with affectation. He was more unlike his neighbors in his thought than in his action. As soon as he had exhausted the advantages of that solitude, he abandoned it. In 1847, not approving some uses to which the public expenditure was applied, he refused to pay his town tax, and was put in jail. A friend paid the tax for him, and he was released. The like annoyance was threatened the next year. But, as his friends paid the tax, notwithstanding his protest, I believe he ceased to resist. No opposition or ridicule had any weight with him. He coldly and fully stated his opinion without affecting to believe that it was the opinion of the company. It was of no consequence if every one present held the opposite opinion. On one occasion he went to the University Library to procure some books. The librarian refused to lend them. Mr. Thoreau repaired to the President, who stated to him the rules and usages, which permitted the loan of books to resident graduates, to clergymen who were alumni, and to some others resident within a circle of ten miles' radius from the College. Mr. Thoreau explained to the President that the railroad had destroyed the old scale of distances—that the library was useless, yes, and President and College useless, on the terms of his rules—that the one benefit he owed to the College was its library—that, at this moment, not only his want of books was imperative but he wanted a large number of books, and assured him that he, Thoreau, and not the librarian, was the proper custodian of these. In short, the President found the petitioner so formidable, and the rules getting to look so ridiculous, that he ended by giving him a privilege which in his hands proved unlimited thereafter.

No truer American existed than Thoreau. His preference of his country and condition was genuine, and his aversation from English and European manners and tastes almost reached contempt. He listened impatiently to news or *bon-mots* gleaned from London circles; and though he tried to be civil, these anecdotes fatigued him. The men were all imitating each other, and on a small mold. Why can they not live as far apart as possible, and each be a man by himself? What he sought was the most energetic nature; and he wished to go to Oregon, not to London. "In every part of Great Britain," he wrote in his diary, "are discovered traces of the Romans, their funereal urns, their camps, their roads, their dwellings. But New England, at least, is not based on any Roman ruins. We have not to lay the foundations of our houses on the ashes of a former civilization."

But, idealist as he was, standing for abolition of slavery, abolition of tariffs, almost for abolition of government, it is needless to say he found himself not only unrepresented in actual politics, but almost equally opposed to every class of reformers. Yet he paid the tribute of his uniform respect to the Anti-Slavery party. One man, whose personal acquaintance he had formed, he honored with exceptional regard. Before the first friendly word had been spoken for Captain John Brown, he sent notices to most houses in Concord that he would speak in a public hall on the condition and character of John Brown, on Sunday evening, and invited all people to come. The Republican Committee, the Abolitionist Committee, sent him word that it was premature and not advisable. He replied, "I did not send to you for advice, but to announce that I am to speak." The hall was filled at an early hour by people of all parties, and his earnest eulogy of the hero was heard by all respectfully, by many with a sympathy that surprised themselves.

It was said of Plotinus that he was ashamed of his body, and 'tis very likely he had good reason for it—that his body was a bad servant, and he had not skill in dealing with the material world, as happens often to men of abstract intellect. But Mr. Thoreau was equipped with a most adapted and serviceable body. He was of short stature, firmly built, of light complexion, with strong, serious blue eyes, and a grave aspect—his face covered in the late years with a becoming beard. His senses were acute, his frame well-knit and hardy, his hands strong and skilful in the use of tools. And there was a wonderful fitness of body and mind. He could pace sixteen rods more accurately than another man could measure them with rod and chain. He could find his path in the woods at night, he said, better by his feet than his eyes. He could estimate the measure of a tree very well by his eye; he could estimate the weight of a calf or a pig, like a dealer. From a box containing a bushel or more of loose pencils, he could take up with his hands fast enough just a dozen pencils at every grasp. He was a good swimmer, runner, skater, boatman, and would probably outwalk most countrymen in a day's journey. And the relation of body to mind was still finer than we have indicated. He said he wanted every stride his legs made. The length of his walk uniformly made the length of his writing. If shut up in the house he did not write at all.

He had a strong common sense, like that which Rose Flammock the weaver's daughter in Scott's romance commends in her father, as resembling a yardstick, which, whilst it measures dowlas and diaper, can equally well measure tapestry and cloth of gold. He had always a new resource. When I was planting forest trees, and had procured half a peck of acorns, he said that only a small portion of them would be sound, and proceeded to examine them and select the sound ones. But finding this took time, he said, "I think if you put them all into water the good ones will sink"; which experiment we tried with success. He could plan a garden or a house or a barn; would have been competent to lead a "Pacific Exploring Expedition"; could give judicious counsel in the gravest private or public affairs.

He lived for the day, not cumbered and mortified by his memory. If he brought you yesterday a new proposition, he would bring you today another not less revolutionary. A very industrious man, and setting, like all highly organized men, a high value on his time, he seemed the only man of leisure in town, always ready for any excursion that promised well, or for conversation prolonged into late hours. His trenchant sense was never stopped by his rules of daily prudence, but was always up to the new occasion. He liked and used the simplest food, yet, when some one urged a vegetable diet, Thoreau thought all diets a very small matter, saying that "the man who shoots the buffalo lives better than the man who boards at the Graham House." He said, "You can sleep near the railroad, and never be disturbed: Nature knows very well what sounds are worth attending to, and has made up her mind not to hear the railroad whistle. But things respect the devout mind, and a mental ecstasy was never interrupted." He noted what repeatedly befell him, that, after receiving from a distance a rare plant, he would presently find the same in his own haunts. And those pieces of luck which happen only to good players happened to him. One day, walking with a stranger, who inquired where Indian arrowheads could be found, he replied, "Everywhere," and, stooping forward, picked one on the instant from the ground. At Mount Washington, in Tuckerman's Ravine, Thoreau had a bad fall, and sprained his foot. As he was in the act of getting up from his fall, he saw for the first time the leaves of the *Arnica mollis*.

His robust common sense, armed with stout hands, keen perceptions and strong will, cannot yet account for the superiority which shone in his simple and hidden life. I must add the cardinal fact, that there was an excellent wisdom in him, proper to a rare class of men, which showed him the material world as a means and symbol. This discovery, which sometimes yields to poets a certain casual and interrupted light, serving for the ornament of their writing, was in him an unsleeping insight; and whatever faults or obstructions of temperament might cloud it, he was not disobedient to the heavenly vision. In his youth, he said, one day, "The other world is all my art; my pencils will draw no other; my jack-knife will cut nothing else; I do not use it as a means." This was the muse and genius that ruled his opinions, conversation, studies, work and course of life. This made him a searching judge of men. At first glance he measured his companion, and, though insensible to some fine traits of culture, could very well report his weight and calibre. And this made the impression of genius which his conversation sometimes gave.

He understood the matter in hand at a glance, and saw the limitations and poverty of those he talked with, so that nothing seemed concealed from such terrible eyes. I have repeatedly known young men of sensibility converted in a moment to the belief that this was the man they were in search of, the man of men, who could tell them all they should do. His own dealing with them was never affectionate, but superior, didactic, scorning their petty ways—very slowly conceding, or not conceding at all, the promise of his society at their houses, or even at his own. "Would he not walk with them?" "He did not know. There was nothing so important to him as his walk; he had no walks to throw away on company." Visits were offered him from respectful parties, but he declined them. Admiring friends offered to carry him at their own cost to the Yellowstone River—to the West Indies—to South America. But though nothing could be more grave or considered than his refusals, they remind one, in quite new relations, of that fop Brummel's reply to the gentleman who offered him his carriage in a shower, "But where will *you* ride, then?"—and what accusing silences, and what searching and irresistible speeches, battering down all defenses, his companions can remember!

Mr. Thoreau dedicated his genius with such entire love to the fields, hills and waters of his native town, that he made them known and interesting to all reading Americans, and to people over the sea. The river on whose banks he was born and died he knew from its springs to its confluence with the Merrimack. He had made summer and winter observations on it for many years, and at every hour of the day and night. The result of the recent survey of the Water Commissioners appointed by the State of Massachusetts he had reached by his private experiments, several years earlier. Every fact which occurs in the bed, on the banks, or in the air over it; the fishes, and their spawning and nests, their manners, their food; the shad-flies which fill the air on a certain evening once a year, and which are snapped at by the fishes so ravenously that many of these die of repletion; the conical heaps of small stones on the river-shallows, the huge nests of small fishes, one of which will sometimes overfill a cart; the birds which frequent the stream, heron, duck, sheldrake, loon, osprey; the snake, muskrat, otter, woodchuck and fox, on the banks; the turtle, frog, hyla and cricket, which make the banks vocal—were all known to him, and, as it were, townsmen and fellow creatures; so that he felt an absurdity or violence in any narrative of one of these by itself apart, and still more of its dimensions on an inch-rule, or in the exhibition of its skeleton, or the specimen of a squirrel or a bird in brandy. He liked to speak of the manners of the river, as itself a lawful creature, yet with exactness, and always to an observed fact. As he knew the river, so the ponds in this region.

One of the weapons he used, more important to him than microscope or alcohol-receiver to other investigators, was a whim which grew on him by indulgence, yet appeared in gravest statement, namely, of extolling his own town and neighborhood as the most favored center for natural observation. He remarked that the flora of Massachusetts embraced almost all the important plants of America—most of the oaks, most of the willows, the best pines, the ash, the maple, the beach, the nuts. He returned Kane's *Arctic Voyage* to a friend of whom he had borrowed it, with the remark, that "Most of the phenomena noted might be observed in Concord." He seemed a little envious of the Pole, for the coincident sunrise and sunset, or five minutes' day after six months: a splendid fact, which Annursnuc had never afforded him. He found red snow in one of his walks, and told me that he expected to find yet the *Victoria regia* in Concord. He was the attorney of the indigenous plants, and owned to a preference of the weeds to the imported plants as of the Indian to the civilized man, and noticed, with pleasure, that the willow bean-poles of his neighbor had grown more than his beans.

"See these weeds," he said, "which have been hoed at by a million farmers all spring and summer, and yet have prevailed, and just now come out triumphant over all lanes, pastures, fields and gardens, such is their vigor. We have insulted them with low names, too—as Pigweed, Wormwood, Chickweed, Shad-blossom." He says, "They have brave names, too—Ambrosia, Stellaria, Amelanchier, Amaranth, etc."

I think his fancy for referring everything to the meridian of Concord did not grow out of any ignorance or depreciation of other longitudes or latitudes, but was rather a playful expression of his conviction of the indifferency of all places, and that the best place for each is where he stands. He expressed it once in this wise: "I think nothing is to be hoped from you, if this bit of mold under your feet is not sweeter to you to eat than any other in this world, or in any world."

The other weapon with which he conquered all obstacles in science was patience. He knew how to sit immovable, a part of the rock he rested on, until the bird, the reptile, the fish, which had retired from him, should come back and resume its habits, nay, moved by curiosity, should come to him and watch him.

It was a pleasure and a privilege to walk with him. He knew the country like a fox or a bird, and passed through it as freely by paths of his own. He knew every track in the snow or on the ground, and what creature had taken this path before him. One must submit abjectly to such a guide, and the reward was great. Under his arm he carried an old music-book to press plants; in his pocket, his diary and pencil, a spy-glass for birds, microscope, jack-knife, and twine. He wore a straw hat, stout shoes, strong gray trousers, to brave scrub-oaks and smilax, and to climb a tree for a hawk's or a squirrel's nest. He waded into the pool for the waterplants, and his strong legs were no insignificant part of his armor. On the day I speak of he looked for the *Menyanthes*, detected it across the wide pool, and, on examination of the florets, decided that it had been in flower five days. He drew out of his breast-pocket his diary, and read the names of all the plants that should bloom on this day, whereof he kept account as a banker when his notes fall due. The *Cypripedium* not due till tomorrow. He thought that, if waked up from a trance, in this swamp, he could tell by the plants what time of the year it was within two days. The redstart was flying about, and presently the fine grosbeaks, whose brilliant scarlet "makes the rash gazer wipe his eye," and whose fine clear note Thoreau compared to that of a tanager which has got rid of its hoarseness. Presently he heard a note which he called that of the night-warbler, a bird he had never identified, had been in search of twelve years, which always, when he saw it, was in the act of diving down into a tree or bush, and which it was vain to seek; the only bird which sings indifferently by night and by day. I told him he must beware of finding and booking it, lest life should have nothing more to show him. He said, "What you seek in vain for, half your life, one day you come full upon, all the family at dinner. You seek it like a dream, and as soon as you find it you become its prey."

His interest in the flower or the bird lay very deep in his mind, was connected with Nature—and the meaning of Nature was never attempted to be defined by him. He would not offer a memoir of his observations to the Natural History Society. "Why should I? To detach the description from its connections in my mind would make it no longer true or valuable to me: and they do not wish what belongs to it." His power of observation seemed to indicate additional senses. He saw as with microscope, heard as with ear-trumpet, and his memory was a photographic register of all he saw and heard. And yet none knew better than he that it is not the fact that imports, but the impression or effect of the fact on your mind. Every fact lay in glory in his mind, a type of the order and beauty of the whole.

His determination on Natural History was organic. He confessed that he sometimes felt like a hound or a panther, and, if born among Indians, would have been a fell hunter. But, restrained by his Massachusetts culture, he played out the game in this mild form of botany and ichthyology. His intimacy with animals suggested what Thomas Fuller records of Butler the apiologist, that "either he had told the bees things or the bees had told him." Snakes coiled round his leg; the fishes swam into his hand, and he took them out of the water; he pulled the woodchuck out of its hole by the tail and took the foxes under his protection from the hunters. Our naturalist had perfect magnanimity; he had no secrets: he would carry you to the heron's haunt, or even to his most prized botanical swamp—possibly knowing that you could never find it again, yet willing to take his risks.

No college ever offered him a diploma, or a professor's chair; no academy made him its corresponding secretary, its discoverer, or even its member. Perhaps these learned bodies feared the satire of his presence. Yet so much knowledge of Nature's secret and genius few others possessed; none in a more large and religious synthesis. For not a particle of respect had he to the opinions of any man or body of men, but homage solely to the truth itself; and as he discovered everywhere among doctors some leaning of courtesy, it discredited them. He grew to be revered and admired by his townsmen, who had at first known him only as an oddity. The farmers who employed him as a surveyor soon discovered his rare accuracy and skill, his knowledge of their lands, of trees, of birds, of Indian remains and the like, which enabled him to tell every farmer more than he knew before of his own farm; so that he began to feel a little as if Mr. Thoreau had better rights in his land than he. They felt, too, the superiority of character which addressed all men with a native authority.

Indian relics abound in Concord—arrowheads, stone chisels, pestles, and fragments of pottery; and on the river-bank, large heaps of clam shells and ashes mark spots which the savages frequented. These, and every circumstance touching the Indian, were important in his eyes. His visits to Maine were chiefly for love of the Indian. He had the satisfaction of seeing the manufacture of the bark-canoe, as well as of trying his hand in its management on the rapids. He was inquisitive about the making of the stone arrowhead, and in his last days charged a youth setting out for the Rocky Mountains to find an Indian who could tell him that: "It was well worth a visit to California to learn it." Occasionally, a small party of Penobscot Indians would visit Concord, and pitch their tents for a few weeks in summer on the river-bank. He failed not to make acquaintance with the best of them; though he well knew that asking questions of Indians is like catechizing beavers and rabbits. In his last visit to Maine he had great satisfaction from Joseph Polis, an intelligent Indian of Oldtown, who was his guide for some weeks.

He was equally interested in every natural fact. The depth of his perception found likeness of law throughout Nature, and I know not any genius who so swiftly inferred universal law from the single fact. He was no pedant of a department. His eye was open to beauty, and his ear to music. He found these, not in rare conditions, but wheresoever he went. He thought the best of music was in single strains; and he found poetic suggestion in the humming of the telegraph-wire.

His poetry might be bad or good; he no doubt wanted a lyric facility and technical skill, but he had the source of poetry in his spiritual perception. He was a good reader and critic, and his judgment on poetry was to the ground of it. He could not be deceived as to the presence or absence of the poetic element in any composition, and his thirst for this made him negligent and per-

haps scornful of superficial graces. He would pass by
many delicate rhythms, but he would have detected
every live stanza or line in a volume, and knew very well
where to find an equal poetic charm in prose. He was so
enamored of the spiritual beauty that he held all actual
written poems in very light esteem in the comparison.
He admired Æschylus and Pindar; but, when someone
was commending them, he said that Æschylus and the
Greeks, in describing Apollo and Orpheus, had given
no song, or no good one. "They ought not to have
moved trees, but to have chanted to the gods such a
hymn as would have sung all their old ideas out of
their heads, and new ones in." His own verses are often
rude and defective. The gold does not yet run pure, is
drossy and crude. The thyme and marjoram are not yet
honey. But if he want lyric fineness and technical merits,
if he have not the poetic temperament, he never lacks
the causal thought, showing that his genius was better
than his talent. He knew the worth of the Imagination
for the uplifting and consolation of human life, and
liked to throw every thought into a symbol. The fact you
tell is of no value, but only the impression. For this reason his presence was poetic, always piqued the curiosity
to know more deeply the secrets of his mind. He had
many reserves, an unwillingness to exhibit to profane
eyes what was still sacred in his own, and knew well
how to throw a poetic veil over his experience. All
readers of *Walden* will remember his mythical record of
his disappointments—

"I long ago lost a hound, a bay horse and a turtle-
dove, and am still on their trail. Many are the travelers
I have spoken concerning them, describing their tracks,
and what calls they answered to. I have met one or two
who have heard the hound, and the tramp of the horse,

and even seen the dove disappear behind a cloud; and they seemed as anxious to recover them as if they had lost them themselves." [1]

His riddles were worth the reading, and I confide that if at any time I do not understand the expression, it is yet just. Such was the wealth of his truth that it was not worth his while to use words in vain. His poem entitled "Sympathy" reveals the tenderness under that triple steel of stoicism, and the intellectual subtility it could animate. His classic poem on "Smoke" suggests Simonides, but is better than any poem of Simonides. His biography is in his verses. His habitual thought makes all his poetry a hymn to the Cause of causes, the Spirit which vivifies and controls his own—

> I hearing get, who had but ears,
> And sight, who had but eyes before;
> I moments live, who lived but years,
> And truth discern, who knew but learning's lore.

And still more in these religious lines—

> Now chiefly is my natal hour,
> And only now my prime of life;
> I will not doubt the love untold,
> Which not my worth nor want have bought,
> Which wooed me young, and wooes me old,
> And to this evening hath me brought.

Whilst he used in his writings a certain petulance of remark in reference to churches or churchmen, he was a person of a rare, tender and absolute religion, a person incapable of any profanation, by act or by thought. Of course, the same isolation which belonged to his original thinking and living detached him from the social religious forms. This is neither to be censured nor re-

---

[1] *Walden:* p. 20.

gretted. Aristotle long ago explained it, when he said, "One who surpasses his fellow-citizens in virtue is no longer a part of the city. Their law is not for him, since he is a law to himself."

Thoreau was sincerity itself, and might fortify the convictions of prophets in the ethical laws by his holy living. It was an affirmative experience which refused to be set aside. A truth-speaker he, capable of the most deep and strict conversation; a physician to the wounds of any soul; a friend, knowing not only the secret of friendship, but almost worshipped by those few persons who resorted to him as their confessor and prophet, and knew the deep value of his mind and great heart. He thought that without religion or devotion of some kind nothing great was ever accomplished: and he thought that the bigoted sectarian had better bear this in mind.

His virtues, of course, sometimes ran into extremes. It was easy to trace to the inexorable demand on all for exact truth that austerity which made this willing hermit more solitary even than he wished. Himself of a perfect probity, he required not less of others. He had a disgust at crime, and no worldly success would cover it. He detected paltering as readily in dignified and prosperous persons as in beggars, and with equal scorn. Such dangerous frankness was in his dealing that his admirers called him "that terrible Thoreau," as if he spoke when silent, and was still present when he had departed. I think the severity of his ideal interfered to deprive him of a healthy sufficiency of human society.

The habit of a realist to find things the reverse of their appearance inclined him to put every statement in a paradox. A certain habit of antagonism defaced his earlier writings—a trick of rhetoric not quite outgrown in his later, of substituting for the obvious word and thought its diametrical opposite. He praised wild mountains and winter forests for their domestic air, in snow and ice he would find sultriness, and commended the wilderness for resembling Rome and Paris. "It was so dry, that you might call it wet."

The tendency to magnify the moment, to read all the laws of Nature in the one object or one combination under your eye, is of course comic to those who do not share the philosopher's perception of identity. To him there was no such thing as size. The pond was a small ocean; the Atlantic, a large Walden Pond. He referred every minute fact to cosmical laws. Though he meant to be just, he seemed haunted by a certain chronic assumption that the science of the day pretended completeness, and he had just found out that the *savants* had neglected to discriminate a particular botanical variety, had failed to describe the seeds or count the sepals. "That is to say," we replied, "the blockheads were not born in Concord; but who said they were? It was their unspeakable misfortune to be born in London, or Paris, or Rome; but, poor fellows, they did what they could, considering that they never saw Bateman's Pond, or Nine-Acre Corner, or Becky Stow's Swamp; besides, what were you sent into the world for, but to add this observation?"

Had his genius been only contemplative, he had been fitted to his life, but with his energy and practical ability he seemed born for great enterprise and for command; and I so much regret the loss of his rare powers of action, that I cannot help counting it a fault in him that he had no ambition. Wanting this, instead of engineering for all America, he was the captain of a huckleberry-party. Pounding beans is good to the end of pounding empires one of these days; but if, at the end of years, it is still only beans!

But these foibles, real or apparent, were fast vanishing in the incessant growth of a spirit so robust and wise, and which effaced its defeats with new triumphs. His study of Nature was a perpetual ornament to him, and inspired his friends with curiosity to see the world through his eyes, and to hear his adventures. They possessed every kind of interest.

He had many elegancies of his own, whilst he scoffed at conventional elegance. Thus, he could not bear to hear the sound of his own steps, the grit of gravel; and therefore never willingly walked in the road, but in the grass, on mountains and in woods. His senses were acute, and he remarked that by night every dwelling-house gives out bad air, like a slaughter-house. He liked the pure fragrance of melilot. He honored certain plants with special regard, and, over all, the pond-lily; then, the gentian, and the *Mikania scandens,* and "life-ever-lasting," and a bass-tree which he visited every year when it bloomed, in the middle of July. He thought the scent a more oracular inquisition than the sight—more oracular and trustworthy. The scent, of course, reveals what is concealed from the other senses. By it he detected earthiness. He delighted in echoes, and said they were almost the only kind of kindred voices that he heard. He loved Nature so well, was so happy in her solitude, that he became very jealous of cities and the sad work which their refinements and artifices made with man and his dwelling. The ax was always destroying his forest. "Thank God," he said, "they cannot cut down the clouds!" "All kinds of figures are drawn on the blue ground with this fibrous white paint."

I subjoin a few sentences taken from his unpublished manuscripts, not only as records of his thought and feeling, but for their power of description and literary excellence—

Some circumstantial evidence is very strong, as when you find a trout in the milk.

The chub is a soft fish, and tastes like boiled brown paper salted.

The youth gets together his materials to build a bridge to the moon, or, perchance, a palace or temple on the earth, and, at length the middle-aged man concludes to build a wood-shed with them.

The locust z-ing.

Devil's-needles zigzagging along the Nut-Meadow brook.

Sugar is not so sweet to the palate as sound to the healthy ear.

I put on some hemlock-boughs, and the rich salt crackling of their leaves was like mustard to the ear, the crackling of uncountable regiments. Dead trees love the fire.

The bluebird carries the sky on his back.

The tanager flies through the green foliage as if it would ignite the leaves.

If I wish for a horse-hair for my compass-sight I must go to the stable; but the hair-bird, with her sharp eyes, goes to the road.

Immortal water, alive even to the superficies.

Fire is the most tolerable third party.

Nature made ferns for pure leaves, to show what she could do in that line.

No tree has so fair a bole and so handsome an instep as the beech.

How did these beautiful rainbow-tints get into the shell of the fresh-water clam, buried in the mud at the bottom of our dark river?

Hard are the times when the infant's shoes are second-foot.

We are strictly confined to our men to whom we give liberty.

Nothing is so much to be feared as fear. Atheism may comparatively be popular with God himself.

Of what significance the things you can forget? A little thought is sexton to all the world.

How can we expect a harvest of thought who have not had a seed-time of character?

Only he can be trusted with gifts who can present a face of bronze to expectations.

I ask to be melted. You can only ask of the metals that they be tender to the fire that melts them. To nought else can they be tender.

There is a flower known to botanists, one of the same genus with our summer plant called "Life-Everlasting," a *Gnaphalium* like that, which grows on the most inaccessible cliffs of the Tyrolese mountains, where the chamois dare hardly venture, and which the hunter, tempted by its beauty, and by his love (for it is immensely valued by the Swiss maidens), climbs the cliffs to gather, and is sometimes found dead at the foot, with the flower in his hand. It is called by botanists the *Gnaphalium leontopodium*, but by the Swiss *Edelweisse*, which signifies *Noble Purity*. Thoreau seemed to me living in the hope to gather this plant, which belonged to him of right. The scale on which his studies proceeded was so large as to require longevity, and we were the less prepared for his sudden disappearance. The country knows not yet, or in the least part, how great a son it has lost. It seems an injury that he should leave in the midst his broken task which none else can finish, a kind of indignity to so noble a soul that he should depart out of Nature before yet he has been really shown to his peers for what he is. But he, at least, is content. His soul was made for the noblest society; he had in a short life exhausted the capabilities of this world; wherever there is knowledge, wherever there is virtue, wherever there is beauty, he will find a home.

CARLYLE

THOMAS CARLYLE is an immense talker, as extrordinary in his conversation as in his writing—I think even more so.

He is not mainly a scholar, like the most of my acquaintances, but a practical Scotchman, such as you would find in any saddler's or iron-dealer's shop, and then only accidentally and by a surprising addition, the admirable scholar and writer he is. If you would know precisely how he talks, just suppose Hugh Whelan (the gardener) had found leisure enough in addition to all his daily work to read Plato and Shakespeare, Augustine and Calvin, and, remaining Hugh Whelan all the time, should talk scornfully of all this nonsense of books that he had been bothered with, and you shall have just the tone and talk and laughter of Carlyle. I called him a trip-hammer with "an Æolian attachment." He has, too, the strong religious tinge you sometimes find in burly people. That, and all his qualities, have a certain virulence, coupled though it be in his case with the utmost impatience of Christendom and Jewdom and all existing presentments of the good old story. He talks like a very unhappy man—profoundly solitary, displeased and hindered by all men and things about him, and, biding his time, meditating how to undermine and explode the whole world of nonsense which torments him. He is obviously greatly respected by all sorts of people, understands his own value quite as well as Webster, of whom his behavior sometimes reminds me, and can see society on his own terms.

And, though no mortal in America could pretend to talk with Carlyle, who is also as remarkable in England as the Tower of London, yet neither would he in any manner satisfy us (Americans), or begin to answer the questions which we ask. He is a very national figure, and would by no means bear transplantation. They keep Carlyle as a sort of portable cathedral-bell, which they like to produce in companies where he is unknown, and set aswinging, to the surprise and consternation of all persons—bishops, courtiers, scholars, writers—and, as in companies here (in England) no man is named or introduced, great is the effect and great the inquiry. Forster of Rawdon described to me a dinner at the *table d'hôte* of some provincial hotel where he carried Carlyle, and where an Irish canon had uttered something. Carlyle began to talk, first to the waiters, and then to the walls, and then, lastly, unmistakably to the priest, in a manner that frightened the whole company.

Young men, especially those holding liberal opinions, press to see him, but it strikes me like being hot to see the mathematical or Greek professor before they have got their lesson. It needs something more than a clean shirt and reading German to visit him. He treats them with contempt; they profess freedom and he stands for slavery; they praise republics and he likes the Russian Czar; they admire Cobden and free trade and he is a protectionist in political economy; they will eat vegetables and drink water, and he is a Scotchman who thinks English national character has a pure enthusiasm for beef and mutton—describes with gusto the crowds of people who gaze at the sirloins in the dealer's shopwindow, and even likes the Scotch night-cap; they praise moral suasion, he goes for murder, money, capital punishment, and other pretty abominations of English law. They wish freedom of the press, and he thinks the first thing he would do, if he got into Parliament, would be to turn out the reporters, and stop all manner of mischievous speaking to Buncombe, and wind-bags. "In the Long Parliament," he says, "the only great Parliament, they sat secret and silent, grave as an ecumenical council, and I know not what they would have done to anybody that had got in there and attempted to tell out-of-doors what they did." They go for free institutions, for letting things alone, and only giving opportunity and motive to every man; he for a stringent government, that shows people what they must do, and makes them do it. "Here," he says, "the Parliament gathers up six millions of pounds every year to give to the poor, and yet the people starve. I think if they would give it to me, to provide the poor with labor, and with authority to make them work or shoot them—and I to be hanged if I did not do it—I could find them in plenty of Indian meal."

He throws himself readily on the other side. If you urge free trade, he remembers that every laborer is a monopolist. The navigation laws of England made its commerce. "St. John was insulted by the Dutch; he came home, got the law passed that foreign vessels should pay high fees, and it cut the throat of the Dutch, and made the English trade." If you boast of the growth of the country, and show him the wonderful results of the census, he finds nothing so depressing as the sight of a great mob. He saw once, as he told me, three or four miles of human beings, and fancied that "the airth was some great cheese, and these were mites." If a Tory takes heart at his hatred of stump-oratory and model republics, he replies, "Yes, the idea of a pig-headed soldier who will obey orders, and fire on his own father at the command of his officer, is a great comfort to the aristocratic mind." It is not so much that Carlyle cares for this or that dogma, as that he likes genuineness (the source of all strength) in his companions.

If a scholar goes into a camp of lumbermen or a gang of riggers, those men will quickly detect any fault of character. Nothing will pass with them but what is real and sound. So this man is a hammer that crushes mediocrity and pretension. He detects weakness on the instant, and touches it. He has a vivacious, aggressive temperament, and unimpressionable. The literary, the fashionable, the political man, each fresh from triumphs in his own sphere, comes eagerly to see this man, whose fun they have heartily enjoyed, sure of a welcome, and are struck with despair at the first onset. His firm, victorious, scoffing vituperation strikes them with chill and hesitation. His talk often reminds you of what was said of Johnson: "If his pistol missed fire he would knock you down with the butt-end."

Mere intellectual partisanship wearies him; he detects in an instant if a man stands for any cause to which he is not born and organically committed. A natural defender of anything, a lover who will live and die for that which he speaks for, and who does not care for him or for anything but his own business, he respects; and the nobler this object, of course, the better. He hates a literary trifler, and if, after Guizot had been a tool of Louis Philippe for years, he is now to come and write essays on the character of Washington, on *The Beautiful,* and on *Philosophy of History,* he thinks that nothing.

Great is his reverence for realities—for all such traits as spring from the intrinsic nature of the actor. He humors this into the idolatry of strength. A strong nature has a charm for him, previous, it would seem, to all inquiry whether the force be divine or diabolic. He preaches, as by cannonade, the doctrine that every noble nature was made by God, and contains, if savage passions, also fit checks and grand impulses, and, however extravagant, will keep its orbit and return from far.

Nor can that decorum which is the idol of the Englishman, and in attaining which the Englishman exceeds all nations, win from him any obeisance. He is eaten up with indignation against such as desire to make a fair show in the flesh.

Combined with this warfare on respectabilities, and, indeed, pointing all his satire, is the severity of his moral sentiment. In proportion to the peals of laughter amid which he strips the plumes of a pretender and shows the lean hypocrisy to every vantage of ridicule, does he worship whatever enthusiasm, fortitude, love, or other sign of a good nature is in a man.

There is nothing deeper in his constitution than his humor, than the considerate, condescending good-nature with which he looks at every object in existence, as a man might look at a mouse. He feels that the perfection of health is sportiveness, and will not look grave even at dullness or tragedy.

His guiding genius is his moral sense, his perception of the sole importance of truth and justice; but that is a truth of character, not of catechisms. He says, "There is properly no religion in England. These idle nobles at Tattersall's—there is no work or word of serious purpose in them; they have this great lying Church; and life is a humbug." He prefers Cambridge to Oxford, but he thinks Oxford and Cambridge education indurates the young men, as the Styx hardened Achilles, so that when they come forth of them, they say, "Now we are proof;

we have gone through all the degrees, and are case-hardened against the veracities of the Universe; nor man nor God can penetrate us."

Wellington he respects as real and honest, and as having made up his mind, once for all, that he will not have to do with any kind of a lie. Edwin Chadwick is one of his heroes—who proposes to provide every house in London with pure water, sixty gallons to every head, at a penny a week; and in the decay and downfall of all religions, Carlyle thinks that the only religious act which a man nowadays can securely perform is to wash himself well.

Of course the new French revolution of 1848 was the best thing he had seen, and the teaching this great swindler, Louis Philippe, that there is a God's justice in the Universe, after all, was a great satisfaction. Czar Nicholas was his hero; for in the ignominy of Europe, when all thrones fell like card-houses, and no man was found with conscience enough to fire a gun for his crown, but everyone ran away in a *coucou,* with his head shaved, through the Barrière de Passy, one man remained who believed he was put there by God Almighty to govern his empire, and, by the help of God, had resolved to stand there.

He was very serious about the bad times; he had seen this evil coming, but thought it would not come in his time. But now 'tis coming, and the only good he sees in it is the visible appearance of the gods. He thinks it the only question for wise men, instead of art and fine fancies and poetry and such things, to address themselves to the problem of society. This confusion is the inevitable end of such falsehoods and nonsense as they have been embroiled with.

Carlyle has, best of all men in England, kept the manly attitude in his time. He has stood for scholars, asking no scholar what he should say. Holding an honored place in the best society, he has stood for the people, for the Chartist, for the pauper, intrepidly and scornfully teaching the nobles their peremptory duties.

His errors of opinion are as nothing in comparison with this merit, in my judgment. This *aplomb* cannot be mimicked; it is the speaking to the heart of the thing. And in England, where the *morgue* of aristocracy has very slowly admitted scholars into society—a very few houses only in the high circles being ever opened to them—he has carried himself erect, made himself a power confessed by all men, and taught scholars their lofty duty. He never feared the face of man.

ROBERT BURNS

Speech at the Celebration of the Burns Centenary,
Boston, January 25, 1859.

M R. PRESIDENT and Gentlemen: I do not know by what untoward accident it has chanced, and I forbear to inquire, that, in this accomplished circle, it should fall to me, the worst Scotsman of all, to receive your commands, and at the latest hour too, to respond to the sentiment just offered, and which indeed makes the occasion. But I am told there is no appeal, and I must trust to the inspirations of the theme to make a fitness which does not otherwise exist. Yet, Sir, I heartily feel the singular claims of the occasion. At the first announcement, from I know not whence, that the 25th of January was the hundredth anniversary of the birth of Robert Burns, a sudden consent warmed the great English race, in all its kingdoms, colonies and States, all over the world, to keep the festival. We are here to hold our parliament with love and poesy, as men were wont to do in the Middle Ages. Those famous parliaments might or might not have had more stateliness and better singers than we—though that is yet to be known—but they could not have better reason. I can only explain this singular unanimity in a race which rarely acts together, but rather after their watchword, Each for himself—by the fact that Robert Burns, the poet of the middle class, represents in the mind of men today that great uprising of the middle class against the armed and privileged minorities, that uprising which worked politically in the American and French Revolutions, and which, not in governments so much as in education and social order, has changed the face of the world.

In order for this destiny, his birth, breeding and fortunes were low. His organic sentiment was absolute independence, and resting as it should on a life of labor. No man existed who could look down on him. They that looked into his eyes saw that they might look down the sky as easily. His muse and teaching was common-sense, joyful, aggressive, irresistible. Not Latimer, not Luther struck more telling blows against false theology than did this brave singer. The Confession of Augsburg, the Declaration of Independence, the French Rights of Man, and the *Marseillaise*, are not more weighty documents in the history of freedom than the songs of Burns. His satire has lost none of its edge. His musical arrows yet sing through the air. He is so substantially a reformer that I find his grand plain sense in close chain with the greatest masters—Rabelais, Shakespeare in comedy, Cervantes, Butler, and Burns. If I should add another name, I find it only in a living countryman of Burns.

He is an exceptional genius. The people who care nothing for literature and poetry care for Burns. It was indifferent—they thought who saw him—whether he wrote verse or not: he could have done anything else as well. Yet how true a poet is he! And the poet, too, of poor men, of gray hodden and the guernsey coat and the blouse. He has given voice to all the experiences of common life; he has endeared the farmhouse and cottage, patches and poverty, beans and barley; ale, the poor man's wine; hardship; the fear of debt; the dear society of weans and wife, of brothers and sisters, proud of each other, knowing so few and finding amends for want and obscurity in books and thoughts. What a love of nature, and, shall I say it? of middle-class nature. Not like Goethe, in the stars, or like Byron, in the ocean, or Moore, in the luxurious East, but in the homely landscape which the poor see around them—bleak leagues of pasture and stubble, ice and sleet and rain and snow-choked brooks; birds, hares, field-mice, thistles and heather, which he daily knew. How many "Bonny Doons" and "John Anderson my Jo's" and "Auld lang Synes" all around the earth have his verses been applied to! And his love songs still woo and melt the youths and maids; the farm-work, the country holiday, the fishing-cobble, are still his debtors today.

And as he was thus the poet of the poor, anxious, cheerful, working humanity, so had he the language of low life. He grew up in a rural district, speaking a *patois* unintelligible to all but natives, and he has made the Lowland Scotch a Doric dialect of fame. It is the only example in history of a language made classic by the genius of a single man. But more than this. He had that secret of genius to draw from the bottom of society the strength of its speech, and astonish the ears of the polite with these artless words, better than art, and filtered of all offence through his beauty. It seemed odious to Luther that the devil should have all the best tunes; he would bring them into the churches; and Burns knew how to take from fairs and gipsies, black-smiths and drovers, the speech of the market and street, and clothe it with melody. But I am detaining you too long. The memory of Burns—I am afraid heaven and earth have taken too good care of it to leave us any-thing to say. The west winds are murmuring it. Open the windows behind you, and hearken for the incom-ing tide, what the waves say of it. The doves perching always on the eaves of the Stone Chapel opposite, may know something about it. Every name in broad Scot-land keeps his fame bright. The memory of Burns— every man's, every boy's and girl's head carries snatches of his songs, and they say them by heart, and, what is strangest of all, never learned them from a book, but from mouth to mouth. The wind whispers them, the birds whistle them, the corn, barley, and bulrushes hoarsely rustle them, nay, the music-boxes at Geneva are framed and toothed to play them; the hand-organs of the Savoyards in all cities repeat them, and the chimes of bells ring them in the spires. They are the property and the solace of mankind.

Journals

Journals

EDITOR'S NOTE

T HE following selection from Emerson's *Journals* is
single and continuous—a section of the famous
work, and not a collection of its best sayings of context. To collect its nuggets is one good way to represent
it, but it is not the only way, and in any case that has
been done: by Bliss Perry, in a volume called *The Heart
of Emerson's Journals*. It was assumed that readers of
the present volume might like to see a solid piece of the
Journals as published in 1909-1914. The piece settled
upon is from the year 1856, when Emerson lectured in
the West, walked in Concord with Thoreau, and wrote
his poem "Brahma." He did still other things, of course:
he read, he reflected, he remembered. And above all he
wrote; for it was in this endless book that he lived as a
writer. "Brahma" is here as, presumably, he first set it
down; but so are passages of prose which were to find
their way into books with titles. The original editors of
the *Journals*, Edward Waldo Emerson and Waldo Emerson Forbes, in most such cases omitted the passages and
cited the titles in footnotes. Their footnotes have been
reprinted with a few exceptions.

It will be observed that Emerson felt differently about
Thoreau on different days, as any man does about anything. Emerson's opinion of Goethe ran a similar course,
from tones of the highest praise to a sour note on the
third volume of the *Autobiography*, whose author
"seems to know altogether too much about himself." His
opinion of himself went radically up and down; in the

early years it was often down, for he found it easy to doubt his powers and his virtues. Daniel Webster comes in and out of favor over decades of speculation concerning the figure he cut. But this is only to say that Emerson was consistent in his view of the *Journals* as a place wherein to expose its author to himself. "Life consists in what a man is thinking of all day." Here is the record of his thought—and of his reading. Anything at all can turn up in these pages. The dream he had last night, a letter he wrote to his Aunt Mary, a sudden memory of Ellen Tucker, his first wife who lived so short a while, a shrewd thing some neighbor said this morning, a paragraph on Plato, a discourse on pantheism, an analysis of someone's character—anything at all may be here, in a great work whose fascination has never yet, in spite of many attempts to do so, been adequately stated. Its final distinction is the grand way it is written: for Emerson alone, since it is his private book, but also for strangers, for imaginary people who want things written well. Good writing is for strangers, and the good writer respects them. The *Journals* are improvised, but they are not slovenly. They are the best a fine writer could do.

JOURNALS

(from RO)

January 1, 1856.

IN DIXON I talked with Mr. Dixon, the pioneer founder of the city. His full-length portrait was hanging in the Town Hall where we were. He is eighty years old and a great favorite with the people. His family have all died, but some grandchildren remain. He, who has made so many rich, is a poor man, which, it seems, is a common fortune here; Sutter, the California discoverer of gold, is poor. It looks as if we must have a talent for misfortune, to miss so many opportunities, as these men who have owned the whole township and not saved a competence. He is a correct, quiet man; was first a tailor, then a stage owner, and mail agent, etc.

I went down the Galena River, once Bean River, Fève, then Fever, now Galena River, four or five miles in a sleigh, with Mr. McMasters to the "Marsden Lead," so called, a valuable lead-mine, and went into it. Marsden, it seems, was a poor farmer here, and sold out his place and went to California; found no gold, and came back, and bought his land again, and, in digging to clear out a spring of water, stumbled on this most valuable "lead" (leed), as they call it, of lead-ore. They can get up 7000 pounds of the ore in a day (by a couple of laborers), and the smelters will come to the spot, and buy the ore at three cents a pound; so that he found California here. He at once called in his brothers, and

divided the mine with them. One of them sold out his
share ("foolishly") for $12,000; the others retain theirs.

Mr. Shetland said seventy-five or a hundred thousand
dollars had already been derived from this mine, and
perhaps as much more remains.

Hon. Mr. Turner, of Freeport, said to me that it is
not usually the first settlers who become rich, but the
second comers. The first, he said, are often visionary
men, the second are practical. The first two settlers of
Rockford died insolvent, and he named similar cases in
other towns; I think Beloit.

An idealist, if he have the sensibilities and habits of
those whom I know, is very ungrateful. He craves and
enjoys every chemical property, and every elemental
force, loves pure air, water, light, caloric, wheat, flesh,
salt, and sugar; the blood coursing in his own veins, and
the grasp of friendly hands; and uses the meat he eats
to preach against matter as malignant, and to praise
mind, which he very hollowly and treacherously serves.
Beware of hypocrisy.

                                    Beloit, January 9.

I fancied in this fierce cold weather—mercury varying from 20° to 30° below zero for the last week—that
Illinois lands would be at a discount, and the agent, who
at Dixon was selling great tracts, would be better advised to keep them for milder days, since a hundred
miles of prairie in such days as these are not worth the
poorest shed or cellar in the towns. But my easy landlord assured me "we had no cold weather in Illinois,
only now and then Indian summer and cool nights." He
looked merrily at his window panes, opaque with a stra-
tum of frost, and said that his was a fashionable first-
class hotel, with window lights of ground glass.

This climate and people are a new test for the wares of a man of letters. All his thin, watery matter freezes; 'tis only the smallest portion of alcohol that remains good. At the lyceum, the stout Illinoisan, after a short trial, walks out of the hall. The Committee tell you that the people want a hearty laugh, and Stark, and Saxe, and Park Benjamin, who give them that, are heard with joy. Well, I think with Governor Reynolds, the people are always right (in a sense), and that the man of letters is to say, These are the new conditions to which I must conform. The architect, who is asked to build a house to go upon the sea, must not build a Parthenon, or a square house, but a ship. And Shakespeare, or Franklin, or Æsop, coming to Illinois, would say, I must give my wisdom a comic form, instead of tragics or elegiacs, and well I know to do it, and he is no master who cannot vary his forms, and carry his own end triumphantly through the most difficult.

Mr. Sweet, a telegraph agent on the Chicago and Rock River line, said he can tell the name of the operator, by the accent of his despatch, by the ear, just as readily as he knows the handwriting of his friends. Every operator has his own manner or accent. An operator usually reads more correctly and quickly by the ear than by the eye. Some good operators never learn to read by the ear. Boys make the best operators, and, in six months, a boy or sixteen was worth $45.00 a month in an office at Chicago. The rule of their experience is never to establish a telegraph line until after a railroad is built. It cannot sooner pay.

At Beloit, on Tuesday night, January eight, the mercury was at 27° and 28° below zero. It has been bitterly cold for a fortnight. A cold night they call *"a singer."*

The hard times of Illinois were from 1837 to 1845 and onward; when pork was worth twelve shillings a hundred, and men journeyed with loads of wheat and pork a hundred miles or more to Chicago, and sold their wheat for twenty-six cents a bushel, and were obliged to sell their team to get home again. Mr. Jenks, a stage agent and livery-stable keeper, told us of his experiences, and when he left Chicago to go eastward, he would not have given $3.00 for a warranty deed of the State of Illinois.

Hoosier meant Southerner. Hoosiers and Yankees would fight for the land. Yankees, when fighting men, would fight by the day; "the Hoosiers are good to begin, but they cave."

Emmons, Esq., of Michigan, said to me that he had said he wished it might be a criminal offence to bring an English lawbook into a court in this country, so foolish and mischievous is our slavery to English precedent.[1] . . .

There are times when the intellect is so active that everything seems to run to meet it. Its supplies are found without much thought as to studies. Knowledge runs to the man, and the man runs to knowledge. In spring, when the snow melts, the maple trees run with sugar, and you cannot get tubs fast enough, but it is only for a few days. The hunter on the prairie at the right season has no need of choosing his ground. East, west, by the river, by the timber, near the farm, from the farm, he is everywhere by his game.

---

[1] The rest is printed in "Power" (Conduct of Life, p. 62).

Here is a road, *Michigan Southern,* which runs
through four sovereign states; a judicial being which
has no judicial sovereign. Ohio, Indiana, Michigan, Illinois franchise has to yield to eminent domain, and the
remedy is appraisal and payment of damages. But unfortunately, when, as now, the Michigan Central is to
be bereaved of its monopoly, which it had bought and
paid for, the jury to appraise the damage done is taken
from the population aggrieved by the Michigan Central.
I asked, why not take a jury from other states?

People here are alive to a benefaction derived from
railroads which is inexpressibly great, and vastly exceeding any intentional philanthropy.[1] . . . My banker here
at Adrian, Mr. L——, is of opinion that, to run on a
bank for gold is a criminal offence, and ought to be
punished by the state's prison! He delights, he frankly
told me, to make such people pay three or four per cent
a month for money.

Seek things in their purity. Well, we try, on each subject we accost, to ascend to principles; to dip our pen in
the blackest of the pot; and to be sure, find the cause of
the trait in some organ, as spleen, or bone, or blood. We
are not nearer; we are still outside. Nature itself is
nothing but a skin, and all these but coarser cuticles. A
god or genius sits regent over every plant and animal,
and causes this, and knits this to that, after an order or
plan which is intellectual. The botanist, the physicist,
is not then the man deepest immersed in nature, as if
he were ready to bear apples or to shoot out four legs,
but one filled with the lightest and purest air, who
sympathizes with the creative spirit, anticipates the tend-

[1] The rest of the passage is printed in "Consideration by the
Way" (*Conduct of Life,* p. 256).

ency, and where the bird will next alight; being himself full of the same tendency.

Hospitality consists in a little fire, a little food, but enough, and an immense quiet. In England, it is a great deal of fine food, and of fire and immense decorum.

When I see the waves of Lake Michigan toss in the bleak snowstorm, I see how small and inadequate the common poet is. But Tennyson, with his eagle over the sea, has shown his sufficiency.

"In the American backwoods there is nothing of those social and artistic enjoyments which ennoble man, whilst they dissatisfy him. What man would live without the poesy of sounds, colors, and rhymes! Unhappy people that is condemned to this privation!"—GERMAN PAPER.

William Little came to church and heard my sermon against minding trifles. He told me had he preached he should have taken the other side. Probably not one hearer besides thought so far on the subject.

The railroads have pretended low fares, and, instead of seventy-five cents, I pay for a passage to Boston from Concord, sixty cents; and the trip costs one hour, instead of two and one-half hours. Well, I have really paid, in the depreciation of my railroad stock, six or seven hundred dollars a year, for the last few years, or, say, a hundred a year, since the roads were built. And I shall be glad to know that I am at the end of my losses on this head.

A writer in the *Boston Transcript* says, that "just in proportion to the morality of a people, will be the expansion of the credit system," which sounds to me like better political economy than I often hear.

Lectures. 1, France; 2, English Civilization; 3, Anglo-American; 4, Stonehenge; 5, The Age; 6, Poetry; 7, Beauty; 8, The Scholar.

For Beauty. Use of gems, in Landor's "Pericles and Aspasia"; in Patmore's "Angel in the House."

They called old France a despotism tempered with epigrams. Wherever the epigrams grow, they are pretty sure to make room for themselves, and temper the despotism. What can you do with a Talleyrand? "Sire, no government has prospered that has resisted me." So in politics with DeRetz; or with Webster. "Where shall I go?" said Webster. There is the Whig Party, and the Democratic Party, and Mr. Webster. It soon appears that the Epigram, or Webster, is a party too. Much more in the courts, where he was really sovereign.

Choate said that, once a candidate for the Presidency, it was impossible to get that *virus* quite out of a man's constitution: as Everett, Webster, Cass, down to Pratt and Mellen.

(From DO)

February 29.

Truth. It is not wise to talk, as men do, of reason as the gift of God bestowed, etc., or, of reasoning from nature up to nature's God, etc. The intellectual power is not the gift, but the presence of God. Nor do we reason to the being of God, but God goes with us into nature, when we go or think at all. Truth is always new and wild as the wild air, and is alive. The mind is always true, when there is mind, and it makes no difference that the premises are false, we arrive at true conclusions.

Mr. Arnold, with whom I talked at New Bedford, saw as much as this, and, when Penn's treacheries were enumerated, replied, "Well, what if he did? it was only Penn who did it." He told of the talking Quaker in Maine who claimed acquaintance with Pyot (?), saying to him, "You know I am your convert." Pyot answered, "Yes, I see thee's my convert, for my Master knows nothing of thee."[1] . . .

Remember the Indian hymn—

God only I perceive, God only I adore.

The Bible will not be ended until the creation is.

If I knew only Thoreau, I should think cooperation of good men impossible. Must we always talk for victory, and never once for truth, for comfort, and joy? Centrality he has, and penetration, strong understanding, and the higher gifts—the insight of the real, or from the real, and the moral rectitude that belongs to it; but all this and all his resources of wit and invention are lost to me, in every experiment, year after year, that I make, to hold intercourse with his mind. Always some weary captious paradox to fight you with, and the time and temper wasted.

---

[1] The first part of this passage, also what follows it, is printed in "Sovereignty of Ethics" (*Lectures and Biographical Sketches,* pp. 195, 196).

I find good sense in the German *Atlantis,* which thinks astronomy overprized, which, at present, is a cold, desert science, too dependent on the mechanic who grinds a lens, and too little on the philosopher. So of chemistry and geology; it finds few deeps in them, no genial universal maxims. The little world of the heart is larger, richer, deeper, than the spaces of astronomy, which take such a row of pompous ciphers to express. And when the same devotion shall be given to ethics and jurisprudence, as now is given to natural science, we shall have ideas and insights and wisdom, instead of numbers and formulas. The most important effect of modern astronomy has been the tapping our theological conceit, and upsetting Calvinism.

I value myself, not when I do what is called the commanding duty of this Monday or Tuesday, but when I leave it to do the duty of a remote day, as, for instance, to write a line, or find a new fact, a missing link, in my essay on "Memory" or on "Imagination."

"Il ne manque à tous les hommes qu'un peu de courage pour être laches," said the Earl of Rochester one day, in a fit of misanthropy.

When the minister presented himself to the North Carolina Unitarian Church Agent to demand his wages for preaching, he asked, "Who sent you here?" "The Lord sent me." "The Lord sent you! I don't believe the Lord knows there is any such man." I have much that feeling about these pretended poets, whom I am sure the Lord of Parnassus knows not of.

Two ways. The most important effect of Copernicus was not on astronomy, but on Calvinism—tapping the conceit of man; and geology introduces new measures of antiquity.

Now and then leaps a word or a fact to light which is no man's invention, but the common instinct. Thus, "all men are born free and equal"—though denied by all politics, is the key-word of our modern civilization.

'Tis strange that Sir John Franklin and his picked men, with all the resources of English art, perished of famine where Esquimaux lived, and found them, and continue to live.

Herschel said, chemistry had made such progress that it would no longer be that men would perish of famine, for sawdust could be made into food. And yet men in Sligo and Cape Verde and New York have been dying of famine ever since. 'Tis answered, yes, you can convert woolen and cotton rags into sugar, but 'tis very expensive; and 'tis like the Duke of Sussex's recommendation, that the poor should eat curry.

'Tis a geographic problem whether the Mississippi, running from the depressed polar zone to the elevated equatorial region, 2500 miles—does it not run uphill?

Manners. If you talk with J. K. Mills, or J. M. Forbes, or any other State Street man, you find that you are talking with all State Street, and if you are impressionable to that force, why, they have great advantage, are very strong men. But if you talk with Thoreau or Newcomb, or Alcott, you talk with only one man; he brings only his own force. But for that very reason (that the conventional requires softness or impressionability to the dear little urbanities in you), if you abound in your own sense, they [i.e., the first] are weak, and soon at your mercy. But the others (those wise hermits), who speak from their thought, speak from the deep heart of men, from a far wide public, the public of all sane and good men, from a broad humanity: and Greek and Syrian, Parthian and Chinese, Cherokee and Kanaka, hear them speaknig in their own tongue.

Mr. Eaton, of Malden, told me, that when Father Taylor was about going to Europe, he heard him preach, and he said, "To be sure, I am sorry to leave my own babes—but He who takes care of every whale, and can give him a ton of herrings for a breakfast, will find food for my babes."

I find it easy to translate all Napoleon's technics into all of mine, and his official advices are to me more literary and philosophical than the *Mémoires* of the Academy. See in *Atlantis* for February, 1856, p. 118, how Carnot translated mechanics into politics.

Sin is when a man trifles with himself, and is untrue to his own constitution.

Everything is the cause of itself.

We have seen Art coming back to Veracity.

Napoleon, from pedantry of old tactics to the making the art of war a piece of common sense. Carlyle, armed with the same realism in his speculation on society and government, red tape, etc.

Nor let the musician think he can be a frivolous person and a parasite; he must be musician throughout, in his vote, in his economy, in his prayer.

Allston said, "His art should make the artist happy."

"A strong nature feels itself brought into the world for its own development, and not for the approbation of the public."—GOETHE.

Here we stand, silent, unknown, dumb as mountains, inspiring curiosity in each other, and what we wish to know is whether there be in you an interior organization as finished and excellent as the body. For if there be, then is there a rider to the horse; then has Nature a lord.[1] Blow the horn at the gate of Egremont Castle, which none but the great Egremont can blow.[2] The outward organization is admirable, the geology, the astronomy, the anatomy, all excellent; but 'tis all a half; and, enlarge it by astronomy never so far, remains a half; it requires a will as perfectly organized: a perfect freedom is the only counterpart to Nature. When that is born, and ripened, and tried—and says, "Here stand I, I cannot otherwise"—Nature surrenders as meekly as the ass on which Jesus rode.[3]

'Tis because the man is by much the larger half; and, though we exaggerate his tools and sciences, yet the moment we face a hero or a sage, the arts and civilizations are *peu de cas*.

There are four sweets in my confectionery—sugar, beauty, freedom, and revenge, said Egyptiacus.

Black star, builders of dungeons in the air.

---

[1] This sentence ends "Country Life" (*Natural History of Intellect*, p. 167).

[2] Referring to Wordsworth's poem.

[3] Part of this passage is found in "Country Life" (pp. 165, 166).

Through Nature's ample range in thought to rove,
And start at man the single mourner there.

—YOUNG.

This passing hour is an edifice,
Which the Omnipotent cannot rebuild.

The Missouri and the Mississippi, after their junction, run forty miles side by side in the same bed before they fully mix. The rate of interest in Illinois runs from ten to forty per cent; in Boston, from five to ten and twelve per cent; yet does not the capital of Boston realize this difference of level and flow down into Illinois. Well, in England and in America there is the widest difference of altitude between the culture of their scholars and that of the Germans, and here are in America a nation of Germans living with the *Organon* of Hegel in their hands, which makes the discoveries and thinking of the English and Americans look of a Chinese narrowness, and yet, good easy dunces that we are, we never suspect our inferiority.

Woman should find in man her guardian. Silently she looks for that, and when she finds, as she instantly does, that he is not, she betakes her to her own defences, and does the best she can. But when he is her guardian, all goes well for both.

Your subject is quite indifferent, if you really speak out. If I met Shakespeare, or Montaigne, or Goethe, I should only aim to understand correctly what they said: they might talk of what they would. When people object to me my topics of England, or France, or natural history, 'tis only that they fear I shall not think on these subjects, but shall consult my ease, and repeat commonplaces. The way to the center is everywhere equally short. "A general has always troops enough, if

he only knows how to employ those he has, and bivou-
acs with them," said Bonaparte. Every breath of air is
the carrier of the universal mind. Thus, for subjects, I
do not know what is more tedious than Dedications, or
pieces of flattery to Grandees. Yet in Hafiz, it would not
do to skip them, since his dare-devil Muse is never better shown.

A practical man is the hobby of the age. Well, when I
read German philosophy, or wrote verses, I was willing
to concede there might be too much of these, and that
the Western pioneer with ax on his shoulder, and still
moving West as the settlements approached him, had
his merits. . . .

On further consideration of this practical quality, by
which our people are proud to be marked, I concede
its excellence; but practice or practicalness consists in
the consequent or logical following out of a good theory.
(See *Atlantis*, February, 1855.) Here are they practical,
i.e., they confound the means with the ends, and lose
the ends thereby out of sight—freedom, worth, and
beauty of life.

Classic and Romantic. The classic art was the art of
necessity: modern romantic art bears the stamp of caprice and chance.[1] . . .

Republics run into romance when they lose sight of
the inner necessity and organism that must be in their
laws, and act from whim.

Wagner made music again classic. Goethe says, "I
call classic the sound, and romantic the sick."

Sainte-Beuve defines classic: *"Un auteur qui a fait
faire un pas de plus, a découvert quelque vérité, qui a*

---

[1] What follows is, in substance, printed in "Art and Criticism"
(*Natural History of Intellect*, pp. 203, 204).

rendu sa pensée dans une forme large et grande, saine et belle en soi," etc. I abridge much. (See *Causeries.*)

Eugène Sue, Dumas, etc., when they begin a story, do not know how it will end; but Walter Scott when he began the *Bride of Lammermoor* had no choice, nor Shakespeare in *Macbeth*.

But Madame George Sand, though she writes fast and miscellaneously, is yet fundamentally classic and necessitated: and I, who tack things strangely enough together, and consult my ease rather than my strength, and often write *on the other side,* am yet an adorer of the *One.*

To be classic, then, *de rigueur,* is the prerogative of a vigorous mind who is able to execute what he conceives.

The classic unfolds: the romantic adds.

The discovery of America is an antique or classic work.

Paris. Of great cities you cannot compute the influences.[1] . . .

April 5.
Walden fired a cannonade yesterday of a hundred guns, but not in honor of the birth of Napoleon.[2]

Aunt Mary said of Talleyrand, that he was not organized for the Future State.

Aunt Mary is jealous of all the newer friends of her friends and cannot bear either X or Y, or the fame of Z.

---

[1] The paragraph is printed in "Boston" (*Natural History of Intellect,* p. 187).

[2] Not for a regiment's parade,
   Nor evil laws or rulers made,
   Blue Walden rolls its cannonade.
   ("May Day," *Poems.*)

She reminds one in these days of an old aristocrat, say Queen Elizabeth shaking the Duchess of —— on her death-bed, or of Sarah of Marlborough, as she walks with her stick to the oyster-shop.

Classic and Romantic. I think I can show that France cleaves to the form, and loses the substance; as, in the famous unities of her drama; and in her poetry itself; in the whole "Classicality" of her turn of mind, which is only apery;

> For France doth ape the lion's shape.

Menander's speech, "that he had finished the comedy, all but the verses," and Burke, who studied the statistics of his speech, but left the illustration and ornament to the impulse of speaking.

Thy voice is sweet, Musketaquid; repeats the music of the rain; but sweeter rivers silent flit through thee, as thou through Concord plain.

Thou art shut in thy banks; but the stream I love, flows in thy water, and flows through rocks and through the air, and through darkness, and through men, and women. I hear and see the inundation and eternal spending of the stream, in winter and in summer, in men and animals, in passion and thought. Happy are they who can hear it.

I see thy brimming, eddying stream, and thy enchantment. For thou changest every rock in thy bed into a gem: all is real opal and agate, and at will thou pavest with diamonds. Take them away from thy stream, and they are poor shards and flints: so is it with me today.[1]

---

[1] The first rhapsody for "The Two Rivers," as it came to mind, sitting by the river, one April day. (See the *Poems*.)

The property proves too much for the man, and now all the men of science, art, intellect, are pretty sure to degenerate into selfish housekeepers dependent on wine, coffee, furnace, gas-light, and furniture. Then things swing the other way, and we suddenly find that civilization crowed too soon; that what we bragged as triumphs were treacheries; that we have opened the wrong door, and let the enemy into the castle; that civilization was a mistake; that nothing is so vulgar as a great warehouse of rooms full of furniture and trumpery; that, in the circumstances, the best wisdom were an auction, or a fire; since the foxes and birds have the right of it, with a warm hole to fend the weather, and no more; that a penthouse, to fend the sun and wind and rain, is the house which makes no tax on the owner's time and thought, and which he can leave when the sun reaches noon.

> What need have I of book or priest?
> And every star is Bethlehem star—
> I have as many as there are
> Yellow flowers in the grass,
> So many saints and saviors,
> So many high behaviors,
> Are there to him
> Who is himself, as thou, alive
> And only sees what he doth give.[1]

Monochord. Aunt Mary cannot sympathize with children. I know several persons whose world is only large enough for one person, and each of them, though he were to be the last man, would, like the executioner in Hood's poem, guillotine the last but one.

Elizabeth Hoar said of Aunt Mary—"She thinks much more of her bonnet and of other people's bonnets than they do"; and she sends Elizabeth from Dan to

---

[1] See the finished verses in *Poems.*

Beersheba to find a bonnet that does not conform; while
Mrs. Hoar, whom she severely taxes with conforming, is
satisfied with anything she finds in the shops. She tram-
ples on the common humanities all day, and they rise as
ghosts and torment her at night.

Kings and Nobles. Tycho Brahe refused (1574) for
a long time to publish his observations upon the remarkable star in Cassiopeia, lest he should thus cast a stain
upon his nobility.

Fame. Copernicus's discoveries "insinuated themselves into ecclesiastical minds by the very reluctance of
their author to bring them into notice."—BREWSTER,
Life of Newton, vol. I, p. 259.

Greatness. To a grand interest a superficial success
is of no account.[1] . . .

States. A man, to get the advantage of the ideal man,
turns himself into several men, by using his eyes today,
when he is loving; and tomorrow, when he is spiteful;
and the third day, when he is merry; and so on; as the
astronomer uses the earth as a cart to carry him to the
two ends of its orbit, to find the parallax of a star.

What a barren-witted pate am I, says the scholar; I
will go see whether I have lost my reason.[2] The right
conditions must be observed. Principally he must have
leave to be himself. We go to dine with M and N and O

---

[1] This passage is printed in "Aristocracy" (*Lectures and Biographical Sketches,* p. 59).
[2] Here follow several passages on unsatisfactory dinner-party conversation which are printed in "Clubs" (*Society and Solitude,* pp.
229, 231, 232).

and P, and, to be sure, they begin to be something else than they were. . . . Keep the ground, feel the roots, domesticate yourself.

I think of Andrews Norton, who did not like toasts and sentiments because they interfered with the hilarity of the occasion. . . . What kind of a pump is that which cannot draw, but only deliver?

I think the Germans have an integrity of mind which sets their science above all other. They have not this science in scraps, this science on stilts. They have posed certain philosophical facts on which all is built, the doctrine of *immanence*, as it is called, by which everything is the cause of itself, or stands there for its own, and repeats in its own all other; "the ground of everything is immanent in that thing." Everything is organic, freedom also, not to add, but to grow and unfold.

They purify, they sweeten, they warm and ennoble, by seeing the heart to be indispensable, not in scraps, not on stilts.

In music, it was once the doctrine, The text is nothing, the score is all; and even, the worse text, the better the score; but Wagner said the text must be fixed to the score and from the first; must be inspired with the score.

So in chemistry, Mülder said—For a good chemist, the first condition is, he shall know nothing of philosophy; but Oersted and Humboldt saw and said that chemistry must be the handmaid of moral science. Do you not see how Nature avenges herself of the pedantry? The wits excluded from the academies met in clubs and threw the academy into the shade.

I know a song which, though it be sung never so loud, few can hear—only six or seven or eight persons: yet they who hear it become young again. When it is sung, the stars twinkle gladly, and the moon bends nearer the earth.

Wafthrudnir. The horse taught me something, the titmouse whispered a secret in my ear, and the Lespedeza looked at me, as I passed. Will the Academicians, in their "Annual Report," please tell me what they said?

I know a song which is more hurtful than strychnine or the kiss of the asp. It blasts those who hear it, changes their color and shape, and dissipates their substance. It is called Time.

> Yet they who hear it shed their age
> And take their youth again.

Whipple said of the author of *Leaves of Grass,* that he had every leaf but the fig leaf.

April 26.

The audience that assembled to hear my lectures in these six weeks was called "the *effete* of Boston."

As Linnæus delighted in finding that seven-stamened flower which alone gave him a seventh class, or filled a gap in his system, so I know a man who served as intermediate between two acquaintances of mine, not else to be approximated.

"I can well wait," said Elizabeth Hoar, "all winter, if sure to blossom, an apple tree, in spring; but not, if, perhaps, I am dead wood, and ought to burn now."

Subject for lecture is, the art of taking a walk. I would not ask Ellery Channing, like the little girl, "Mamma wishes, Sir, you would begin to be funny." Indeed, quite the reverse: for his written fun is very bad; and as to his serious letter, the very best, that to Ward in Europe, is unreproducible. Would you bottle the efflux of a June noon, and sell it in your shop? But if he could be engaged again into kindly letters, he has that which none else could give. But 'tis rare and rich compound of gods and dwarfs, and best of humanity, that goes to walk. Can you bring home the summits of Wachusett and Monadnoc, and the Uncanoonuc, the savin fields of Lincoln, and the sedge and reeds of Flint Pond, the savage woods beyond Nut Brook towards White Pond? He can.

Do you think I am in such great terror of being shot?[1] . . .

It is curious that Thoreau goes to a house to say with little preface what he has just read or observed, delivers it in lump, is quite inattentive to any comment or thought which any of the company offer on the matter, nay, is merely interrupted by it, and when he has finished his report departs with precipitation.

Materialists. Economical geology; economical astronomy, with a view (to annexation, if it could be) to navigation: and chemistry and natural history, for utility. Yes, rightly enough: but is there no right wishing to know what is, without reaping a rent or commission? Now, their natural history is profane. They do not know the bird, the fish, the tree they describe. The ambition that "hurries them after truth, takes away the power to attain it."

---

[1] This and what follows, purporting to be quoted from "a humorist," but mainly autobiographical, is printed in *Society and Solitude* (p. 5).

This charge that I make against English science, that it bereaves Nature of its charm, lies equally against all European science.

"Mathematics," said Copernicus to the Pope, "are written for mathematicians."

The comfort of Alcott's mind is, the connection in which he sees whatever he sees. He is never dazzled by a spot of color, or a gleam of light, to value that thing by itself; but forever and ever is prepossessed by the undivided one behind it and all. I do not know where to find in men or books a mind so valuable to faith. His own invariable faith inspires faith, in others. I valued Miss Bacon's studies of Shakespeare, simply for the belief they showed in cause and effect; that a first-rate genius was not a prodigy and stupefying anomaly, but built up step by step as a tree or a house is, with a sufficient cause (and one that, with diligence, might be found or assigned) for every difference and every superiority to the dunce or average man. For every opinion or sentence of Alcott, a reason may be sought and found, not in his will or fancy, but in the necessity of Nature itself, which has daguerred that fatal impression on his susceptible soul. He is as good as a lens or a mirror, a beautiful susceptibility, every impression on which is not to be reasoned against, or derided, but to be accounted for, and until accounted for, registered as an indisputable addition to our catalogue of natural facts. There are defects in the lens, and errors of refraction and position, etc., to be allowed for, and it needs one acquainted with the lens by frequent use, to make these allowances; but 'tis the best instrument I have ever met with.

Every man looks a piece of luck, but he is a piece of the mosaic accurately measured and ground to fit into the gap he fills, such as Parker or Garrison, or Carlyle, or Hegel is, and with good optics, I suppose, we should find as nice fitting down to the bores and loafers.

I admire that poetry which no man wrote, no poet less than the genius of humanity itself, and which is to be read in my theology, in the effect of pictures, or sculptures, or drama, or cities, or sciences, on me.

My son is coming to get his Latin lesson without me. My son is coming to do without me. And I am coming to do without Plato, or Goethe, or Alcott.

To carry temperance very high and very thoroughly into life and into intellect, and that with insight of its necessity and efficacy!

Conversation. I ought to have said above, in respect to Conversation, that our habit is squalid and beggarly.[1] . . .

In a parlor, the unexpectedness of the effects. When we go to Faneuil Hall, we look for important events: facts, thoughts, and persuasions, that bear on them. But in your parlor, to find your companion who sits by your side start up into a more potent than Demosthenes, and, in an instant, work a revolution that makes Athens and England and Washington politics old carrion and dust-barrels, because his suggestions require new ways of living, new books, new men, new arts and sciences—yes, the lecture and the book seem vapid. Eloquence is

---

[1] The rest of the passage is found in "Considerations by the Way" (*Conduct of Life*, p. 271).

forever a power that shoves usurpers from their thrones, and sits down on them by allowance and acclaim of all.

These black coats never can speak until they meet a black coat: then their tongues are loosed, and chatter like blackbirds. The "practical" folks in the rail-car meet daily, and to their discourse there is no end.

Once more for Alcott it is to be said that he is sincerely and necessarily engaged to his task and not wilfully or ostentatiously or pecuniarily. Mr. Johnson at Manchester said of him, "He is universally competent. Whatever question is asked, he is prepared for."

I shall go far, and see many, before I find such an extraordinary insight as Alcott's. In his fine talk, last evening, he ran up and down the scale of powers, with as much ease and precision as a squirrel the wires of his cage, and is never dazzled by his means, or by any particular, and a fine heroic action or a poetic passage would make no impression on him, because he expects heroism and poetry in all. Ideal Purity, the poet, the artist, the man, must have. I have never seen any person who so fortifies the believer, so confutes the skeptic. And the almost uniform rejection of this man by men of parts, Carlyle and Browning inclusive, and by women of piety, might make one despair of society. If he came with a cannonade of acclaim from all nations, as the first wit on the planet, these masters would sustain the reputation: or if they could find him in a book a thousand years old, with a legend of miracles appended, there would be churches of disciples: but now they wish to know if his coat is out at the elbow, or whether somebody did not hear from somebody, that he had got a new hat, etc., etc. He has faults, no doubt, but I may safely know no more about them than he does; and some that are most severely imputed to him are only the omissions of a preoccupied mind.

Paris vaut bien un messe. Her great names are Carnot and Francis Arago. The last did not duck to the second Napoleon, nor did Carnot nor Lafayette to the first.

Carnot's Theorem was, "Avoid sudden alterations of speed; since the loss of living power is equal to the living power which all the parts of the machine or system would possess, if you should give to every one of them the speed which it lost in the moment when the sudden alteration occurred." (See *Atlantis,* February, 1856, p. 118.)

Maupertuis's Theorem. "La quantité d'action nécessaire pour produire un changement dans le mouvement des corps est toujours un minimum."

Il entendait par quantité d'action le produit d'une masse par sa vitesse et par l'espace qu'elle parcourt. ("Principes de l'équilibre, et du mouvement," CARNOT.)

Education. Don't let them eat their seed-corn; don't let them anticipate, ante-date, and be young men, before they have finished their boyhood. Let them have the fields and woods, and learn their secret and the base- and football, and wrestling, and brickbats, and suck all the strength and courage that lies for them in these games; let them ride bareback, and catch their horse in his pasture, let them hook and spear their fish, and shin a post and a tall tree, and shoot their partridge and trap the woodchuck, before they begin to dress like collegians and sing in serenades, and make polite calls. 'Tis curious that there is not only an apotheosis of every power or faculty of mind and body, but also of every element, material, and tool we use; as, of fire, water, air, earth, the hammer of Thor, the shoe of Mercury, the belt of Venus, the bracelet, balance, waterpot.

One man is born to explain bones and animal architectures; and one, the expression of crooked and casual lines, spots on a turtle, or on the leaf of a plant; and one, machines, and the application of coil springs and steam and water-wheels to the weaving of cloth or paper; and one, morals; and one, a pot of brandy, and poisons; and the laws of disease are as beautiful as the laws of health. Let each mind his own, and declare his own.

The Affirmative. To awake in man and to raise the feeling of his worth; to educate his feeling and his judgment, that he must scorn himself for a bad action. My friend Anna W. refuses to tell her children whether the act was right or wrong, but sends them away to find out what *the little voice* says, and at night they shall tell her.

It must be admitted, that civilization is onerous and expensive; hideous expense to keep it up; let it go, and be Indians again; but why Indians?—that is costly, too; the mud-turtle and trout life is easier and cheaper, and oyster, cheaper still.

> . . . *Pater ipse colendi*
> *Haud facilem esse viam voluit:* . . .
> . . . *curis acuens mortalia corda.*[1]

Play out the game, act well your part, and if the gods have blundered, we will not.

[1] The Father himself willed not the farmer's lot an easy one, sharpening men's minds by Care. (Virgil, *Georgics*, I, pp. 121-123.)

I have but one military recollection in all my life. In
1813, or 1814, all Boston, young and old, turned out to
build the fortifications on Noddle's Island; and the
schoolmaster at the Latin School announced to the boys,
that, if we wished, we might all go on a certain day to
work on the Island. I went with the rest in the ferry-
boat, and spent a summer day; but I cannot remember
that I did any kind of work. I remember only the pains
we took to get water in our tin pails, to relieve our intolerable thirst. I am afraid no valuable effect of my
labor remains in the existing defences.

May 21.

Yesterday to the Sawmill Brook with Henry. He was
in search of yellow violet (*pubescens*) and *menyanthes*
which he waded into the water for; and which he concluded, on examination, had been out five days. Having
found his flowers, he drew out of his breast pocket his
diary and read the names of all the plants that should
bloom this day, May 20; whereof he keeps account as a
banker when his notes fall due; *Rubus triflora, Quercus,
Vaccinium,* etc. The *Cypripedium* not due till tomorrow.
Then we diverged to the brook, where was *Viburnum
dentatum,* Arrow-wood. But his attention was drawn to
the redstart which flew about with its *cheap, cheap
chevet,* and presently to two fine grosbeaks, rose-
breasted, whose brilliant scarlet "bids the rash gazer
wipe his eye," and which he brought nearer with his
spyglass, and whose fine, clear note he compares to that
of a "tanager who has got rid of his hoarseness." Then
he heard a note which he calls that of the night-warbler,
a bird he has never identified, has been in search of for
twelve years, which, always, when he sees it, is in the
act of diving down into a tree or bush, and which 'tis

vain to seek; the only bird that sings indifferently by
night and by day. I told him, he must beware of finding and booking him, lest life should have nothing more
to show him. He said, "What you seek in vain for half
your life, one day you come full upon—all the family
at dinner. You seek him like a dream, and as soon as you
find him, you become his prey." He thinks he could tell
by the flowers what day of the month it is, within two
days.

We found *Saxifraga Pennsylvanica,* and *Chrysosple-
nium oppositifolium,* by Everett's spring, and *Stellaria*
and *Cerastium* and *Arabis rhomboidea* and *Veronica
anagallis,* which he thinks handsomer than the cultivated
Veronica, Forget-me-not. *Solidago odora,* he says, is
common in Concord, and pennyroyal he gathers in
quantity as *herbs* every season. *Shad-blossom* is no
longer a *pyrus,* which is now confined to choke-berry.
Shad-blossom is *Amelanchier botryapium.* Shad-blossom
because it comes when the shad come.

Water is the first gardener: he always plants grasses
and flowers about his dwelling. There came Henry with
music-book under his arm, to press flowers in; with
telescope in his pocket, to see the birds, and microscope
to count stamens; with a diary, jack-knife, and twine; in
stout shoes, and strong gray trousers, ready to brave the
shrub-oaks and smilax, and to climb the tree for a
hawk's nest. His strong legs, when he wades, were no
insignificant part of his armor. Two alders we have,
and one of them is here on the northern border of its
habitat.

Pantheism. In the woods, this afternoon, it seemed
plain to me, that most men were Pantheists at heart,
say what they might of their theism. No other path is,
indeed, open for them to the One, intellectually at least.

Man delights in freedom even to license, and claims infinite indulgence, from the Powers seen, and unseen, to
whom he would give indulgence on those [terms?]. In a
word, he would conquer and surrender in his own way;
living no less open to the power of soul than of State,
swayed by gods and demons, he is never, in his fresh
morning-love, quite himself. His audacity is immense.
His impieties are his pieties: he wins and loses, to win
and lose. He reveres, dallies with, defies, and overcomes
every god and demigod of the Pantheon, in quest of his
freedom, and thus liberates Humanity from the demons
by these twelve labors.

[The brutal attack on Senator Sumner by Preston
Brooks, of South Carolina, which resulted in painful and
disabling illness for years, had roused the indignation of
Massachusetts.]

May 27.

I am impressed at the indignation meeting last night,
as ever, on like occasions, with the sweet nitrous oxide
gas which the speakers seem to breathe. Once they taste
it, they cling like mad to the bladder, and will not let it
go. And it is so plain to me that eloquence, like swimming, is an art which all men might learn, though so few
do.[1] . . .

Sumner's attack . . . only a leaf of the tree; it is not
Sumner who must be avenged, but the tree must be cut
down. But this stroke rouses the feeling of the people,
and shows everybody where they are. All feel it. Those
who affect not to feel it must perforce share the shame,
nor will hiding their heads, and pretending other tasks
and a preoccupied mind, deceive themselves or us. We

---

[1] The rest of the passage is found in "Eloquence" (*Letters and
Social Aims*, p. 119).

are all in this boat of the State, and cannot dodge the duties.

This history teaches the fatal blunder of going into false position. Let us not compromise again, or accept the aid of evil agents.

Our position, of the Free States, very like that of Covenanters against the Cavaliers.

Massachusetts uniformly retreats from her resolutions.

Suppose we raise soldiers in Massachusetts. Suppose we propose a Northern Union.

June 2.

The finest day, the high noon of the year, went with Thoreau in a wagon to Perez Blood's[1] auction: found the *Myrica* flowering; it had already begun to shed its pollen one day, the lowest flowers being effete; found the English hawthorn on Mrs. Ripley's hill, ready to bloom; went up the Assabet, and found the *Azalea nudiflora* in full bloom, a beautiful show; the *Viola Muhlenbergi,* the *Ranunculus recurvatus;* saw swamp white oak (chestnut-like leaves), white maple, red maple—no chestnut oak on the river.

Henry told his story of the *Ephemera,* the manna of the fishes, which falls like a snowstorm one day in the year, only on this river, not on the Concord, high up in the air as he can see, and blundering down to the river (the shad-fly), the true angler's fly; the fish die of repletion when it comes, the kingfishers wait for their prey.

Around us the *pee pee pee* of the kingbird kind was noisy. He showed the history of the river from the banks, the male and the female bank. The *Pontederia* keeps the female bank, on whichever side.

---

[1] The old farmer had died who has been alluded to in earlier journals as having spent much of his inheritance on a telescope, globes, and books on astronomy.

"Avec un grand génie, il faut une grande volonté."

"Les faiblesses de Voltaire! Que nous importe à nous ses heritiers sous benefice d'inventaire? Nous ne sommes solidaires que de ses vertus."—LANFREY.

I go for those who have received a retaining fee to this party of Freedom, before they came into the world. I would trust Garrison, I would trust Henry Thoreau, that they would make no compromises. I would trust Horace Greeley, I would trust my venerable friend Mr. Hoar, that they would be staunch for freedom to the death; but both of these would have a benevolent credulity in the honesty of the other party, that I think unsafe.

The vote of a prophet is worth a hundred hands. If he knows it to be the true vote, it will be decisive of the question for his country. The want of profound sincerity is the cause of failures.

South Carolina is in earnest. I see the courtesy of the Carolinians, but I know meanwhile that the only reason why they do not plant a cannon before Faneuil Hall, and blow Bunker Hill Monument to fragments, as a nuisance, is because they have not the power. They are fast acquiring the power, and if they get it, they will do it.

There are men who as soon as they are born take a bee-line to the axe of the inquisitor, like Giordano Bruno. In France, the fagots for Vanini. In Italy, the fagots for Bruno. In England, the pillory for Defoe. In New England, the whipping-post for the Quakers. Algernon Sydney a tragic character; and Sumner is; no humor.

Wonderful the way in which we are saved by this unfailing supply of the moral element.

[In 1855, the Emigrant Aid Society was formed in New England to advise, and help where needful, would-be settlers in the prairie country. In the following year George L. Stearns, an able, patriotic and generous Boston merchant, a resident of Medford, organized the Massachusetts State Kansas Committee to ensure that territory from the adoption of a constitution per- mitting slavery, by helping good men of "free state" principles to go thither with their families as *bona fide* settlers. Funds were furnished to aid them to establish themselves, and when they were attacked by pro-slavery settlers and also by parties from Missouri who crossed the river to ensure pro-slavery elections, Sharp's rifles were also sent in quantities for defense.[1]]

June 14.

At our Kansas relief meeting, in Concord, on June 12, $962.00 were subscribed on the spot. Yesterday, the subscription had amounted to $1130.00; and it will probably reach $1200.00, or one per cent on the valuation of the town.

$1360.00 I believe was the final amount.

Cant. "A character more common in the modern world is that of ambition without belief (with the mask of religion, deceiving men to enslave them), seeing in a dogma nothing but a two-edged glaive, to strike them down." (See LANFREY.)

Voltaire enrolled fashion on his side—the mode— good society—*il est de bon ton d'être libre penseur.*

To get the hurra on our side is well; but if you are a gentleman, you must have the hurra of gentlemen on your side.

---

[1] See "George L. Stearns" (*Lectures and Biographical Sketches*).

The government has been an obstruction, and nothing but an obstruction. The people by themselves would have settled Iowa, and Utah, and Kansas, in a sufficient way. The government has made all the mischief. This for the people; then for the upper classes, who acquiesce in what they call law and order of a government which exists for fraud and violence—they are properly paid by its excessive vulgarity. The refined Boston upholds a gang of Rhynderses, and Toombses, and Brookses, before whom it is obliged to be very quiet and dapper like a dear little rabbit, as it is, among the wolves. The Choates and Winthrops, and, at long interval, the H——s, we see through them very clearly, and their abject attitude.

I was to say at the end of my narrative of Wordsworth, that I find nothing, in the disparaging speeches of the Londoners about him, that would not easily be said of a faithful scholar who rated things after his own scale, and not by the conventional. He almost alone in his generation has treated the Mind well.

Jesuits. "*Et chaque fois que le dogme embarrassa la marche triomphante des conquérants, ils laissèrent le dogme en chemin.*"—LANFREY.

Montesquieu said, "*Dans les pays où l'on a le malheur d'avoir une religion que Dieu n'a pas donnée, il est toujours nécessaire qu'elle s'accorde avec la morale.*"— LANFREY (p. 156).

Literature. "*Le temps fera distinguer ce que nous avons pensé de ce que nous avons écrit,*" said Diderot and Voltaire.

Lorsqu'on cherche à préciser le rôle et l'influence des

femmes à une époque donnée, une chose frappe tout d'abord l'esprit, c'est leur radicale inaptitude à généraliser, à embrasser de vastes horizons, à dégager les causes de leurs effets. Est-ce à dire qu'elles soient condamnées à perpétuité aux servitudes intellectuelles ou seulement à le rôle, noble assurèment, mais un peu sacrifié, des Sabines?—LANFREY (p. 202).

"It is the quality of words that they imply a speaker." —MISS BACON.

Professor Poikilus had one advantage over the rest of the University, that when the class gaped or began to diminish, he would with great celerity throw his heels into the air, and stand upon his head, and continue his lecture in that posture, a turn which seemed to invigorate his audience, who would listen with marked cheerfulness as long as he would speak to them in that attitude.

When I said of Ellery's new verses that "they were as good as the old ones," "Yes," said Ward, "but those were excellent promise, and now he does no more." He has a more poetic temperament than any other in America, but the artistic executive power of completing a design, he has not. His poetry is like the artless warbling of a vireo, which whistles prettily all day and all summer in the elm, but never rounds a tune, nor can increase the value of melody by the power of composition and cuneiform determination. He must have construction also.

July 23.

Returned from Pigeon Cove, where we have made acquaintance with the sea, for seven days. 'Tis a noble friendly power, and seemed to say to me, "Why so late and slow to come to me? Am I not here always thy proper summer home? Is not my voice thy needful music: my breath, thy healthful climate in the heats; my touch, thy cure? Was ever building like my terraces? was ever couch so magnificent as mine? Lie down on my warm ledges and learn that a very little hut is all you need. I have made thy architecture superfluous, and it is paltry beside mine. Here are twenty Romes and Ninevehs and Karnacs in ruins together, obelisk and pyramid and giant's causeway—here they all are prostrate or half piled."

And behold the sea, the opaline, plentiful and strong, yet beautiful as the rose or the rainbow, full of food, nourisher of men, purger of the world, creating a sweet climate, and, in its unchangeable ebb and flow, and in its beauty at a few furlongs, giving a hint of that which changes not, and is perfect.[1]

"Until man is able to compress the ether like leather, there will be no end of misery, except through the knowledge of God."—*Upanishad.*

"From whom the sun rises, and in whom it sets again, him all the gods entered; from him none is separated; this is that.

"What is here, the same is there, and what is there, the same is here. He proceeds from death to death who beholds here difference.

"He (Brahma, or the Soul) does not move; is swifter than the mind: not the gods (the senses) did obtain

---

[1] The day after our return from this visit to the rocks of Cape Ann, to which Rev. Cyrus Bartol had led the way, my father came up to my mother's room looking much pleased, and said, "I came in yesterday from the rocks and wrote down what the ocean had said to me, and today when I open my book, I find it blank verse by omitting a word here and there. Listen"; and he read the above passage from the *Journal.* Compare with the "Seashore," in the *Poems.* E.W.E.

him, he was gone before. Standing, he outstrips all the other gods, how fast soever they run.

"He moves, he does not move. He is far, and also near."

SONG OF THE SOUL (BRAHMA)

If the red slayer think he slays,
Or if the slain think he is slain,
They know not well the subtle ways
I keep, and pass, and turn again.

Far or forgot to me is near;
Shadow and sunlight are the same;
The vanished gods not less appear;
And one to me are shame and fame.

They reckon ill who leave me out;
When me they fly, I am the wings;
I am the doubter and the doubt,
And I the hymn the Brahmin sings.

The strong gods pine for my abode,
And pine in vain the sacred Seven;
But thou, meek lover of the good!
Find me, and turn thy back on heaven.

"Know that which does not see by the eye; and by which they see the eyes, as Brahma, and not what is worshipped as this.

"Know that which does not think by the mind, and by which they say the mind is thought, as Brahma, and not what is worshipped as this.

"The soul declared by an inferior man is not easy to be known, but when it is declared by a teacher who beholds no difference, there is no doubt concerning it, the soul being more subtle than what is subtle, is not to be obtained by arguing."

Letters

EDITOR'S NOTE

EMERSON as a letter-writer has been slow in making himself known. His correspondence with Carlyle was published soon after his death, and that correspondence—represented here—is one of the best things of its kind. But it shows only one side of Emerson, who had many sides to show, and who in the whole of his correspondence adapted himself with singular simplicity to the persons he addressed. With each person he became the man whom that person understood him to be. He has many styles, none of which is wrong. He genuinely communicates, and in the process of doing so reveals once more his genius for comprehending persons. He seems at times to have doubted that he had such a genius; he wondered whether he had a right to claim success in friendship; but his letters prove the right. This has become evident as further collections of the correspondence have appeared, in the *Memoir* by Cabot and elsewhere. It is finally evident in the six large volumes of *Letters* published by Ralph L. Rusk in 1939.

Emerson's early letters were family affairs, full of secrets and absurdities, somewhat in the manner of Mozart's famous correspondence. As he grew older and busier he had less time for such play, and indeed less inclination. The letters that follow are of various sorts and to various people. The people include Emerson's Aunt Mary, Carlyle, Lidian Emerson (born Lydia Jackson), and Margaret Fuller. The subject in more than one instance is the death of Emerson's first child, his son Waldo, in 1842 at the age of five. This death was a blow from which the father did not soon recover; as he did so, gradually, he became capable of writing the "Threnody" which appeared in his *Poems* of 1846. But "Threnody" had taken shape in the letters, or certain phrases of it had, as the following pages will suggest. No subject ever touched Emerson more deeply. Yet he was often touched deeply, by Carlyle and every other friend he had. The record of his letters, incomplete though it must be, is not the least revealing record left by this man who was at once so genial and so proud.

Emerson's open letter to President Van Buren belongs here only, perhaps, because of its form. In substance it was a protest, for public consumption, against a public outrage, the removal of the Cherokees from their lands in Georgia. Emerson confided to his *Journal* that he hated doing such things—"this stirring in the philanthropic mud gives me no peace. . . . I fully sympathize, be sure, with the sentiments I write; but I accept it rather from my friends than dictate it. It is not my impulse to say it, and therefore my genius deserts me; no muse befriends; no music of thought or word accompanies." "It is like dead cats around one's neck," he remarked years later. Yet he went through with what he must, and he underestimated the force, even the music, of his letter to Van Buren. It is a right music, like the others that he mastered.

The letters dated 1835 and 1842 are reprinted from Volumes I and III of Professor Rusk's *Letters of Ralph Waldo Emerson* (Columbia University Press). Thanks are due to Professor Rusk, to the publishers, and to the Ralph Waldo Emerson Memorial Association.

LETTERS

TO MARY MOODY EMERSON

Boston, January 6, 1829.

My dear Aunt,—You know—none can know better —on what straitened lines we have all walked up to manhood. In poverty and many troubles the seeds of our prosperity were sown. Now all these troubles appeared a fair counterbalance to the flatteries of fortune. I lean always to that ancient superstition (if it is such, though drawn from a wise survey of human affairs) which taught men to beware of unmixed prosperity; for Nemesis kept watch to overthrow the high. Well, now look at the altered aspect. William has begun to live by the law. Edward has recovered his reason and his health. Bulkeley was never more comfortable in his life. Charles is prospering in all ways. Waldo is comparatively well and comparatively successful, far more so than his friends, out of his family, anticipated. Now I add to all this felicity a particular felicity which makes my own glass very much larger and fuller, and I straightway say, Can this hold? Will God make me a brilliant exception to the common order of his dealings, which equalizes destinies? There's an apprehension of reverse always arising from success. But is it my fault that I am happy, and cannot I trust the Goodness that has uplifted to uphold me? I cannot find in the world, without or within, any antidote, any bulwark against this fear. like this: the frank acknowledgment of unbounded dependence. Let into the heart that is filled with prosperity the idea of God, and it smooths the giddy precipices of human pride to a substantial level; it harmonizes the condition of the individual with the economy of the universe. I should be glad, dear aunt, if you, who are my oldest friend, would give me some of your meditations upon these new leaves of my fortune. You have always promised me success, and now when it seems to be coming I choose to direct to you this letter, which I enter as a sort of protest against my Ahriman; that, if I am called, after the way of my race, to pay a fatal tax for my good, I may appeal to the sentiment of collected anticipation with which I saw the tide turn and the winds blow softly from the favoring west.

TO LYDIA JACKSON

Concord, 1, February [1835].

One of my wise masters, Edmund Burke, said, "A wise man will speak the truth with temperance that he may speak it the longer." In this new sentiment that you awaken in me, my Lydian Queen, what might scare others pleases me, its quietness, which I accept as a pledge of permanence. I delighted myself on Friday with my quite domesticated position and the good understanding that grew all the time, yet I went and came without one vehement word—or one passionate sign. In this was nothing of design, I merely surrendered myself to the hour and to the facts. I find a sort of grandeur in the modulated expressions of a love in which the individuals, and what might seem even reasonable personal expectations, are steadily postponed to a regard for truth and the universal love. Do not think me a metaphysical lover. I am a man and hate and suspect the over refiners, and do sympathize with the homeliest pleasures and attractions by which our good foster mother Nature draws her children together. Yet am I well pleased that between us the most permanent ties should be the first formed and thereon should grow whatever others human nature will.

My Mother rejoices very much and asks me all manner of questions about you, many of which I cannot answer. I don't know whether you sing, or read French, or Latin, or where you have lived, and much more. So you see there is nothing in it but that you should come here and on the Battle-Ground stand the fire of her catechism.

Under this morning's severe but beautiful light I thought, dear friend, that hardly should I get away from Concord. I must win you to love it. I am born a poet, of a low class without doubt, yet a poet. That is my nature and vocation. My singing be sure is very 'husky,' and is for the most part in prose. Still am I a poet in the sense of a perceiver and dear lover of the harmonies that are in the soul and in matter, and specially of the correspondences between these and those. A sunset, a forest, a snow-storm, a certain river-view, are more to me than many friends and do ordinarily divide my day with my books. Wherever I go therefore I guard and study my rambling propensities with a care that is ridiculous to people, but to me is the care of my high calling. Now Concord is only one of a hundred towns in which I could find these necessary objects, but Plymouth I fear is not one, Plymouth is streets; I live in the wide champaign.

Time enough for this, however. If I succeed in preparing my lecture on Michel Angelo Buonarotti for

Thursday, I will come to Plymouth on Friday. If I do not succeed—do not attain unto the Idea of that man—I shall read of Luther, Thursday, and then I know not when I shall steal a visit.

Dearest, forgive the egotism of all this letter. Say they not, "The more love the more egotism"? Repay it by as much and more. Write, write to me. And please, dear Lidian, take that same low counsel and leave thinking for the present and let the winds of heaven blow away your dyspepsia.

WALDO E.

TO THOMAS CARLYLE

Concord, 13 September, 1837.

MY DEAR FRIEND,—Such a gift as the *French Revolution* demanded a speedier acknowledgment. But you mountaineers that can scale Andes before breakfast for an airing have no measures for the performance of low-landers and valetudinarians. I am ashamed to think, and will not tell, what little things have kept me silent.

The *French Revolution* did not reach me until three weeks ago, having had at least two long pauses by the way, as I find, since landing. Between many visits received, and some literary haranguing done, I have read two volumes and half the third: and I think you a very good giant; disporting yourself with an original and vast ambition of fun: pleasure and peace not being strong enough for you, you choose to suck pain also, and teach fever and famine to dance and sing. I think you have written a wonderful book, which will last a very long time. I see that you have created a history, which the world will own to be such. You have recognized the

existence of other persons than officers, and of other
relations than civism. You have broken away from all
books, and written a mind. It is a brave experiment, and
the success is great. We have men in your story and not
names merely; always men, though I may doubt sometimes whether I have the historic men. We have great
facts—and selected facts—truly set down. We have
always the co-presence of Humanity along with the imperfect damaged individuals. The soul's right of wonder
is still left to us; and we have righteous praise and doom
awarded, assuredly without cant. Yes, comfort yourself
on that particular, O ungodliest divine man! thou cant-
est never. Finally we have not—a dull word. Never was
there a style so rapid as yours—which no reader can
outrun; and so it is for the most intelligent. I suppose
nothing will astonish more than the audacious wit and
cheerfulness which no tragedy and no magnitude of
events can overpower or daunt. Henry VIII loved a
Man, and I see with joy my bard always equal to the
crisis he represents. And so I thank you for your labor,
and feel that your contemporaries ought to say, All hail,
Brother! live forever: not only in the great Soul which
thou largely inhalest, but also as a named person in this
thy definite deed.

I will tell you more of the book when I have once
got it at focal distance—if that can ever be—and muster
my objections when I am sure of their ground. I insist,
of course, that it might be more simple, less Gothically
efflorescent. You will say no rules for the illumination
of windows can apply to the Aurora Borealis. However,
I find refreshment when every now and then a special
fact slips into the narrative couched in sharp and busi-
nesslike terms. This character-drawing in the book is
certainly admirable; the lines are ploughed furrows; but
there was cake and ale before, though thou be virtuous.

Clarendon surely drew sharp outlines for me in Falkland, Hampden, and the rest, without defiance or skyvaulting. I wish I could talk with you face to face for one day, and know what your uttermost frankness would say concerning the book.

I feel assured of its good reception in this country. I learned last Saturday that in all eleven hundred and sixty-six copies of *Sartor* have been sold. I have told the publisher of that book that he must not print the *History* until some space has been given to people to import British copies. I have ordered Hilliard, Gray, & Co. to import twenty copies as an experiment. At the present very high rate of exchange, which makes a shilling worth thirty cents, they think, with freight and duties, the book would be too costly here for sale, but we confide in a speedy fall of Exchange; then my books shall come. I am ashamed that you should educate our young men, and that we should pirate your books. One day we will have a better law, or perhaps you will make our law yours.

I had your letter long before your book. Very good work you have done in your lifetime, and very generously you adorn and cheer this pilgrimage of mine by your love. I find my highest prayer granted in calling a just and wise man my friend. Your profuse benefaction of genius in so few years makes me feel very poor and useless. I see that I must go [on and] [1] trust to you and to all the brave for some longer time, hoping yet to prove one day my truth and love. There are in this country so few scholars, that the services of each studious person are needed to do what he can for the circulation of thoughts, to the end of making some counterweight to the money force, and to give such food as he may to the nigh starving youth. So I religiously read

---

[1] Covered by the seal.

lectures every winter, and at other times whenever summoned. Last year, "the Philosophy of History," twelve lectures; and now I meditate a course on what I call ' Ethics." I peddle out all the wit I can gather from Time or from Nature, and am pained at heart to see how thankfully that little is received.

Write to me, good friend, tell me if you went to Scotland—what you do, and will do—tell me that your wife is strong and well again as when I saw her at Craigenputtock. I desire to be affectionately remembered to her. Tell me when you will come hither. I called together a little club a week ago, who spent a day with me—counting fifteen souls—each one of whom warmly loves you. So if the *French Revolution* does not convert the "dull public" of your native Nineveh, I see not but you must shake the dust from your shoes and cross the Atlantic to a New England. Yours in love and honor.

R. WALDO EMERSON.

May I trouble you with a commission when you are in the City? You mention being at the shop of Rich in Red-Lion Square. Will you say to him that he sent me some books two or three years ago without any account of prices annexed? I wrote him once myself, once through S. Burdett, bookseller, and since through C. P. Curtis, Esq., who professes to be his attorney in Boston —three times—to ask for this account. No answer has ever come. I wish he would send me the account, that I may settle it. If he persist in his self-denying contumacy, I think you may immortalize him as a bookseller of the gods.

I shall send you an Oration presently, delivered before a literary society here, which is now being printed. Gladly I hear of the Carlylet—so they say—in the new Westminster.

TO MARTIN VAN BUREN,
PRESIDENT OF THE
UNITED STATES

Concord, Mass., April 23, 1838.

Sir,—The seat you fill places you in a relation of credit and nearness to every citizen. By right and natural position, every citizen is your friend. Before any acts contrary to his own judgment or interest have repelled the affections of any man, each may look with trust and living anticipation to your government. Each has the highest right to call your attention to such subjects as are of a public nature and properly belong to the chief magistrate; and the good magistrate will feel a joy in meeting such confidence. In this belief and at the instance of a few of my friends and neighbors, I crave of your patience a short hearing for their sentiments and my own: and the circumstance that my name will be utterly unknown to you will only give the fairer chance to your equitable construction of what I have to say.

Sir, my communication respects the sinister rumors that fill this part of the country concerning the Cherokee people. The interest always felt in the aboriginal population—an interest naturally growing as that decays—has been heightened in regard to this tribe. Even in our distant State some good rumor of their worth and civility has arrived. We have learned with joy their improvement in the social arts. We have read their newspapers. We have seen some of them in our schools and colleges. In common with the great body of the American people, we have witnessed with sympathy the painful labors of these red men to redeem their own race from the doom of eternal inferiority, and to borrow and domesticate in the tribe the arts and customs of the Caucasian race. And notwithstanding the unaccountable apathy with which of late years the Indians have been sometimes abandoned to their enemies, it is not to be doubted that it is the good pleasure and the understanding of all humane persons in the republic, of the men and the matrons sitting in the thriving independent families all over the land, that they shall be duly cared for; that they shall taste justice and love from all to whom we have delegated the office of dealing with them.

The newspapers now inform us that, in December, 1835, a treaty contracting for the exchange of all the Cherokee territory was pretended to be made by an agent on the part of the United States with some persons appearing on the part of the Cherokees; that the fact afterwards transpired that these deputies did by no means represent the will of the nation; and that, out of eighteen thousand souls composing the nation, fifteen thousand six hundred and sixty-eight have protested against the so-called treaty. It now appears that the government of the United States choose to hold the Cherokees to this sham treaty, and are proceeding to execute the same. Almost the entire Cherokee nation stand up and say, "This is not our act. Behold us. Here are we. Do not mistake that handful of deserters for us"; and the American President and the Cabinet, the Senate and the House of Representatives, neither hear these men nor see them, and are contracting to put this active nation into carts and boats, and to drag them over mountains and rivers to a wilderness at a vast distance beyond the Mississippi. And a paper purporting to be an army-order fixes a month from this day as the hour for this doleful removal.

In the name of God, sir, we ask you if this be so. Do the newspapers rightly inform us? Men and women with pale and perplexed faces meet one another in the streets and churches here, and ask if this be so. We have inquired if this be a gross misrepresentation from the party opposed to the government and anxious to blacken it with the people. We have looked in the newspapers of different parties, and find a horrid confirmation of the tale. We are slow to believe it. We hoped the Indians were misinformed, and that their remonstrance was premature, and will turn out to be a needless act of terror.

The piety, the principle that is left in the United States—if only in its coarsest form, a regard to the speech of men—forbid us to entertain it as a fact. Such a dereliction of all faith and virtue, such a denial of justice, and such deafness to screams for mercy were never heard of in times of peace and in the dealing of a nation with its own allies and wards, since the earth was made. Sir, does this government think that the people of the United States are become savage and mad? From their mind are the sentiments of love and a good nature wiped clean out? The soul of man, the justice, the mercy that is the heart's heart in all men, from Maine to Georgia, does abhor this business.

In speaking thus the sentiments of my neighbors and my own, perhaps I overstep the bounds of decorum. But would it not be a higher indecorum coldly to argue a matter like this? We only state the fact that a crime is projected that confounds our understandings by its magnitude—a crime that really deprives us as well as the Cherokees of a country; for how could we call the conspiracy that should crush these poor Indians our government, or the land that was cursed by their parting and dying imprecations our country, any more? You, sir, will bring down that renowned chair in which you sit into infamy if your seal is set to this instrument of perfidy; and the name of this nation, hitherto the sweet omen of religion and liberty, will stink to the world.

You will not do us the injustice of connecting this remonstrance with any sectional and party feeling. It is in our hearts the simplest commandment of brotherly love. We will not have this great and solemn claim upon national and human justice huddled aside under the flimsy plea of its being a party-act. Sir, to us the questions upon which the government and the people have been agitated during the past year, touching the prostration of the currency and of trade, seem but motes in comparison. These hard times, it is true, have brought the discussion home to every farmhouse and poor man's house in this town; but it is the chirping of grasshoppers beside the immortal question whether justice shall be done by the race of civilized to the race of savage man —whether all the attributes of reason, of civility, of justice, and even of mercy, shall be put off by the American people, and so vast an outrage upon the Cherokee nation and upon nature shall be consummated.

One circumstance lessens the reluctance with which I intrude at this time on your attention my conviction that the government ought to be admonished of a new historical fact, which the discussion of this question has disclosed, namely, that there exists in a great part of the Northern people a gloomy diffidence in the *moral* character of the government.

On the broaching of this question, a general expression of despondency, of disbelief that any good will accrue from a remonstrance on an act of fraud and robbery, appeared in those men to whom we naturally turn for aid and counsel. Will the American government steal? Will it lie? Will it kill? we ask triumphantly. Our counsellors and old statesmen here say that ten years ago they would have staked their life on the affirmation that the proposed Indian measures could not be executed; that the unanimous country would put them down. And now the steps of this crime follow each other so fast, at such fatally quick time, that the millions of virtuous citizens, whose agents the government are, have no place to interpose, and must shut their eyes until the last howl and wailing of these tormented villages and tribes shall afflict the ear of the world.

I will not hide from you, as an indication of the alarming distrust, that a letter addressed as mine is, and suggesting to the mind of the executive the plain obligations of man, has a burlesque character in the apprehensions of some of my friends. I, sir, will not beforehand treat you with the contumely of this distrust. I will at least state to you this fact, and show you how plain and humane people, whose love would be honor, regard the policy of the government, and what injurious inferences they draw as to the minds of the governors. A man with your experience in affairs must have seen cause to appreciate the futility of opposition to the moral sentiment. However feeble the sufferer and however great the oppressor, it is in the nature of things that the blow should recoil upon the aggressor. For God is in the sentiment, and it cannot be withstood. The potentate and the people perish before it; but with it, and as its executor, they are omnipotent.

I write thus, sir, to inform you of the state of mind

these Indian tidings have awakened here, and to pray
with one voice more that you, whose hands are strong
with the delegated power of fifteen millions of men, will
avert with that might the terrific injury which threatens
the Cherokee tribe.

With great respect, sir, I am your fellow citizen,

RALPH WALDO EMERSON.

TO MARY MOODY EMERSON

Concord, 28 January, 1842.

MY DEAR AUNT,—My boy, my boy is gone. He was
taken ill of Scarlatina on Monday evening, and died last
night. I can say nothing to you. My darling and the
world's wonderful child, for never in my own or another
family have I seen any thing comparable, has fled out
of my arms like a dream. He adorned the world for me
like a morning star, and every particular of my daily life.
I slept in his neighborhood and woke to remember
him. . . .

This thought pleases me now, that he has never been
degraded by us or by any, no soil has stained him, he
has been treated with respect and religion almost, as
really innocence is always great and inspires respect.
But I can only tell you now that my angel has vanished.
You too will grieve for the little traveler, though you
scarce have seen his features.

Farewell, dear Aunt.

WALDO E.

TO MARGARET FULLER

Dear Margaret,—I am not going to write you a letter but only to say in reply to your request, that we are finding again our hands and feet after our dull and dreadful dream which does *not* leave us where it found us. Lidian, Elizabeth, and I recite chronicles, words, and tones of our fair boy and magnify our lost treasure to extort if we can the secretest wormwood of the grief, and see how bad is the worst. Meantime the sun rises and the winds blow. Nature seems to have forgotten that she has crushed her sweetest creation, and perhaps would admonish us that as this Child's attention could never be fastened on any death, but proceeded still to enliven the new toy, so we children must have no retrospect, but illuminate the new hour if possible with an undiminished stream of rays.

WALDO E.

2 Feb. [1842]

TO THOMAS CARLYLE

Concord, 14 May, 1846.

Dear Friend,—I daily expect the picture, and wonder—so long as I have wished it—I had never asked it before. I was in Boston the other day, and went to the best reputed Daguerrotypist, but though I brought home three transcripts of my face, the house-mates voted them rueful, supremely ridiculous. I must sit again; or, as true Elizabeth Hoar said, I must not sit again, not being of the right complexion which Daguerre and iodine delight in. I am minded to try once more, and if the sun will not take me, I must sit to a good crayon sketcher, Mr. Cheney, and send you his draught. . . .

Good rides to you and the longest escapes from London streets. I too have a new plaything, the best I ever had—a wood-lot. Last fall I bought a piece of more than forty acres, on the border of a little lake half a mile wide and more, called Walden Pond—a place to which my feet have for years been accustomed to bring me once or twice a week at all seasons. My lot to be sure is on the further side of the water, not so familiar to me as the nearer shore. Some of the wood is an old growth, but most of it has been cut off within twenty years and is growing thriftily. In these May days, when maples, poplars, oaks, birches, walnut, and pine are in their spring glory, I go thither every afternoon, and cut with my hatchet an Indian path through the thicket all along the bold shore, and open the finest pictures.

My two little girls know the road now, though it is nearly two miles from my house, and find their way to the spring at the foot of a pine grove, and with some awe to the ruins of a village of shanties, all overgrown with mullein, which the Irish who built the railroad left behind them. At a good distance in from the shore the land rises to a rocky head, perhaps sixty feet above the water. Thereon I think to place a hut; perhaps it will have two stories and be a petty tower, looking out to Monadnoc and other New Hampshire Mountains. There I hope to go with book and pen when good hours come.

I shall think there, a fortnight might bring you from London to Walden Pond. Life wears on, and do you say the gray hairs appear? Few can so well afford them. The black have not hung over a vacant brain, as England and America know; nor, white or black, will it give itself any Sabbath for many a day henceforward, as I believe. What have we to do with old age? Our existence looks to me more than ever initial. We have come to see the ground and look up materials and tools. The men who have any positive quality are a flying advance party for reconnoitring. We shall yet have a right work, and kings for competitors. With ever affectionate remembrance to your wife, your friend,

R. W. EMERSON.

TO THOMAS CARLYLE

Concord, 8 December, 1862.

MY DEAR FRIEND,—Long ago, as soon as swift steamers could bring the new book across the sea, I received the third volume of *Friedrich*, with your autograph inscription, and read it with joy. Not a word went to the beloved author, for I do not write or think. I would wait perhaps for happier days, as our President Lincoln will not even emancipate slaves, until on the heels of a victory, or the semblance of such. But he waited in vain for his triumph, nor dare I in my heavy months expect bright days. The book was heartily grateful, and square to the author's imperial scale. You have lighted the glooms, and engineered away the pits, whereof you poetically pleased yourself with complaining, in your sometime letter to me, clean out of it, according to the high Italian rule, and have let sunshine and pure air enfold the scene. First, I read it honestly through for the history; then I pause and speculate on the Muse that inspires, and the friend that reports it. 'Tis sovereignly written, above all literature, dictating to all mortals what they shall accept as fated and final for their salvation. It is Mankind's Bill of Rights and Duties, the royal proclamation of Intellect ascending the throne, announcing its good pleasure, that, hereafter, *as heretofore,* and now once for all, the World shall be governed by Common Sense and law of Morals, or shall go to ruin.

But the manner of it! the author sitting as Demiurgus, trotting out his manikins, coaxing and bantering them, amused with their good performance, patting them on the back, and rating the naughty dolls when they misbehave; and communicating his mind ever in measure, just as much as the young public can understand; hinting the future, when it would be useful; recalling now and then illustrative antecedents of the actor, impressing the reader that he is in possession of the entire history centrally seen, that his investigation has been exhaustive, and that he descends too on the petty plot of Prussia from higher and cosmical surveys. Better I like the sound sense and the absolute independence of the tone, which may put kings in fear. And, as the reader shares, according to his intelligence, the haughty *coup d'œil* of this genius, and shares it with delight, I recommend to all governors, English, French, Austrian, and other, to double their guards, and look carefully to the censorship of the press. I find, as ever in your books, that one man has deserved well of mankind for restoring the Scholar's profession to its highest use and dignity. I find also that you are very wilful, and have made a covenant with your eyes that they shall not see anything you do not wish they should. But I was heartily glad to read somewhere that your book was nearly finished in the manuscript, for I could wish you to sit and taste your fame, if that were not contrary to law of Olympus. My joints ache to think of your rugged labor. Now that you have conquered to yourself such a huge kingdom among men, can you not give yourself breath, and chat a little, an Emeritus in the eternal university, and write a gossiping letter to an old American friend or so? Alas, I own that I have no right to say this last—I who write never.

Here we read no books. The war is our sole and doleful instructor. All our bright young men go into it, to be misused and sacrificed hitherto by incapable leaders. One lesson they all learn—to hate slavery, *teterrima causa*. But the issue does not yet appear. We must get ourselves morally right. Nobody can help us. 'Tis of no account what England or France may do. Unless backed by our profligate parties, their action would be nugatory, and, if so backed, the worst. But even the war is better than the degrading and descending politics that preceded it for decades of years, and our legislation has made great strides, and if we can stave off that fury of trade which rushes to peace at the cost of replacing the South in the *status ante bellum*, we can, with something more of courage, leave the problem to another score of years—free labor to fight with the Beast, and see if bales and barrels and baskets cannot find out that they pass more commodiously and surely to their ports through free hands, than through barbarians.

I grieved that the good Clough, the generous, susceptible scholar, should die. I read over his *Bothie* again, full of the wine of youth at Oxford. I delight in Matthew Arnold's fine criticism in two little books. Give affectionate remembrances from me to Jane Carlyle, whom——

——'s happiness and accurate reporting restored to me in brightest image.

Always faithfully yours,

R. W. EMERSON.

TO THOMAS CARLYLE

Concord, 16 May, 1866.

MY DEAR CARLYLE,—I have just been shown a private letter from Moncure Conway to one of his friends here, giving some tidings of your sad return to an empty home. We had the first news last week. And so it is. The stroke long threatened has fallen at last, in the mildest form to its victim, and relieved to you by long and repeated reprieves. I must think her fortunate also in this gentle departure, as she had been in her serene and honored career. We would not for ourselves count covetously the descending steps after we have passed the top of the mount, or grudge to spare some of the days of decay. And you will have the peace of knowing her safe, and no longer a victim. I have found myself recalling an old verse which one utters to the parting soul—

> For thou hast passed all change of human life,
> And not again to thee shall beauty die.

It is thirty-three years in July, I believe, since I first saw her, and her conversation and faultless manners gave assurance of a good and happy future. As I have not witnessed any decline, I can hardly believe in any, and still recall vividly the youthful wife, and her blithe account of her letters and homages from Goethe, and the details she gave of her intended visit to Weimar, and its disappointment. Her goodness to me and to my friends was ever perfect, and all Americans have agreed in her praise. Elizabeth Hoar remembers her with entire sympathy and regard.

I could heartily wish to see you for an hour in these lonely days. Your friends, I know, will approach you as tenderly as friends can; and I can believe that labor— all whose precious secrets you know—will prove a consoler—though it cannot quite avail, for she was the rest that rewarded labor. It is good that you are strong, and built for endurance. Nor will you shun to consult the awful oracles which in these hours of tenderness are sometimes vouchsafed. If to any, to you.

I rejoice that she stayed to enjoy the knowledge of your good day at Edinburgh, which is a leaf we would not spare from your book of life. It was a right manly speech to be so made, and is a voucher of unbroken strength—and the surroundings, as I learn, were all the happiest—with no hint of change.

I pray you bear in mind your own counsels. Long years you must still achieve, and, I hope, neither grief nor weariness will let you "join the dim choir of the bards that have been," until you have written the book I wish and wait for—the sincerest confessions of your best hours.

My wife prays to be remembered to you with sympathy and affection.

Ever yours faithfully,

R. W. EMERSON.